Entrepreneur
MAGAZINE'S

ULTIMATE

GUIDE TO

PAY-PER-CLICK
ADVERTISING

Join the top 3% Capturing Sales from Search Advertising – and Outsmart 97% of the Competition

RICHARD STOKES

EP
Entrepreneur.
Press

Publisher: Jere Calmes
Cover Design: Beth Hansen-Winter
Editorial and Production Services: CWL Publishing Enterprises, Inc., Madison, Wisconsin, www.cwlpub.com

This publication is designed to provide accurate and authoritative information in regard to the subject matter covered. It is sold with the understanding that the publisher is not engaged in rendering legal, accounting, or other professional services. If legal advice or other expert assistance is required, the services of a competent professional person should be sought.

> —From a Declaration of Principles jointly adopted by a
> Committee of the American Bar Association and
> a Committee of Publishers and Associations

ISBN 13: 978-1-59918-363-3
       10: 1-59918-363-3

Library of Congress Cataloging-in-Publication Data

Stokes, Richard L.
  Ultimate guide to pay-per-click advertising / by Richard Stokes.
     p. cm.
ISBN 1-59918-363-3 (alk. paper)
. Internet marketing. 2. Internet advertising. I. Title.
HF5415.1265.S753 2009
659.14'4--dc22

                              2009030580

Printed in Canada
14 13 12 11 10   10 9 8 7 6 5 4 3 2 1

to Kelly, Brendan, and Brittain

Contents

Foreword

by Perry Marshall

PAY-PER-CLICK IS SO INCREDIBLY COOL THAT WHEN YOU SHOW IT TO SOMEONE WHO'S unfamiliar, they can hardly believe it's been around for 10 years.

Few people have any idea how big it is, how deep it is or how much there is to know about it.

When Google introduced AdWords in 2002, the success formula was "Do lots of crazy experiments and keep track of the results." Those of us who were "in the know" tried everything we could think of, and some of it worked handsomely. We experienced success—and the thrill of discovering a new form of advertising.

Today we know what works. But even guys who've bought millions of dollars of clicks and know AdWords like a jockey knows his winning horse still don't know what Richard Stokes knows. Richard brings a completely new perspective.

Richard's perspective is that of someone who's built a giant engine (AdGooroo.com) for analyzing millions of Google ads and millions of keywords—an engine that generates reports every month and monitors the tiny adjustments Google makes to their own machine.

Outside of the Googleplex, there may not be anyone else who knows more than Richard about how the Google AdWords algorithm actually works.

Now if that was all I could say about Richard, then what we'd have is an exceptionally good analyst. (Ho-hum.) But Richard is more than that.

He's also a guy who began just as thousands of other people do, as an affiliate marketer, using AdWords to generate an admirable part-time income. He spent hours and hours mastering the art of AdWords street fighting.

If that's all I could say about Richard, then what we'd have would be a world-class Google AdWords practitioner.

But there's another thing: He's built AdGooroo from basement operation to full-tilt growing company. He's made the transition from scrappy entrepreneur to captain of industry. He understands the needs of medium and large corporations and speaks their language. This is a chasm that few cross.

Those three things truly set him apart and make this book worthy of your time and attention.

Warning: Pay-per-click is trickier than it looks. It has become one of those things that can be made to appear very simple and easy, but in reality demands well-honed chops, close attention to trends, and a good bit of art and intuition.

Juggling these things is a lot harder if you're not even quite sure how Google's machine works in the first place. Google won't tell you nearly as much as Richard will.

As you read this book and delve into the world of pay-per-click, I hope you'll cultivate the following high-level skills:

- Pay-per-click itself is relatively straightforward and mechanical. I know what you're thinking: "Perry, that's easy for you to say . . ." Trust me: even many of the nuances of Google can be mastered, and this book will be a crucial resource in helping you do that. But that's not the only thing . . .
- There is a conversation inside your customer's head and a story—before he or she even clicks on your ad. Ultimately, your success in this game has more to do with your ability to understand a human being than to understand a giant advertising machine or the internet.
- It's more important to understand a specific market than it is to understand marketing. You need to be able to read your customers' diary.
- There is a path you need to take your customer on to drive that conversation forward. Your customers don't want to stay where they are; they want to conquer their problems and give their stories happy endings. It's not enough to promise that: you need to deliver it.
- Online marketing is 50% science and 50% art. Yes, there is an "art factor." It's not just color-by-numbers. If it was, some giant corporation would just hire drones with crayons and give them coloring books. That's where your opportunity lies—in using formulas and techniques on one hand, but bringing your own uniqueness and art on the other.
- Selling on the internet is about rifle shots and extreme specificity. It's often about very narrow niches and very tight communities of people. Online businesses need to answer the question: "Why should I buy from you instead of anybody else in the whole world?"
- You should regard your first few weeks and months of using Google AdWords as an educational investment. You set reasonable budgets, you make sure you're not going to lose your shirt the first week, and you wade into dangerous waters sensibly. It's competitive out there. If you have the right expectations going in, you'll be resilient and you'll bounce

back from inevitable disappointments.

- The "online marketer's dream" really is true. There really are people who run micro-empires from their spare bedrooms. There really are savvy people at big companies who alone possess the expertise to bring in the traffic.

- Once your online business is running the way you envision it, there are few things that compare. It's a thrill to log into your shopping cart and have a record sales day. It's rewarding to know that people all over the world are responding positively to your uniqueness in the world.

- Your mission, should you choose to accept it, is to see to it that once a person clicks on your ad, they never search for that thing again. From that point forward, they are so enthralled with what you offer, so engaged in your story, that they'd never consider going anywhere else. Google rewards you for doing just that, by the way, as you'll see in the pages of this book.

Wherever you are in your pay-per-click journey and your evolution as an entrepreneur or marketing professional, I wish you the very best of success. You've already done more than most people will do—you've picked up an excellent book by a world-class expert. So you deserve it.

Now, sit at Richard's feet and hear what wisdom he has to share.

—Perry Marshall
Author, *The Definitive Guide to Google AdWords*
www.perrymarshall.com

Preface

I N THE EARLY 2000S, AFTER MANY STOPS AND STARTS, I HIT MY FIRST MAJOR-LEAGUE HOMERUN on the internet with an antivirus software review website I created as a side project while working full-time at a well-known global advertising agency. My first weekend, I made $29. I remember thinking at the time that if I could only make $500 a month from the site, it would be a huge success.

Fortunately, I was among the first wave of early adopters taking advantage of Google AdWords to drive cheap, targeted traffic to my websites. AdWords was wildly profitable back then … and easier, as well. No matter how bad your ads were, you could make money. That $29 turned into $200 by the end of the week. My first month's revenues totaled over $3,000. Small? Sure. But I'm still pretty proud of that growth curve. And it was entirely due to pay-per-click advertising.

However, success cannot (and never does) go unanswered. My competitors caught on quickly. As they increased the sophistication of their campaigns, the bar was set higher, and it became more difficult (and expensive) to generate traffic from the search engines.

Even though they were making it tough on me, I was able to steadily increase the profits my websites were generating throughout this period. Why? Because I had made it my business to study the search tactics my competitors were using. Every time they tried something new—whether it was a new keyword, better ad copy, or a specific bidding strategy—I tested it and applied the winning practices to my own campaigns.

By 2005, the PC security industry had topped out, yet I continued to pull in good profits for several years while most of the competing websites quit advertising altogether.

I did not achieve this success through some magic marketing technique. Rather, I achieved it by being just a little bit better than each of my competitors in many different areas. I surmised that if I could discover the best tactics of each competitor and apply them to my campaign, then, taken together as a whole, this would put me far ahead of the pack.

My secret for doing this was a sophisticated software program I wrote that would actively hunt for my competitors' ads and tell me everything it could about them. By the end of my first year of business, this software allowed me to grow my sales sixfold, all while working less than 10 hours a week.

It was when I cashed my first $100,000 check that I realized that this technology could probably help many other companies as well. We named the software AdGooroo and quietly sold it by word of mouth only.

As time passed, we acquired more customers. Today, AdGooroo has grown from a tiny software company to a global presence. Our software is used by more than two-thirds of the largest interactive agencies in the world, as well as thousands of other consultants, agencies, and in-house brand advertisers. Our quarterly reports on the state of the search engine industry are eagerly consumed and reported by the media.

As busy as AdGooroo keeps me, I still make time to run our PPC campaigns. I talk daily with other search marketers and attend five to 10 trade shows a year. And perhaps most importantly, the AdGooroo database grants me insider access to the search marketing activity and rankings of virtually every advertiser in every imaginable type of business on the planet. I have the luxury of seeing what works and what doesn't.

It was from this vantage point that I wrote my first book, *Mastering Search Advertising— How the Top 3% of Search Advertisers Dominate Google AdWords*. In it, I revealed several little-known strategies that savvy search marketers were using at the time to gain an edge on the competition. I chose those strategies because each of them had the potential for big rewards and none of them required a lot of time or money to implement.

The book was more popular than I anticipated, but there was some criticism: it was too short and could have been better served with more extensive examples and tutorials. The strategies presented were basic and easily implemented, but even at the time we knew that the most successful search marketers were using techniques far more sophisticated than the ones discussed.

At the encouragement of Entrepreneur Press, I've decided to dive much deeper into advanced strategies and research in this all-new book. All of the strategies covered in my previous work are included here. However, you'll find new insights and techniques we've gained from research conducted after the first book was published. Where the material overlaps, it has been updated to reflect the latest developments on the search engines. Some of these changes (primarily those in Google's quality score algorithm, which seems to be in a state of constant flux) have required me to include new sections on the essentials of landing page optimization and analytics. While to the newcomer these areas may seem tangential to the business of pay-per-click advertising, I will explain in due course why you simply cannot compete without being somewhat competent in these areas.

The book you are holding in your hands represents the current state of the art in search marketing. With it, you have the tools you need to propel your business into the top tier of search advertisers.

Good luck!

—Rich

ACKNOWLEDGMENTS

I'd like to express my thanks to Rick Carlson, CEO of Surf Secret, and Dave Gobel and Roger Holzberg, both executive members of the Methuselah Foundation, for sharing their marketing data with me for use in this book.

I am also very grateful to Jere Calmes and the rest of the team at Entrepreneur Press for their vision and assistance during the preparation of this work.

Many thanks go out to Perry Marshall (author, *The Definitive Guide to Google AdWords*), Tim Seward and Jeremy Aube of ROI Revolution, Josh Dreller of Fuor Digital, Matt Van Wagner of Find Me Faster, Tim Ash (author, *Landing Page Optimization*), and Howie Jacobson (author, *AdWords for Dummies*) for their contributions. These are some of the finest search marketers in the world, and anyone interested in pay-per-click advertising would be well advised to follow their advice closely.

My thanks also to Jamie Crouthamel, Matt McCall, and Randy Glein for their vision in recognizing the power that quantitative data would someday hold in internet marketing. Without their help, AdGooroo would never have come to be, nor would this book.

To those clients who have allowed me to share some of their techniques mentioned in Chapter 19, you have my appreciation.

Finally, this book would not have been possible without the patience of my family, Kelly, Brendan, and Brittain, throughout many months of marathon writing sessions.

ABOUT THE AUTHOR

An internet marketer for more than 13 years, Richard Stokes is the founder and president of AdGooroo, LLC, a leading provider of search marketing intelligence. Prior to founding AdGooroo, Richard was a senior technology executive at Publicis Groupe/Leo Burnett. He has a

BS in computer engineering from the University of Illinois and an MBA in entrepreneurship and technology management from the Kellogg Graduate School of Management (Northwestern University). Richard is a regular speaker on search marketing topics and is certified as a conversion optimization professional.

ABOUT ADGOOROO

Based in Chicago, AdGooroo provides competitive intelligence to search engine marketers through its suite of products, including AdGooroo Express, SEM Insight, and Trademark Insight. Over 1,000 companies rely on these keyword tracking tools and other unique products to provide them with quantifiable insights they can use to rise above the competition and build a long-term competitive advantage in search engine marketing.

LEGAL NOTES

AdGooroo is not affiliated with Google, Yahoo!, or the Google AdWords™ program. Our views and opinions do not reflect those of any search engine or any entity other than our own.

Inside This Book

PEER INSIDE THE PLAYBOOKS OF THE WORLD'S TOP SEARCH MARKETERS AND LEARN THE insider pay-per-click techniques and strategies used by leading search agencies, consultants, and brands to steal impressions from competitors, multiply traffic, and explode sales.

Inside:

- The analytics reports you really need to succeed as a search marketer
- How to create traffic maps—a powerful tool that will tell you where your visitors are coming from, why they are leaving, and why they are buying
- A crash course in landing page optimization
- Why only 3% of search advertisers dominate Google AdWords (and what you can do to join them!)
- How to make your competitors pay outrageous prices for their ads (or risk losing their ad placements altogether)
- An inside peek into Google's quality score algorithm
- How to use the Visitor Intention model to guide your ad copy, pick the best landing pages, and set bid prices
- The one feature the search engines provide that you must never, ever use
- How to find "super-converter" keywords—phrases that can drive 80% or more of your total website revenue
- The world's best affiliate ads (deconstructed so you can write your own!)
- Why you should never take your search campaign reports at face value

In other works, a guide for serious marketers who are ready to bust through the noise!

Ultimate Guide to Pay-per-Click Advertising

CHAPTER 1

Pay-Per-Click Requires a Solid Foundation

B EFORE WE DIVE INTO PAY-PER-CLICK, WE NEED TO HAVE A WORD ABOUT THE PROPER ORDER IN which to tackle things.

When most advertisers go about starting their pay-per-click campaigns, they begin by creating an advertising account (usually on Google), randomly choose some keywords, create an ad (or two), and pick a starting bid price out of thin air. The clicks start coming in, but more often than not, the profits fail to follow.

These undisciplined campaigns rarely pay for themselves. This is a real shame, because although pay-per-click is a cutthroat business, it's still as easy as shooting fish in a barrel if you know how to do it right.

The reality that these advertisers fail to take into account is that no matter what business you're in, someone has probably been there before you. Blindly rushing in with a half-baked website is a guaranteed way to ensure that your competitors will outbid (and outsell) you.

Starting a campaign without having access to analytics is marketing suicide. You need tracking to know how much you can profitably spend for each of your ads. You'll also need it to learn which pages on your site should be sending visitors from the search engines. (I'll teach you plenty more techniques for boosting your search advertising results with analytics in the next section.)

And if you have tracking installed on your website but haven't optimized your website's ability to convert visitors into buyers, you probably won't be able to compete for the best possible placement for your ads. As a result, your ads will appear infrequently, buried deep within the search results pages. And more importantly, you'll only be capturing a small percentage of the sales you would have captured by identifying and eliminating sales bottlenecks.

Only after you've taken these preliminary steps will your website be ready to hold its own against the competition. Here again, though, neophyte search marketers are all too quick to jump into a campaign without really knowing what they are doing. Consequently, their campaigns end up a mishmash of poorly aligned keywords, ad copy, and landing pages. Impressions are slowly choked off and first-page bid prices rise until their ads are shut out of what could be the most profitable keywords in the campaign.

Instead, I encourage you to take a disciplined approach, the one I outline in this book. I've honed this approach through years of creating pay-per-click campaigns. If you follow these steps in the order I've laid them out for you, you should be able to capture a majority of the available impressions and generate high clickthrough rates at a fraction of the price most of your competitors are paying. Figure 1-1 captures these ideas.

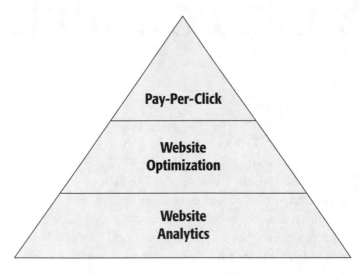

FIGURE 1-1. Effective Pay-per-click advertising campaigns must be built on a solid foundation of analytics and website optimization

Installing and Using Analytics

Your Marketing Will Fail Without Tracking

PRETEND FOR A MOMENT THAT INSTEAD OF PROMOTING YOUR BUSINESS OVER THE WEB, YOU were to take a more traditional approach such as television advertising. You might be prepared to spend upwards of a quarter-million dollars just for production, to be followed by potentially millions of dollars of national media buys.

With so much at stake, it seems unlikely that you would simply write a check and forget about it. Not by a long shot. I bet you'd be watching the sales figures like a hawk to see if your campaign was bringing customers in. And if it didn't perform, you'd cut your losses quickly (and probably fire your marketing manager).

Most of our businesses will never grow to the scale where we can afford big-ticket television buys. Fortunately, internet advertising now gives us a way to purchase smaller, more reasonably priced blocks of traffic.

The downside of this is that these less expensive campaigns tend to fall off the radar of most managers and entrepreneurs. There is a false sense of security that comes from spending "only" $500 a month or so on search. We tell ourselves, "Maybe it will come in, maybe it won't," or "Let's just start it and see what happens."

This is nothing more than a shortcut to failure, and I don't want you to fall into that trap. So please take this firm, but friendly, piece of advice:

If you don't track your campaign, you will lose. Period.

If you blow off the numbers behind your business, your marketing will be mediocre because it will be built on opinion and guesswork.

Guesses and opinions are the enemies of good marketing. If you let the numbers tell you the truth, you'll make your website better. You'll make your advertising better. Your sales will end up 5x, 10x, even 100x over where you started.

Marketing Sherpa[1] reports that 90% of search marketers use some form of analytics. While I personally believe that this figure is highly inflated (the majority of advertisers I talk to have no website tracking in place or never look at their reports), the fact remains that any serious competitors will be relying on their website tracking to improve their returns. You need to do the same if you want to level the playing field.

You must have tracking installed on your website. There are no ifs, ands, or buts about it.

The next few chapters will show you exactly how to set up a basic tracking system and how to make the best use of it.

Note

1. *Marketing Sherpa Search Benchmark Guide*, 2009. "4.03 Chart: Who Uses Web Analytics for Search?"

CHAPTER 3

Installing Tracking on Your Website

WEBSITE ANALYTICS IS THE STUDY OF ONLINE USER BEHAVIOR FOR THE PURPOSE OF improving sales. By adding analytics capabilities to your website, you will be able to measure:

- Where visitors are coming from (e.g., search engines, type-in traffic, banner ads, etc.)
- What pages they are visiting the most
- How much and how often they convert (e.g., buy your products, sign up for your e-mail newsletters, request more information, etc.)
- How long they stay on each page
- How quickly they leave
- How much every page on your site is worth to you

With this information, you can make your site *better*.

You'll have the insights you need to improve your site design, create a better user experience, and streamline your conversion pages.

The end result? Higher return on every advertising dollar you spend.

These insights will be contained in your website analytics reports. These will be your new best friend.

THE TWO APPROACHES TO COLLECTING WEBSITE DATA

Analytics packages utilize two basic approaches to gathering traffic data from your website: log file analysis and page tagging.

Log File Analysis

Log file analysis was the original approach to tracking visitors. The web server on which your site is hosted records all user access information in a log file. This file contains such information as the visitor's IP address, the time of the request, and the URL of the page they visited. Some analytics packages use this data to generate their analytics reports.

The data contained in these log files are not always accurate due to the presence of web caches. If a visitor revisits a page, the second request can be retrieved from this visitor's cache. In this case, no request will be made to the web server, and the visitor's path through your website will be lost. Similarly, log files tend to have difficulties distinguishing visitors who connect to the internet via large ISPs or those who have dynamic IP addresses.

> ### Conversions
>
> Whenever this book refers to conversions, it may mean sales, leads, signups, donations, or whatever it is you're trying to get your visitors to do on your website.

In order to set up an in-house logging system, you'll need access to your web servers. You'll also need to purchase, install, and configure the software. This is ordinarily only cost-effective if you already have a high-volume website with at least a six-figure revenue stream.

For more modest sites, we'll want to consider the next alternative.

Page Tagging

With the page tagging approach, a small snippet of JavaScript code is inserted on every page of your website. When a visitor reads one of your pages, the code passes along certain identifying pieces of information about the page and the visitor to an outside web analytics company. They maintain all of the hardware and software and generate your traffic reports on a near real-time basis (usually under 24 hours).

Page tagging eliminates errors caused by web caches. Even if a visitor fetches your page from their local browser cache, the JavaScript code is still executed and the information is saved. Also, it is much easier to record additional information such as the size of the order, the SKUs that were purchased, browser capabilities, and so on. In fact, some tracking services can even generate heat maps that will show you what links and images attract your visitors' attention. Now that's power!

However, page tagging isn't perfect. Some visitors will have JavaScript turned off and will never be tracked. Sometimes the tracking data gets lost in transmission over the internet and the visitor's information is not recorded. Also, this approach requires you to share sensitive financial information with an outside party, and this may conflict with your company's data security policies.

Which Is Better?

Both approaches are useful and can typically be used interchangeably. However, for the purposes of this book, we will recommend page tagging. Page tagging is fairly accurate and easy to set up; moreover, there are free packages available, so the price is right.

However, there is one very important consideration to be aware of with page tagging. In my experience, this approach will understate your traffic by about 10-15%. Thus, it is very important that your site is getting sufficient traffic so that this error is minimized. If you are only getting 20 sales a month and your package loses track of three of them, your decision-making ability will be compromised.

The solution to this is to ensure that your site is getting a reasonable amount of traffic before you begin to take your analytics data too seriously. A great way to do this, of course, is by using pay-per-click advertising. We'll go into great depth on this in the third part of this book. For now, let's get started with analytics.

If you have the resources at your disposal, you can use two separate tracking software packages. I opted to do this for a very large website that was getting over 2,000,000 visits per day and had a small army of developers working on it. By cross-referencing the reports generated by the different analytics packages against each other on a regular basis, we were able to quickly identify situations in which new pages were rolled out with either tracking or HTML errors.

MY PICK: GOOGLE ANALYTICS

For all of the above reasons, we're going to recommend Google Analytics. It's a solid, robust package that won't overwhelm the first-time web marketer, and it's extremely popular (see Figure 3-1). Best of all, it's free. (For an expert counterpoint, see the sidebar, "Top 10 Reasons Not to Use Google Analytics.")

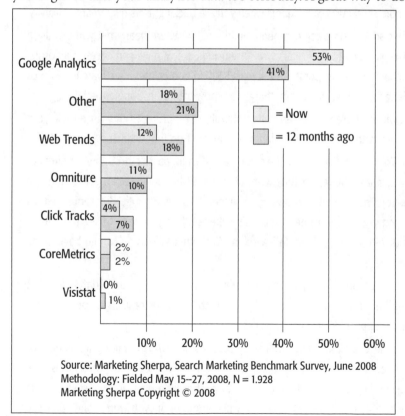

Source: Marketing Sherpa, Search Marketing Benchmark Survey, June 2008
Methodology: Fielded May 15--27, 2008, N = 1.928
Marketing Sherpa Copyright © 2008

FIGURE 3-1. What analytics programs are used the most?

Top 10 Reasons Not to Use Google Analytics
Joshua Dreller Director, Media Technology & Analytics Fuor Digital

I like Google Analytics. Really, I do. But sometimes it's not the right tool for the job. Here are 10 reasons you may want to consider using an alternative website analytics package:

1. **Google Gets All of Your Data**. Personally, I don't mind that much, but for some companies, privacy is a big concern.

2. **No Technical Support**. The best you get from Google is a help forum or a referral to one of their Certified agencies (which are not free). With an Omniture or a Web Trends, you get toll-free support from experts.

3. **You Only Get Four Conversion Goals (per profile)**. This is one of the big differences in my book. With most analytics solutions, you can have *way more* conversions in your report suite. I'm surprised GA hasn't expanded this feature yet.

4. **Advanced Reporting**. Google Analytics is fine for the basics, but when you need to pull multiple advanced reports on a consistent basis, you'll need something a bit heavier than GA.

5. **Cookie Window**. Google Analytics' max length for a cookie is six months. That's still a ton of data they're tracking for free. However, it may completely skew your numbers when you are tracking users over years of activity.

6. **Advanced Segmentation**. GA has added some segmentation, but it's still nowhere near what you can do in an advanced analytics suite. When you want to see users who "are using Firefox, have come from California, visited at least three times in the last six weeks, purchased at least $500 in goods, and have watched four or more videos in your downloads section," you need something more powerful than Google Analytics.

7. **Industry Integration**. Do you want to share cookies and integrate full-on reporting from your e-mail, your ad server, your survey solution, etc. with your analytics platform? You can't do that with Google Analytics.

8. **Data Recording Methodology**. With Google Analytics, the raw data comes in, passes through your filters (if you have any), and then gets written into the report suite. With other tools, the raw data can get written into a data warehouse and then hit your report suite (through your filters). This is a subtle difference, but it's important to note—especially when you realize three months after the fact that you want to see the data in a new way. With GA, you're stuck with the way the data is written. With other tools, you can go back to the raw stream and reanalyze.

9. **Lack of Flexibility**. There's not much opportunity to make modifications to the system. That still makes Google Analytics fine for 95% of the things you need to do, but the inability to customize it to perform that last 5% might one day become a real problem for your business.

10. **So Many Other Little Reasons**. There are too many other small reasons that GA isn't the right solution for full-on web analytics. If all you need are page views, visitors, some basic conversions, etc., then GA is fine. But if you are doing serious business on the web, there are so many other little bells and whistles you get with a robust suite that certainly justify the expense. Do a demo with Omniture or Web Trends and you'll see the difference immediately.

INSTALLING TRACKING SCRIPTS

Getting your website tagged with basic tracking scripts is easy and can often be done in under an hour, although a little more time will be needed to implement advanced order tracking.

Step 1: Create a Google AdWords Account

If you don't already have a Google AdWords account, you'll need to set one up now. We'll be using the same account to both run your PPC campaigns and access your website analytics reports.

Start by navigating over to the Google AdWords site (google. com/adwords). Click the "Start now" button to begin the sign-up process (Figure 3-2).

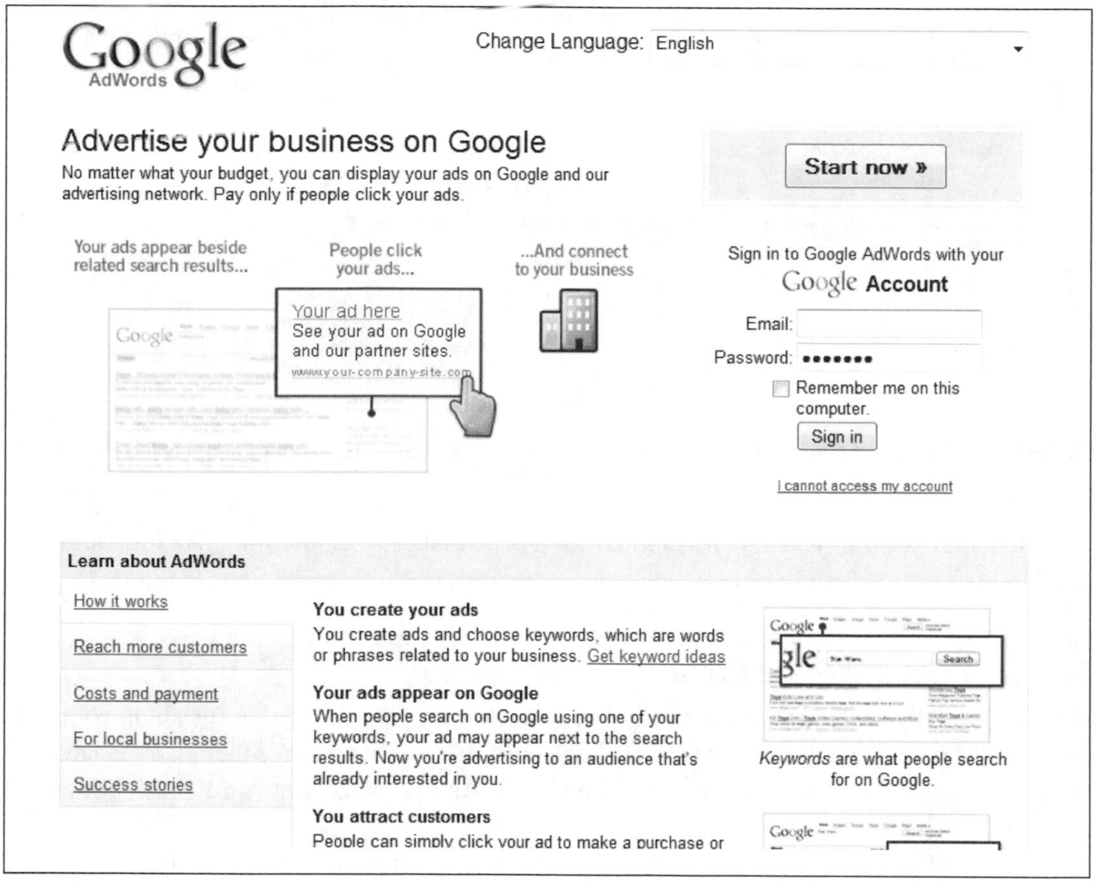

FIGURE 3-2. The main Google AdWords page

On the first page, you will be asked to sign up for "Starter Edition" or "Standard Edition." Be sure to select "Standard Edition." Don't waste your time with a starter account, as it won't allow you to do most of the things you'll need it to (Figure 3-3).

On the next several pages, you'll be asked to create a username and password, set your currency preferences, and verify your e-mail address. These are all straightforward and full instructions are provided. If you have any problems, you can contact a Google representative via live chat.

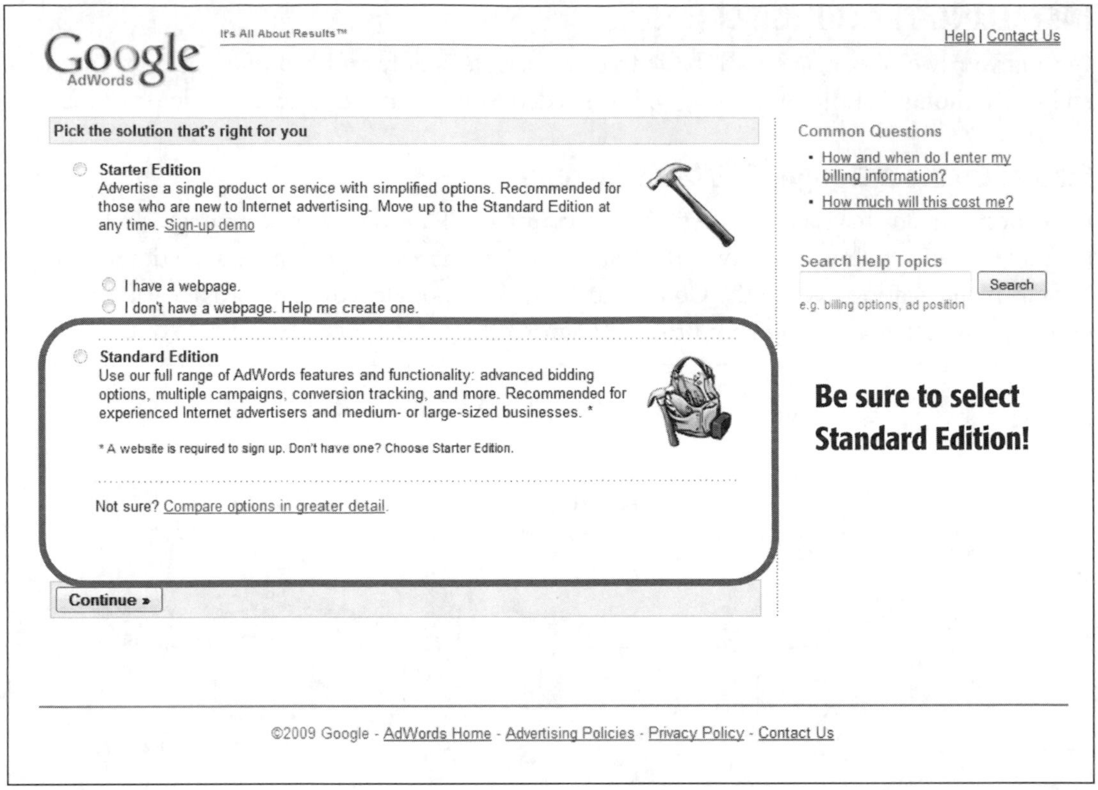

FIGURE 3-3. Select the Standard Edition when setting up a new account. The Starter Edition is too limited for our purposes.

When your account is ready, you should see a page that looks something like the following. Don't worry about creating a campaign yet; the tracking needs to come first (Figure 3-4).

Step 2: Create a Website Profile

Next, we'll configure Google Analytics and generate the scripts you need to install on your site.

From the Google AdWords account, click the tab at the top of the page that reads "Analytics." Select the option that reads "Create my free Google Analytics account" and click "Continue" (Figure 3-5).

Next, you'll be asked for the domain name of your website. You can also assign an easy-to-remember name for the set of reports for this particular website, but in most cases it suffices if the account name and domain name are the same.

There are two other settings here: "Destination URL Auto-tagging" and "Apply Cost Data." Leave these on for now, as they will save you a lot of work when creating your PPC campaigns later. While you can turn them off, you only need to do so in select situations (Figure 3-6).

Next, you'll be asked to agree to the terms of service. You must do so before you will be allowed to use Google Analytics. Finally, you'll be directed to a page which will contain the tracking code for your site (Figure 3-7).

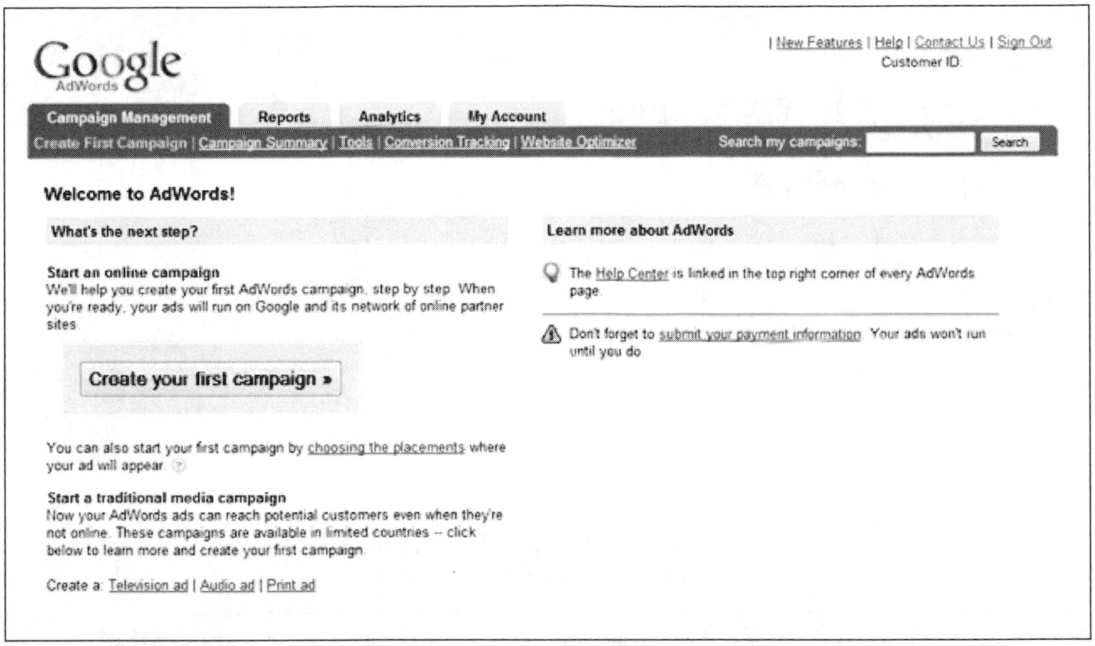

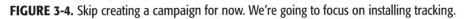

FIGURE 3-4. Skip creating a campaign for now. We're going to focus on installing tracking.

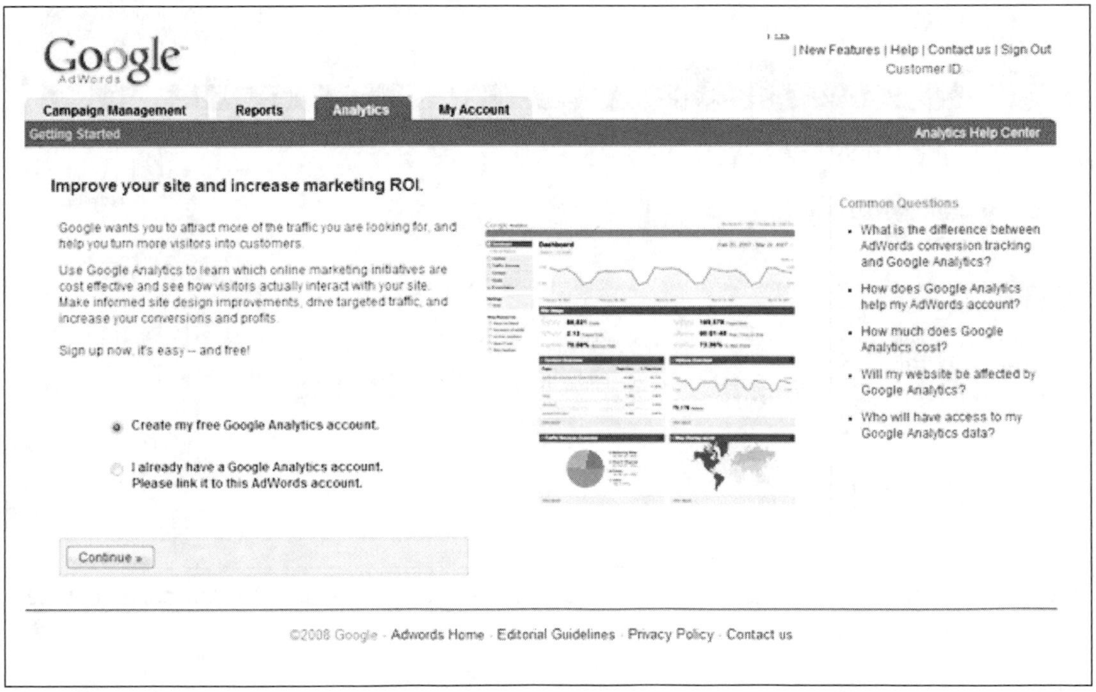

FIGURE 3-5. Create a new Google Analytics account

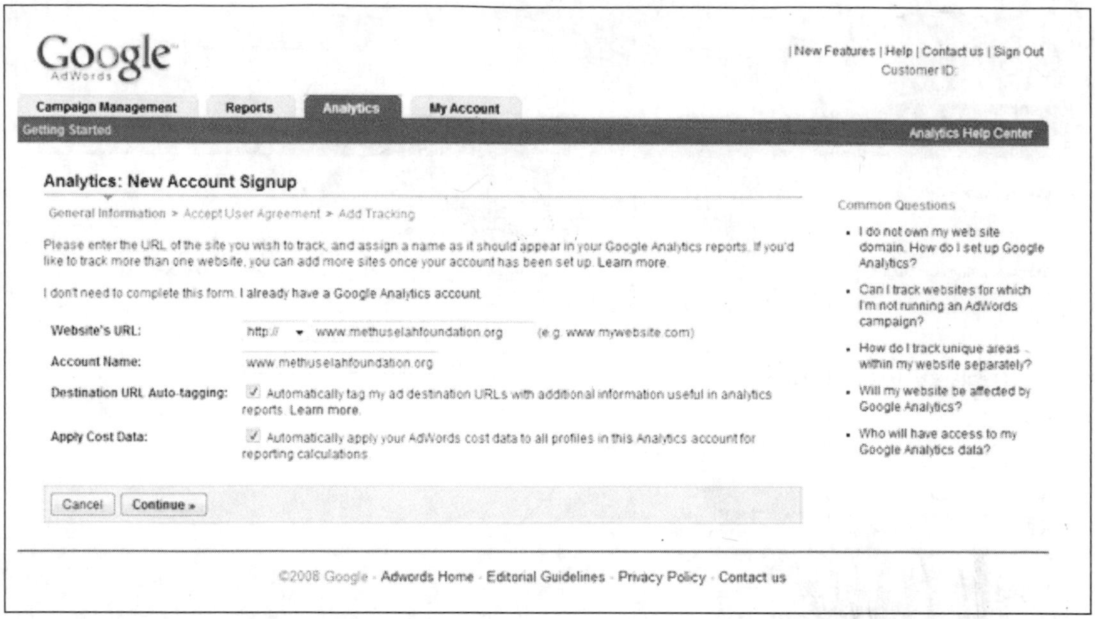

FIGURE 3-6. You'll need to provide Google Analytics with the name of your website. Make sure that "Destination URL Auto-tagging" and "Apply Cost Data" are checked for now.

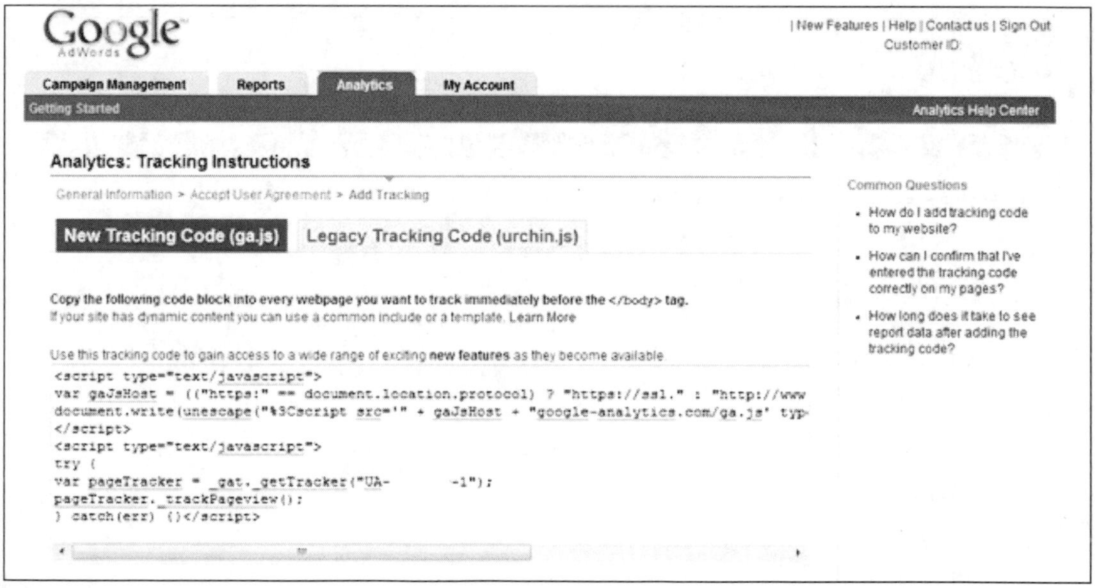

FIGURE 3-7. The final step will give you the tracking script. This should be inserted verbatim into every page of your site.

Step 3: Tag Your Site

You now have to copy the script shown on this page to your site. You will want to do this on every page of your site (this is usually very easy to do if your website uses templates—most modern sites do).

Insert the code just before the </body> tag in your page, like so:

```
<!DOCTYPE HTML PUBLIC "-//W3C//DTD HTML 4.0I//EN" "http://www.w3.org/TR/html4/strict.dtd">
<meta http-equiv="Content-Type" content="text/html; charset=iso-8859-1" />
<html>
  <head>
    <title>The Methuselah Foundation-Welcome to The Methuselah
        Foundation</title>
  </head>
<body>
… Your Website Content Goes Here …
<script type="text/javascript">
var gaJsHost = (("https:" = document.location.protocol) ? "https://ssl." : "http://www.");
document.write(unescape("%3Cscript src='" + gaJsHost + "google-analytics.com/ga.js'
type='text/javascript'%3E%3C/script%3E"));
</script>
<script type="text/javascript">
try {
var pageTracker = _gat._getTracker("UA-7345580-1");
pageTracker._trackPageview();
} catch(err) {}</script>
</body>
```

That's it! Your site is now tagged and the traffic will start showing up on your analytics reports in a matter of hours.

Why Is the Tracking Script Placed at the End of the Page?

While the script location is not absolutely critical, it is recommended that you place it at the end of each page on your website. This ensures that your visitors see your website immediately and aren't waiting for the Google Analytics script to execute. While the script is usually fast, there's always a chance it could introduce a few seconds of delay to your page load time.

There are two exceptions to this rule. The first is when you are split-testing your pages using the Google Website Optimizer (GWO) tool (see Chapter 9). The second is when you are tracking individual order sizes (see "Advanced E-Commerce Goal Tracking" below).

Both e-commerce order and GWO tracking scripts should be placed after the standard Google Analytics tracking script.

Finding This Script Later

The first time you set up Google Analytics, you are automatically directed to the page containing the script. However, finding it later is truly an exercise in frustration (Figure 3-8).

You can return to this page again by clicking the "Edit" link next to your profile on the main Google Analytics page. From there, you'll be taken to the "Profile Settings" page. There is a link on this page that reads "Check Status." Click this link and you'll be taken to the script page (Figure 3-9).

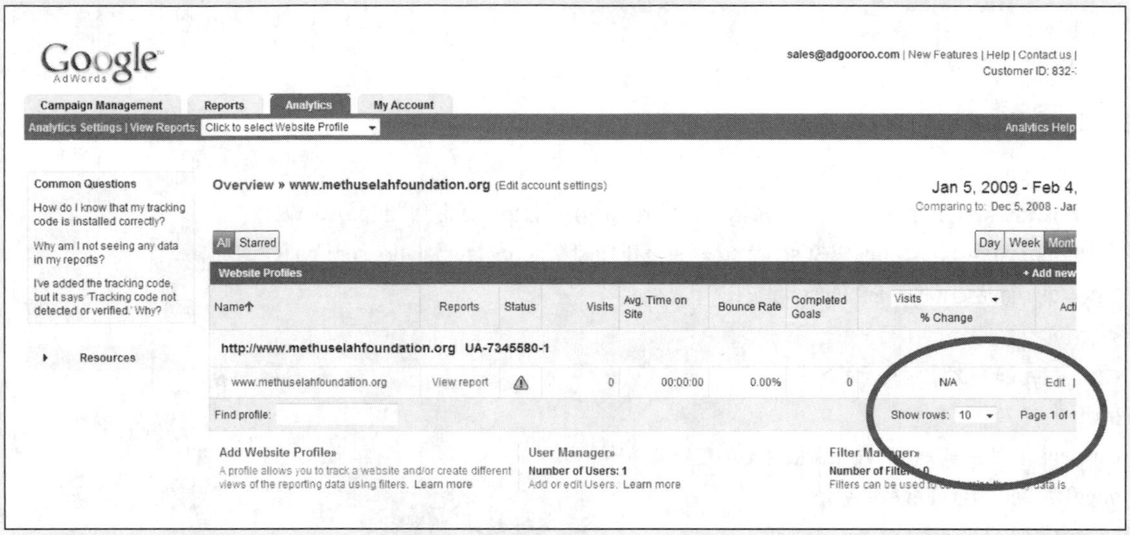

FIGURE 3-8. It's not easy to find the Google Analytics script after the initial setup process. Should you need to return to it, click on the "Edit" link next to your profile.

COMMON PROBLEMS
Missing or Mangled Scripts

If you don't see any traffic on your tracking reports within 24 hours, you should check to make sure the script is actually installed on your site.

If the script is on your site, make sure the script hasn't been altered in any way. Well-meaning developers sometimes insert comments around the code in an effort to provide backwards compatibility with older browsers. This is not necessary and will break the tracking script. If there's any doubt, delete the old script and paste the new one (unaltered) from the Google Analytics website back into your pages.

Also, be sure that any third-party shopping cart pages are tagged properly. A very common problem is that pages on the main site are tagged, but the shopping cart pages are overlooked. These are the most important pages on your site, so you will need data on them to fully optimize your site later on.

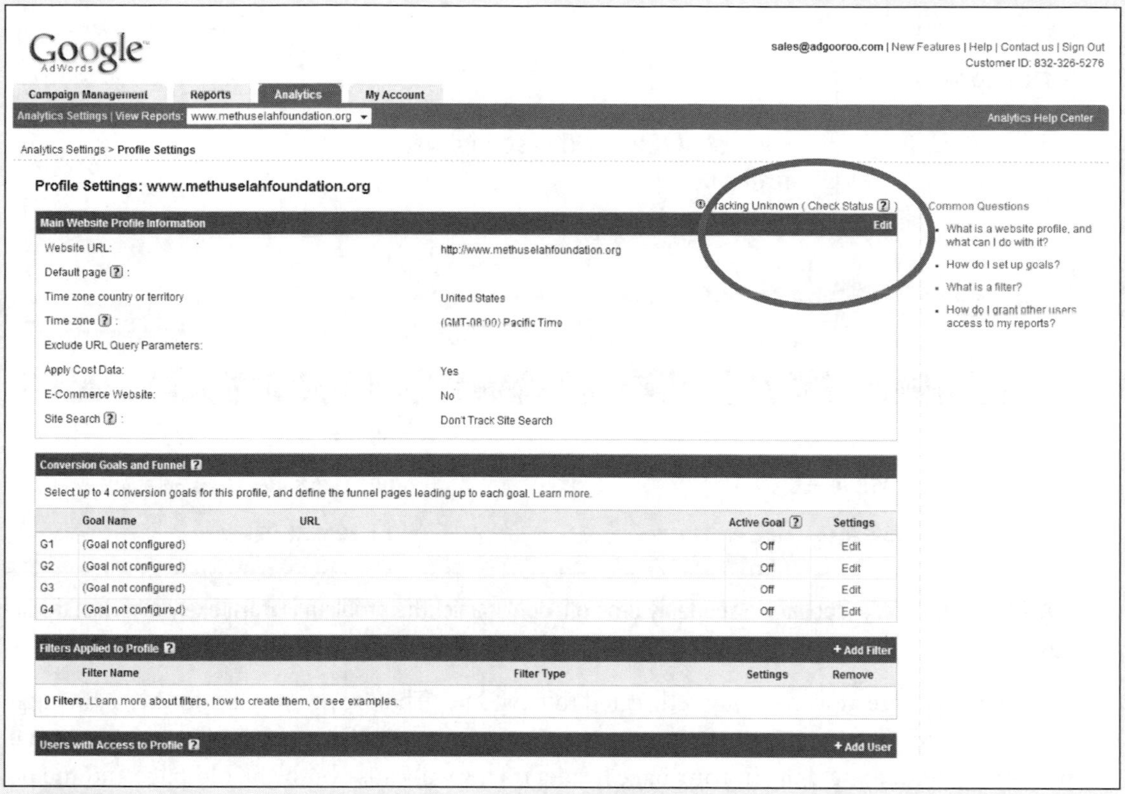

FIGURE 3-9. Next, click on the "Check Status" link. You will then be directed to the page containing the tracking code.

Wrong Account Number

The Google tracking script contains an account number and profile ID that uniquely identify your site. When working with multiple sites, it's easy to accidentally paste a script from a different profile than the one you intended.

If this happens, your site traffic will not be recorded in the proper account. If you seem to be missing data in your reports, double-check that the account number matches the one in Google Analytics (Figure 3-10).

Improper Redirects on Your Site

It is a common SEO practice to use redirects to ensure that visitors who were intending to go to

While we were writing this book, this very thing happened to us. We noticed a large drop in traffic on the Methuselah Foundation website after a site rebrand. No other marketing changes were happening at the time, so the prime suspect was a broken script. Upon further investigation, we discovered that the developer had inadvertently updated the tracking code with a new account number, causing most of our traffic data to disappear.

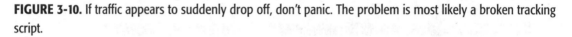

FIGURE 3-10. If traffic appears to suddenly drop off, don't panic. The problem is most likely a broken tracking script.

obsolete pages are automatically redirected to new ones. The proper way to do this is through a 301 or 302 redirect. Under no circumstances should you use a client-side redirect script (usually performed with a meta tag in your page header). This will cause both the old page and the new one to be rendered on your visitors' browsers, resulting in your traffic being counted twice.

DEFINING CONVERSION GOALS

Next, you'll need to tag your order confirmation pages with information such as product names, quantities, and order amounts. We'll be using this information later to reverse-engineer your customers' browsing and buying habits.

Start by figuring out what your conversion goal is. Is it an e-mail signup or a product sale? You'll have at least one on your website, but many sites have two or more. (At AdGooroo, we track e-mail signups, free trials, report downloads, and paid subscriptions all as separate conversion goals.)

Next, you'll need to assign a value to each goal. Here are some typical ways this is done:

- **E-mail signups.** If your e-mail subscribers purchase products from you in a predictable fashion, then you may be able to calculate the lifetime value of a typical subscriber. Otherwise, you can simply assign a value of $0 and track the signup rate as a percentage (from one to one hundred).
- **Leads.** Use an average order amount based on your conversion rate. It's best to average everything into a single estimate, but it's not always possible. For instance, if you find that your leads from Google's search result pages convert at twice the rate of Yahoo's, you'll

need to consider using separate goals for each source or possibly incorporating the source of the click into your conversion tracking code (see below).

- **Sales.** This is the "classic" case, and it's the easiest to get set up. Just insert the order details (at a minimum, the total order amount) into the conversion tracking script on your "thank you" page, and Google Analytics will do the rest.

BASIC GOAL TRACKING

Use this method if you simply want to define a fixed value for every conversion goal. This is what you would typically do when recording a lead or e-mail signup. For conversion goals where the order amount may change, use the advanced method in the next section.

Begin by logging into your Google Analytics account. On your main page, you'll see a listing of your active profiles. Click on the one you wish to work with. Then, from within the Google Analytics website, click the "Goals" menu on the left navigation bar (Figure 3-11, page 20).

If you've never set up goals before, you'll see an introductory page. Click the link at the bottom that reads "Learn how to set up goals and funnels." You'll then be taken to your profile settings page.

Note: if you've worked with goals before, just click the "Edit" button next to your profile when you log in (Figure 3-12, page 21).

The section that reads "Conversion goals and funnels" is where you set up your goals. Click the "Edit" link next to any row to set up a goal.

> ### A Tip For Selling Downloadable Products
>
> If you're selling downloadable goods such as ebooks or software, don't provide users with direct links to the files. Instead, create an intermediary download page that streams the file to the user. This accomplishes two things. First, you can control access by preventing users from bookmarking the direct link to the file (and possibly sharing the link with non-paying customers). Second, you can add analytics and goal tracking scripts to the download page. This will allow you to track downloads and even tie them back to the originating traffic sources. This is incredibly valuable data.

On the next page, you can tell Google Analytics what your goal consists of. I'll show you how I set it up for the Methuselah Foundation newsletter signup conversion path.

I chose the following settings:

- **Active Goal:** "On"
- **Match Type:** I chose "Head Match." Use it if your URL is the same every time. If your "thank you" page URL can change, click the help button for advanced options.
- **Goal URL:** Enter the URL of your "thank you" or "order receipt" page here.
- **Goal Name:** Here you enter a name that describes what this funnel does. I chose "Newsletter Signup."
- **Case Sensitive:** I usually leave this unchecked. You should only check it if your website makes use of case-sensitive URLs (a bad practice).

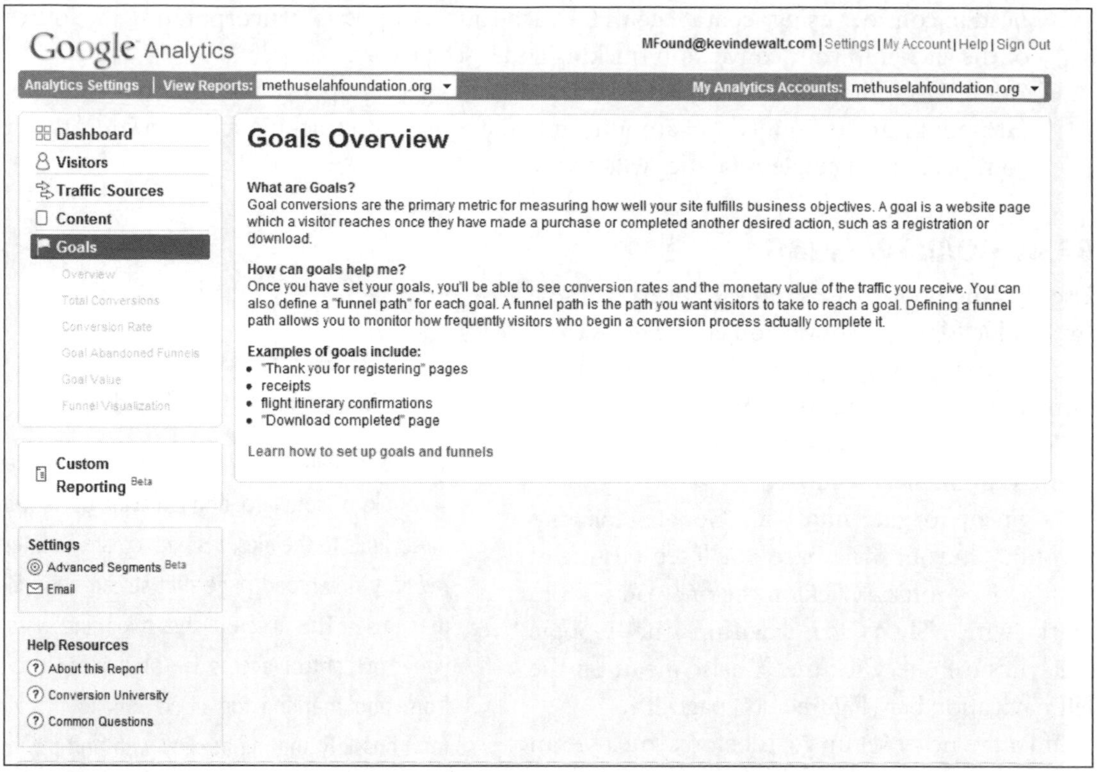

FIGURE 3-11. You'll see a page similar to this one prior to setting up any goals.

- **Goal Value:** Enter whatever dollar value you've assigned to this goal. I've entered zero, as I'll track conversions as a percentage.

The second section of this page allows you to define a conversion funnel for your checkout pages. A conversion funnel is simply a sequence of pages that you'd ideally like your customers to follow. It always ends with your conversion goal. For instance, your conversion funnel may consist of a product page, a shopping cart page, a page to gather account and payment details, and finally, a goal ("thank you") page.

Defining your entire conversion funnel here activates a special funnel report in the Google Analytics interface that may come in handy (more on this in Chapter 8).

Conversion funnel tracking is also useful for segmenting visitors who arrive at the same goal page from different source pages (this could happen if you have two separate e-mail signup pages and only one "thank you" page). Each source of traffic may exhibit different conversion rates, and this is impossible to determine unless you have a means of distinguishing between them. Defining a funnel and setting the "required step" function will allow you to track your visitors through each funnel independently of one another (Figure 3-13, page 22).

ADVANCED E-COMMERCE GOAL TRACKING

If the amounts of your orders vary, you'll need to create an e-commerce tracking script to tell

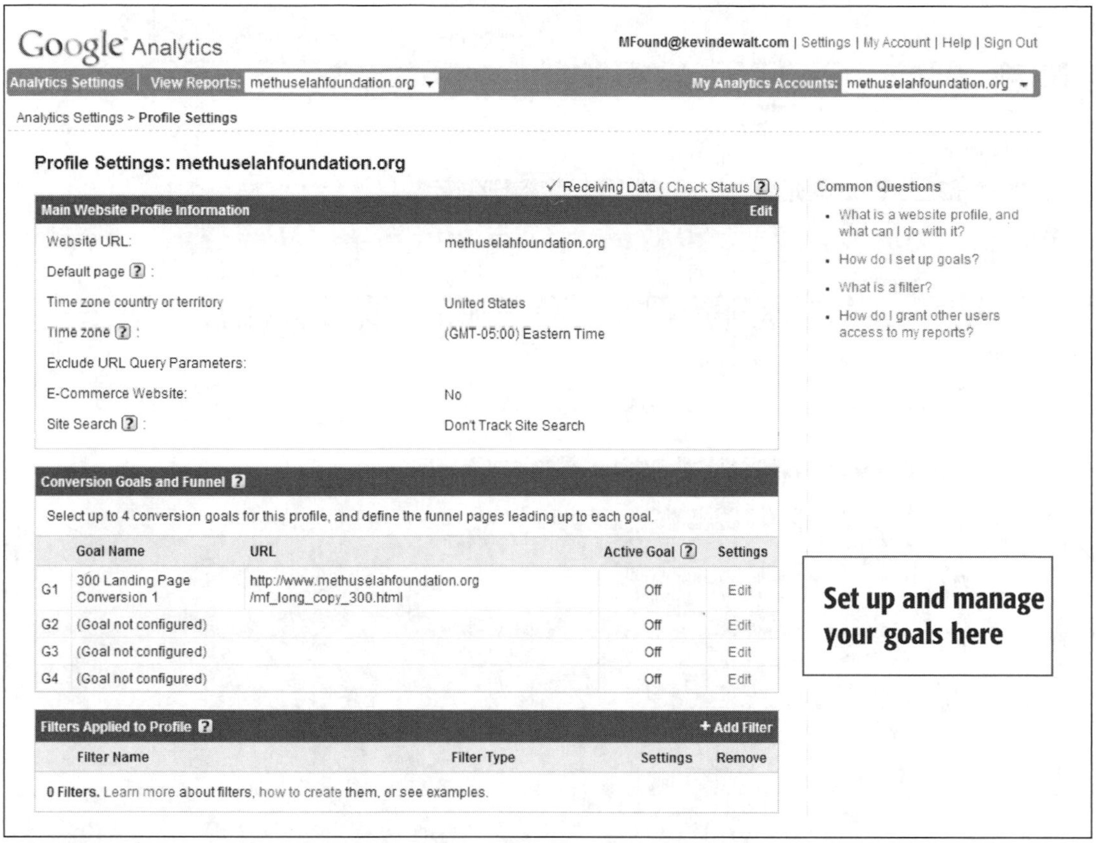

FIGURE 3-12. Your Google Analytics profile page allows you to set up to four goals.

Google Analytics what products were purchased, the individual amounts, and the grand total. You can track other helpful information (such as taxes, the geographic location of the order, etc.), but for our purposes, we'll stick with the basics. This method is not necessary if you are tracking goals that don't directly lead to orders (such as leads or e-mail signups). *Instead, just use goal tracking as described above.*

To activate e-commerce tracking, you'll need to modify your "thank you" page (or ask your developers to do it for you).

You'll add tracking for your order amounts by calling two Google Analytics functions designed specifically for this purpose. The first, _addTrans(), tracks the total order amount. The second, _addItem(), is used to track individual line items. These functions need to be called after the basic Google Analytics tracking script described earlier in this chapter.

An example is shown on pages 22-23.

This simple example is sufficient if your order processing takes place all on the same domain. However, e-commerce tracking tends to be more complicated than that. If you process your orders through a third-party shopping cart or a dedicated subdomain (for instance, https://store. yourdomain.com), you'll need to customize your tracking scripts as described in the next section.

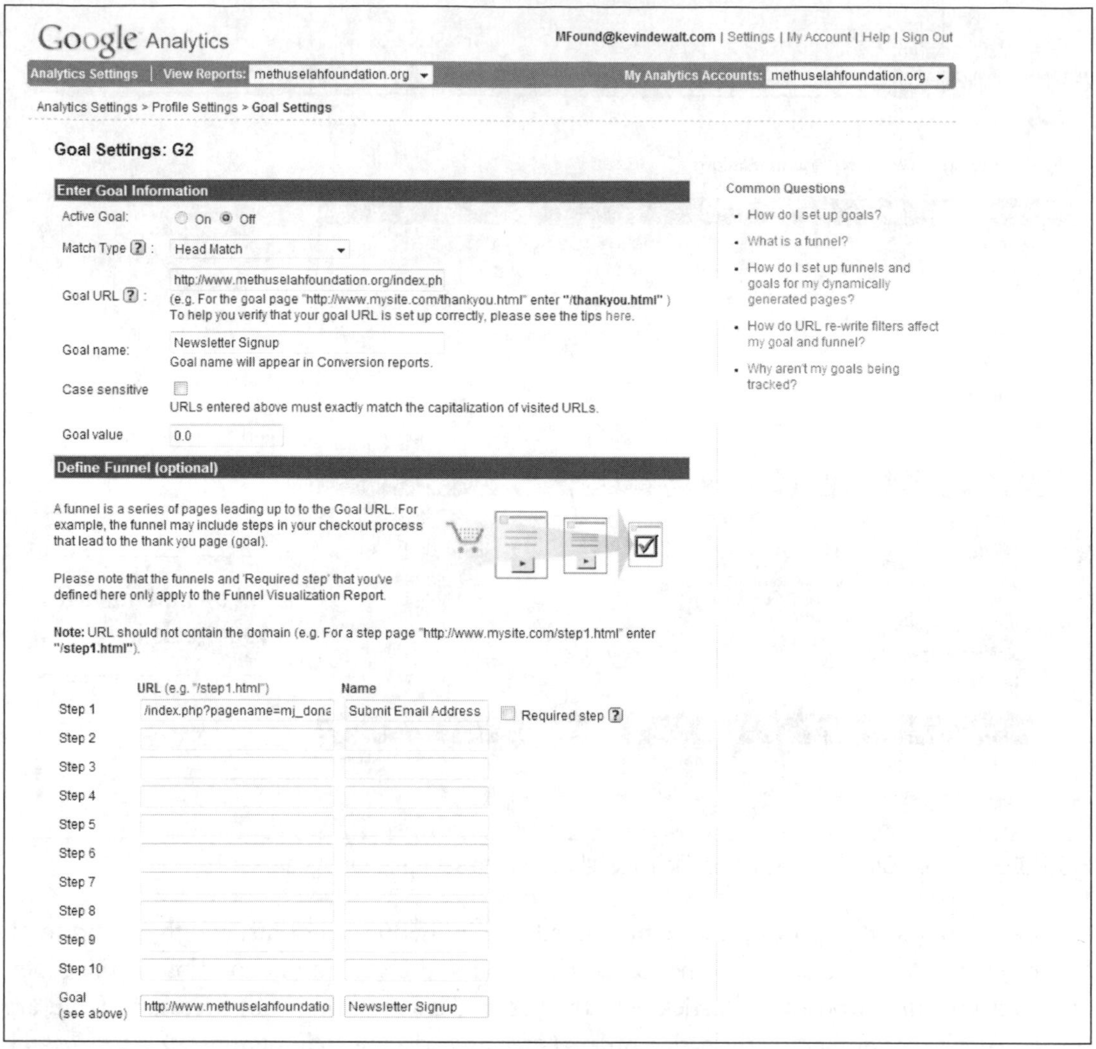

FIGURE 3-13. Use the Goal Settings page to define a new goal, assign a conversion value, and create a funnel.

```
<script type="text/javascript">
// This is the standard Google Analytics script
var gaJsHost = (("https:" == document.location.protocol) ? "https://ssl." : "http://www.");
document.write(unescape("%3Cscript src='" + gaJsHost + "google-analytics.com/ga.js'
```

```
type='text/javascript'%3E%3C/script%3E"));
</script>
// End standard Google Analytics script
// E-commerce goal tracking script starts here. Insert your account number
// in the _getTracker() function call.
<script type="text/javascript">
var pageTracker = _gat._getTracker("UA-XXXXX-1");
pageTracker._trackPageview();
// This first call records your total order amount and other information.
pageTracker._addTrans(
  "1234",              // Order ID
  "Authorize.NET",     // Affiliation
  "29.99",             // Total
  "1.29",              // Tax
  "0",                 // Shipping
  "Chicago",           // City
  "Illinois",          // State
  "USA"                // Country
);
// This next section of code records the individual line items. This
// is optional, but definitely helpful.
pageTracker._addItem(
  "23883",             // Order ID
  "PP2009",            // SKU
  "Privacy Protector", // Product Name
  "Software",          // Category
  "29.99",             // Price
  "1"                  // Quantity
);
// This line sends the order information to Google. Required.
pageTracker._trackTrans();
</script>
</body>
```

E-Commerce Tracking with Third-Party Shopping Carts

Jeremy Aube
Web Analytics & Optimization Specialist
ROI Revolution, Inc.
www.roirevolution.com

Google Analytics integrates well with most third-party shopping carts. Many third-party shopping carts even offer an automated method of integration that does most of the work for you.

For those shopping carts without automatic Google Analytics integration, tracking e-commerce presents a special type of challenge. First, e-commerce tracking requires you to get access to the details of every order placed via the shopping cart. The third-party site typically makes this data available to you either through the query string or through POST variables. You will need to work with your shopping cart vendor to determine what data can be made available and in what form it will appear.

Even after you've figured out how to retrieve the order details, there are still other considerations that need to be made. Storing transaction data within Google Analytics is only useful insofar as it allows you to assign those transactions back to specific sources, mediums, campaigns, keywords, and landing pages.

To make this happen, you need a page where the order details are available, the Google Analytics tracking code can be placed correctly, and the referral data for the customer is also available. This is usually the "thank you" page that is displayed to the visitor after they've successfully placed an order.

Because Google Analytics uses first-party cookies, it's easiest to track orders if the entire site exists on a single domain. In the case of an outside shopping cart, you'll need to pass the visitor's referral data for that visitor to that third-party domain.

Sites that use third-party shopping carts to process orders basically come in two types:

- Those where the "thank you" page occurs on the main site
- Those where the "thank you" page occurs on the shopping cart

Regardless of which situation you're dealing with, you need to make sure that you've installed the Google Analytics tracking script correctly throughout your main site. Next, you need to determine if the standard tracking code given to you by Google will suffice, or if you will need to make changes. There are many cases where minor tweaks will be necessary to address the particular needs and characteristics of your site's structure. If your site spans multiple domains or subdomains, this will almost certainly apply to you.

We'll discuss some of the more common changes below. The exact order in which they appear in the script doesn't matter in most situations. The following example code indicates the proper locations where any changes should go:

```
<script type="text/javascript">
var gaJsHost = (("https:" == document.location.protocol) ? "https://ssl." : "http://www.");
```

```
document.write(unescape("%3Cscript src='" + gaJsHost + "google-analytics.com/ga.js'
ype='text/javascript'%3E%3C/script%3E"));
</script>
<script type="text/javascript">
try {
var pageTracker = _gat._getTracker("UA-XXXXXXX-1");
// Changes Go Here ...
pageTracker._trackPageview();
} catch(err) {}</script>
```

Rolling Up Subdomain Traffic

One type of change that's extremely useful is to set the cookie domain to the root level domain. This is useful in situations where your site has multiple subdomains, and also helps if visitors can get to your site both with and without a leading www.

To do this, just add this line to your tracking script:

```
pageTracker._setDomainName("example.com");
```

In this case, "example.com" is the root level domain for your site. This line will tell Google Analytics to use the same set of cookies before the transaction and at the time of the transaction, even if the visitor is on example.com before the transaction and www.example.com at the time of the transaction (or on entirely different subdomains altogether).

"Thank You" Page on the Main Site

This situation is by far the easier one to deal with. Because visitors are coming back to the main site, we have the option of completely ignoring the visitor while they are on the third-party shopping cart and resuming tracking once they get back to the main site.

The problem here is that there is a potential for the visitor's original referral data to be overwritten with a referral from the third-party site. There are a number of ways to prevent this.

Usually, the easiest way to prevent referrals from the third-party site is to change the return URL, the URL that the shopping cart sends visitors to when they've completed their transaction, so that it includes the parameter utm_nooverride=1:

```
http://www.example.com/thanks.html?utm_nooverride=1
```

Adding this parameter ensures that previous referral data will not be overwritten.

If for some reason you are unable to change the return URL in this way, you can instead add the following lines:

```
pageTracker._addIgnoredRef("www.thirdpartysite.com");
```

```
pageTracker._addIgnoredRef("thirdpartysite.com");
```

Notice that we're using _addIgnoredRef for both www.thirdpartysite.com and thirdpartysite.com. This illustrates the fact that the value you pass to _addIgnoredRef needs to be exactly the domain visitors see when they get to the shopping cart. If there's more than one subdomain for that domain, even if it's just www and non-www, then you need an _addIgnoredRef line for each subdomain.

You may also want to consider extending the session timeout on the page immediately before visitors are taken to the shopping cart. The default session timeout is 30 minutes, but if you wanted to extend this to two hours, you'd add the following line to your Google Analytics tracking code:

```
pageTracker._setSessionTimeout("7200");
```

Notice that 7200 is the number of seconds in two hours. You can change this amount to match the needs of your site. By adding this line, you will allow plenty of time for visitors to fill in their order information on the shopping cart.

"Thank You" Page on the Shopping Cart

If the only place your "thank you" page can exist is on the third-party site, then you must be able to track the visitor across domains. To do this, you will need to add the following lines to your Google Analytics tracking code:

```
pageTracker._setAllowHash(false);
pageTracker._setAllowLinker(true);
pageTracker._setAllowAnchor(true);
```

The first line makes your cookie data compatible with both sites. The second line enables the linking functions that pass referral data from one site to the other. The third line tells Google Analytics to look for referral data in the anchor in addition to the query string.

After adding the above lines, determine how your visitors are getting from your site to the third-party shopping cart. This is usually done either via a regular link or through a form submit.

For links, you'll add an onclick event that passes the referral information to the third-party cart:

```
<a href="http://www.thirdpartysite.com/buynow/" onclick="javascript:pageTracker._link(this.href,
true); return false;">Buy Now!</a>
```

If visitors get to your third-party cart through form submissions, you'll add some special tracking code to the onsubmit event of the form element:

```
<form action="http://www.thirdpartysite.com/shoppingcart/" method="POST"
onsubmit="javascript:pageTracker._linkByPost(this, true);">
```

For both of these functions, I am adding the optional "true" parameter so that referral data is passed in the anchor instead of the query string. Shopping carts tend to modify query strings more often than anchors, so this makes sure that referral data is successfully passed to the shopping cart.

For forms that use the "GET" method, passing referral data through the anchor is the only option. When a "GET" form is submitted, the query string is stripped from the action parameter to make way for the form's input values.

There's a lot to consider when setting up e-commerce tracking for a third-party shopping cart, but the steps described above will work in the vast majority of scenarios. Be sure to consult the Google Analytics support site (google.com/support/googleanalytics/) for up-to-date solutions.

SUMMARY

You've made it this far, so you now know what tracking is, why it's important, and how to set it up. In the next chapter, you'll learn how to get answers to the most common questions using the Google Analytics reporting website.

CHAPTER 4

Using Your Analytics Software

Google Analytics comes with a dizzying array of graphs and statistics, far more than most marketers need. The trick to using this software successfully is to become familiar with the critical, high-level reports and then drill down into the details when necessary.

Analytics is an indispensable part of search marketing. You simply can't succeed without it. But don't make the mistake of taking the data it provides at face value. In fact, my experience has shown me that most of the data provided by Google Analytics and other analytics packages can be inaccurate or even downright wrong at times.

The data is inaccurate for a variety of reasons: users delete cookies, tracking scripts get removed or modified, and sometimes the data just gets lost in transmission. (Don't believe me? Just try matching up your orders as reported by Google Analytics with your in-house order tracking system. Consider yourself lucky if the two come within 10% of each other.)

But this doesn't make it useless. Far from it! Instead, consider the reporting data you get from Google Analytics as directional. It tells a story that a smart marketer (you!) can use to figure out how to drive more traffic, deepen your relationship with your site's visitors, and increase sales.

In this chapter, I'll give you a whirlwind tour through the most important reporting features of Google Analytics as well as a few of my techniques for turning this data into a story that you can act on.

THE DASHBOARD

The very first screen you'll see when you log in to Google Analytics is the dashboard. It should look something like the screenshot shown in Figure 4-1.

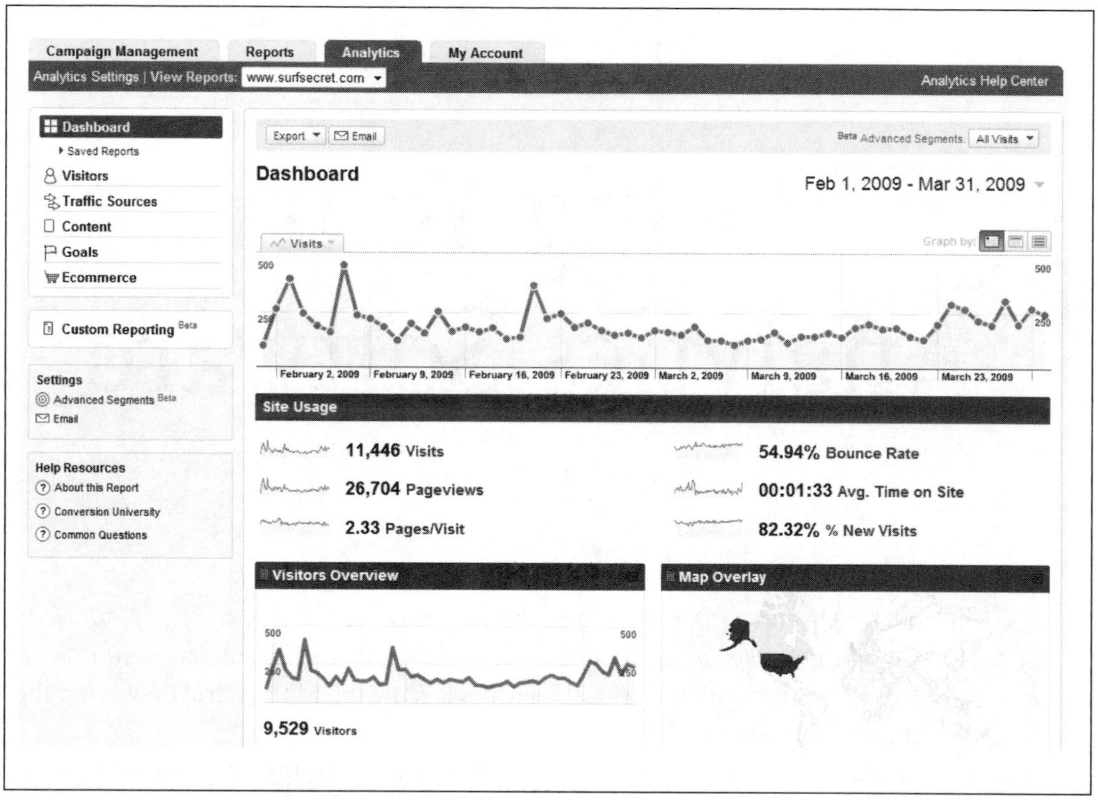

FIGURE 4-1. The Google Analytics dashboard

On this page are a number of key statistics:

- **The primary charting area**—the number of visits to your site over time is displayed here by default, but you can also plot other statistics by clicking on the dropdown at the upper left of the graph.
- **Visits** is the most important statistic on this page. It tells you the number of unique sessions initiated by visitors to your site. A session is considered to be a series of page requests from the same uniquely identified visitor that occur near each other. After 30 minutes of inactivity, the session is considered to be over. You will most likely want your visits counter to increase over time.

- **Pageviews** indicates the number of pages on your site that were loaded by your visitors. A visit always consists of at least one pageview, so this figure will always be higher than the visits statistic. Only pages tagged with the Google Analytics script will be counted in this figure.

- **Pages/Visit** is calculated by dividing pageviews by visits. This figure is interesting in that it tells you how "sticky" your site is. Generally speaking, the longer visitors hang around your site, the easier it is to get them to engage in your desired action. The best way to do this is to provide high-value content and plenty of cross-linking. For most commercial sites, I consider a value of two to be low, while three or higher is quite good. Your mileage may vary!

- **Bounce Rate** indicates the percentage of visitors who enter and exit at the same page without visiting any other pages on the site. The overall statistic presented on this page isn't particularly useful, but there are some excellent uses for it which I'll discuss in more detail below.

The "Visits" Graph Can Tell You When Your Tracking Is Broken

Sudden drops in site traffic are unusual, so if you see one, your first thought should be to look for broken Google Analytics tracking scripts. If you're using a CMS system to publish your website, it is usually a good idea to lock down any template files containing this tracking script to eliminate the possibility of someone deleting them (Figure 4-2).

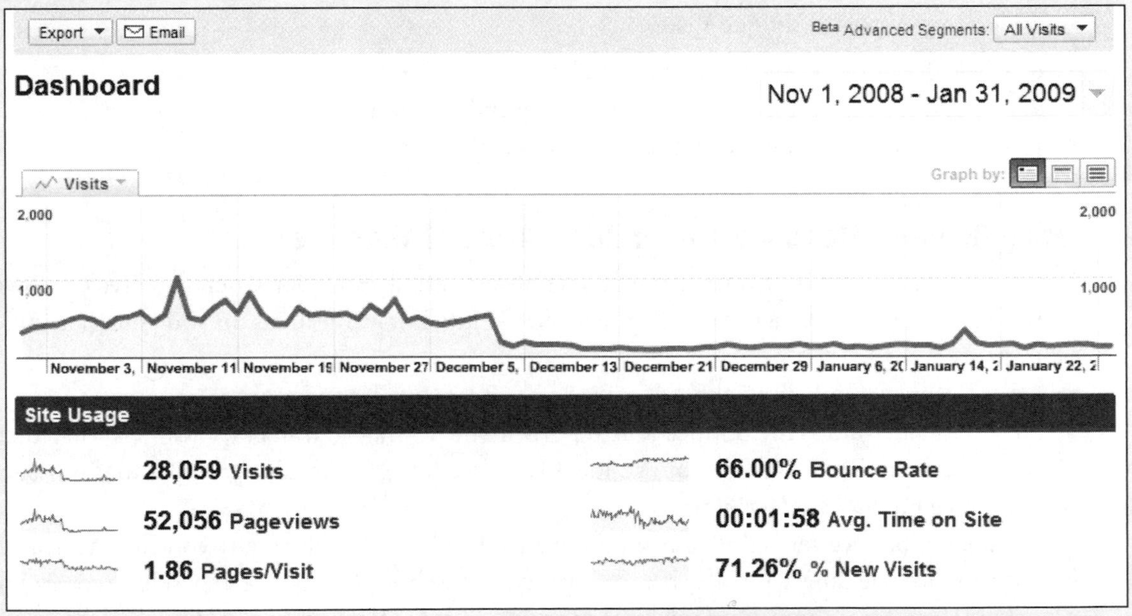

FIGURE 4-2. Sudden drops in site traffic such as this are usually the result of broken or mangled Google Analytics tracking scripts.

- **Avg. Time on Site** attempts to measure the average period of time that each session lasts. This is complicated by the fact that Google Analytics cannot determine the length of time the visitor spent on the final page.
- **% New Visits** measures first-time visits as a percentage of total visits. For brand-new sites, this statistic will be very high. It tends to decline as sites age and accumulate repeat visitors.

ESTIMATING MARKETING POTENTIAL USING ABSOLUTE UNIQUE VISITORS

While this page is a good starting point, there's another statistic I find to be of great importance: **Absolute Unique Visitors.** This statistic counts each unique client only once during the time period. In other words, it's a pretty good estimate of how many actual people visited your site, regardless of how many times they may have visited it. Keep in mind that it is just an estimate. If someone visits your site on different browsers or computers, they will be counted multiple times.

The dashboard report indicated that we had 11,446 visits in February and March. The Absolute Unique Visitor report (shown below) tells you that there were 9,529 actual people behind these visits.

This figure may help you to plan your marketing initiatives if you know the size of your potential audience. For instance, if you estimate that there are 200,000 potential customers on the internet for your service and you are reaching 10,000 of them a month, you have a lot of room for growth in your customer acquisition and/or branding activities. On the other hand, if you reached all 200,000 in a single month, you may be at the end of the runway in terms of new customer acquisition. In that event, you might look at focusing on repeat business, product expansion, and so forth (Figure 4-3).

To look up Absolute Unique Visitors:

- Click "Visitors" on the left navigation bar
- Expand the "Visitor Trending" submenu by clicking on it.
- Click "Absolute Unique Visitors" in the submenu.

Using Bounce Rate to Identify Problem Areas of Your Site

Bounce rate, measured over your entire site, is not very useful. However, when you break it down by traffic source, it can be a helpful diagnostic to identify low-value areas on your site that could be improved.

Let's take an example from the AdGooroo free site (http://free.adgooroo.com).

First, we'll navigate to the Bounce Rate report (on the left navigation bar, click "Visitors," then "Visitor Trending," and finally, "Bounce Rate"). We see from the resulting report that our site-wide bounce rate is 79.46% (Figure 4-4).

Although a bounce rate of 80% is on the high side, it's hard to draw any conclusions from it because bounce rate can vary widely based on the type of website. In this case, the website consists of a large number of free competitive intelligence reports. Some of these reports rank well on the search engines for various keywords, so the site tends to draw in a high volume of untargeted visitors.

On one hand, you may (reasonably) think that the free site is a failure because of the high

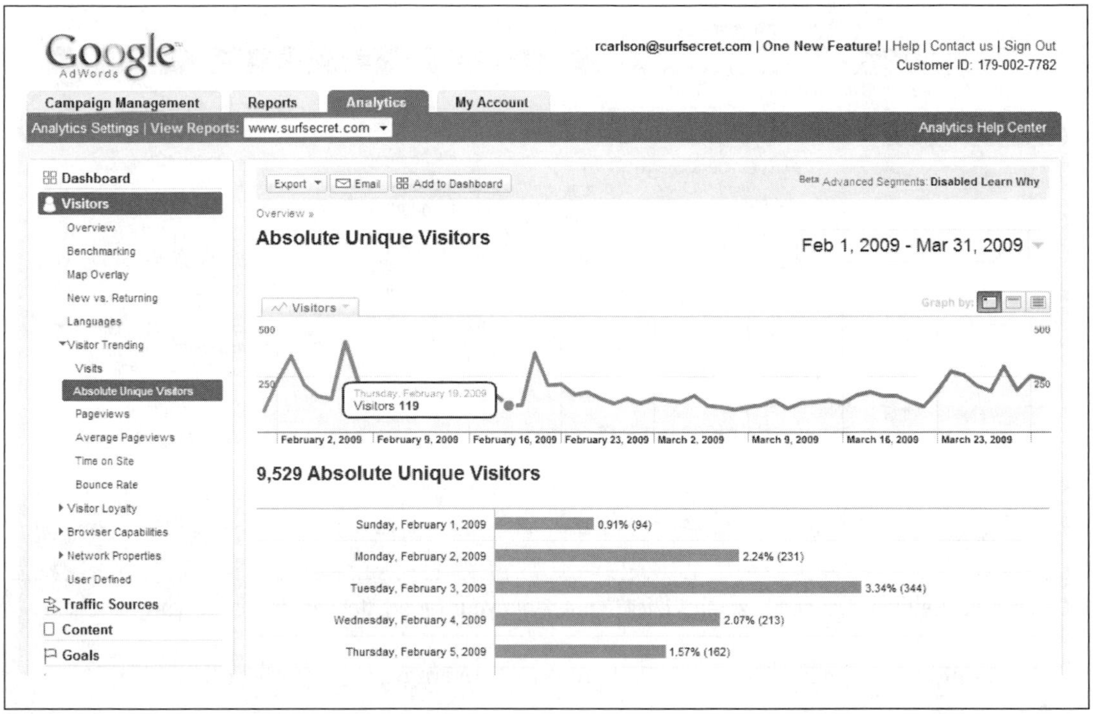

FIGURE 4-3. Absolute Unique Visitors is a vital statistic for any site.

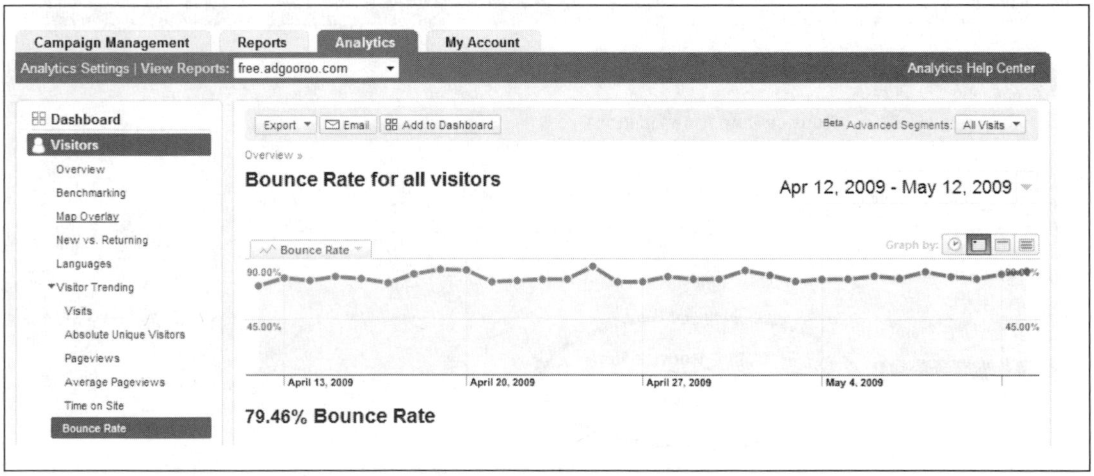

FIGURE 4-4. Find your site-wide bounce rate on the Bounce Rate report.

bounce rate. On the other, you could argue that 80% is remarkably low, considering that most of the visitors had no prior knowledge of our website!

We can shed some more light on the situation by segmenting our traffic out by new vs. repeat visitors. We can do this by clicking the "All Visits" button next to the "Advanced Segments" label at the top right of the graphing area. This will open an expanded area where we can segment out our traffic. Here I'll pick "New Visitors" and "Returning Visitors" (Figure 4-5).

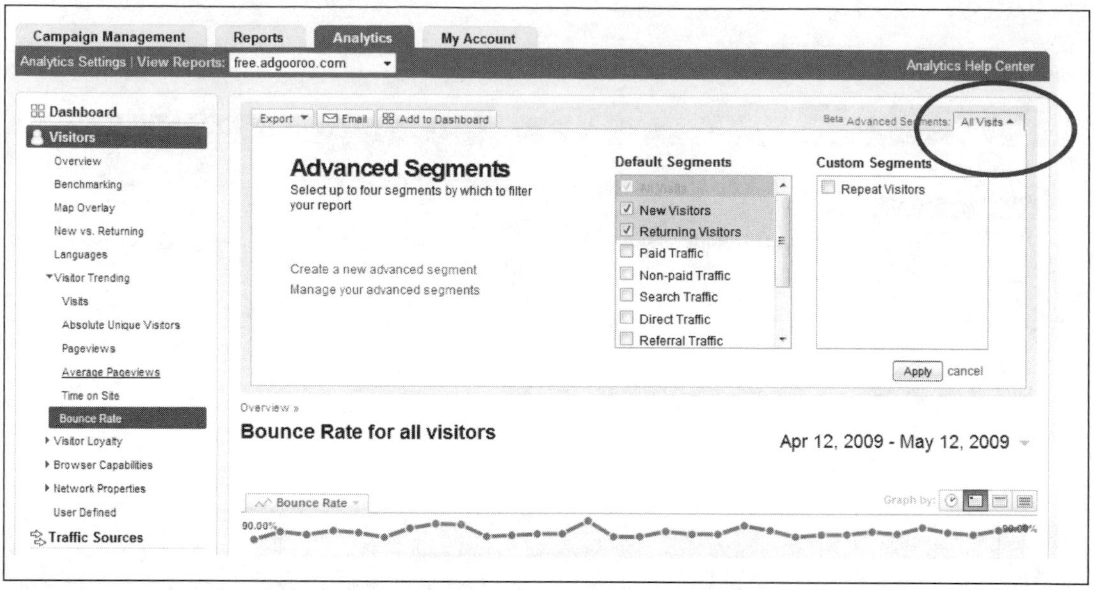

FIGURE 4-5. Use the Advanced Segments filter to break out your report statistics by visitor type.

After applying these changes, a very different picture emerges (Figure 4-6).

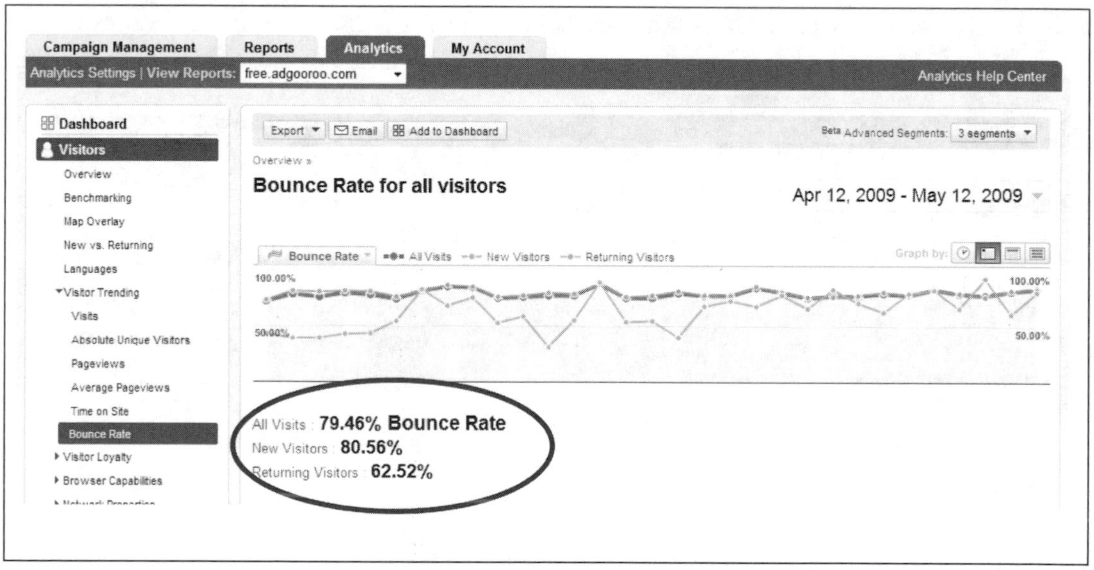

FIGURE 4-6.

We see here that among first-time visitors, we have a high bounce rate of around 81%. However, among repeat visitors, the bounce rate is less than 63%. This tells us that we're getting a much higher degree of involvement with certain people. This is an indicator that the website is delivering value to interested prospects and that we're on the right path after all.

IDENTIFYING HIGHLY MOTIVATED BUYERS WITH THE TRAFFIC SOURCES REPORT

Other reports I use frequently are those located in the "Traffic Sources" menu on the left navigation bar. The reports here allow you to segment your data by direct traffic, traffic referred from other sites, and search engine traffic (both paid and natural).

In particular, I use the paid search engine keyword report on an almost daily basis. To navigate to it, click on "Traffic Sources," then "Search Engines" in the submenu underneath. From here, you can further refine the report by clicking on a search engine as well as the "paid" link just below the graph shownin Figurc 4-7.

The resulting report will give you basic performance metrics for each of your paid search keywords. For instance, you can compare the Bounce Rate, Avg. Time on Site, and Pages/Visit for each keyword against the site as a whole (Figure 4-8).

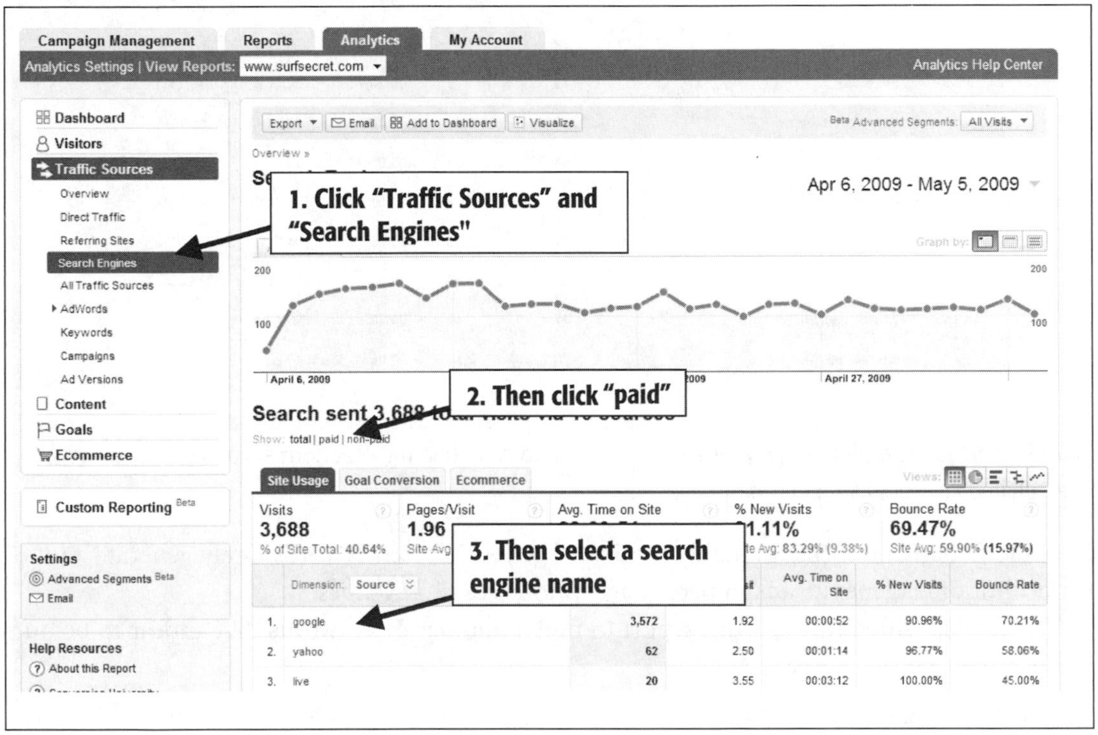

FIGURE 4-7.

In this example, the site-wide Bounce Rate is 75.8%, Pages/Visit is 1.66, and the Avg. Time on Site is 37 seconds. These are the benchmarks for all of my Google AdWords paid search traffic.

Most people focus on optimizing their high-traffic keywords first. My philosophy is different. High-traffic keywords often have high assist rates (see Chapter 31), so I believe that cutting them prematurely is a mistake. Instead, I start maximizing sales by looking for those keywords that

Site Usage	Goal Conversion	Ecommerce				Views:

Visits	Pages/Visit	Avg. Time on Site	% New Visits	Bounce Rate
2,428	**1.66**	**00:00:37**	**93.12%**	**75.82%**
% of Site Total: 31.83%	Site Avg: 2.46 (-32.33%)	Site Avg: 00:02:10 (-71.54%)	Site Avg: 81.99% (13.58%)	Site Avg: 57.79% (31.20%)

	Dimension: Keyword	Visits ↓	Pages/Visit	Avg. Time on Site	% New Visits	Bounce Rate
1.	search history	363	1.46	00:00:28	93.39%	76.31%
2.	web history	362	1.55	00:00:29	93.37%	76.52%
3.	computer history	180	1.54	00:00:55	93.89%	77.78%
4.	delete internet history	146	1.37	00:00:13	97.26%	81.51%
5.	clear google history	144	1.39	00:00:23	94.44%	82.64%
6.	google history	133	1.31	00:00:27	96.24%	86.47%
7.	history remove	86	1.53	00:01:04	97.67%	81.40%
8.	remove history	78	1.29	00:00:29	98.72%	85.90%
9.	clear cache	72	1.46	00:00:12	100.00%	86.11%
10.	history of computer	49	1.65	00:00:22	89.80%	85.71%
11.	surfsecret	47	5.23	00:03:38	36.17%	36.17%
12.	erase history	41	1.78	00:00:22	87.80%	70.73%
13.	remove files	37	1.78	00:00:19	94.59%	72.97%
14.	erase aol history	35	1.49	00:00:23	94.29%	74.29%
15.	clear internet history	27	1.44	00:00:11	96.30%	81.48%
16.	erase internet history	26	2.50	00:00:20	76.92%	80.77%
17.	get rid of history	26	1.50	00:00:13	88.46%	84.62%

FIGURE 4-8. You can sift through your paid search keywords to find underperformers and outperformers. The outlined keywords are in need of improvement.

have the potential to bring in highly motivated buyers. These keywords rarely generate a lot of traffic, but often generate a high percentage of total search revenues.

To do this, I sifted through this report to find a number of keywords that appear to be out-performing these averages:

- **Internet privacy protector:** 27% bounce rate, 4:24 on site, and 5.73 pages/visit
- **Hard drive cleaner:** 42% bounce rate, 3:07 on site, and 2.42 pages/visit
- **History cleaner free:** 48% bounce rate, 56 seconds on site, and 2.9 pages/visit

These are the keywords my best prospects are typing into the engines. If I wanted results fast, these would be the keywords I would focus my initial efforts on. For instance, I would immediately "Peel & Stick" them into separate ad groups (see Chapter 24) and then create dedicated landing pages for each. I'd also take measures to improve my quality score and possibly raise my bid prices.

After I've spent some time tailoring my site to accommodate these visitors, I then use this same report to cut high-cost, low-ROI terms out of my account. Here, you look for keywords that are getting lots of clicks but have high bounce rates, low pages/visit, and short average time spent on site. In this example, I've identified a number of keywords that are candidates for trimming:

- **Search history:** bounce rate 76%, 28 seconds on site, and 1.5 pages/visit
- **Web history:** bounce rate 76%, 32 seconds on site, and 1.5 pages/visit
- **Computer history:** bounce rate 77%, 52 seconds on site, and 1.5 pages/visit

I wouldn't immediately cut these terms. Rather, I would first look for possible negative matches to cut down on the amount of unqualified traffic being sent through them (see Chapter 23). Then I would "Peel & Stick" these terms into separate ad groups and optimize them as before. If after taking all of these steps I still couldn't get them to perform better than the site-wide averages, I'd consider dropping their bids or deleting them from my campaign altogether.

Streamline the Sales Process Using the Funnel Report

The funnel report is one of my favorites for making conversion funnels more efficient. This report is only available if you've set up goals for your site as described in the previous chapter. Access it by clicking the "Funnel Visualization" link in the "Goals" menu on the left-hand navigation bar (Figure 4-9).

This report shows you the completion rate for each stage of your conversion funnel. The way I use it is quite typical: simply look at the percentage of visitors who complete each stage and then optimize those pages with the lowest clickthrough rates. Your goal is to get your visitors further and further into the funnel until eventually they reach the final step (a conversion).

In the sample funnel report shown in Figure 4-9, the first two stages have approximately the same clickthrough rate, so I would focus my optimization efforts on the first stage (it has higher traffic, so my tests will return results faster). For more on this, see the next section, which focuses on conversion optimization.

Prioritizing Paid and Organic Optimization Efforts

Website owners often ask whether they should focus more on paid search or search engine optimization (SEO). There's no pat answer for this. Contrary to popular belief, having high organic rankings doesn't always translate to higher sales. In fact, many sites get much higher conversion rates with paid search than they do from organic traffic.

At the end of the day, it depends entirely on your business and your visitors. The best approach to answering this question is an empirical one. Try both and see what happens.

This doesn't mean you have to break the bank. Instead, you can experiment with small campaigns and then see which performs better. And Google Analytics' segmenting feature is a great way to measure this.

Here's an example. In Figure 4-10, I've broken out the conversion rate report by both "paid" and "unpaid" traffic. You can see that the conversion rate for organic traffic is more than four times the rate of paid traffic. This is a strong indicator that we should be focusing more on SEO than PPC.

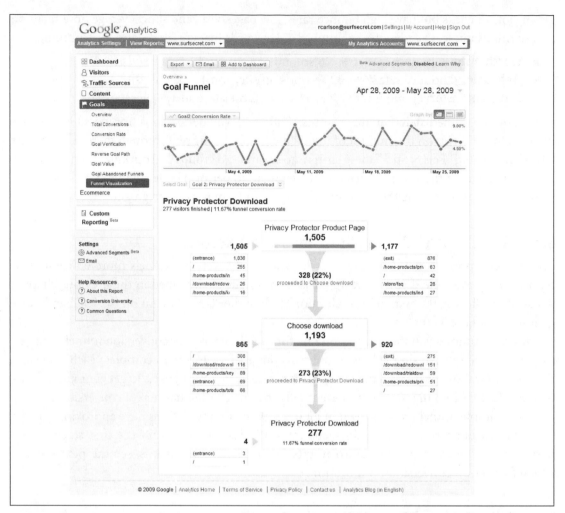

FIGURE 4-9. The Funnel Visualization report comes in handy for diagnosing problems with sales funnels.

The Granddaddy of All Google Analytics Metrics: The "Dollar Index"

For years, I considered this to be my most powerful weapon for increasing website sales and kept it a closely guarded secret. It's now included as a standard metric within Google Analytics, so the cat's out of the bag.

The $/Index ("Dollar index") tells you how much every page on your site contributed to your revenue. It's calculated by first calculating the total revenue generated by visitors to that page and then dividing that by the total number of views of that page (including visitors who didn't purchase anything).

Here's an example. Assume that a particular page was viewed 360 times and that visitors to that page generated $18,184 in sales. The $/Index is calculated as follows:

$$\frac{\$}{\text{Index}} = \frac{\$18,184}{360} = \$50.51$$

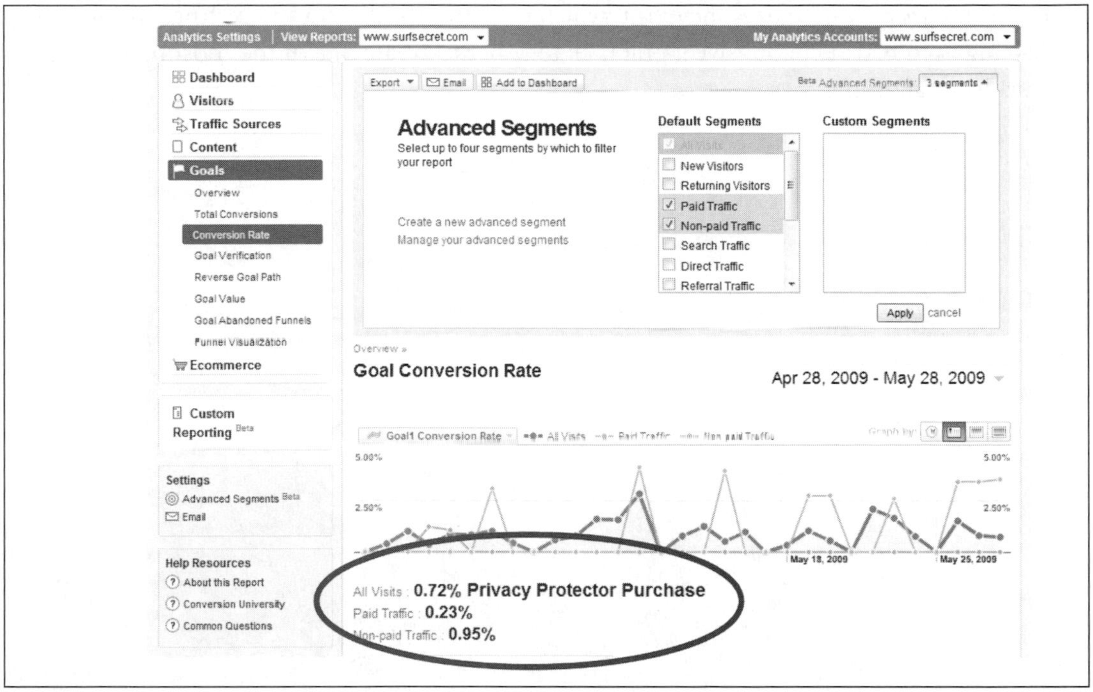

FIGURE 4-10. Google Analytics' segmenting features make it easy to compare results from paid and organic traffic sources.

By itself, the figure is interesting. For instance, if you find high $/index pages that aren't in your sales funnels, you may want to test them (or portions of them) as potential landing pages.

However, the $/Index statistic becomes far more valuable when it's calculated for every page on your site (this is difficult to do by hand, so it's a welcome addition to Google Analytics). You can then layer this data on top of your website traffic map (see the next chapter) to identify high-value pages. For instance, in the early days at AdGooroo we discovered that our pricing page had a high $/index, despite being buried somewhat deeply in the site. As a result, we took this page and linked to it prominently from the top of every page. Today, this page is one of the most viewed pages on our site and assists in driving a significant portion of our sales.

> Analytics is a deep subject and we've just scratched the surface. If you want to further your knowledge, I recommend *Advanced Web Metrics with Google Analytics* by Brian Clifton.

SUMMARY

If you want to succeed at PPC, you'll need to have at least a rudimentary grasp of the reports provided by your analytics software. In this chapter, we gave you the keys to using Google Analytics to explore your visitors' behavior on your website. These reports tell you where your visitors came from, what pages they visit, which ones they find most interesting, and why they are leaving. In the next chapter, we'll pull it all together to create one of the most powerful tools at your disposal: traffic maps.

Use Traffic Maps to Get to Your Destination

THE MOST IMPORTANT LEVER YOU CAN PULL TO ENSURE YOUR SUCCESS AS A PAY-PER-CLICK advertiser has nothing to do with the search engines. Rather, it's largely determined by the efficiency of your website in converting visitors into revenue.

If every thousand visitors to your site generate $1,000 in revenue, then you can afford to pay up to $1 each and still break even. If, on the other hand, a thousand visitors generate only $100 of revenue, then you can pay only a dime each before you begin losing money.

Only a fraction of PPC advertisers appear to grasp this fundamental tenet of search advertising. They rush into starting a Google campaign with very little understanding of how all the parts fit together. This is where all the work we've accomplished together so far pays off.

We're now going to create a blueprint of your website traffic. With it, you'll learn where your prospects are coming from, what pages they're visiting, what they buy, and how they buy it. This map will be the key to your success with PPC advertising.

HOW DOES A TRAFFIC MAP HELP YOU?
You'll Know … Not Guess … Where Your Sales Are Coming From

First, it will allow you to clearly articulate where your sales are coming from. Few marketing managers have a grasp on exactly where the revenue is being generated on their sites. They spend days or weeks working on projects that often bear little fruit. Most of the time, it's not because they failed. Rather, it's because they succeeded at optimizing areas that have little revenue-generating potential.

If you don't know where your sales are coming from, it's very difficult to identify low-risk/high-reward efforts that can be exploited quickly with a minimum of effort. The traffic map, which usually takes less than an hour to create, will arm you with low-risk/high-reward marketing projects that can literally multiply your sales.

You'll Find Bottlenecks in Your Conversion Funnels

Second, the process of creating this map will invariably turn up sales bottlenecks on your site that result in lost revenue. As an example of this, a traffic map I created for a well-known computer security site showed that their main bottleneck was occurring on a single page in the checkout process, where 53% of all visitors were abandoning their orders.

You'll Redirect Traffic from Low-Value Pages to High-Converting Ones

For them, the map acted as a type of focusing lens. It told us exactly where we had to concentrate our efforts. In just a matter of days, we were able to narrow down the problems to a few specific areas:

- The order form was lengthy and confusing
- A European VAT (tax) notice was being displayed to U.S. users
- Brittle validation scripts on the order entry fields caused users to give up on placing orders out of frustration
- The shopping cart was sometimes "forgetting" customers' items during the checkout process

This site, which received over 100,000 visitors a day, consisted of hundreds of pages. It was no small feat to be able to narrow the problems down to a few quick projects with the potential to make a noticeable impact on sales.

You'll Learn How to Convert More Visitors into Revenue

As a result of addressing the above problems, the cost-per-acquisition (CPA) on the site dropped by 30% almost overnight. In other words, we were making $1.30 for every $1.00 we had made before. This allowed us to increase the spend for all of our advertising buys and drive larger volumes of traffic to the site.

You'll Identify New Landing Pages

Another important discovery was made in the process of creating the traffic map for this site. We discovered a few pages that had a high $/Index value and were not included in our regular sales funnel. We tested these pages and found one that wildly outperformed the original landing page.

In the process of creating your map, you'll also be looking at the $/Index values for many of the important pages on your site. These pages often perform well in the landing page tests you'll need to run when optimizing your PPC campaigns.

You'll No Longer Be Held Hostage by Your Designers

Web designers love to create beautiful and innovative new page layouts. They'll insist that you need to have navigation on a certain page, that your pages are created according to certain proportions, that the font choice is critical to the integrity of the site, that the Flash animation is absolutely necessary … well, you get the idea.

But the fact of the matter is that they are often wrong—at least when it comes to designing sites that drive sales. With most businesses, creative needs to serve the functional, not the other way around. With a map in hand, you will have logical and defensible reasons for insisting on certain design decisions and you won't be easily swayed by the latest trends in web design. No, you won't win many points with your designers, but we're all in business to make money, aren't we?

You'll Make Life Much More Difficult for Your Competitors

The changes you'll identify as part of the mapping process are often subtle and not at all obvious to the untrained eye. A competitor who scours your site to find the secret of your success will lack the numbers behind your page flow and design decisions. They will be subject to the same guesswork and opinions that I am insisting you not rely on—and if you're lucky, their designers will insist that you're doing it all wrong! As a result, their conversions will suffer and you'll be able to outbid them for paid search traffic.[1]

BEFORE YOU CAN CREATE A TRAFFIC MAP, YOU'LL NEED SOME WEBSITE TRAFFIC

You can't construct a traffic map without traffic. If you don't already have a reasonable amount of traffic on your site, you're facing a "chicken and egg" problem. The solution? Start a simple PPC campaign so that you can begin to gather some analytics data. (PPC is covered in the third section of this book.)

You don't need to break the bank on this, but you will need to send enough traffic to reach deep into your funnels and generate some actionable data. Ideally, you'd like to get no less than 25 conversions on each funnel (100 is even better). This can easily add up to several thousand clicks.

If your website is already generating sales (presumably through organic search traffic), it may only cost you a few hundred dollars to get the required traffic. But for those of you starting from scratch, this may be a tall order, as your conversion funnels may be in bad shape.

Fortunately, there's an easy workaround. Instead of mapping out your entire site, just map the first page or two of your funnels. If you can get 25 people even halfway through the sales process, you'll learn a lot and can focus on getting some quick wins under your belt. As your site improves, more and more people will find their way into the deeper pages of your funnels, giving you the traffic you need to conduct split tests.

It may take a while to make your first sale, but don't give up. Progress comes slowly at first, but as visitors begin to trickle closer and closer to the final "thank you" pages, the improvements will come faster. It's not uncommon to spend months making your first sale, only to have dozens more follow up in the subsequent few days.

THE FIRST MAP IS ALWAYS THE HARDEST

Creating your first traffic map can be frustrating at times because of the obstacles you'll encounter:

- You will find critical errors such as broken links on the site that need to be fixed
- You'll find pages where the tracking code wasn't installed properly
- You may not yet have enough traffic to generate a map (remember, you need around 100 conversions at the tail end of each of your funnels to have confidence in your map)

If you have a large site that has plenty of traffic and sales, the process will probably be easy, as your main problem will be broken tracking scripts (these can be quickly fixed). If you don't have a lot of traffic, you'll need to fix any errors you encounter and then wait until your analytics software collects sufficient data to create the map. This can take days, or it can take months—so get started!

The good news is that after you complete the process the first time, you'll be able to easily update your map at any time in under an hour.

HOW TO CREATE A TRAFFIC MAP

The steps you'll follow to create your traffic map are as follows:

1. Collect site-wide statistics.
2. Identify the most popular page on your site.
3. Find out how most people get to your site.
4. Identify follow-up pages.
5. Repeat for your sales funnel pages.
6. Identify any "cross-feeders."
7. Calculate theoretical CPA (non-revenue-generating funnels).

Once you've constructed a traffic map using these steps, you'll need to interpret it. An invaluable metric for this purpose is the $/Index ("dollar index"). This is best demonstrated with the following tutorial.

TRAFFIC MAP TUTORIAL

We're now going to walk through the process of creating a simple map. We'll use real data from a real site, MethuselahFoundation.org, to illustrate the process.

Step 1: Collect Site-Wide Statistics

Begin by picking a date range long enough to capture a few thousand visits in your analytics reports. The date range you select should also reflect ordinary traffic conditions. You want to eliminate any one-time traffic bursts, such as holiday promotions, mentions on Slashdot, etc. Visitors who arrive during these periods may be more or less motivated than your regular visitors and may throw off your findings.

Next, consult your analytics reports to pull the following data:

- Total visits
- Total absolute unique visitors
- Site-wide bounce rate

You'll find this information on the "Visitors Overview" report in Google Analytics (click on "Visitors" in the left navigation bar) (Figure 5-1).

FIGURE 5-1. Your primary website analytics metrics include Visits, Absolute Unique Visitors, and Bounce Rate. These can be found on the "Visitors Overview" report.

I chose a six-day period for Methuselah Foundation: February 2-7, 2009. The statistics I recorded were:

Total visits: 3,596

Total absolute unique visitors: 2,904

Site-wide bounce rate: 57.42%

Step 2: Identify the Most Popular Page on Your Site

For many domains, this will be the homepage. There's no need to guess, however. You can conclusively identify this page by consulting the "Top Content" report in Google Analytics (found under the "Content" menu on the left navigation bar) (Figure 5-2).

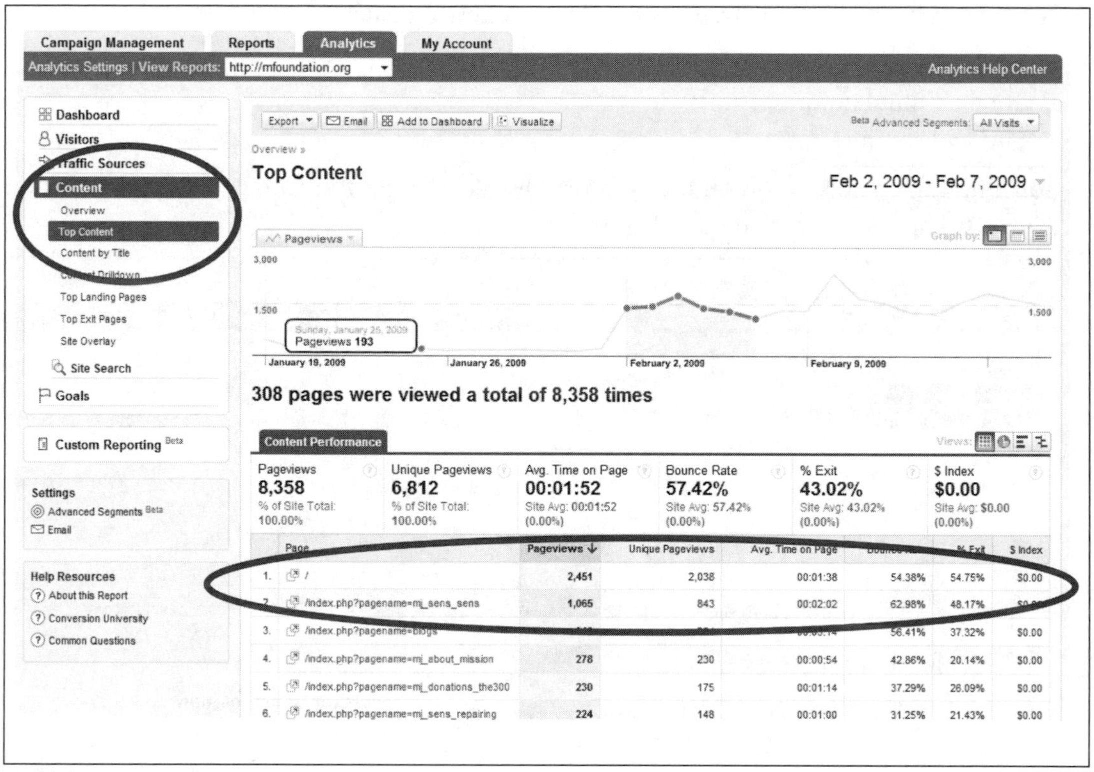

FIGURE 5-2. Identify your most popular page using the "Top Content" report.

The "Top Content" report indicates that the most popular page on Methuselah-Foundation.org is the root page ("/"). This report also contains three mandatory statistics that we'll collect for every page on our map: unique pageviews, bounce rate, and exit rate. Jot the information you've gathered so far on a piece of paper like this:

MethusalehFoundation.org Traffic Analysis
February 2--7, 2009

All Pages
Visits: 3,596
Unique Visitors: 2,904
Bounce Rate: 57.42%

UP: 2,038
Bounce 54.4%
Exit: 54.8%

Step 3: Find Out How People Get to Your Site

Most of your visitors are probably arriving on your site through your homepage (the same page we identified in step 2). However, some sites make heavy use of landing pages, and we want to find this out now.

To get this information, visit the "Top Landing Pages" report in Google Analytics (again, under the "Content" menu). This report will indicate what page is making the first impression with your visitors. If it's the same page as above, record the entrance rate on your map by drawing an inbound arrow on the first box. If it's a different page, add that page to your map, fetch the same statistics we gathered in step 2, and record that data as well (Figure 5-3).

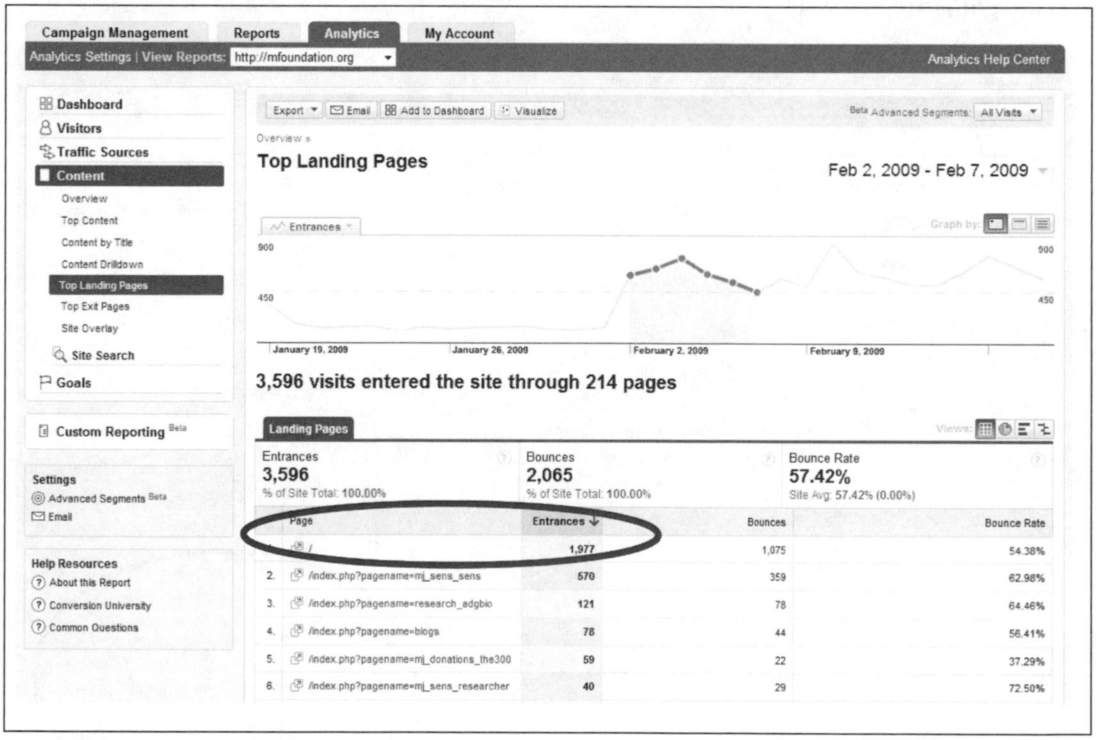

FIGURE 5-3. The first row of the "Top Landing Pages" report will tell you how most of your visitors are arriving at your site.

Here's how our map looks at this point:

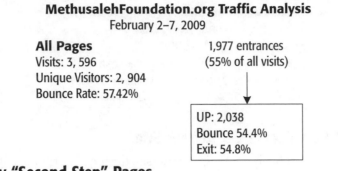

MethusalehFoundation.org Traffic Analysis
February 2–7, 2009

All Pages
Visits: 3, 596
Unique Visitors: 2, 904
Bounce Rate: 57.42%

1,977 entrances
(55% of all visits)

UP: 2,038
Bounce 54.4%
Exit: 54.8%

Step 4: Identify "Second Step" Pages

Now we want to identify what pages your visitors are going to after they arrive at your site. There will likely be dozens, maybe even hundreds, of these follow-up pages. Don't waste time overanalyzing the situation, though. Instead, focus on just the top five.

Retrieve this data by navigating back to the "Top Content" report and clicking on the page in the first row. This will bring you to the "Content Detail" report. Click the link that reads "Navigation Summary." The right column of the page will tell you where your homepage visitors are going (Figure 5-4).

FIGURE 5-4.

The first row is often the same destination page as the source. This indicates that users may be reloading the page. Don't worry about it unless it's significantly higher than 10% (in which case, you should investigate further to find out why people are finding it necessary to refresh the page).

Ignoring the first row, record the next five pages on your map (leaving space for the additional statistics). Draw an arrow from your most important page to each of the "second step" pages and record the percentage of clicks shown on this report.

Feel free to write down any notes while you're constructing the map if ideas begin to jump out at you (or if you simply need to remember what a cryptic URL points to).

To complete this step, go back to the "Top Content" report and fill out the missing statistics for each of the pages you just added.

Our map now looks like as shown in Figure 5-5, page 50.

Step 5: Map Your Funnel Pages

When constructing a traffic map, it usually becomes apparent at this point that there are two sets of important pages on our sites: the pages that visitors are actually visiting and the pages we want them to visit (our conversion funnel pages).

If these two sets of pages don't overlap (which will usually be the case for all but single-page, long copy sites), you'll need to repeat the above process for your funnel pages.

Start with the first page in your funnel and retrieve the clickthrough rate from the page before, as well as the unique page views and bounce/exit rates. Continue to do this for each page in your funnel until it's complete (use the "Top Content" and "Page Navigation" reports), then continue the process for any remaining funnels you have (Figure 5-6, page 51).

Step 6: Look Out for "Cross-Feeders"

Notice that we haven't filled in the percentage of traffic coming from the email newsletter signup form to our "thank you" page. That's because we're now going to work backwards to figure out how people are joining our email list. This allows us to identify "cross-feeder" pages.

A "cross-feeder" is a funnel page that is receiving significant traffic from two or more pages (Figure 5-7, page 51).

Developers and designers like using cross-feeders because it saves them time (they only have to code the page once). However, they cause no end of headaches for search marketers. They require you to manually separate out your traffic statistics for each source, and if there are any significant differences in clickthroughs or conversion rates, you will be forced to unravel your data to answer questions like the following:

- Why is Page A converting at so much higher of a rate than Page B?
- Why is Page B driving so much more traffic?
- What makes Page A visitors different from Page B visitors?

It can be very difficult to answer these questions with any confidence, so when I design a sales

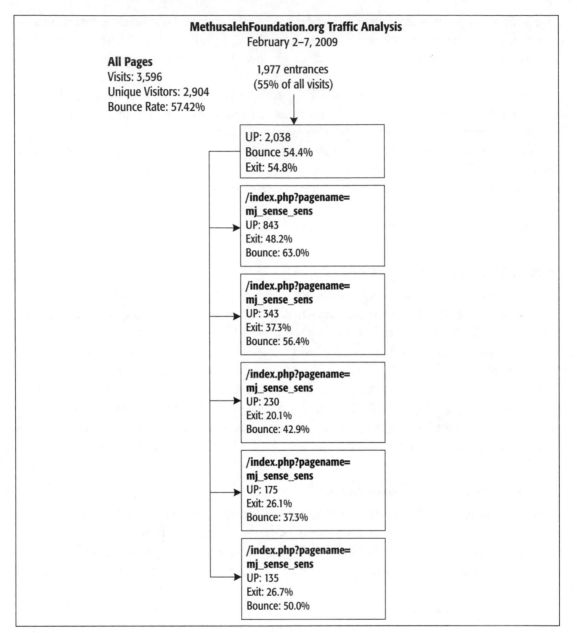

FIGURE 5-5.

funnel, I avoid using cross-feeders if at all possible. Instead, I duplicate these important pages and give them distinct URLs. Good developers don't like to do things this way, so expect some pushback.

If you aren't building a site from scratch, you don't have that luxury. You'll need to use the "Navigation Summary" report on your funnel pages to determine if you have any cross-feeders.

Click the link for your sales funnel page on the "Top Content" report. You'll be directed to the

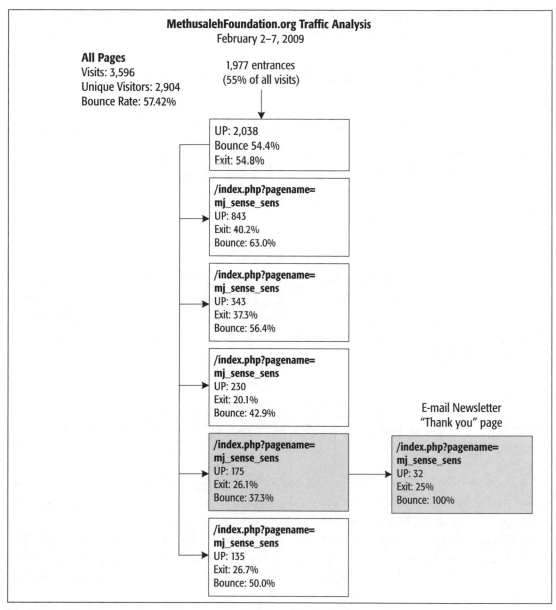

MethusalehFoundation.org Traffic Analysis
February 2–7, 2009

All Pages
Visits: 3,596
Unique Visitors: 2,904
Bounce Rate: 57.42%

1,977 entrances
(55% of all visits)

UP: 2,038
Bounce 54.4%
Exit: 54.8%

/index.php?pagename=
mj_sense_sens
UP: 843
Exit: 40.2%
Bounce: 63.0%

/index.php?pagename=
mj_sense_sens
UP: 343
Exit: 37.3%
Bounce: 56.4%

/index.php?pagename=
mj_sense_sens
UP: 230
Exit: 20.1%
Bounce: 42.9%

E-mail Newsletter
"Thank you" page

/index.php?pagename=
mj_sense_sens
UP: 175
Exit: 26.1%
Bounce: 37.3%

/index.php?pagename=
mj_sense_sens
UP: 32
Exit: 25%
Bounce: 100%

/index.php?pagename=
mj_sense_sens
UP: 135
Exit: 26.7%
Bounce: 50.0%

FIGURE 5-6. Traffic map after adding sales funnel pages. The shaded pages indicate our email newsletter signup path.

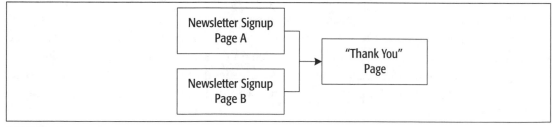

Newsletter Signup
Page A

Newsletter Signup
Page B

"Thank You"
Page

FIGURE 5-7.

"Navigation Summary" report. Look in the left column to determine if there are any significant sources of traffic feeding the page that aren't already on your map (Figure 5-8).

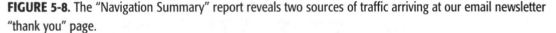

FIGURE 5-8. The "Navigation Summary" report reveals two sources of traffic arriving at our email newsletter "thank you" page.

This report allowed us to identify a second page sending traffic to our newsletter signup "thank you" page. In essence, we have two sales funnels being merged into one. We'll now add this page to our map along with the statistics from the "Top Content" page.

We can also use this page to figure out the conversion rate for each of the feeder pages. The "Navigation Summary" report above indicates that only 3.12% of the 32 visitors (1 visitor) came from the first email newsletter signup form. The remaining 93.75% (31 visitors) came from another page, which is not currently on our map.

Use the reports in a similar fashion to figure out how people are getting to this second newsletter signup page. Add this information to the map as you collect it (Figure 5-9).

It's obvious that we have a real mystery on our hands here. In this case, the two pages were virtually identical, yet one had a much higher conversion rate (29.2% vs. 0.6%). I had to sort through a number of different reports to try and figure out what the difference was. It turned out that the reason was because most visitors arrived on the second email signup page only after clicking through various other pages on the site. As a general rule, the more clicks it takes to get to a page, the fewer visitors you'll get, but the ones who make it there will be very motivated! I call this "Darwinnowing."

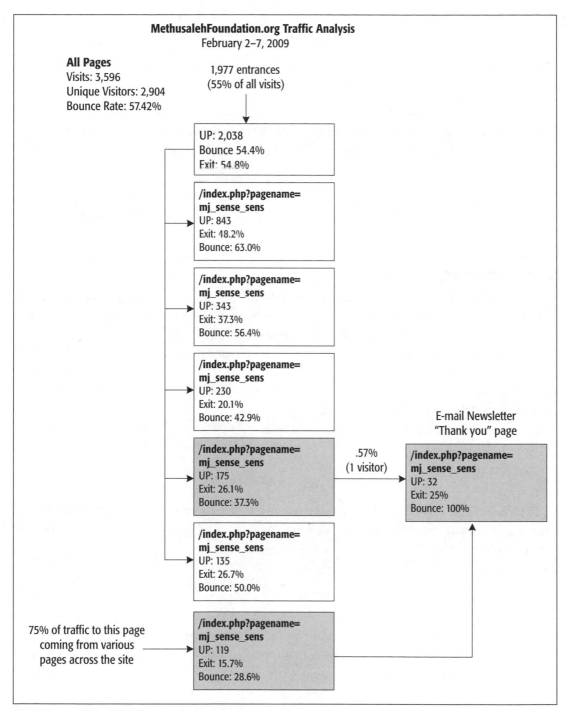

FIGURE 5-9. The updated map now includes two cross-feeders.

> ## Darwinnowing
>
> Darwinnowing[2] is the process of filtering out all but your most patient and motivated visitors, often through the use of poor navigation and graphic design.
>
> It's Darwinnowing that explains why two otherwise identical pages can produce dramatically different conversion rates depending on where they live on your site. If it takes six clicks to reach your funnel page, you can expect it to have a great conversion rate because most of the herd was killed off in the process of getting there.
>
> Remember, the goal is not to maximize your conversion rate; it's to maximize your total conversions. You can ensure that you aren't Darwinnowing your visitors by following the procedure laid out in Chapter 8.

Step 7: Calculate Theoretical CPA

If your conversions aren't measured in actual dollars (for instance, you are generating leads or signups for an email newsletter), then you're almost done. If you aren't tracking order amounts, then your job is considerably easier than the one outlined in step 8.

Instead, you're going to figure out how much each conversion would cost you if you paid $0.25 per visitor. This is a lower cost-per-click price than you would typically pay on Google AdWords. Being conservative here will help to ensure that we can indeed be competitive when it comes time to start our PPC campaign.

In our example, 32 people signed up for the email newsletter during the six-day analysis period. We had 2,904 visitors total, so the site-wide conversion rate is simply:

$$\frac{32}{2,904} \times 100\% = 1.10\%$$

This means that on average, 1.10% of the site visitors sign up for the email newsletter. Divide the conversion rate into $0.25 to calculate how much it would cost you (on average) to get an email newsletter subscriber.

$$\frac{\$0.25}{0.0110} = \$22.72$$

What this tells us is that it will cost us nearly $23 to get someone on our email list from Google AdWords, and that's using a conservative $0.25 cost-per-click estimate. That's far too high a price for the Methuselah Foundation (a nonprofit) to pay. This exercise has shown us that starting a PPC campaign at this point would be premature.

INTERPRETING TRAFFIC MAPS

Once you've created your traffic map, you'll want to use it to piece together the "story" of your website. How are people arriving? What are they buying? Why are they leaving?

To give you an example of how to do this, I've constructed a similar traffic map for Surf

Secret, a company that sells privacy software on the internet.

For many people, this example will be closer to what you might encounter when you map your own website. The SurfSecret website is more complex than the previous one. While the shopping cart consists of a linear sequence of order form pages, the rest of the site consists of a wide variety of content, product, and download pages hyperlinked somewhat chaotically between one another. Visitors often visit the site once or twice, download a trial, and come back at a later date to buy. In addition, we are trying to optimize not one, but three separate products. Needless to say, this makes the tracking data quite messy.

To make sense of it all, you'll need to apply inductive reasoning to the spaghetti bowl of data to formulate some likely scenarios of what might be happening on the site. When doing this, don't worry too much about being wrong. Rather, the goal is to generate testable ideas that you can come back to later.

One of the things that will help us with that is the $/Index metric discussed in the previous chapter. We can use this in conjunction with the traffic map to figure out what the analytics data is trying to tell us. I've layered this data on top of the traffic map as well(Figure 5-10, page 56).

Looking at the data in this fashion provides some interesting insights. For instance, we see that 27% of our visitors are arriving at the site through a landing page—more than through the home page. However, this landing page has a $/Index of only $0.17. In contrast, the website homepage has a $/Index of $0.23, six cents higher. Product pages are supposed to have a higher conversion rate than less-targeted homepages. The fact that this isn't the case here suggests a couple of possibilities:

The product page may not be doing a good job of converting visitors. (While looking at the page, I notice that the free trial download button is quite prominent, while the "buy now" buttons are buried well below the fold. This is a prime suspect.)

The traffic coming to this page is not appropriate for this product. We can use Google Analytics to track down this problem as well.

As this is one of the most prominent pages on our site, this should be one of the first things we take a look at as part of our optimization efforts (Figure 5-11, page 57).

Another interesting observation is that the generic download page (/download/index.shtml) is generating virtually no revenue for the site. This could mean that the free trial model ("try before you buy") isn't working and that we should test a paid-up-front approach. It may also indicate that the product download links are broken. Whatever it means, it deserves some investigation.

Next, let's look at the shopping cart pages (shaded boxes on the right side of the traffic map). The first page is the Privacy Protector special offer page (/store/surfsecret_privacy_protector_2009) (Figure 5-12, page 59).

This page generates a whopping $4.11 per visitor! However, of the 6,358 unique visitors to our product page, only 0.83% actually made it here. This is a miserable clickthrough rate. (I would aim for getting no less than 10-15% of the visitors on the main product page to put the product in the cart.) This is almost certainly due to the below-the-fold placement of the "buy now" button on the product page.

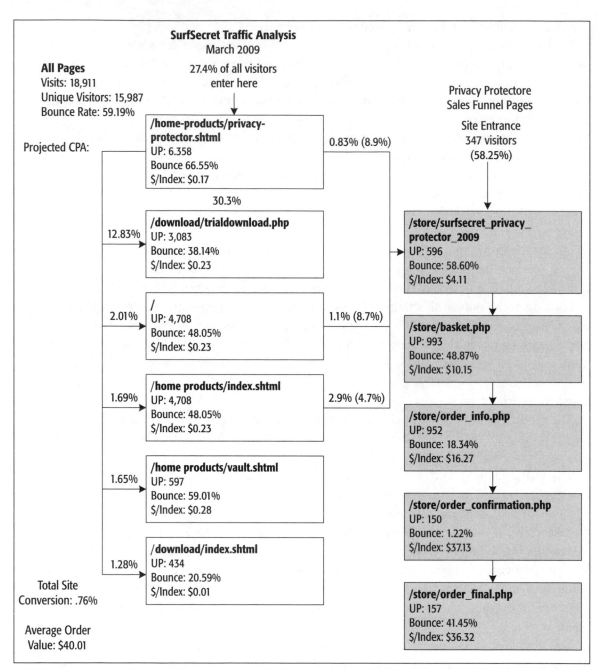

FIGURE 5-10. Our Surf Secret traffic map. The shaded boxes represent shopping cart pages, while the unshaded boxes indicate high-traffic pages from other areas of the website.

As good as this page appears to be, the $10.15 average value on the next page in the shopping cart (/store/basket.php) makes me wonder if perhaps we shouldn't get rid of it altogether. To dig up some more data, I turned back to the Google Analytics funnel report discussed in the previous chapter:

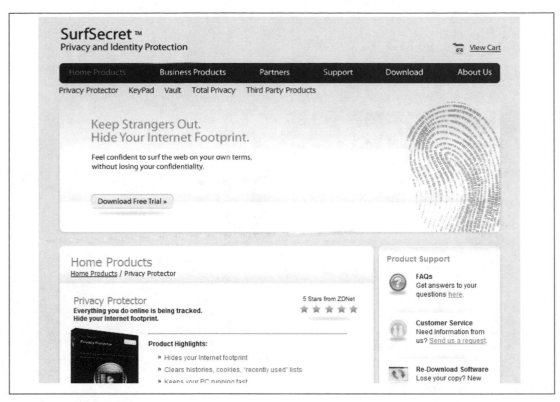

FIGURE 5-11. Privacy Protector Home Version product page

There are two main differences between this report and the traffic map:

1. The traffic map shows average values for all visitors (including those purchasing other products), while the funnel visualization report includes only those visitors who began purchasing the Privacy Protector product. This makes the funnel visualization report more precise (but at the cost of having less data to work with).

2. The traffic map includes the $/Index values. The funnel visualization report does not.

The funnel visualization report tells us that only 36% of the people who saw the "special offer" page decided to continue on to the next page (or in other words, a 64% abandon rate on this page). This is an extremely high drop-off rate. My marketing senses are telling me that the occasional $59.99 upgrade I might make as a result of this page isn't enough to make up for all of the lost sales from visitors who are abandoning their carts at this point. This is something I'll want to test as soon as possible.

As you can see, both reports are useful to have on hand for this exercise. On the other hand, if you haven't set up any goals within Google Analytics, you can get a rough estimate of the number of people who drop off between any two pages by looking at the ratio of their $/Index values:

$$\text{Dropoff} \ = \ \frac{\$ \text{ Index on page 1}}{\$ \text{ Index on page 2}} \ = \ \$4.11 = 40.1\%$$

FIGURE 5-12. Privacy Protector Special Offer page

This is relatively close to the same figure we got from the funnel visualization. The difference can be explained by the fact that the traffic map data includes all traffic data, while the funnel visualization report only includes data from the Privacy Protector product.

Continuing on in this fashion, I also take note of the 48% clickthrough rate on the customer order form (order_info.php). Any time I lose half of my visitors on a single page, there's probably something I can do there to make that page a lot better for my customers.

Finally, the last things I'll look for in the traffic map are potential landing pages. The $/Index tells me the theoretical value of each visitor on a particular page. This is essentially the maximum possible amount I can pay to acquire a visitor. So while I could pay up to $0.17 to send a visitor from AdWords to the Privacy Protector Home Version page (/home-products/privacy-protector.shtml), I could pay up to $0.65 per visitor to send them to the Home Products page (/home-products/index.shtml). If I had to start a PPC campaign today, this would be the landing page I chose.

This exercise, which took less than an hour, revealed three problem areas of the website that can be easily tested and optimized and have the potential to pay off.

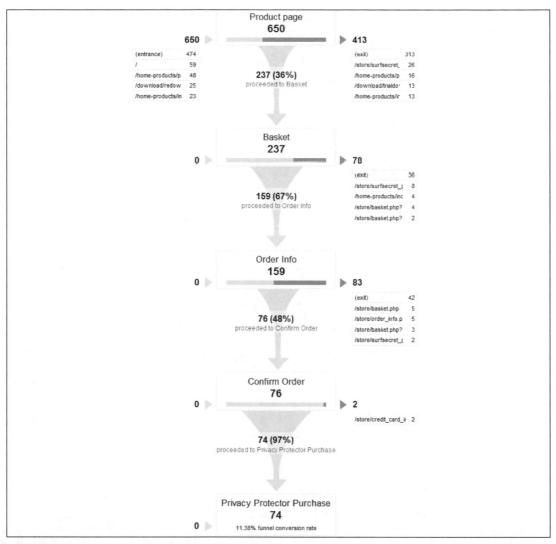

FIGURE 5-13. The Funnel Visualization report provided by Google Analytics can be extremely useful for answering questions traffic maps cannot.

SUMMARY

Most advertisers rush into starting a Google AdWords campaign without ever taking an honest assessment of their traffic. By doing so, they end up limiting the revenue potential of their site as well as the maximum amount they can profitably bid for ad placement on the search engines.

Smart advertisers, on the other hand, begin with the creation of a traffic map. This allows them to identify (and fix) bottlenecks on their websites that are resulting in lost sales and easily outbid most of their competitors.

In addition, the traffic map tips you off to the best landing page candidates on your website, further increasing the chance that your PPC campaign will be profitable from day one.

Notes

1. For a classic example of this, see this response to a critique of one of our landing pages: www.adgooroo.com/why_we_have_a_38_percent_clickthrough_rate.php.

2. The term *Darwinnowing* was coined by Dave Gobel, CEO and resident "wordventor" of Methuselah Foundation.

Website
Optimization

Your Primary Goal as an Internet Marketer

HANDS DOWN, THE SUREST WAY TO IMPROVE YOUR PPC RESULTS IS TO IMPROVE YOUR website's efficiency at converting visitors into buyers.

Too many marketers hope that adding an AdWords campaign will redeem a low-performing website or product. If that doesn't fix their business, they compound their error by raising their bids. They make the same mistake that many dot-com companies made during the late '90s—pouring money into a losing business in a mistaken attempt to "grow to profitability."

To do it right, you have to accept pay-per-click advertising for what it is: a way to multiply your existing business. If you add PPC to a bad business, you'll simply lose money faster. On the other hand, if you add PPC to a good business, you will make more money … if you do it right.

A proven technique for improving the efficiency of your online business is website optimization. Website optimization is the art and science of enhancing the user experience of a website with the goal of converting visitors into customers.

To see why this is important, you need to become familiar with the concept of cost-per-action (CPA). CPA is simply the average cost you incur for turning a visitor into a customer.

To calculate it, you add up the entirety of your variable costs for a given time period (which for most websites consists largely of traffic acquisition costs) and divide by the total number of customers during that same time. For instance, if in a given month your website generated 25 customers and you spent $1,000 on acquiring traffic, then your CPA is $40.

Your priority as a marketer is to minimize your CPA. It should be well below your average order size (ideally, no more than half). The difference between them tells you how much profit your website is generating.

If your average order size was $60 during a time when your average CPA was $40, then you made money to the tune of $20 per customer. If, on the other hand, your average order size was only $30, then you lost $10 per customer.

As you can see, CPA is a convenient way for general managers to measure the overall profitability of a website. However, as this example shows, it provides no guidance on how to actually go about improving your profitability. You need a better set of measures if you hope to succeed.

A BETTER WAY TO MEASURE WEBSITE PROFITABILITY

The inability of CPA to lead to any actionable strategies has led to the creation of two alternate measures by which you can assess the profitability of a website: cost-per-visitor (which in pay-per-click advertising translates to *cost-per-click*, or CPC) and $/Index.

The $/Index is calculated by dividing your total revenue by the total number of visitors. Unlike the CPA metric we discussed above, $/Index can be calculated for any page on a website. This makes it very useful as a tool for measuring the effectiveness of a page (we discussed how to do this in the previous chapter).

In other words, you can directly compare the $/Index to the average price you're paying for each visitor to tune your bid prices.

A quick example to illustrate these points: Let's take a one-page website that purchased 1,000 clicks from Google AdWords for $2,350, and another 300 visitors from Microsoft Bing for $150. Through the process of converting visitors on this page, the website generated 25 customers at an average order size of $100, for a grand total of $1,875 in revenue (Figure 6-1).

FIGURE 6-1.

We calculate the CPA by dividing our total traffic acquisition costs ($2,100) by the total number of customers (25) to arrive at $84/customer. This is well below the $100 average order size, so you know we turned a profit. If you stopped here, though, you would be leaving quite a bit of money on the table.

This becomes apparent when we calculate the $/Index for the page. This figure is equal to $1.92, which we arrive at by dividing the total revenue ($2,500) by the total number of visitors (1,300). This figure gives you a sense of how much a typical visitor to this page is worth to us.

Next, we compare that with the average cost-per-click (CPC) that we're paying each engine. The CPC for Google AdWords is $1.95 ($1,950 total cost divided by 1,000 visitors). The CPC for Microsoft Bing is $0.50 ($150 divided by 300 visitors).

This is actionable information. These figures tell us that we're actually losing a few cents per visitor from our Google AdWords traffic. In contrast, we're paying a very attractive price for visitors from Bing. We could immediately improve profitability by lowering our average CPC for the Google AdWords traffic (we would get less traffic as a result). At the same time, we would raise our average bid price for Bing traffic to increase the amount of traffic from that source.

Later in the book are various strategies for profitability adjusting your average CPC (either up or down). For now, though, we want to consider another possible outcome of this exercise. What if, instead of adjusting our bid prices on the search engines, we made this landing page better?

In our example above, the landing page converted visitors at the rate of 25 out of 1,300. Dividing these figures gives you a conversion rate of 1.92%.

If we found a way to improve this landing page so that it converted at a slightly higher rate— say, 35 out of 1,300 customers (2.7% conversion rate)—our $/Index would increase to $2.69 ($3,500 total revenue divided by 1,300 visitors). This means we wouldn't have to lower our average CPC on Google; we could even possibly raise it and get even more traffic!

While this example is overly simplified, it is quite representative of the interplay between bid prices and landing page conversion rates that we encounter in the real world. Website owners are usually in a big hurry to get their PPC campaigns rolling, but this is a huge mistake if they've never given a moment's attention to their landing page conversion rates.

SUMMARY

You should always start your optimization efforts by building a traffic map, as covered in the previous chapter. Next, you'll use this map to determine and optimize the length of your sales funnels by eliminating unnecessary pages. Finally, you'll carefully assess and improve the remaining pages to maximize their contribution to your overall revenue.

CHAPTER 7

Optimizing the Length of Your Sales Funnels

THERE ARE TWO FUNDAMENTAL APPROACHES TO IMPROVING YOUR WEBSITE CONVERSION rate:

1. Reduce the number of pages in your sales funnels, and/or …
2. Optimize individual pages

The quickest path to improving sales on most sites is by eliminating unnecessary pages from the checkout or lead generation processes.

Internet marketers tend to spend a great deal of time on their flashy product pages and not enough on the more boring, but far more important, checkout pages. The tendency is to hand these pages off to a designer with the mandate to collect as much information as possible about the customer in order to maximize their chances of selling to them again in the future.

The designers usually accept this assignment without much resistance, perhaps breaking the data collection process up into a number of pages, each designed to collect a few pieces of data from the customer (after all, who wants to fill out a form with 25 fields on it?) They tack an "order confirmation" page to the end and perhaps a "special one-time offer" page to the beginning and move on to the next job.

The result of this (sadly typical) process is a lengthy series of checkout pages designed with little thought given to the user experience. The resulting hodgepodge of pages serves only to chase potential customers away at exactly the moment when they are closest to buying!

The next chartFigure 7-1 illustrates shows a real-world example of the results of the above process at a company selling computer security software over the internet. When they came to me, they were utilizing a seven- page checkout process:

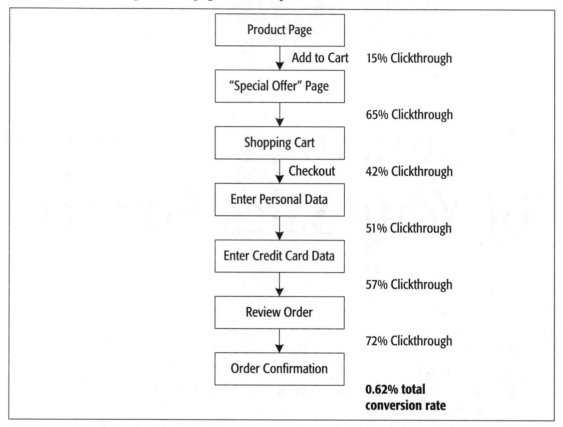

FIGURE 7-1. Actual sales funnel results of a well-known software company. Notice the higher click-through rates in the later stages. This is a sign of Darwinnowing.

At each stage, a percentage of the visitors abandoned their carts, never to return. As you can see by multiplying the clickthrough rates at each stage, their site-wide conversion rate was only 0.62% (about 1 in every 162 visitors).

As low as the starting conversion rate may seem, it's actually the norm for a website to convert at well under 1%. Higher conversion rates are almost always the result of sustained testing and optimization efforts.

And that's exactly what we ended up doing next (Figure 7-2). Compare the above to the results we achieved by eliminating two of the pages from the checkout process. Although our clickthrough rates on each page were lower than before, we eliminated enough friction from the sales funnel to increase our sales by 248%!

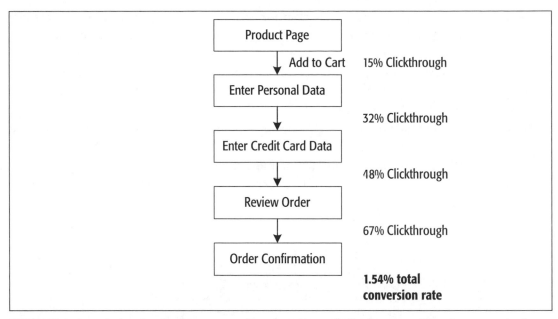

FIGURE 7-2. By reducing the checkout process from seven pages to five, we were able to increase sales by nearly 250%.

HOW LONG SHOULD YOUR SALES FUNNEL BE?

There is no "correct" answer to how many pages a checkout process should have. It is determined largely by your customer base and the dollar amount of your orders (with free and low-priced goods requiring shorter checkout processes.). While most marketers who have gone public with their own data have stated that a two- or three- page checkout process is optimal, there are others who claim longer processes performed better. (I recently sat in on a panel at a search engine strategies conference where a speaker claimed that exhaustive testing revealed a seven-page checkout process was optimal for their B2B site.)

One good way to get an idea of how long your checkout process should ideally be is by looking at your competitors' websites. If they've been in business for any significant length of time, they've probably done some testing to optimize their checkout processes, and you can leverage that information for your own benefit.

At the end of the day, however, the best way to determine the optimal number of steps is by testing checkout processes of various lengths to see which works best for you.

TECHNIQUES FOR ELIMINATING PAGES

With a site that has been optimized already, it can be quite difficult to further reduce the number of pages in a checkout process. There's a direct tradeoff between form length and the number of pages. If you absolutely require a customer to fill out 16 fields, you are looking at no less than three pages in your checkout process (two to collect the information and an additional "thank you" page).

Fortunately, most sites have had little to no prior optimization. The way to start is to carefully consider eliminating every field which you ask your visitors to fill out. Are they all truly necessary? We had many conversations along these lines at AdGooroo. For instance, while it was important for us to ask for an address for people downloading research reports (in the event that we wanted to send a physical copy of the report to them later), we did not need to ask for an address for the purpose of starting a free trial.

By systematically eliminating any field that wasn't absolutely required for sales and marketing purposes, we were able to reduce the number of fields on our free trial forms from nearly twenty 20 down to six (the research report conversion funnel remained a separate process). As a result, we were able to eliminate an entire page from our checkout procedure: (Figure 7-3).

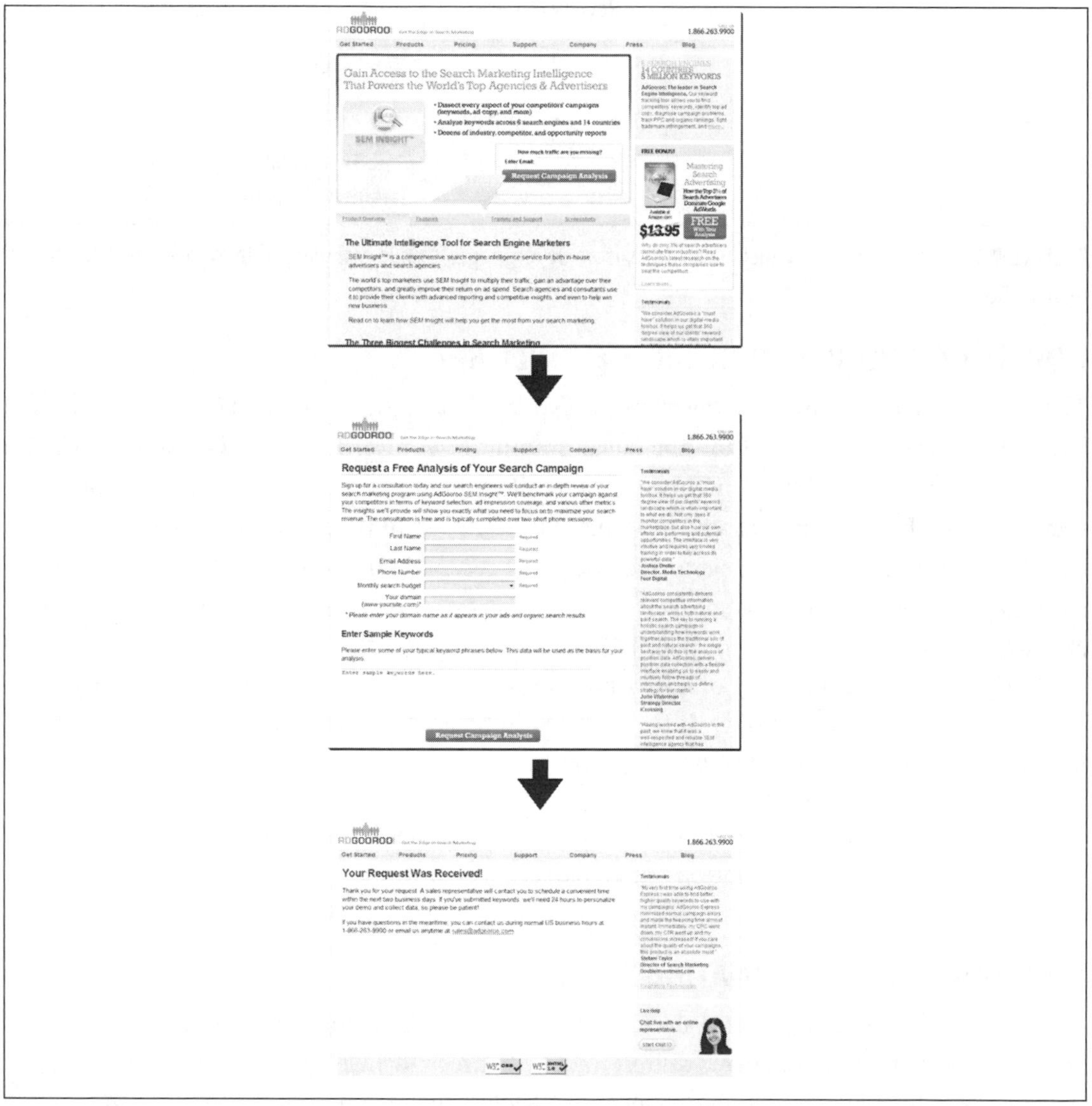

FIGURE 7-3. By aggressively doing away with unnecessary form fields, we were able to reduce our checkout process to just three pages, only one of which requires visitors to provide personal information.

Next, you want to look for pages that may seem "obvious" to have. Often, they are not.

A common example is the ubiquitous "special offer" page which that pops up just as prospects are trying to complete their orders. These pages annoy visitors and lead to high abandonment rates. Be sure to test them to determine if the lift in average order size outweighs the lost sales which that result from the additional step (Figure 7-4).

How Many Form Fields Per Page?

A simple rule of thumb for figuring out approximately how many pages your checkout process will require is to divide the number of data fields you ask for by ten10. This is about the most you can cram on a form before visitors start abandoning your page out of frustration.

FIGURE 7-4. "Special Offer" pages should be avoided unless you are prepared to test them in a controlled fashion.

Another common mistake is requiring visitors to register before they can shop on your website. Not only will this requirement scare away many would-be customers, it's often implemented in such a manner that adds an additional other page to the checkout process. If you absolutely require visitors to log in, consider moving this step as deep into your conversion funnel as possible.

The page in Figure 7-5 taken from the AbeBooks website is a good example of what you should try to avoid. The requirement to either sign in or create a new account presents an unnecessary obstacle to new users who simply want to buy a book .

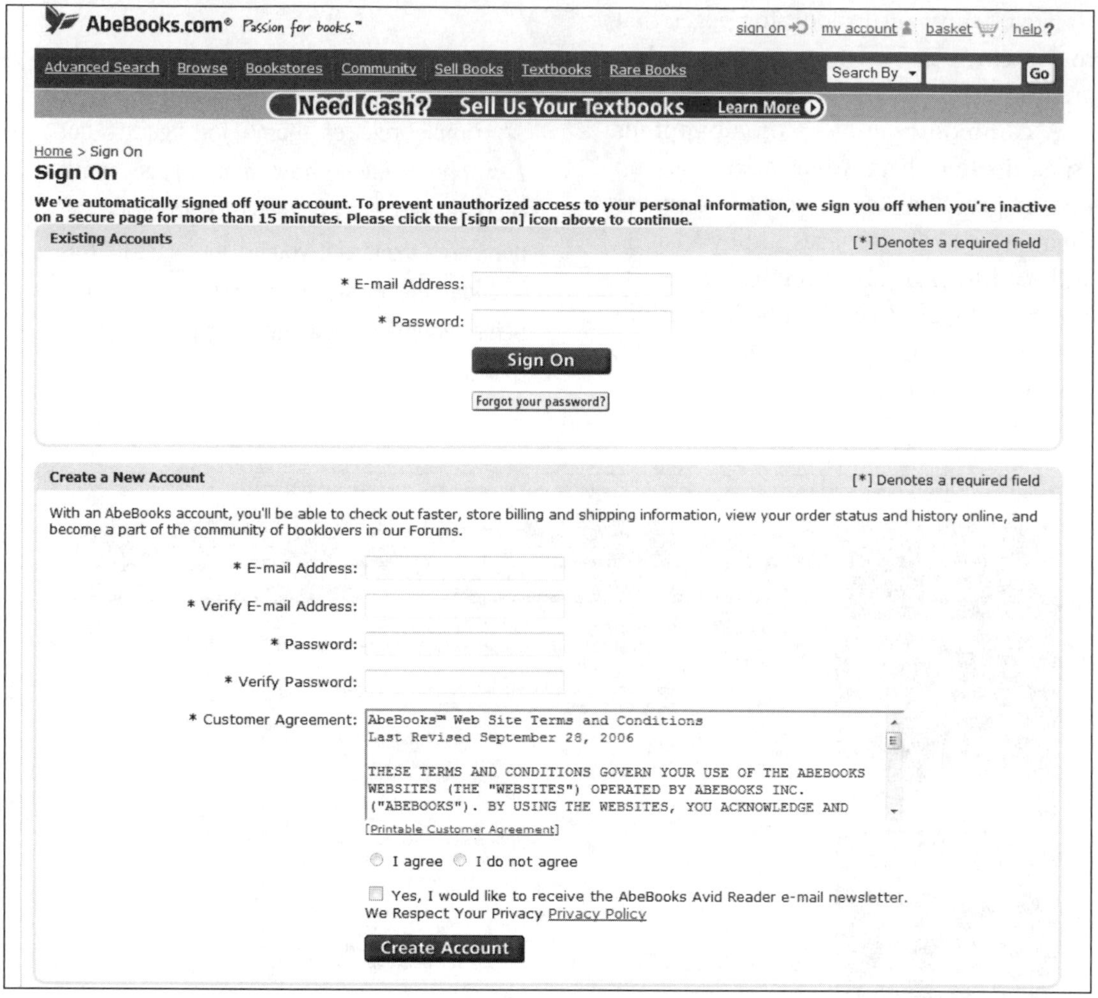

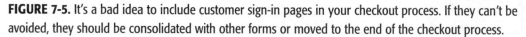

FIGURE 7-5. It's a bad idea to include customer sign-in pages in your checkout process. If they can't be avoided, they should be consolidated with other forms or moved to the end of the checkout process.

A better way is the approach taken by Grisoft, makers of the popular AVG antivirus product (Figure 7-6). Instead of forcing new customers to make a choice between signing in or creating a new account, it assumes everyone is a new customer. Those few customers who do want to sign in (and can actually remember their login information) are provided with a link to do so. This eliminates an entire page and no small amount of confusion from the checkout process.

Another great way to eliminate pages from a checkout process is to combine payment and customer information on a single form (most e-commerce sites use at least two forms to collect this data). You have to be very careful to test this carefully, though, as asking for this much information on a single form can scare away customers.

Again, Grisoft provides an excellent example in Figure 7-7.

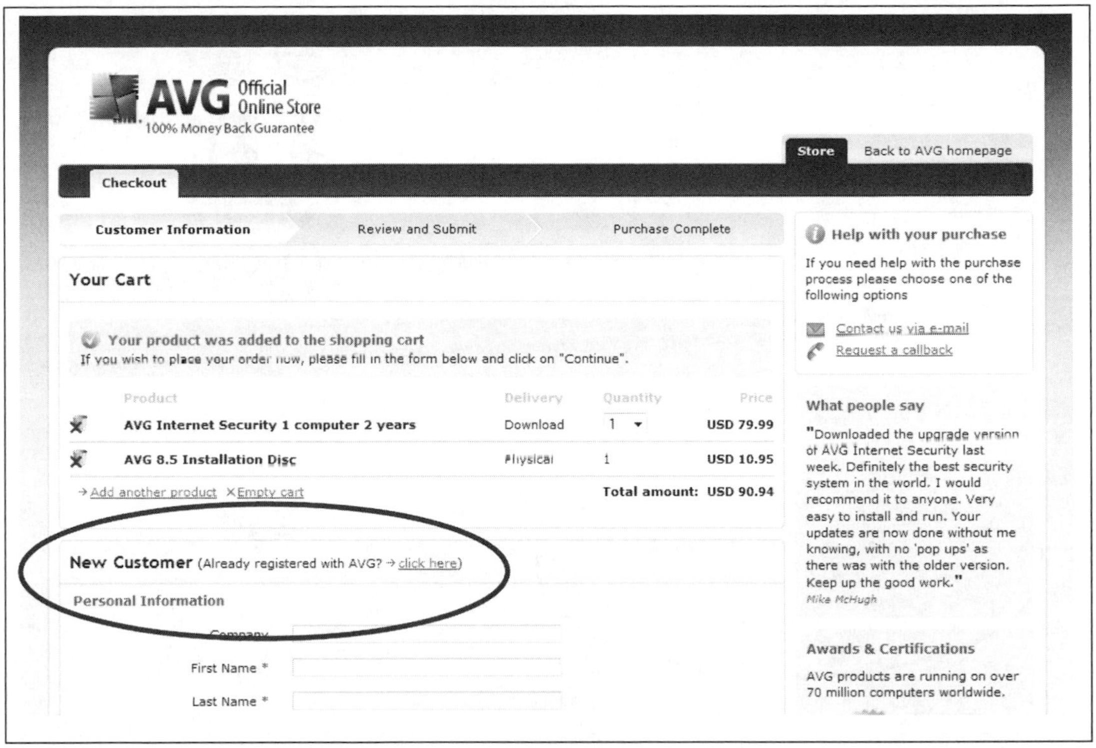

FIGURE 7-6. A better way to accommodate returning customers is to provide them with a sign-in link.

While your site may vary considerably from the few examples presented here, there is a technology that may help you considerably when streamlining your own checkout process: AJAX.

AJAX is a set of web development techniques that can be used to create highly interactive web applications. It works by retrieving data from the server in the background without interfering with the display of the existing page. Used wisely, this can eliminate a page or two from your checkout processes.

For instance, at AdGooroo we require every customer to have a unique username. A couple of years ago, this meant that after filling out the customer information page, we'd have to perform a round trip to the server to see if the username was actually available. If it wasn't, an error message would be displayed and the customer would need to try again. This frustrating little exercise cost us more than 10% of our sales.

Today, the first piece of information we ask for on our free trial forms is the username. While the visitor is completing the rest of the form, we use AJAX to check if the username is available. If the username is already in use, we display a warning message next to the username text box—often before the visitor has completed filling in their password. This eliminates the frustration that people feel when they complete a sign-up form, only to have the page refreshed with error messages (Figure 7-8).

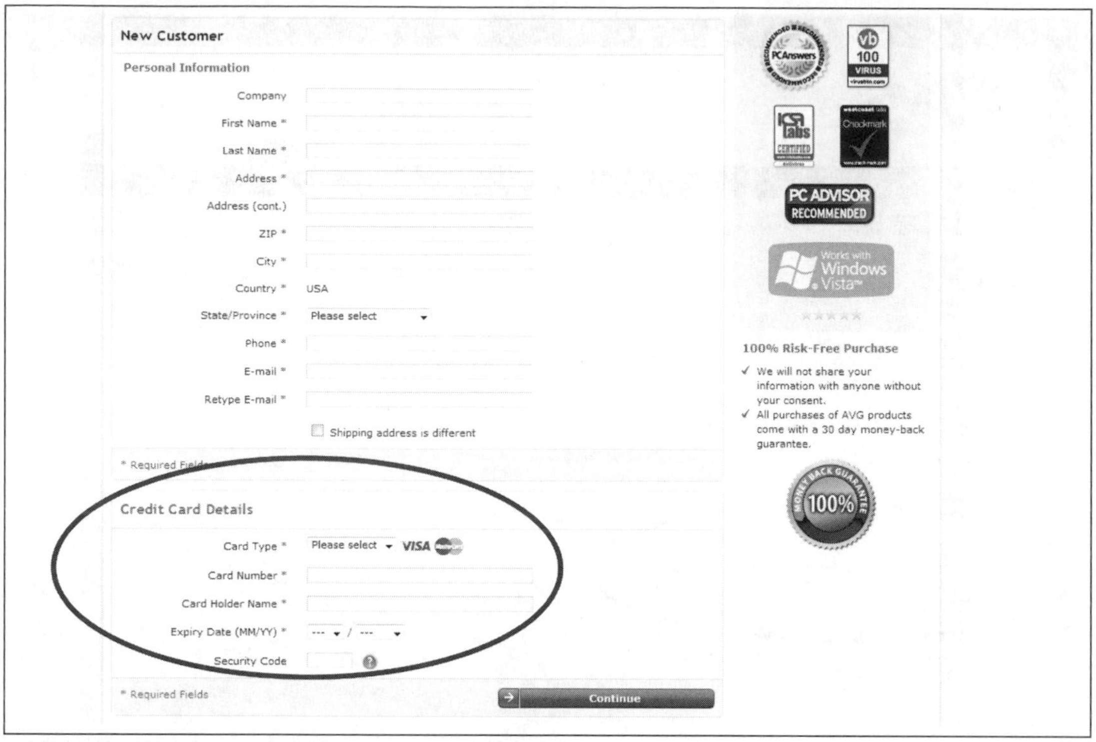

FIGURE 7-7. Asking for payment information on the same page as the customer information can be an effective way to eliminate checkout pages.

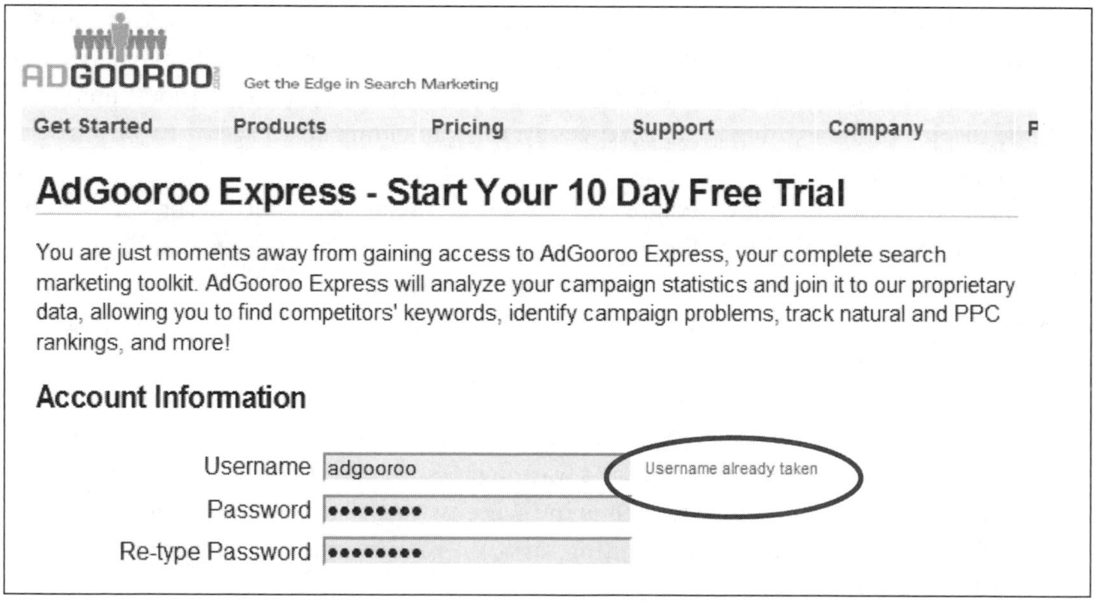

FIGURE 7-8. We use AJAX to check for duplicate usernames while visitors fill out the free trial forms. If they've selected a username that's already in use, they'll find out before they finish filling out the form.

Be careful with AJAX, as it can bloat the page. This can result in slow load times and poor quality scores (much more on this in Chapter 18). AJAX is also notorious for causing cross-browser compatibility problems (which means that your Firefox visitors may see something different than your IE and Chrome visitors). Finally, if it's used inappropriately or in excess, it can even make your site less usable, resulting in a lower conversion rates.

SUMMARY

The easiest way to increase sales on most websites is to reduce the number of pages found in the sales funnels. Any funnel with more than a few steps is suspect, so your first priority will be to find ways to shorten them. After you've done this (and have thoroughly tested your improvements), per Chapter 9, it's time to move on to optimizing individual pages.

Crash Course in Conversion Optimization

THIS CHAPTER MAY BE THE MOST IMPORTANT OF THIS BOOK. IN IT, I'M GOING TO OUTLINE the essentials of my personal website optimization program. I've used this very same methodology many times to secure a 3-10 times increase in sales on sites in many different verticals (including both B2B and B2C categories). Once you complete these steps for your website, you should have a high enough conversion rate to turn a profit on even the highest-priced keywords in your pay-per-click program.

HUNT OPTIMIZATION OPPORTUNITIES WITH A RIFLE, NOT A SHOTGUN

Throughout the previous chapters in the book, I have repeatedly stated that you should do a careful assessment of your site if you expect to make much progress with improving your sales. If you've been working along up to now, you have that assessment in the form of a traffic map (if not, now is the time to go back to Chapter 5 and follow the instructions there to create one).

Creating a traffic map allows you to avoid a rookie mistake: picking pages for optimization at random (the shotgun approach). Optimization is painstaking work, so to avoid wasting your time on pages that will have little impact on the final outcome, you start by assessing each page to find a few promising targets (the rifle approach).

For each page in your sales funnel, you need to compare the number of visitors coming in to the number of visitors clicking through to the next page. Look for pages with a high drop-off rate relative to the rest of the pages in your shopping cart.

If you've defined a goal within Google Analytics, the Funnel Visualization report will come in handy for this purpose. Let's take a look at this report for SurfSecret (Figure 8-1).

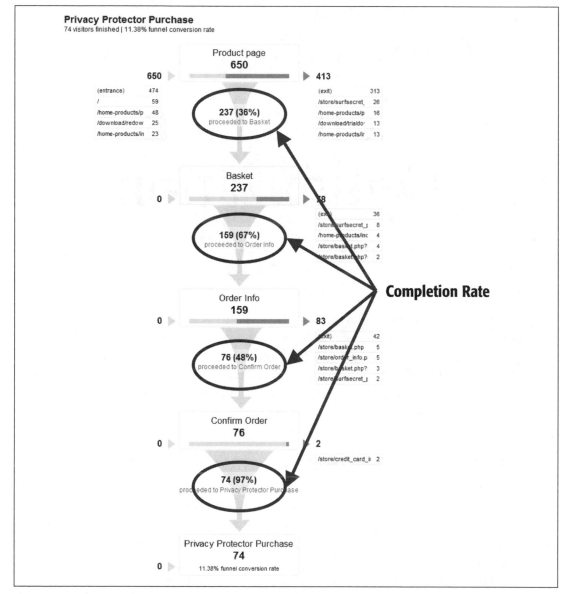

FIGURE 8-1. The Funnel Visualization Report shows the completion rate at each stage in a sales funnel.

This report shows the completion rate at each stage in the funnel. The lowest completion rates are on the product page (36%) and the order info page (48%), so these are the pages we want to take a look at first. The basket page has a completion rate of 67% (60% or higher is pretty good for shopping cart pages), while the order confirmation page has a completion rate of 97%, so no action is required there.

In addition to looking at the completion rate of each page, you also have to take into consideration the potential for improvement. In other words, how much can you realistically expect to improve a page through optimization?

Unfortunately, this is one of those areas that defies simple rules of thumb. You have to make a best guess based on personal judgment and past experience. For instance, once a shopping cart page is getting a greater than 70% clickthrough rate, you have virtually no hope of improving it. Free trial download pages tend to top out around 15 or 20%, while e-mail newsletter pages max out at around 30%.

Product pages, on the other hand, vary considerably based on the industry, product, and traffic source. A site receiving relatively little traffic may have a very high clickthrough rate on the product page, but once you add PPC traffic into the mix, the conversion rate may drop considerably.

Nevertheless, if you've never optimized your pages before, it's not at all uncommon to get a 100-500% increase in completion rate from just a few simple changes. Hope for the best, but be conservative in your estimates.

The $/Index figure can really help to put things in perspective when prioritizing your potential optimization projects. Take the example of a shopping cart page that receives 100 visitors a day and has a $/Index of $2.00. Multiplying these two figures together gives a total daily page value of $200.

If you believe that you can achieve a 40% increase in completion rate as a result of optimizing this page, then the value of optimizing that page is $80/day, or about $2,400/month. Not bad for an experiment that may just take a few hours of actual work!

Let's return to the Methuselah Foundation traffic map to see how this plays out in practice (Figure 8-2).

We are looking at a very simple, three-page sales funnel:

- Homepage—clickthrough rate to the e-mail newsletter signup page is 2.1%.
- E-mail newsletter signup page—completion rate is 0.57%.
- E-mail newsletter "thank you" page

To get the signup rate for these three pages in conjunction with each other, you convert the conversion rate percentages to decimals and then multiply them:

Signup Rate = 2.1% x 0.57%
Signup Rate = 0.021 x 0.0057
= 0.00012 (0.012%)

E-mail newsletter signup pages are pretty easy to optimize. And because they don't require the visitor to pay for anything, you can typically get very high clickthrough rates. While my personal

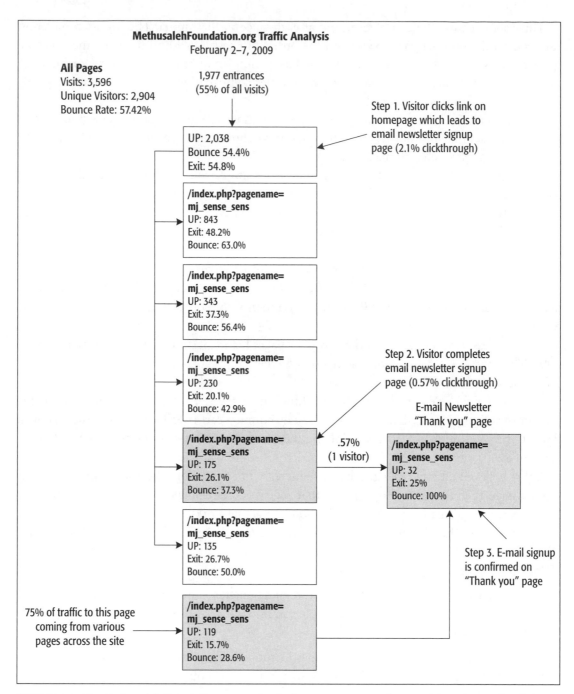

FIGURE 8-2. The Methuselah Foundation uses a simple three-page process for e-mail newsletter subscriptions.

record is over 30%, I typically aim for 15-20% (depending on how motivated I think the website's visitors are). Because the Methuselah Foundation's visitors tend to find the site through mentions in books or documentaries, I believe that I could (conservatively) raise the conversion rate to 15%.

Next we should take a look at the homepage. Visitors are only clicking through to the e-mail newsletter page at a rate of 2.1%. This isn't terrible, but I think we could do a lot better. I'd aim for around 10% here.

The new conversion rate scenario for this particular sequence of pages plays out like so:

- 2,038 unique visitors to the homepage.
- 10% of them, or 204 unique visitors, click through to the e-mail newsletter signup page.
- 15%, or about 30 unique visitors, actually sign up for the e-mail newsletter.

We only had one conversion from these two pages before, so we'd expect to have 29 more e-mail newsletter subscribers than we did before (assuming that we aren't cannibalizing any of the subscribers who signed up through the cross-feeder page).

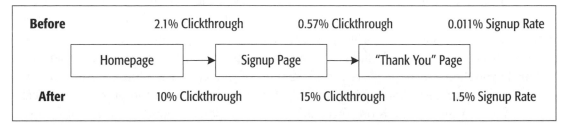

What effect would this have in practice? As you may recall, we previously calculated our site-wide conversion rate to be 1.10% (32 e-mail subscribers out of 2,904 total visitors to the site).

We then divided this number into an average $0.25 cost-per-click price to come up with our theoretical CPA: $22.72.

$$\text{Theoretical CPA} \quad \frac{\$0.25}{0.011} = \$22.72$$

We now expect to have 29 more e-mail subscribers. This makes a total of 61 subscriptions from the same 2,038 visitors. Dividing the two gives us a new site-wide conversion rate of 3.00%.

$$\text{Site-wide Converstion Rate} \quad \frac{(32 + 29)\ \text{Signups}}{2,038\ \text{Visitors}} = 3.0\%$$

We then divide the new number into the theoretical CPA formula to get a new projected cost for an e-mail newsletter signup:

$$\text{Theoretical CPA} \quad \frac{\$0.25}{0.0300} = \$8.33$$

So if we succeed at optimizing these two pages, we are looking at a 70% reduction in costs (from $22.72 to $8.33) to acquire an e-mail subscriber. This will allow the Methuselah Foundation to afford much higher ad placement when it finally gets around to starting its pay-per-click campaign.

OTHER FACTORS TO KEEP IN MIND WHILE PRIORITIZING OPTIMIZATION PROJECTS

There are a few other factors that you have to consider when estimating the impact of your optimization efforts.

First, keep Darwinnowing in mind (see sidebar in Chapter 5). If your visitors have to hunt through your website to find your sales funnel, you will be starting off with artificially high clickthrough rates. Basing estimates off of these figures is useless. In this case, you have to start bringing these pages closer to the primary entry point on your site (this is functionally the same as reducing the number of pages in your sales funnel, per Chapter 7).

Another rule of thumb to keep in mind is that as you increase the number of visitors to a page, your clickthrough rates will tend to decline. As you increase the volume, the audience becomes less targeted, and thus a smaller percentage of visitors complete that stage of the pipeline. So don't be surprised if while you're optimizing one stage of your sales funnel, the completion rate at the next stage declines (you can always optimize that page later if necessary).

Finally, you should focus on pages at the beginning of your conversion funnel first. As we'll see in the next chapter, a test will require around 100 successful conversions to produce statistically valid results. If your website is only generating 50 conversions a month, then it will take you around two months to optimize the latter pages of your shopping cart. By focusing on the initial pages, you'll not only increase sales, but also decrease the total time needed to optimize your site.

THE EIGHTFOLD PATH TO CONVERSION NIRVANA

Once you've identified the pages you wish to optimize, it's time to figure out exactly what needs to be optimized. The following checklist will help you with this.

1. **Single Conversion Goal**
   - Does every page in your sales funnel have a primary call to action?
   - Can the purpose of the page be understood by a typical visitor in less than five seconds?
   - Is the intended goal of the page clearly spelled out in a headline?
   - Is the purpose of the page clearly visible "above the fold"?

2. **Eyeline**
   - Do the shapes and colors of the page clearly lead the eye to the desired call to action?
   - Are you using no more than two columns in your page layout?

3. **Anxiety**
   - Are you asking for data the visitor may not want to give?
   - Are you offsetting the user's anxiety with a payoff?
   - Can you use testimonials?
   - Can you use third-party trust seals to improve credibility?

4. **Friction**
   - Are there too many elements on the page?
   - Are there too many links or navigation elements?

- Is there sufficient white space on the page?
- Are you using a font appropriate for your visitors?
- Are form fields aligned with one another?
- Are links and buttons used appropriately?
- Are you asking for unnecessary information?
- Do the labels on form fields clearly convey what is required of the visitor?
- Are you limiting the use of Flash or other third-party technologies?
- Can you use AJAX to eliminate unnecessary page reloads?

5. Length

- Is the page copy of the appropriate length?
- Are there 10 or fewer form fields on the page?

6. Congruency

- Does the page look similar to the ones immediately before and after it?
- Is the page hosted on a third-party domain?

7. Load Time

- Does the page load in under five seconds in both Internet Explorer and Firefox?
- Is the page size under 150k?

8. Urgency

- Do customers feel a strong need to not only buy your product, but to but it *now*?
- If not, can you offer an incentive to boost response rates?
- Is the incentive something that would be useful to your ideal customer?

SINGLE CONVERSION GOAL

The first and most important rule of conversion optimization is that every important page on your site must have a single goal, or call to action.

Not two. Not three. Just one.

With few exceptions, every sales funnel page must be assigned a singular positive outcome. Here are some examples:

- Subscribe to your opt-in e-mail newsletter list.
- Add a product to the shopping cart.
- Accept a special offer.
- Complete a contact information form.
- Confirm the order.

Relatively few websites heed this advice. In the course of an average day, I come across many pages on popular websites that either have no clear purpose or have too many of them competing with one another.

Furthermore, the purpose of the page must be clearly conveyed to the visitor within a very short period of time: no more than five seconds. This is usually accomplished through headlines and supporting graphics.

This does not mean that the page should be entirely devoid of navigation or other links (like the spammy, single-page long-copy websites that were popular in 2003). Rather, the most important action on the page should stand out so that the casual visitor doesn't have to think about what to click. Other actions that may compete with the primary goal should be de-emphasized (visitors looking for them will be more motivated to hunt for them).

Some examples will help to illustrate this important principle. The e-mail marketing company AWeber has a landing page that demonstrates a clear, singular conversion goal. The headline is well above the fold and is easily distinguished from the rest of the page. The button reading "FREE Test Drive" hammers home the next step that visitors should take: signing up for a free trial (Figure 8-3).

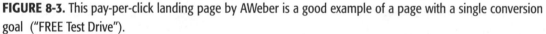

FIGURE 8-3. This pay-per-click landing page by AWeber is a good example of a page with a single conversion goal ("FREE Test Drive").

In contrast, the page from the Symantec site for All-in-One security software products (Figure 8-4) presents a number of products competing with each other, with little to distinguish one from another. Furthermore, it's not clear at all what the next action is because there are no buttons or underlined hyperlinks. (I finally figured out that you are supposed to click the light orange prices to add items to your cart. I doubt most people are as patient as I was.)

It's pages like this that drive customers away from shopping sites. It could be easily improved by changing the headline to "Choose a Security Software Product" and adding some "Add to Cart" buttons next to the products (Figure 8-4).

Of course, you can't always have a single conversion goal on a page. Online shopping sites present a challenging example because browsing is an important customer activity. How can these sites present a variety of products to their visitors while still following this principle?

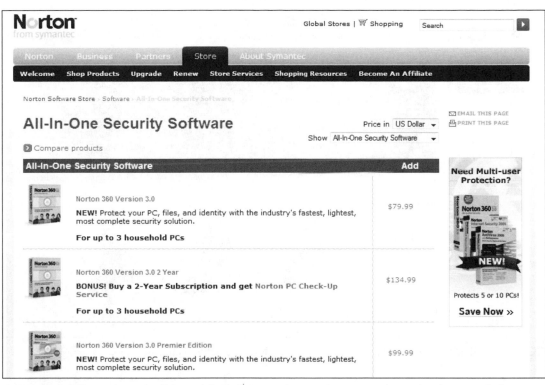

FIGURE 8-4. This product selection page from Symantec has no clear conversion action (or several obscure ones, depending on your perspective).

The shoe company Aldo shows us how (Figure 8-5). This landing page, which was served for the phrase *black pumps* on Google, has a matching headline, and the purpose of the page is clear; the visitor is there to browse a selection of popular women's heeled shoes. Notice that other page elements such as the site navigation have been de-emphasized to minimize distractions from the page content (this will come up again in the section on friction).

In contrast, the corresponding landing page from Piperlime (Figure 8-6) buries the headline ("Sandals") in reverse-type at the top of the page. And while the primary purpose of the page is to browse sandals, the page also encourages visitors to "Narrow it down" (in very small type). While the images of the shoes are probably enough to save this page, it could be improved dramatically by simply changing some of the font sizes and colors to make the important elements of the page stand out.

There is absolutely no confusion about what this next website (Figure 8-7) is asking its visitors for.

In contrast, this page (Figure 8-8) from one of my favorite local pizza joints has no clear call to action. The headline reads, "Order Online!" but there is no button or link to click. How am I supposed to place an order here? On Facebook?

Choosing a single goal for every page can be frustrating at times, particularly with larger organizations. The need to accommodate multiple stakeholders is one of the primary reasons the websites of certain large corporations tend to do a poor job of converting visitors into customers.

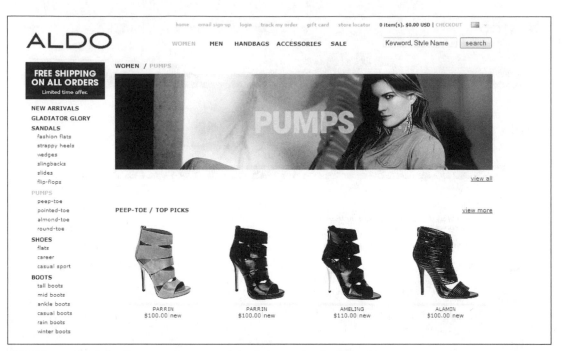

FIGURE 8-5. Aldo's landing page for women's heels has a clearly defined purpose.

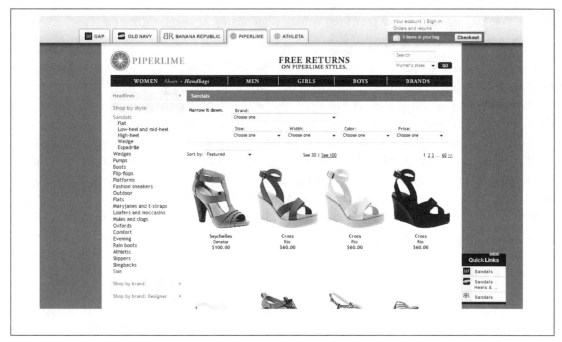

FIGURE 8-6. Visitors have to work much harder to browse this shoe site.

One example of how conflicting priorities undermine the effectiveness of a website can be found at AmericanAirlines.com (Figure 8-9). The homepage is cluttered with a variety of links,

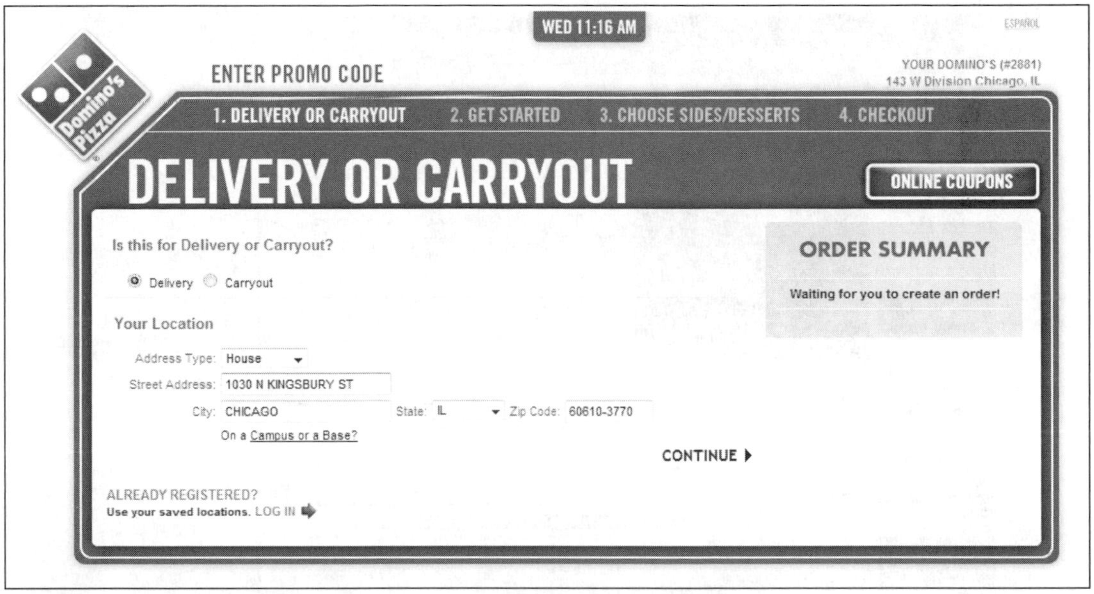

FIGURE 8-7. This page from Domino's Pizza has a single, well-defined purpose.

FIGURE 8-8. You have to be really hungry to order pizza from this website.

navigation, discounts, and alerts. It was designed to please everyone at corporate HQ, but just ends up alienating customers.

On the other end of the spectrum is Dell. While they, too, have a bewildering variety of activities that a visitor can undertake on their site, they've managed to reduce this problem somewhat by allowing visitors to segment themselves into home, small and medium business, public

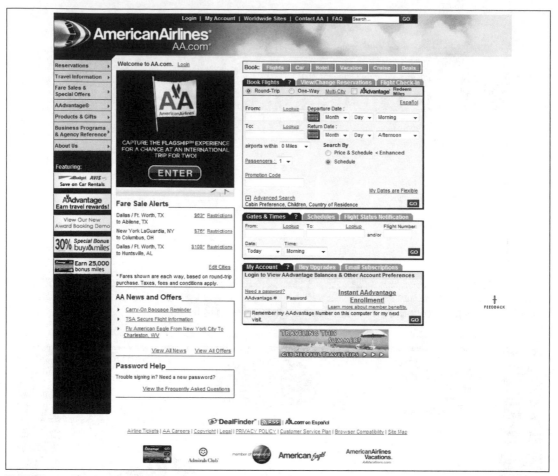

FIGURE 8-9. The American Airlines homepage consists of a confusing array of options. There are too many conversion goals on this page.

sector, and large-enterprise customers. These options are clearly presented at the top of the page. While the headline in the large graphic below still competes with this, it's a step in the right direction (Figure 8-10).

EYELINE

Eyeline is the path that your visitors' gazes (and mouse clicks) naturally follow as they skim a page. It is guided by the use of color, contrast, and visual interest. Through careful use of these elements on your pages, you can subtly direct visitors to your desired action.

To see where the eyeline leads on a page, start at the top left of the page and follow the line of color. On most sites, the logo is found in the top left corner, and after years of training, most of us begin reading there (of course, if your visitors read from right to left, you would start at the upper right).

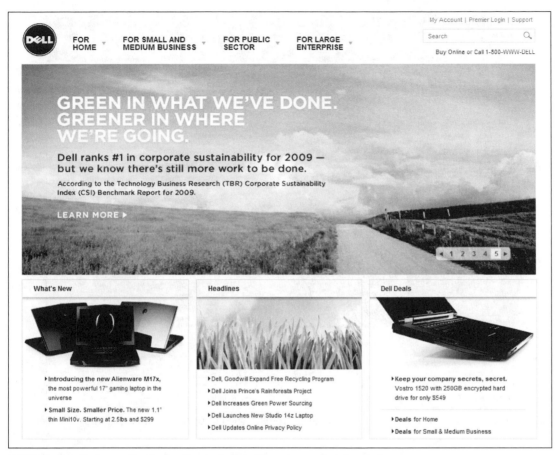

FIGURE 8-10. Dell uses the top toolbar to invite visitors to segment themselves.

Here are three examples. These were all taken from the mortgage industry to illustrate how looking at competitive sites within a given category can help to uncover important principles. (See Chapter 19 for more on using competitors' websites to help your own campaign.)

The eyeline on the page from Mortgage Marvel (Figure 8-11) starts at the top left. From there it proceeds downward, into the photo. Photographs are often used to direct eyeline due to their high visual interest, color, and contrast. From the bottom of the photo, it proceeds right into the "action area." This small colored box consists of three fields that the visitors fill out to receive their mortgage quotes.

This next page from E-Loan (Figure 8-12) uses the same technique. The eyeline starts at the upper left, follows the dark blue bar to the right, and then jumps down into the "No Hidden Fees, Great Rates" headline. From there, the eyeline jumps to the yellow button below the action area.

Here's an example of how to apply this technique in a slightly different manner (Figure 8-13). The photo anchors the gaze at the top left, while an orange arrow, dark blue navbar, and orange button direct visitors where they need to go.

FIGURE 8-11. The eyeline on this landing page leads from the logo through the photo and into the action area.

Finally, this page from Xerox (Figure 8-14) was put together with little thought given to eyeline. Starting at the upper left, the visitor's eye is dropped at the navbar and abandoned, as neither the headline nor the "Start Saving" button has sufficient contrast or interest. Not only do these elements blend into the page; they are competing with the bright, interesting photo off to the right.

The page could be improved dramatically by moving the photo to the left of the copy area and increasing the contrast of the headline and button (Figure 8-15). I'd expect to see a 20-30% increase in clickthrough rate from these changes.

It takes a fair amount of practice to be able to correctly spot the path of least visual resistance through a page, so many companies opt to have their pages tested by usability labs. These labs produce heat maps—graphic visualizations of where site visitors are paying the most attention (Figure 8-16).

This type of study is rather expensive, so years ago I created a software package that could track both mouse movements and clicks on my pages. While it couldn't track where users were actually looking, this information still proved incredibly valuable in my testing efforts.

Today, you can do the same thing on the cheap with a tool called *CrazyEgg* (www.crazyegg.com). This service starts at $9/month, putting it within reach of virtually every website (Figure 8-17).

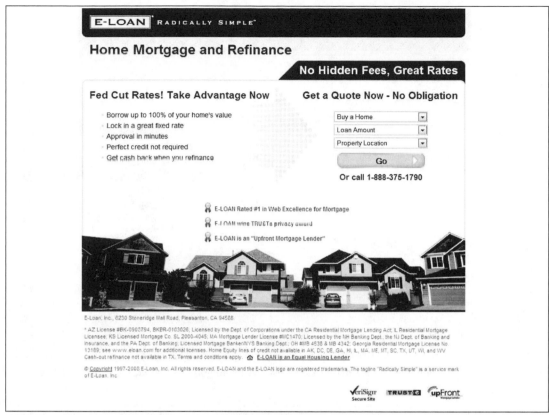

FIGURE 8-12. E-Loan used a similar technique on this page.

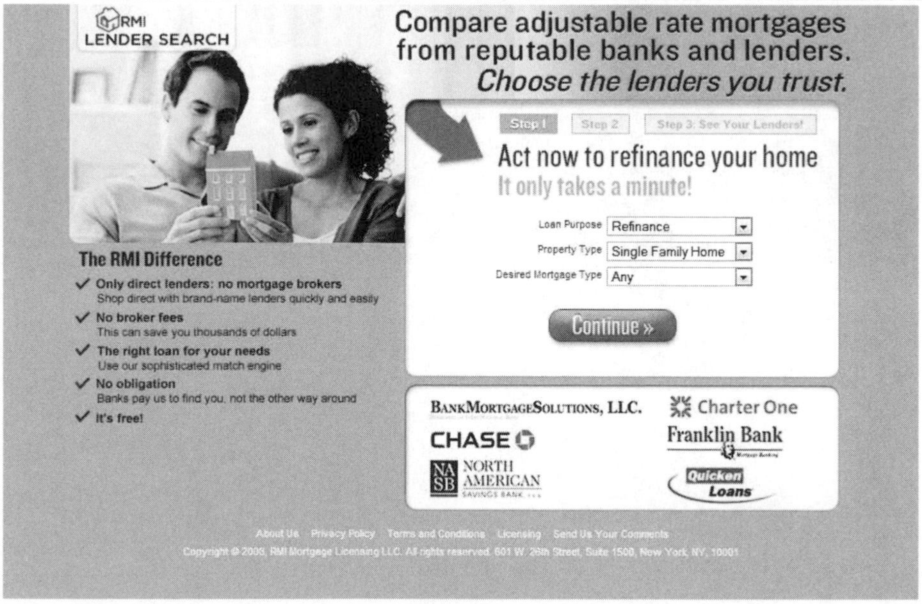

FIGURE 8-13. A third example of how to use eyeline to direct visitors to the action area.

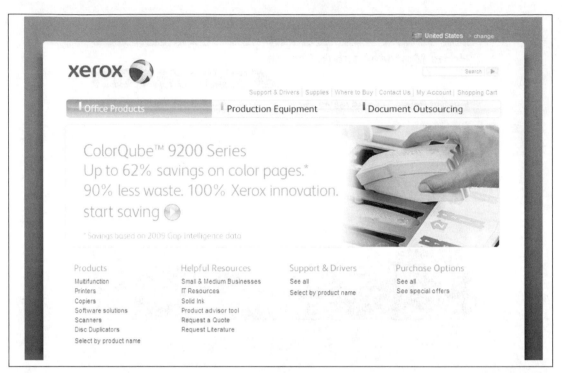

FIGURE 8-14. This landing page from Xerox does not use eyeline to good effect, but could be improved dramatically with just a few minor tweaks.

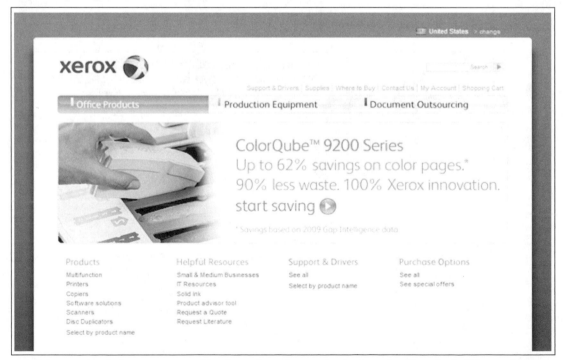

FIGURE 8-15. Here's the same page with a few minor changes. Notice how the "Start Saving" button is much more prominent now.

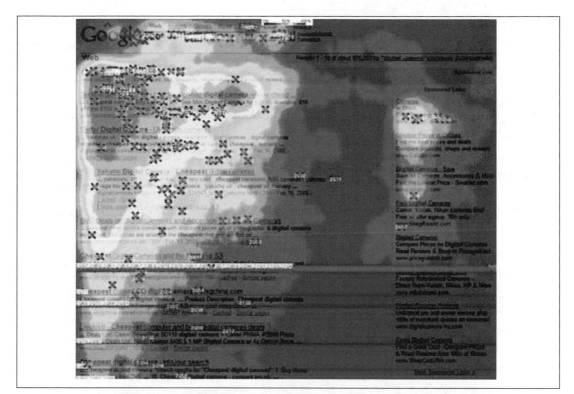

FIGURE 8-16. Heat maps are a useful tool to see where your visitors are looking (and clicking).

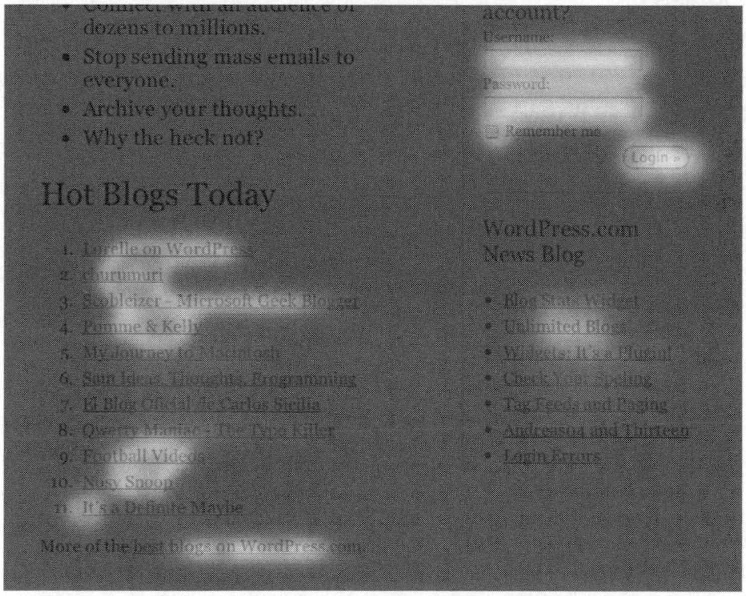

FIGURE 8-17. CrazyEgg is an inexpensive tool you can use to generate click maps, an inexpensive substitute for heat maps.

ANXIETY

Anxiety refers to the reluctance of your site visitors to provide personal information. While designing your sales pages, you should be sensitive to the concerns visitors may have when you ask them for their addresses, phone numbers, e-mail addresses, and of course, credit card data.

As we stated previously, your best bet here is to carefully consider what information you require for visitors to complete an action on your site. Eliminate all but the most necessary data fields.

However, you cannot eliminate anxiety from your pages completely! In order for prospects to buy from you, they must provide some payment information. If you want visitors to sign up for a newsletter, they must provide their e-mail addresses.

Therefore, you need to offset their anxiety in some manner. The best way to do this is to establish your credibility. Here are some common techniques for reassuring visitors to your site that their personal information is safe:

- Prominently display company phone numbers.
- Provide a contact page with mailing and e-mail addresses.
- Place (authentic) customer testimonials in sidebars.
- Include a privacy policy on your site.
- Allow customers to submit and browse product reviews directly on the site.
- Link to third-party reviews of your products and services.
- Provide live chat capabilities.
- Display third-party trust seals on checkout pages.

And here are some common mistakes that can actually harm your credibility:

- Fake testimonials.
- Use of certain third-party trust seals that can hurt sales because they make your site look cheap.
- Poorly written copy that makes outlandish or unbelievable claims.
- Use of false addresses or PO boxes; with the advent of Google Street View, anyone can check to see who's really at your address.
- Offshore phone support and live chat.

Here's a site that makes many of these mistakes (Figure 8-18). The homepage copy is poorly written and makes use of logos unrelated to the business—why is there an NFL logo on an auto transport website? Even the Better Business Bureau logo (which is normally a good thing) has been faked. An actual BBB lookup shows that this company has received nothing but complaints from dissatisfied customers.

Clicking through to the "Contact Us" page (Figure 8-19) shows a physical address, but no e-mail or phone number. Google Street View shows that there is actually a mailbox store at this address. Run, don't walk, from this website.

Your site's visitors will naturally get a little nervous when asked for credit card information. This is an area where you should spend time reassuring them. The checkout page at Back to Basics Toys (Figure 8-20) uses a third-party trust seal from McAfee to let customers know their credit card information will be transferred via a secure connection. This page is pretty good, but

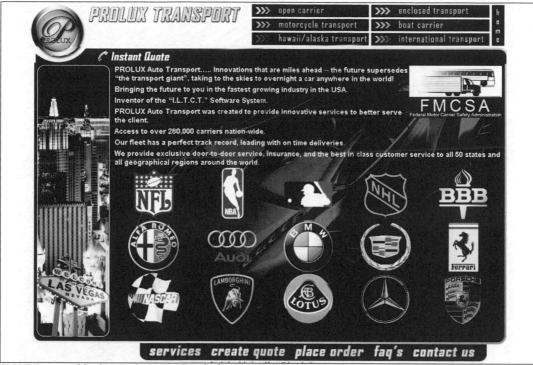

FIGURE 8-18. This site sends many signals that it can't be trusted.

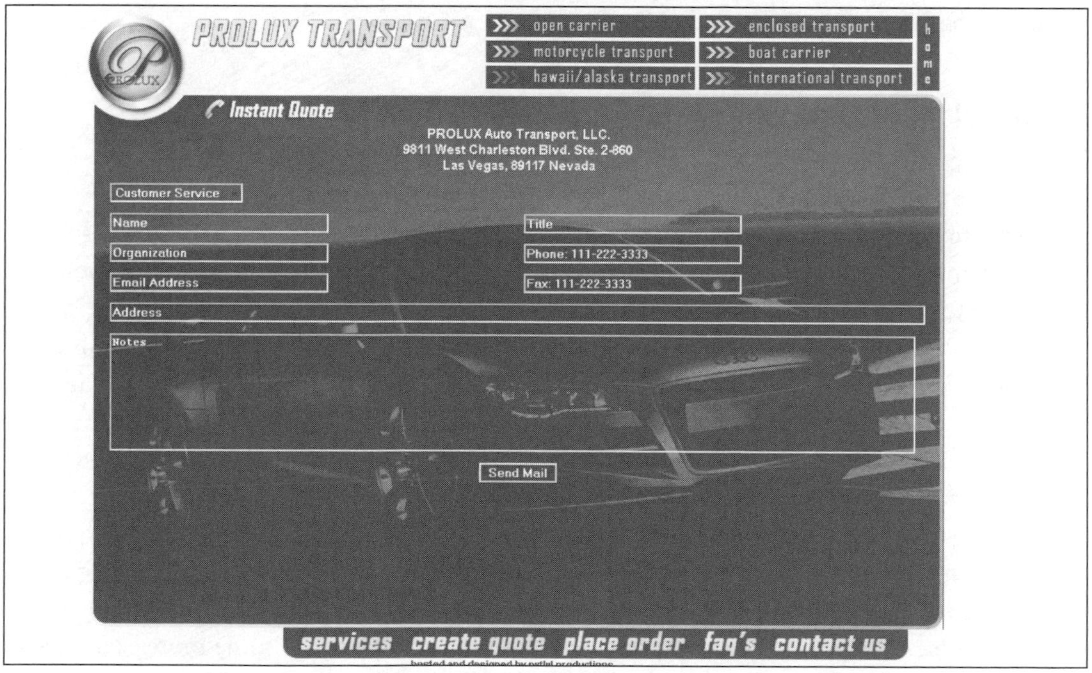

FIGURE 8-19. The contact page shows a fake address for this business.

it could be improved further by including testimonials from customers who were happy about how their orders were handled.

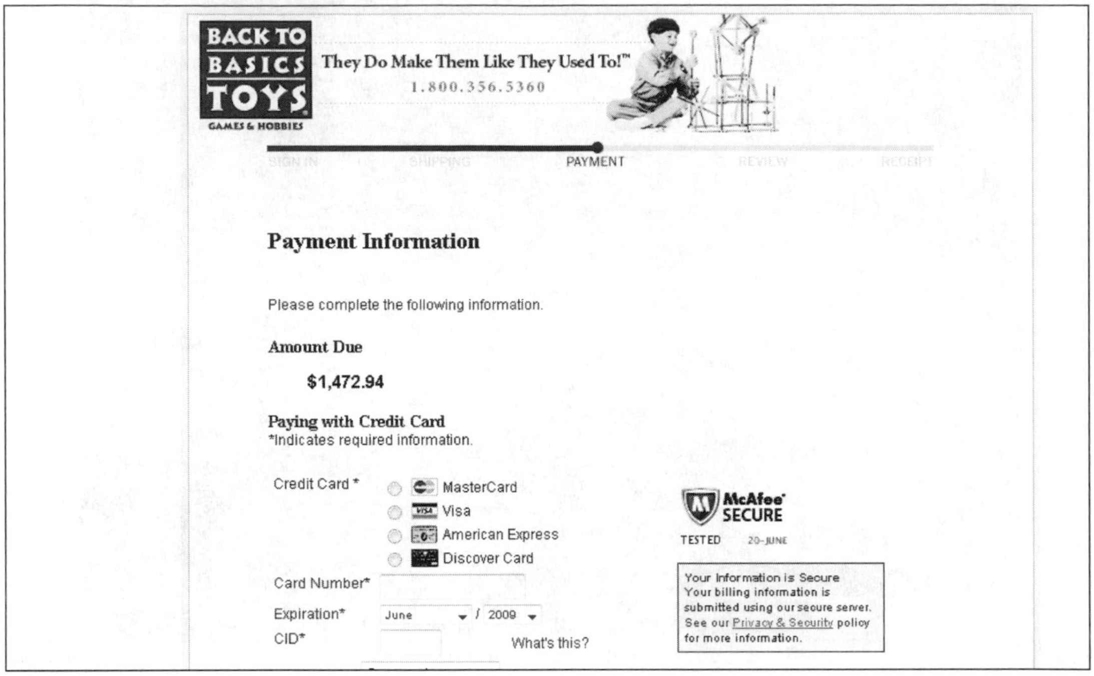

FIGURE 8-20. Reassure customers using third-party trust seals. This site would also benefit from placing testimonials on this page.

FRICTION

Friction can be thought of as page elements that cause confusion for visitors and increase the likelihood that they will abandon the page.

There are many ways in which poor design can cause friction for visitors, so I'll cover only the most common ones. Low-friction pages aren't particularly instructional, so this section will demonstrate this concept through bad examples.

The first, and by far, most common way that sites confuse their visitors is by including too many elements (links, navigation items, and form fields) on a page. This is often compounded by poor use of eyeline.

The American Airlines site mentioned earlier (Figure 8-9) has this problem, but the worst offender I've come across is HavenWorks.com (Figure 8-21).

Even pages with relatively few links can cause major confusion for visitors. If you're serious about website optimization, you should avoid the use of clever "metaphor" navigation schemes such as the one shown in Figure 8-22.

The website of Sarasota Tampa Express (www.stexps.com) provides some more examples of what not to do. The page makes use of annoying flashing graphics, including a circa-1996 effect that displays a text message wherever the mouse cursor moves. Navigation is included at the top,

FIGURE 8-21. HavenWorks.com: A case study in friction.

FIGURE 8-22. Keep your designer on a tight leash, or you may end up with a navigation scheme like this one.

left, and bottom of the page. And for the trifecta, every page on the site plays MIDI-style classical music (Figure 8-23).

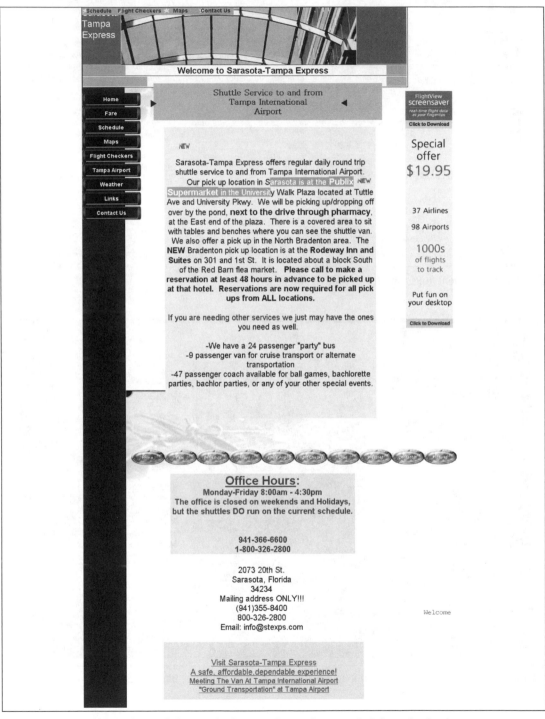

FIGURE 8-23. One of the few websites on the internet that makes use of triple navigation bars.

Many sites fail to use hyperlinks in the proper way. Either through "creativity" or neglect, these sites end up making navigation extremely difficult for their users.

Here are some basic rules you should follow when using hyperlinks on your site:

- Links should be clearly labeled with meaningful and understandable names.
- Use underlines to distinguish links from other elements on the page. Avoid using underlines anywhere else, as this only serves to confuse visitors.
- Most of the time, you should use text, rather than graphics, for links. If you opt to use graphics for your links, split-test them against text-only versions, as this often has a profound impact on sales.
- All links on your site should have the same format so that visitors can distinguish them from other elements on the site.

Another common (and important) question that comes up in optimizing your web design is whether to use links or buttons. The rule of thumb I follow is that if clicking the link will complete a transaction of some sort, use a button. Otherwise, use a link. The rationale for this is that most people experience a certain degree of anxiety when clicking a button—much more than they feel when clicking links. Therefore, only use buttons when you want to signal to your users that they will be doing something with a consequence (such as placing an order).

Figure 8-24 shows a page that uses buttons when it should be using links.

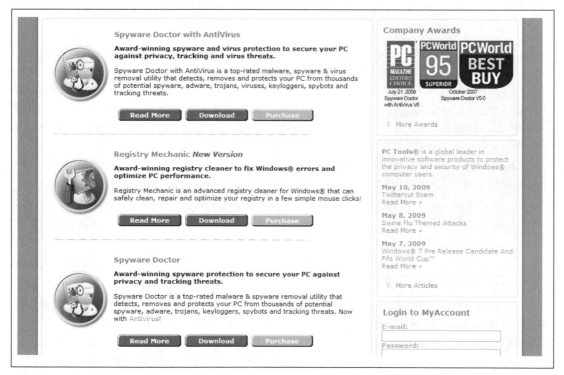

FIGURE 8-24. Buttons should only be used when the visitor is submitting information or completing a transaction. Replacing these buttons with links would probably lift sales.

Here is an example from Dell that uses buttons to good effect (Figure 8-25). Although the page is packed with information, the buttons give visitors a hint about where they should click next.

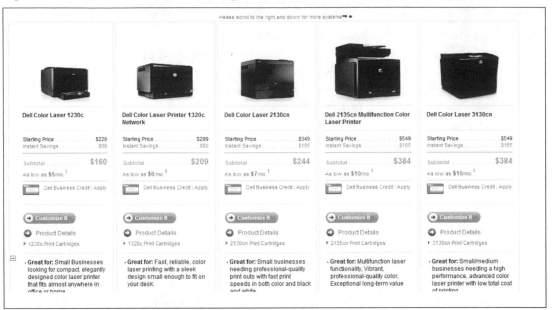

FIGURE 8-25. Effective use of buttons on the Dell printers website.

An area that should be tested far more extensively than you may think is the font style and size. Many sites use fonts that are either too small or too large for their target audience. For instance, if your B2B site caters to executives, your font size should be no less than 12 pixels, because many people past the age of 35 have difficulty reading fonts smaller than this. Conversely, using a font size greater than 15 pixels on page copy can convey an unprofessional tone that is best avoided.

Friction may also stem from the technologies that your developers use behind the scenes. For instance, Flash is a favorite of many designers. However, it has some serious drawbacks:

- Flash can increase the overall size and load time of the page.
- Flash animations often add a few seconds of rendering time to the page, especially for those visitors using slower computers.
- Flash is not available on certain mobile devices (most notably, the iPhone). Its use may also be restricted in corporate environments.

For these reasons, I almost always shy away from using Flash except in product demo videos, and even then, only after split-testing against static HTML versions of the same page.

AJAX can be a very useful technology for eliminating unnecessary pages from your sales funnels (see Chapter 7), but you do need to be careful to test it on a wide variety of platforms and browsers. I have seen cases where the AJAX calls were broken only in Firefox, making it impossible for Firefox users to purchase anything. The problem went undetected for months because Internet Explorer users were able to complete the checkout process successfully.

The final source of friction can be traced back to minor cosmetic issues on your pages. Seemingly trivial problems such as misaligned text boxes or insufficient white space can depress conversions to a small degree, so again, be sure to thoroughly test your site on a wide variety of browsers.

LENGTH

The lengths of your pages and sales funnels will dramatically affect conversions.

First, your ad copy length should be appropriate to the product or service that you're offering. Note that this doesn't mean copy needs to be as short as possible: on the contrary, high-commitment transactions often require lengthy copy in order to sell. This is because copy length (generally) needs to be proportional to the price of the product. An e-mail newsletter signup form should require no more than a few sentences to convince visitors to subscribe. A seminar costing $700 will probably require five or more page lengths of copy.

Next, your pages should each have no more than 10 data entry fields on them. When longer forms are unavoidable, try splitting them out on separate pages to maximize completion rates.

Incidentally, if you do end up splitting your pages out, one way to reduce the perceived length of your sales funnel is through the use of a progress indicator at the top of the page (see Figure 8-26).

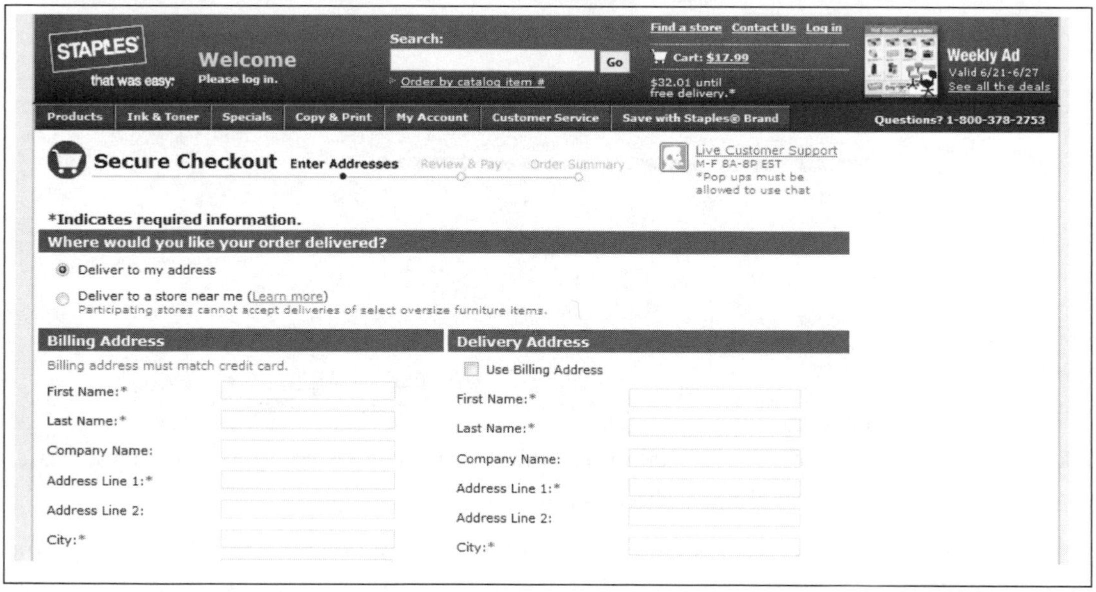

FIGURE 8-26. Staples.com uses a progress indicator to reduce the perceived length of the checkout process.

Another very important optimization task is to reduce the height of your important sales funnel pages. Your conversions will jump dramatically if you can squeeze your content in "above the fold" at a 1024 x 768 browser resolution. Your options here are (again) to reduce the number of fields you ask your customers to fill out or to use a double-column format. Staples.com makes use of this latter technique, but the checkout form is still far longer than the optimal length (see Figure 8-27).

FIGURE 8-27. The entire Staples checkout form is nearly three pages long. Eliminating several of these sections as well as the footer would likely result in a large jump in online sales.

Finally, take a look at the actual size of your pages in bytes (in Firefox, right-click the page and select "View Page Info"). Page size should be as small as possible, certainly no more than 150k. We'll touch on the reasons for this shortly.

CONGRUENCY

All of the pages in your sales funnel should share as many common elements as possible (with the exception of the content areas, of course). When visitors see dramatic changes in page layouts, they are far more likely to abandon your site. These common elements should include the page header, sidebars, navigation menus, and to a small extent, footers.

Another common cause of lost conversions is the use of third-party shopping carts, particularly those hosted on a separate domain. Nothing kills sales faster than when customers are abruptly switched from your site to a third-party domain with a completely different look and feel. If you have a choice, keep the shopping cart hosted on your own domain.

LOAD TIME

The load time of your pages will have a profound impact on your conversion rate. Your click-through rate will start taking a hit after five seconds. After eight seconds, most visitors will abandon the page (unless they've already filled in a good number of data fields on prior forms).

Many marketers make the mistake of assuming that if a page loads quickly on their own computer, it will load quickly for most or all of their visitors. This is a mistake because page load time is dependent on a wide variety of factors:

- Database calls made by the page. The effect of database calls and other page logic is usually apparent to all users (even ones at your corporate headquarters), so this is usually optimized away by the developers.
- Total page size in bytes. This will affect visitors with slow internet connections and those that are geographically far away.
- Number of external files (CSS, JavaScript, and images) referenced by the page. This will tend to affect visitors more or less randomly based on their network latency, their bandwidth, and even the type of browser they are using.
- The HTML Doctype that the page adheres to (such as HTML 4 Transitional, HTML 4.01 Strict, XHTML, and so forth). This seemingly minor detail will have a profound impact on your page load speed that is particularly dependent on the browser version your visitors are using.

Your developers and designers should be well informed on this subject. Here are some general guidelines to follow, however:

- Minimize the total page size in bytes. You can see how large your pages are by right-clicking them in Firefox and selecting "View Page Info" from the pop-up menu. Ask your developers to remove unnecessary code from the page and consider switching your website to a CSS-based design, such as XHTML, if you haven't already (Figure 8-28).
- Minimize the number of external files referenced by your page. An easy way to do this is by combining all of your JavaScript code into a single global include file. The same can be done for your CSS files. Even images referenced by your site can be merged into a single sprite file to minimize load time. Your designers will know how to do all of this.
- Utilize design tricks such as loading indicators, AJAX, and (subtle) animations to reduce the perceived page load time experienced by your users. Note that this won't reduce the actual page load time, so you won't get a boost to your quality scores from this technique.
- If you're using ASP.Net to host your website, ask your developers to devote attention to

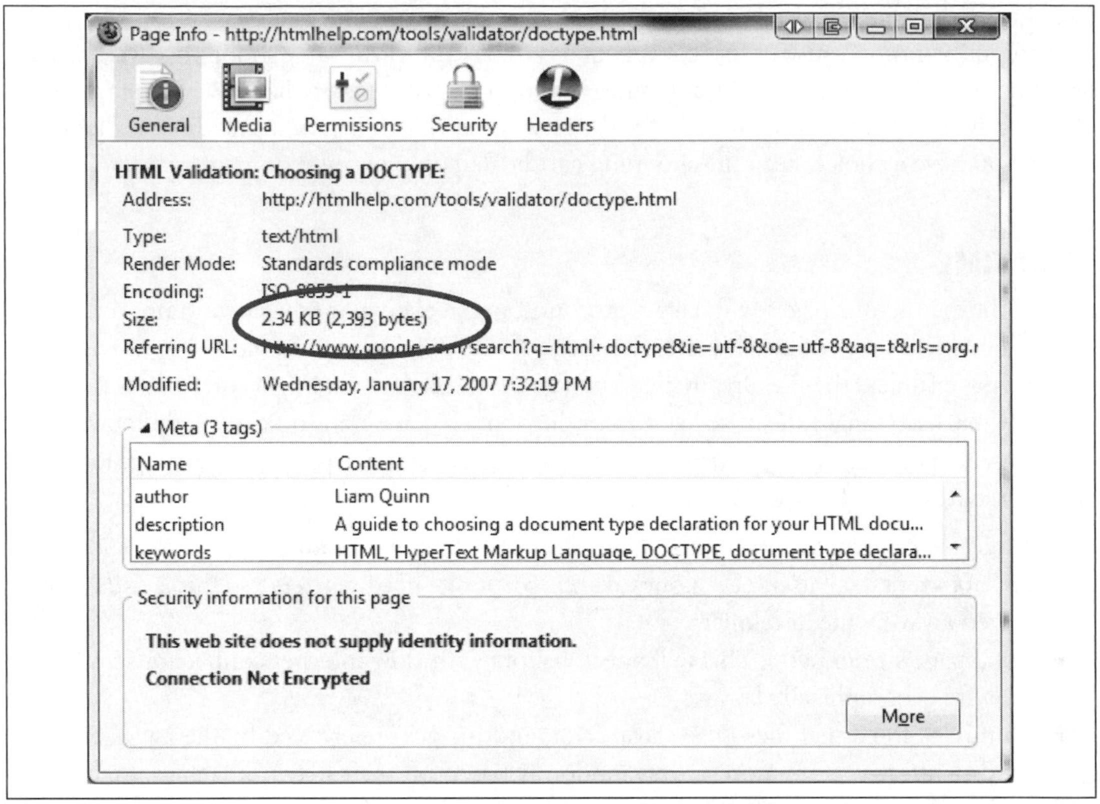

FIGURE 8-28. View the size of your pages using the Page Info pop-up dialog in Firefox.

minimizing the viewstate data contained in the page. By default, ASP.Net uses far more storage within viewstate than necessary. This adds considerable bloat to the page and can seriously increase your page load times (both perceived and actual). At AdGooroo, we use ASP.Net only for our internal reporting pages because these tend to be more complex. For the external marketing pages, we stick with lightweight languages such as PHP and Perl.

- Don't go overboard with AJAX! AJAX can be useful to reduce your sales funnel length, but many sites use far too much of it. This can be annoying to users, prevent your pages from being indexed properly, hurt your quality scores, and significantly increase the size of your pages. Use it sparingly.

One of the best tools for speeding up your pages is the Google Page Speed add-on for Firefox (http://code.google.com/speed/page-speed/). This free plug-in analyzes your pages and generates specific recommendations that your developers can implement to reduce your load time.

URGENCY

A classic sales technique for improving close rates is to create a sense of urgency. This works on landing pages as well!

The technique is simple: offer something of value to your potential customers to encourage them to complete the conversion process. This generally works well but you have to be careful, as it can also increase the number of bogus orders.

Contrary to popular belief, incentives work just as well with B2B websites as they do with B2C ones. The key is to ensure that the incentive provides value to your target audience. Corporate executives are unlikely to be swayed by a pen or plastic toy, but they are far more likely to download a proprietary research study.

We make use of this technique at AdGooroo. We experimented with many types of incentives, ranging from corporate swag to free subscriptions. The most successful incentive turned out to be a copy of my previous book, *Mastering Search Advertising*. Not only did this incentive increase free trials by 48%; it also helped to educate many new search advertisers, some of whom later came back as subscribers (Figure 8-29).

FIGURE 8-29. At AdGooroo, we encourage visitors to sign up for a campaign analysis by offering a free book.

AN EXAMPLE OF CONVERSION OPTIMIZATION AT WORK

Now that we've gone through the eight optimization areas, it's your turn! Figure 8-30 shows the actual e-mail newsletter signup form from the Methuselah Foundation as it looked at the beginning of 2009. Work through the checklist and see how many optimization opportunities you can find.

During the optimization process, I performed this same exercise by marking up a printout of the page. Here are some of the problem areas I found:

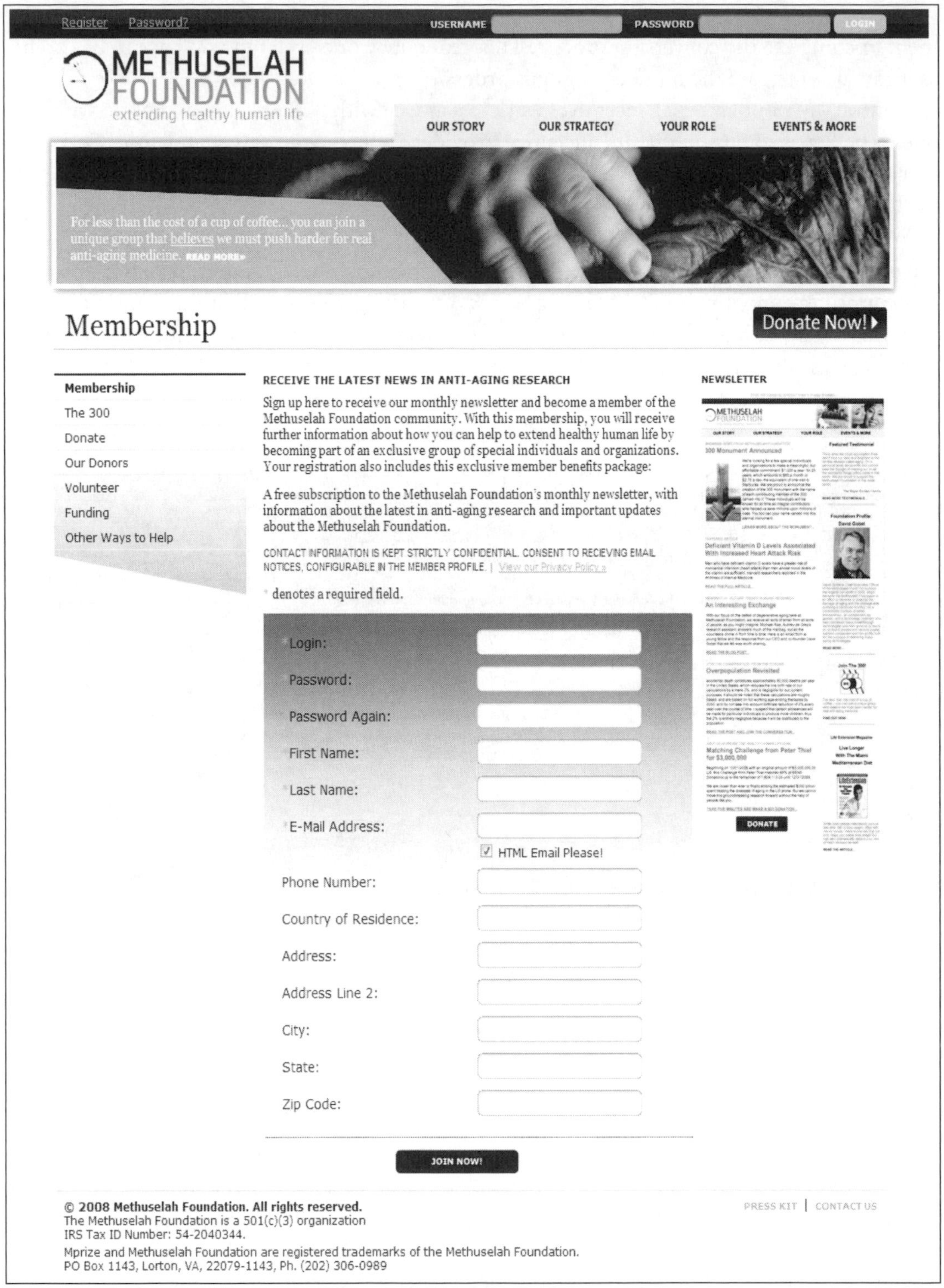

FIGURE 8-30. The Methuselah Foundation e-mail newsletter signup page as it looked prior to optimization.

- The page doesn't appear to have a single purpose. Rather, it's a confusing collection of links, images, navigation bars, and form fields.
- The form is nearly three pages in length.
- The login area (along the top of the page) competes with the rest of the page elements.
- Menu items above the photo offer the user conflicting choices and push the important areas further down the page.
- A second left-hand navigation menu competes with the top menus.
- A third column is required to contain the left-hand navigation menu. This breaks up the eyeline.
- The form and "join now" button are below the page fold at a standard 1024x768 resolution.
- A large, red "Donate Now!" button sits prominently above the fold.
- The photo is interesting, but it drags the eyeline to the right (directly into the "Donate Now!" button).
- The copy is three paragraphs in length. This may be too much for an e-mail newsletter signup page.
- The newsletter thumbnail graphic to the right pulls the eyeline right, away from the form fields.
- The primary headline ("Membership") does not clearly convey the purpose of the page.
- A secondary headline ("Receive the latest news in anti-aging research") does a better job of describing the page, but is in small type.
- The area containing the form fields has a red background. This may increase anxiety on the part of the user.
- This simple e-mail newsletter signup form is asking for too much personal information. The following fields could be eliminated:
  - Login
  - Password
  - Password verification
  - "HTML E-mail Please!" check box (all e-mails should be sent in both HTML and plain text)
  - Phone number
  - Country
  - All address fields
- More competing links ("press kit" and "contact us") are found at the bottom of the page (Figure 8-31).

My notes gave me a clear direction for where I wanted to take this page. I eliminated everything that I felt wasn't necessary and rearranged the remaining elements to come up with the following testing candidate (Figure 8-32).

Here are both pages placed next to each other for comparison (Figure 8-33, page 110).

Although it seemed obvious at this point that the new page would outperform the original, we still needed to test them to be sure. We'll see how this turned out in the next chapter.

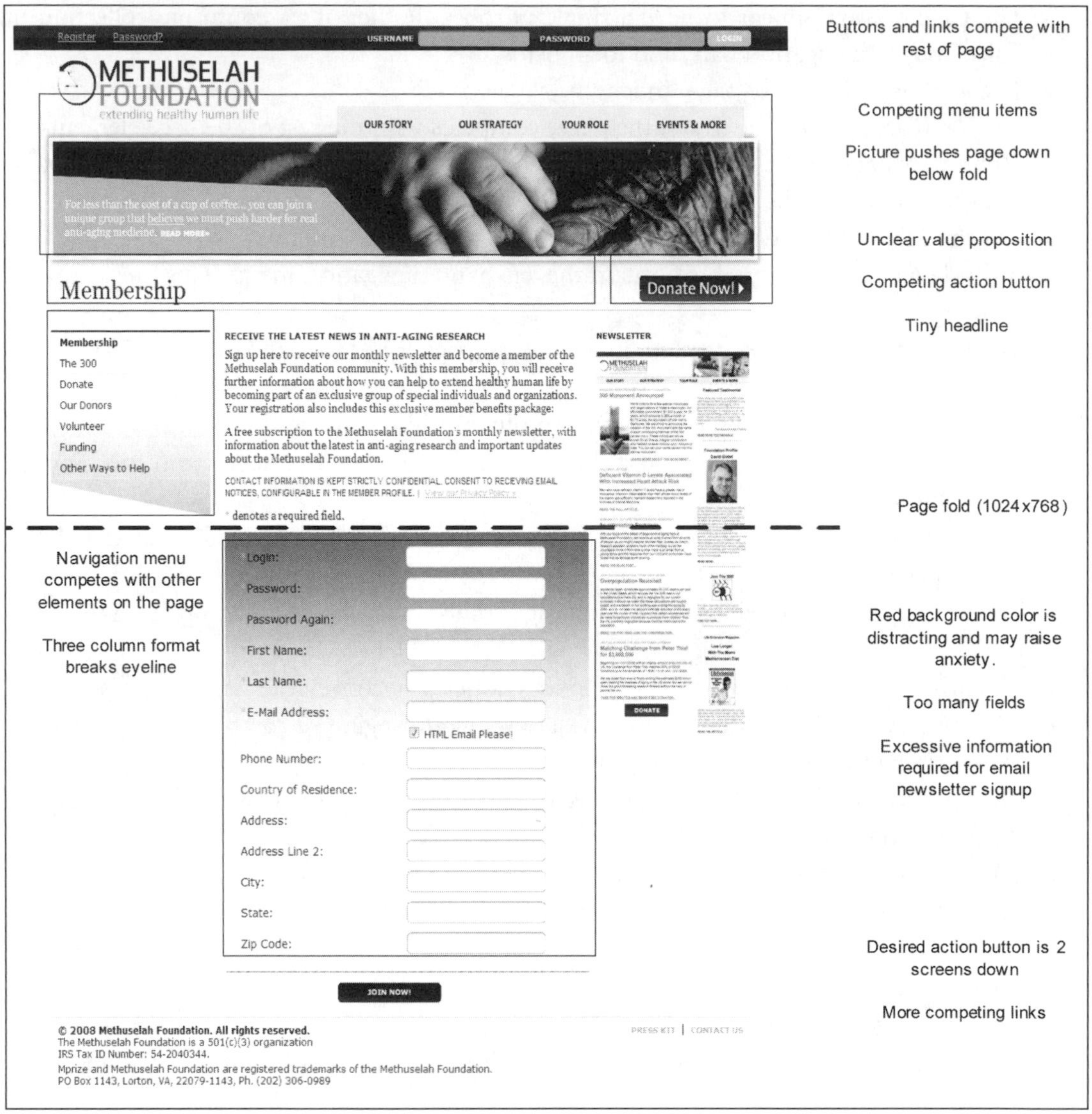

FIGURE 8-31. My actual notes from this optimization exercise.

FIGURE 8-32. The redesigned e-mail newsletter signup page.

FIGURE 8-33. The before and after pages placed side by side for comparison. Notice how much shorter and cleaner the new page looks.

How to Split-Test Your Site

A N INTEGRAL PART OF INTERNET MARKETING IS SPLIT-TESTING. THIS IS THE PROCESS BY which we can test one or more components of our marketing materials in a live environment. This is usually a page on a website, but this same process can be applied to ad copy or promotional emails.

The rules laid out in the last chapter may have made it sound as if testing is optional. It is not.

Testing makes continuous improvement of your website possible. The most important thing it achieves is the elimination of guesswork. If you are a decent internet marketer, your optimization decisions might be correct 50% of the time. However, the other half of the time when you are wrong could easily wipe out all of your gains.

And even if you're a great internet marketer who's spot on 80% of the time, all it takes to crush your conversion rate is a single mistake. Split-testing prevents this from happening because it allows you to identify when you've taken a step in the wrong direction.

Still, I've seen some marketers modify critical portions of their websites without as much as a passing thought given to testing their changes. They fall into this error for one reason: some things are easy to predict.

For instance, if a page started off with 9px Comic Sans font, you can be fairly confident that switching to 12px Arial will improve your conversions (see Figure 9-1).

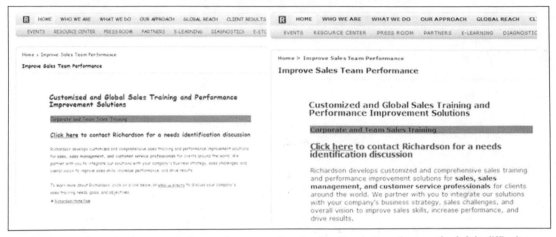

FIGURE 9-1. It doesn't take a marketing genius to see that the tiny Comic Sans font on the left is difficult to read and will lower conversions.

But what if the page was already in 12px Arial? Would 13px boost sales? There's no way to tell without testing.

There are many gray areas like this. On the Methuselah Foundation email newsletter signup form I designed in the previous chapter, you may have noticed that I placed the newsletter thumbnail on the right of the form. I felt that this was more aesthetically pleasing, but someone at the Foundation pointed out that this broke the eyeline and led the visitor off to the right. In the end, we decided to test two alternate versions with the image in different positions (I'll have more to say about this at the end of the chapter).

The same holds true for copy, colors, navigation elements, and so forth. As marketers, we'd all like to have reliable guidelines, but these are elusive. Even the recommendations in my checklist, while based on past experience, need to be thoroughly tested in a live environment before you will know for certain that they work.

Testing will tell us conclusively what works best on our sites. But it comes with a few complications.

CONTROL VARIABLES

One thing that you learn as you go along is that testing is very sensitive to outside conditions. Only a few errant clicks can wildly throw off your results, so you must eliminate as many outside variables as possible in an effort to isolate your testing variables.

In the product marketing world, this lands us squarely in the realm of focus groups, usability studies, and conjoint analysis. This type of market research is way out of reach of most of our budgets. And besides, the best subjects are those who don't know they are being tested.

This is why we like to split-test in a live environment. The problem is that this makes it much

Landing Page Optimization: Guessing vs. Testing

Tim Ash
CEO, SiteTuners.com
Author, "Landing Page Optimization"

You can, within the limits of ethics and accuracy, represent yourself any way that you want on the internet. Your landing page is not written on stone tablets. In fact, it is the most ethereal of objects—a set of bits that resides on a computer hard disk and is accessible to the world.

The only obstacles keeping you from creating more compelling landing pages could be a lack of attention and imagination. You are as free as an artist in front of a blank canvas, but the promise of high-performing landing pages is often tempered by a fear of making things worse than they already are; it's impossible to know in advance what will or won't work, yet you are supposed to be the expert.

But don't worry—you already have access to thousands of willing "experts." You are interacting with them on a daily basis. The real experts on the design of your landing pages are your website visitors.

Landing page optimization can be viewed as a giant online marketing laboratory. The actions (or inactions) of your "test subjects" allow you to improve your appeal to a similar population of people.

Websites have three desirable properties as a testing laboratory:

High data rates: Many websites have significant traffic rates and an ample supply of test subjects. In aggregate, all of your traffic sources result in a particular traffic mix unique to your website. With high website traffic volumes, statistical analysis allows you to find verifiably better landing pages and to be confident in your answer. The best versions are proven winners. Unlike previous designs, they are no longer based solely on subjective opinions. Nor are they the results of political popularity contests within your company.

Accurate tracking: Web analytics software supports the accurate tracking and recording of every interaction within your website. Each visit is recorded along with a mind-numbing amount of detailed information. Although web analytics software is not perfect, it provides a standard of data collection accuracy that is almost unheard of in any other marketing medium.

Easy content changes: Internet technology offers the ability to easily swap or modify the content that a particular website visitor sees. The content can be customized based on the source of the traffic, the specific capabilities of the visitor's computer or web browser software, their behavior during the particular visit, or their past history of interactions with your site. In other experimental environments, it is very expensive and time-consuming to come up with an alternative version or prototype. On the internet, countless website content variations can be created and managed at minimal cost for a landing page optimization test.

So stop guessing and start testing—it will make your cash register ring more often!

harder to isolate our changes. In practice, we can never perfectly control for outside influences. Nevertheless, split-testing can get close enough if we test our pages under identical conditions.

This means that you absolutely must test your pages at the same time to eliminate the effects of seasonality, weekends, holidays, and other time-based shifts in demand.

When you test alternate versions of pages, they need to share the same traffic sources as the original. If you send organic visitors to your original page and PPC visitors to your alternate version, you won't be able to rely on the results of your test. Similarly, internal links pointing to your original page should drive visitors equally (and at random) to your testing variations. If you don't follow this rule, one of your pages may experience artificially high clickthrough rates as a result of Darwinnowing.

You should avoid testing during one-time promotions, email blasts, or other periods of atypical traffic. This can bring in highly motivated visitors who destroy the integrity of your test and artificially inflate your clickthrough rates. This means you should coordinate your testing efforts with your marketing department or anyone else who may be responsible for driving traffic to your site.

Sampling error can also creep into your tests if you forget to filter out your home and office IPs from the testing pages. You'll be sorely tempted to check your pages (especially when a favorite page is underperforming), but any meddling with the page will corrupt (or at least delay) your testing results.

This brings us to another important point.

HOW LONG DO SPLIT TESTS NEED TO RUN?

This is hard to predict unless you are good at statistics (for those of you who are, check out Tim Ash's book *Landing Page Optimization* to get deep into the math behind split-testing). I can give you some guidelines, though. The most important determining factor for testing time is the difference in the clickthrough rate of each of your pages. This means that a test consisting of two pages with clickthrough rates of 3% and 7% will finish much more quickly than one consisting of pages with clickthrough rates of 4% and 5%, because the first test has a larger difference in clickthrough rates.

The testing time is also highly dependent on the number of conversions and the volume of traffic you send to your pages. This is why I recommend that you optimize the higher-trafficked pages in your sales funnel first. Resist pressure from your marketing team to optimize low-traffic areas, as doing so could result in very long testing times indeed.

As a general rule of thumb, you'll probably need at least 1,000 visits (or roughly between 25 and 150 conversions) to each of your testing pages before you have statistically valid results. The nice thing about this rule is that it allows you to generate a ballpark estimate for how long your test will take. Instead of relying on complicated statistics, just look at your traffic map and figure out how long it will take to send 1,000 visitors to each of your testing pages. It may not actually take this long, but it's better to be conservative for planning purposes.

Your testing time will also increase with the number of variations you are testing. Testing four pages does not take twice as long as two pages. It could take much longer, because you are increasing the chance that two of your pages have similar clickthrough rates, which will extend your test significantly. So, for the quickest results, I recommend that you test only two variants in a standard A/B split test at first (we'll cover the different types of tests momentarily).

Limiting yourself to two pages per test brings up another concern however. It's rather easy to take an unoptimized page and identify dozens of potential improvements (we did exactly this in the last chapter). If you test each of these improvements individually, it can take months (or even years) to get valid results for so many variations.

My approach to solving this problem is the blue sky test. I group the improvements in which I am most confident into a single new page design and test that against the original. I usually make huge gains in this single test. If further gains are needed, I can do a series of follow-up tests to measure variants that I am less confident about. This allows me to make large gains quickly and then allot additional time later to squeeze every possible click out of a page.

> ### What If You Don't Have Enough Traffic to Complete a Split Test?
>
> The math behind my recommendations indicates that you'll need a minimum of 2,000 visits to your testing page to complete your tests (2 pages x 1,000 visitors each).
>
> If your site doesn't get that much traffic, you should skip ahead to the pay-per-click chapters and get a simple campaign up and running. Don't break the bank, and don't spend a lot of time optimizing your campaign just yet. Your goal should be to drive just the minimum amount of traffic to your site needed to start optimizing.

TYPES OF TESTS

My aim in this chapter is not to get bogged down in complex math or industry terminology. Nevertheless, there are a few types of tests you are going to encounter often, so we should touch on them briefly.

The most common type of test is the standard A/B split test, which involves the simultaneous testing of two (sometimes three) independent pages against each other. It's the easiest to set up, and because it limits the number of pages you can test, it usually produces quick results. I'll teach you how to run an A/B split test in this chapter.

The next type of test is known as a multivariate test. This is used when you would like to test two or more variables on a page. Each variable could have two or more variations. Here's an example:

- Variable 1: Headline
  - Variation 1: "Buy now and save"
  - Variation 2: "Buy one, get one free"

- Variable 2: Headline color
  - Variation 1: Midnight blue
  - Variation 2: Black
  - Variation 3: Orange
- Variable 3: Supporting graphic
  - Grandfather and granddaughter
  - Hand of a baby holding the hand of a grandparent
  - Young woman
  - Young family

A multivariate test allows you to test every permutation of your variables in a single run. However, you need a lot of traffic to make this pay off, because the number of variables means that your tests will require far more traffic to generate valid results.

If you have the necessary traffic to support a multivariate test, it offers a couple of big advantages.

First, you won't need to code separate tests for each permutation. Most multivariate testing software packages will require you only to place a few scripts on your test page and upload your variants as small code snippets to a master administration panel. To run a simple A/B test incorporating six variables with three variations each, you would need to code (and debug) 18 separate pages. This could take days. A multivariate test could be put together in a fraction of the time.

The second advantage is that a multivariate test can identify pages with correlated testing variables. For instance, you may be testing to see if the presence of a privacy policy link and the text "We value privacy" helps boost email newsletter signup rates. A multivariate test may help

Super-Advanced Testing: Taguchi Testing

Let's say you have to test five headlines, three section headings, four different font styles, ten submit buttons, and six supporting graphics. You are looking at a whopping 3,600 unique pages, which will require around 7,200,000 visitors to test.

Obviously A/B split-testing is out of the question. Multivariate testing on that many page variations could take years, even if your site is getting hundreds of thousands of visitors a month.

The answer? Taguchi testing.

Taguchi testing is a technique that grew out of the automotive industry. It enabled design engineers to test thousands of variations with a surprisingly small number of actual models. You can apply this same technique to make massive gains in your conversion rate in a surprisingly short amount of time with far less traffic than the equivalent multivariate test.

This is one of my favorite techniques for optimizing high-traffic sites. The math is complicated, but if you want to learn more, Tim Ash's book *Landing Page Optimization* is a good primer on the subject.

you discover that both elements together significantly boost conversions over either element alone. This is something that you may miss with a series of simple A/B tests.

TESTING GOALS

Defining your testing goal is simple, but important. For the purposes of this book, we are going to concern ourselves with testing clickthrough (or conversion) rates. This is sufficient for the vast majority of tests you'll need to undertake when optimizing your own site.

You can also test your average order size, but this is much harder to do (I don't know of any off-the-shelf software that will do the job for you). If you absolutely must use order size as your testing criteria, you will need to cookie your visitors and collect the information manually. This isn't something that can be done simply with Google Analytics. Fortunately, this scenario doesn't come up too often.

TESTING TOOLS

There are two tools that I will introduce you to in this chapter. The first can be found at www.splittester.com. This is a very simple tool that you can use if you are testing two variations and already have a system or report that will generate clicks and clickthrough data for you (for instance, if you are split-testing ads against each other, Google AdWords will tell you the clicks and clickthrough rate for each of your variations) (Figure 9-2).

FIGURE 9-2. Just plug your numbers into SplitTester, and it will do all of the math for you!

Just enter the number of clicks (or conversions) and the clickthrough rate for your variations, and it will tell you how confident (expressed as a percentage between 0 and 100%) you can be that the results are valid. If this tool tells you that you can have 95% confidence in the results, your test is complete (99% is better, but takes longer).

For most of your testing needs, however, you will need something more robust. Years ago, I had to create my own testing software to get the job done. Then Google came out with a terrific free tool: Google Website Optimizer (GWO). This has served me well for the past few years and has (almost) completely eliminated the need for custom software.

SETTING UP YOUR FIRST GWO TEST

1. Before you start, you'll need at least two distinct pages on your site that you wish to test. This is usually your original page and a new testing variation. You'll also need to identify your successful conversion page. This will typically be the page immediately following your original (Figure 9-3).

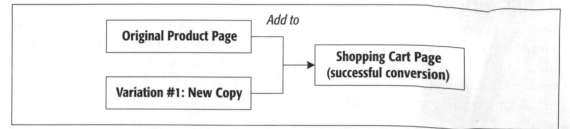

FIGURE 9-3. For your first A/B split test, you will need to work with your original page, an alternate test version, and a successful conversion page.

2. Log in to AdWords, and click the "Website Optimizer" link on the top toolbar (Figure 9-4).
3. If this is your first time using GWO, you will see a short description of the tool. You may also have to accept some terms and conditions at this point (Figure 9-5).
4. Click on the "Create a new experiment" link (Figure 9-6).
5. On the next screen, you may choose between an A/B experiment and a multivariate test. Multivariate testing is for more advanced users. For now, select the option to create an A/B experiment (Figure 9-7).
6. You'll be presented with a checklist. Read this page carefully to make sure that you understand the instructions. Check the check box at the bottom of the page and click "Create" (Figure 9-8).
7. Enter the URLs of your test pages and successful conversion action page. GWO will check to make sure that these pages are accessible before allowing you to proceed to the next step (Figure 9-9).
8. The next page will ask if you are setting up your scripts or if your web team will do this work. If your team will, then the following page will allow you to send instructions to them. We'll assume that you are for this tutorial. Select that option, and press the "Continue" button.

9. The next page will give you a set of scripts to install on the pages of your site (Figure 9-10).

Installing the scripts is easy, but it can be helpful to understand what they do. Here's a brief explanation of each.

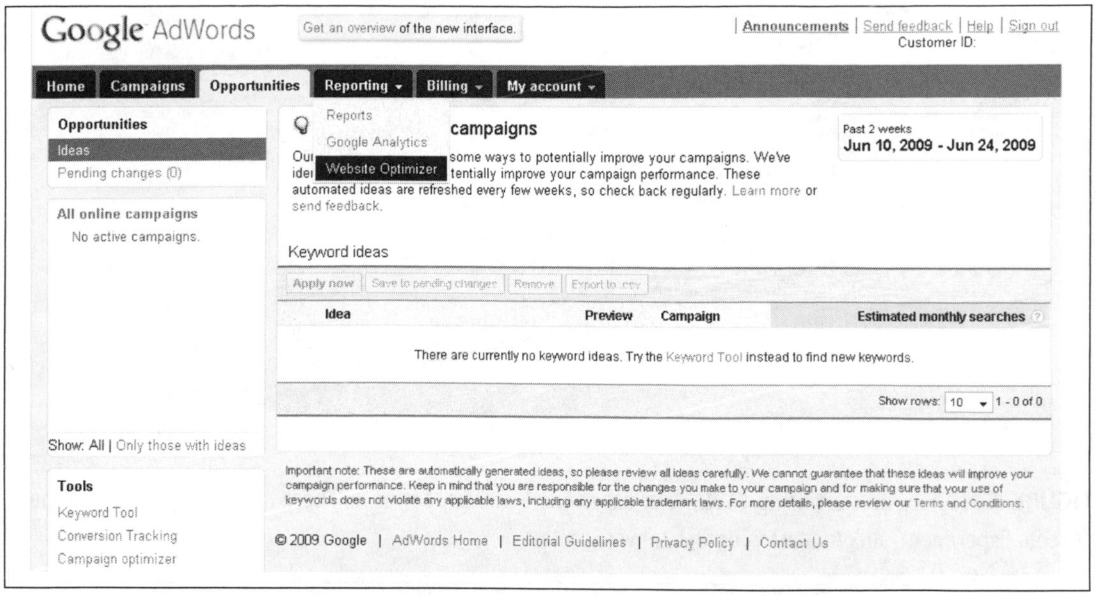

FIGURE 9-4. You can find the Website Optimizer link in the Reporting menu within the AdWords interface.

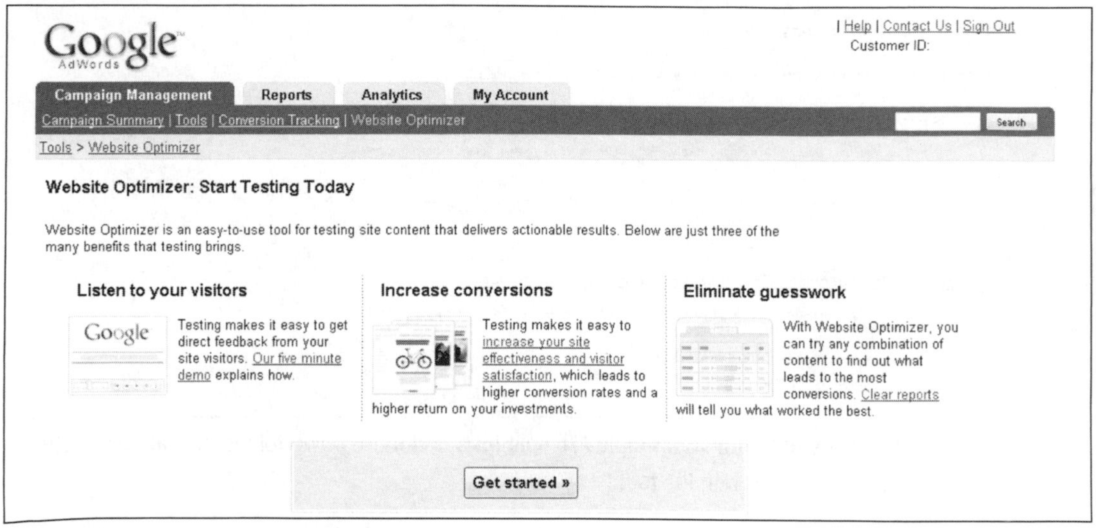

FIGURE 9-5. The GWO "Getting Started" page.

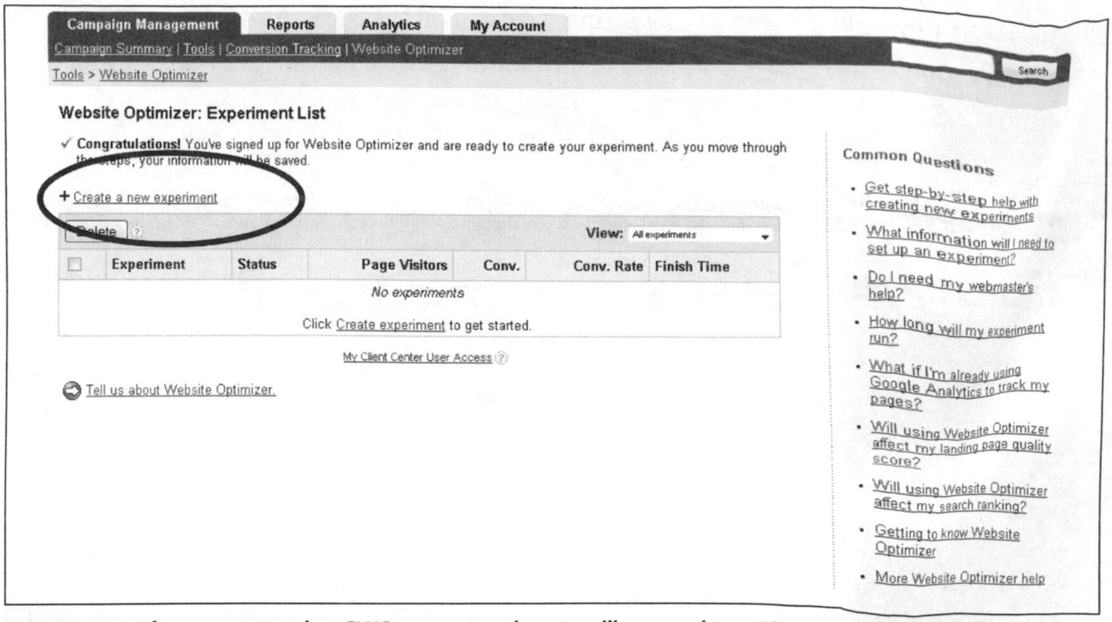

FIGURE 9-6. After you start using GWO, your experiments will appear here. There are none yet, so click the "Create Experiment" link to start your first conversion test.

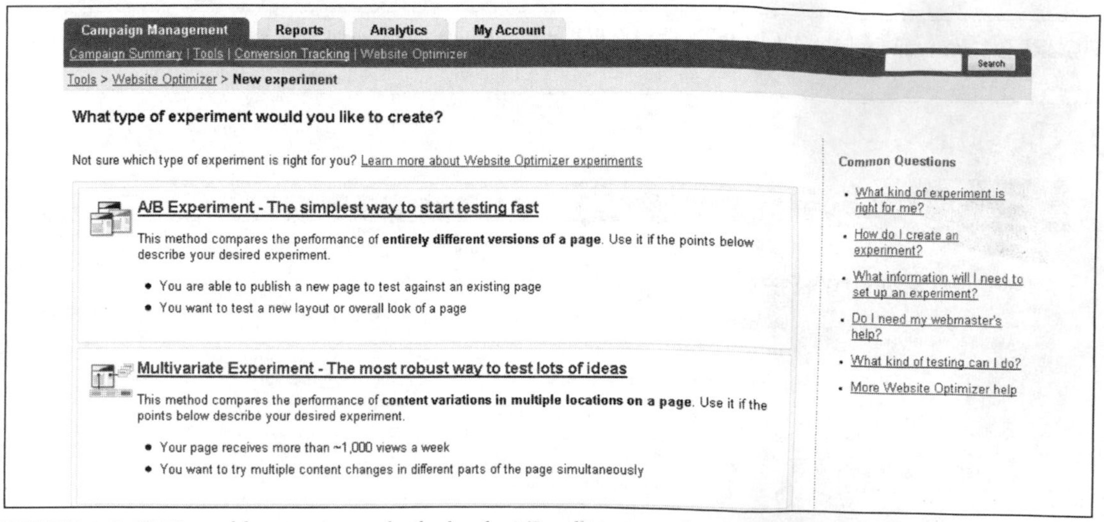

FIGURE 9-7. GWO enables you to run both simple A/B split tests and more powerful multivariate tests. Stick with A/B tests until you get familiar with the tool.

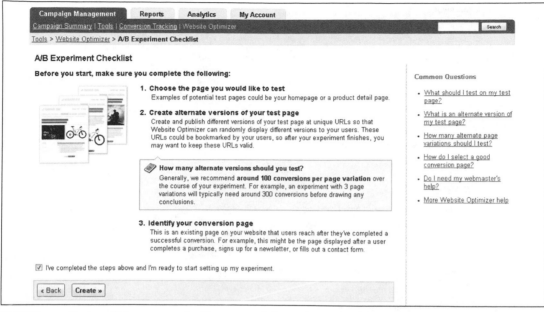

FIGURE 9-8. Next you'll be presented with a recap of the testing process. Review the instructions before proceeding.

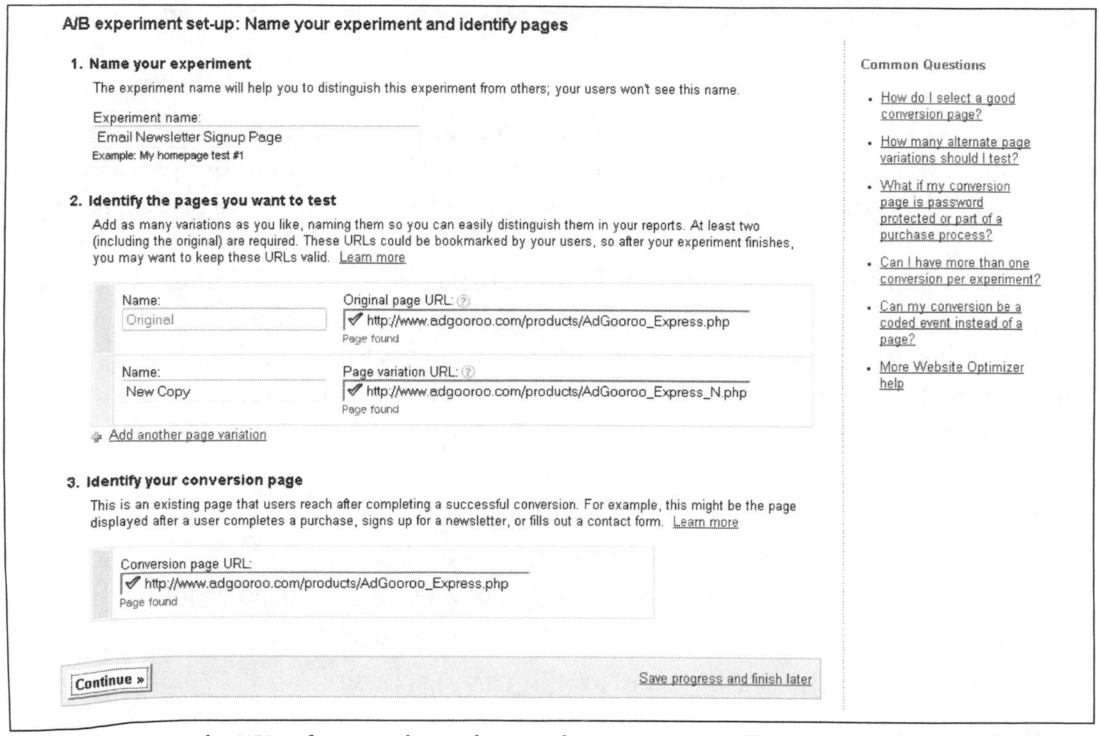

FIGURE 9-9. Enter the URLs of your testing and conversion pages. GWO will validate them before allowing you to proceed.

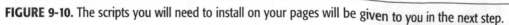

FIGURE 9-10. The scripts you will need to install on your pages will be given to you in the next step.

Control Script

Every time a visitor attempts to view the page with the control script, it will call back to Google to get a list of your alternate testing pages and randomly redirect a percentage of your visitors to your testing pages. The remaining visitors will be allowed to view the original page (this is your control page).

This tiny snippet of code performs the rather remarkable function of eliminating much of the noise that would otherwise distort your testing results as a result of running in a live environment. It divides your visitors up at random, which eliminates sample bias. It also prevents distortions that may arise from sending different traffic sources to your test pages. All in all, it's quite a remarkable piece of code.

```
<script>
function utmx_section(){}function utmx(){}
(function(){var k='[TEST_NUMBER]',d=document,l=d.location,c=d.cookie;function f(n){
if(c){var i=c.indexOf(n+'=');if(i>-1){var j=c.indexOf(';',i);return c.substring(i+n.
length+1,j<0?c.length:j)}}}var x=f('__utmx'),xx=f('__utmxx'),h=l.hash;
d.write('<sc'+'ript src="'+
'http'+(l.protocol=='https:'?'s://ssl':'://www')+'.google-analytics.com'
```

```
+'/siteopt.js?v=1&utmxkey='+k+'&utmx='+(x?x:'')+'&utmxx='+(xx?xx:'')+'&utmxtime='
+new Date().valueOf()+(h?'&utmxhash='+escape(h.substr(1)):'')+
'" type="text/javascript" charset="utf-8"></sc'+'ript>')})();
```

Tracking Script

The tracking script counts the number of visitors who viewed each of your pages. Similar code is placed on each of your testing pages, including the original. This script should be placed at the end of your page, near the closing </body> tag. This ensures that only visitors who waited for the complete page to load actually get counted (visitors who bounced immediately will not be counted).

This script also cookies your visitors, ensuring that they see the same page should they leave your site and come back.

```
<script type="text/javascript">
if(typeof(_gat)!='object')document.write('<sc'+'ript src="http'+
(document.location.protocol=='https:'?'s://ssl':'://www')+
'.google-analytics.com/ga.js"></sc'+'ript>')</script>
<script type="text/javascript">
try {
var pageTracker=_gat._getTracker("UA-XXXXXXX-2");
pageTracker._trackPageview("/[TEST_NUMBER]/test");
}catch(err){}</script>
```

Conversion Tracking Script

This script should be placed at the end of your conversion page. It's used to track the number of successful clickthroughs for each of your testing pages. It also reads the cookie that was set by the prior tracking script to filter out visitors who didn't click on one of your test pages (e.g., those who may have bookmarked your conversion page).

It's important that this script is not found anywhere else on your site, or your test will register false testing results.

```
<script type="text/javascript">
if(typeof(_gat)!='object')document.write('<sc'+'ript src="http'+
(document.location.protocol=='https:'?'s://ssl':'://www')+
'.google-analytics.com/ga.js"></sc'+'ript>')</script>
<script type="text/javascript">
```

```
try {
var pageTracker=_gat._getTracker("UA-XXXXXXX-2");
pageTracker._trackPageview("/1964489370/goal");
}catch(err){}</script>
```

Troubleshooting Three Common Installation Problems

1. If you already have a Google Analytics tracking script installed, it should appear after the control script but before the tracking scripts.

2. Don't mix the old (Urchin) Google Analytics scripts with the new GWO scripts. This can result in unpredictable traffic and conversion figures. This is one of the most common problems people have when trying to install GWO for the first time.

3. If you are testing pages on multiple domains (such as product pages that link to a third-party shopping cart), then you won't be able to use an A/B test. Instead, you'll need to create a multivariate experiment and follow the instructions at this link: google.com/support/websiteoptimizer/bin/answer.py?hl=en&answer=62999.

As you can see, the purpose of each of these scripts is quite straightforward. Each is absolutely necessary to conduct your test successfully. If the scripts are mangled, removed, or placed on pages where they don't belong, your test results will be incorrect. GWO checks to ensure that the scripts are installed correctly on your testing pages, but it's up to you to ensure that they aren't found anywhere else on your site.

After validating your pages, you should receive the go-ahead to launch your test. If you're ready, go ahead and launch. Otherwise, you can save your test and launch at a later date.

Now it's waiting time. You can come back to the GWO reports page at any time to check your progress.

You won't see results right away. It can take up to 12 hours for impressions to show up. Clicks come a little later. Your stats will be updated on roughly an hourly basis after that. If you don't see results after a full day, check your Google Analytics reports to ensure that all of your testing and conversion pages are actually receiving traffic. If they are and your GWO report doesn't reflect this data, this means your scripts may have been installed incorrectly.

GWO will crunch the numbers for you and tell you when you have statistically valid results. The winning page will be clearly highlighted. When you reach this happy point, it's time to start your next test!

I mentioned previously that a good rule of thumb is that you'll need at least 1,000 visitors per page before your test will complete. However, sometimes tests with high variance in click-through rates can finish much more quickly.

Here's an example of one that completed in just under a day. Although each page had fewer than 60 visitors, one of the variations outperformed the others by such a wide margin that further testing was unnecessary (Figure 9-11).

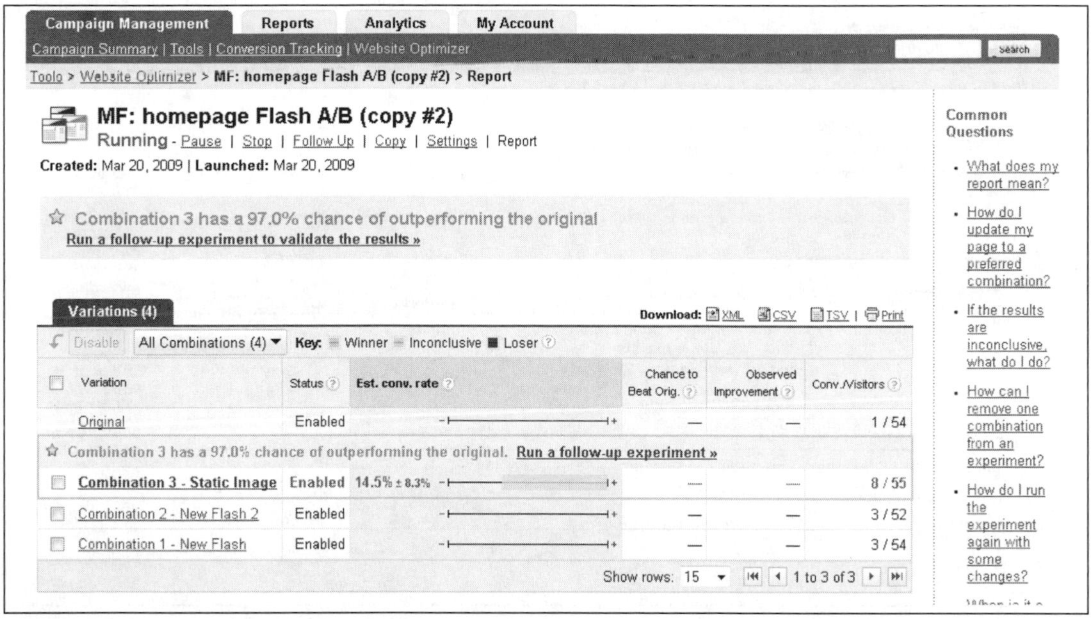

FIGURE 9-11. A test that completed much more quickly than anticipated due to a large improvement in conversion rate.

GWO GONE WILD

If you're working on a larger website, be sure to coordinate your efforts so that others don't accidentally delete your GWO scripts. Another problem may arise if your developers unknowingly install GWO scripts in site-wide header or footer templates instead of just the pages that need them.

Unfortunately, this happens all the time. You might see something similar to Figure 9-12 if your scripts were installed improperly.

Notice that each of the pages (even the original) is registering a conversion rate between 56% and 66%. I knew that this was wrong because the traffic map showed a 2.1% click-through rate for the page (also see Chapter 5).

Abort Tests That Drag On

If you test three or more pages simultaneously, you may end up in a situation where two of your alternatives soundly beat the original, but have close to the same conversion rate. In this case, your test may drag on for a long time while GWO attempts to declare a winner. I usually stop the test at this point and just pick one to optimize further. When it comes to conversion optimization, time is money. Don't get sidetracked by avoidable delays.

METHUSELAH FOUNDATION RESULTS

We'll wrap up this chapter with the results of the blue sky test doesn't seem to be mentioned until p. 115 of this chapter. My design had the thumbnail on the right, but the Methuselah Foundation

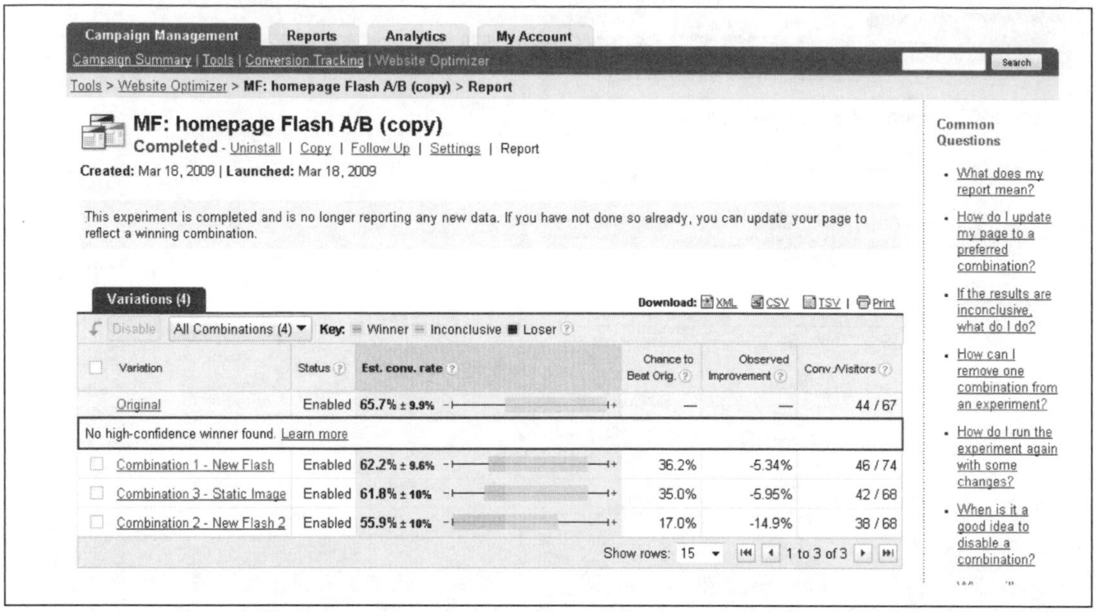

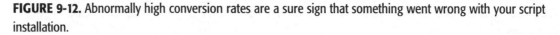

FIGURE 9-12. Abnormally high conversion rates are a sure sign that something went wrong with your script installation.

executives suggested that we run the same design with the thumbnail on the left because it had a better eyeline. We ran this page (Figure 9-13) against the original shown in Chapter 8.

FIGURE 9-13. The two new "blue sky" testing variants for the Methuselah Foundation email newsletter signup page. Note that they vary only by the placement of the thumbnail image.

The original scored a conversion rate of 23.6%. This sounds like a pretty incredible completion rate for an email newsletter signup page, but remember that many of the visitors to this page had to actively hunt through the site to find it. They wanted the information desperately enough at that point that they were signing up in droves (Darwinnowing at work). This skews all of our conversion rates upwards.

My blue sky design (the one with the thumbnail on the right) had a 45.2% clickthrough rate, absolutely blowing the original away. However, the page with the thumbnail on the left lifted the conversion rate to an astonishing 60%!

It turns out that even with all of my years of practice in optimizing websites, they made the right call. Testing trumps experience. This tiny change lifted conversions by nearly 33%. Had we simply relied on my checklist and not tested this variation, we would have missed out on what may end up being the most successful email subscriber signup page of my entire career (Figure 9-14).

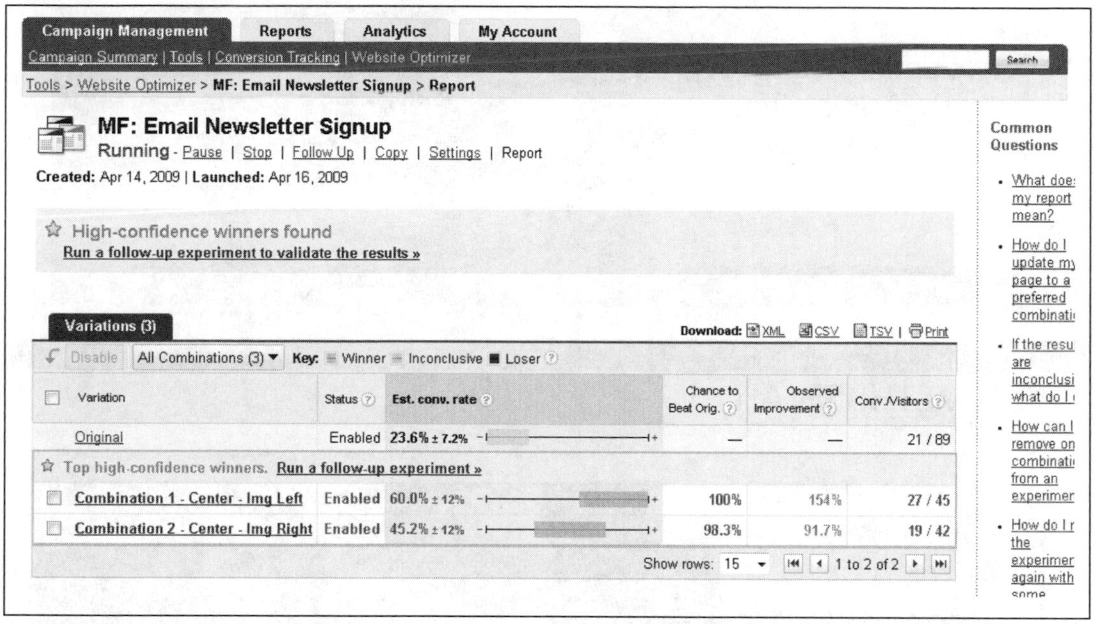

FIGURE 9-14. Testing results of our upgraded Methuselah Foundation email newsletter signup pages.

HOW MUCH DID CONVERSION OPTIMIZATION HELP THE METHUSELAH FOUNDATION?

We ran only two optimization tests for the Foundation over the course of writing this book. The first was a design change on their homepage to optimize the clickthrough rate of the email newsletter signup link. The original page used an animated Flash graphic and a button that read "Donate Now!" The button faded in at the end of the graphic, so it wasn't visible for the first few seconds after the page loaded.

We hypothesized that many visitors were not waiting long enough to see the button. We also knew that the button text was scaring people away. Furthermore, the Flash animation wasn't visible at all on many mobile devices, such as the iPhone.

Our final page replaced the Flash animation with a static image. The button was immediately visible and the text was changed to "Join Now!" We also made the entire image clickable, instead of merely the button.

The optimization results are shown in Figure 9-15. The original clickthrough rate was a mere 1.9% (one conversion out of 54 visitors). Our change increased the clickthrough rate to 14.5%—7.7 times better.

FIGURE 9-15. The original homepage (top) and the winning testing alternative. A few simple changes to the homepage image, button text, and file format type improved clickthrough to the email newsletter signup page by 770%.

We already discussed the extensive changes we made to the email newsletter signup page. The improvements we made increased the email newsletter signup rate from 23.6% to 60.0%, an increase of 2.5 times.

Together, these two optimizations increased email signups by over 1,900%. As you may recall from Chapter 8, we calculated our theoretical CPA to be $22.72. This is roughly the average amount we would have to pay to acquire one new subscriber if we paid $0.25 average CPC. After optimization, this figure dropped to $1.16, a decrease of nearly 95%.

It is unlikely that you'll be able to reduce your AdWords costs by 95% no matter how hard you try. Yet we were able to achieve exactly that with two short optimization experiments (and there are probably many more optimizations waiting to be discovered). It's improvements such as these that will stretch your PPC dollars a long way.

Without a doubt, conversion optimization is the single best means at your disposal of improving your PPC results.

SUMMARY

I hope that this chapter has shown you the importance of testing. Rely on your intuition and past experience only for radical blue sky redesigns of existing pages. Otherwise, you should scrupulously test even the smallest of changes on your funnel pages. You never know which one will push your conversions into the stratosphere.

Once you've brought your projected CPA (cost-per-action) down to a reasonable level, you'll finally be ready to get your hands dirty with an actual pay-per-click campaign.

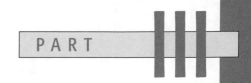
Advanced Pay-per-Click Strategies

Is Pay-per-Click Advertising for You?

C HANCES ARE YOU'VE HEARD ABOUT THE AMAZING ROI THAT CAN BE HAD WITH PAY-PER-click. A return of 300% or even higher is not at all unusual with this form of advertising. (Back in 2003, I was making more than $10 for every $1 I spent on Google AdWords.)

When it works, it works well. But what we don't usually hear are the stories of people who lost their entire ad spend. As with anything else in business, it's best to be realistic from the onset about your chances of success. In this chapter, we'll talk about who usually wins with PPC and who often loses.

PPC WORKS FOR DIRECT RESPONSE MARKETERS

Direct response marketing is a specific form of marketing that sends its messages directly to consumers, usually asking them to take a specific action (for instance, to call a free phone number or fill out a request for more information). Typical businesses that make use of direct response marketing include software companies, newspapers and magazines, sellers of information products, and online retailers.

Traditional direct response marketing relies heavily on having access to performance statistics, such as open and response rates. PPC provides access to many comparable statistics (such as clickthrough rate, conversion rate, coverage, and many more), so the performance-based marketer should feel right at home with this channel.

PPC WORKS FOR BRAND ADVERTISERS

On the other end of the spectrum lie brand advertisers. The goal of these advertisers is to build a psychological construct (the "brand image") in the minds of their target audience. This image can be highly successful in convincing consumers to pay high prices for products that are extremely cheap to make. In a very real sense, this additional margin is what gives a brand its value.

Brand advertisers depend less on the types of performance-based statistics mentioned above, and more on statistics that attempt to measure the penetration of the brand in the minds of their target consumers. These statistics include brand awareness, brand recognition, and top-of-mind awareness.

While pay-per-click doesn't provide access to these statistics, it does offer other valuable advantages to the brand manager. First, PPC is extraordinarily cheap in comparison with typical advertising channels (such as television advertising). This gives brand advertisers the ability to pay for the top search results spots while hardly making a dent in their budgets.

It's even cheaper when you consider the fact that impressions are free! Advertisers only pay when visitors click on their ads, not when they merely view them. Yet these impressions continue to build brand recognition in the minds of consumers at no cost.

Finally, PPC gives brand advertisers unprecedented control over their message, allowing them to vary their copy based on searcher intention, geography, culture, and so on.

WHY PPC MAY NOT WORK FOR YOU

Only about 5% of those companies using search can be considered brand advertisers. The vast majority fall into the direct response marketing category. It's these advertisers that tend to run into problems that prevent PPC from being a viable advertising medium.

There are typically six reasons why PPC campaigns fail. Three of these are fully under the control of the advertiser, while the remaining three are somewhat out of the control of the advertiser.

By far, the most common reason for failure is that the advertisers are unwilling or unable to manage their PPC campaigns properly. PPC campaigns cannot be ignored if you expect to turn a profit. We'll talk more about this in Chapter 13.

Another reason search advertising campaigns tend to fail is a lack of tracking. Without tracking, you'll be unable to figure out which keyword buys are working and which are not. You won't be able to tune your campaign and cut out the waste. Installing tracking is a low-cost, one-time effort. There's really no reason other than negligence or ignorance not to do this. Tracking was covered in the first section of the book.

Finally, if your conversion rate or your average order size is too low, you'll be unable to afford even the most modest PPC buys. Your profit margin on successful transactions needs to absorb the cost of acquiring not only the customers, but also all of the other visitors who didn't buy from you. The reason why most affiliate marketers have been priced out of Google AdWords is that they're earning only a small commission (5-10%) on every completed order. Having high conversion rates on your website is such a fundamental contributor to pay-per-click success that we devoted an entire section of this book to it.

There are three other reasons why PPC campaigns might not be a good fit for your business. These are somewhat out of your control, but there can be workarounds.

The first problem arises if your target customers aren't looking on the search engines for the types of products you sell. In this case, you'll need to identify alternative advertising channels (see sidebar by Perry Marshall).

Another common problem is that your products or services require a high-touch sales process to sell successfully. If prospects only buy from you after they talk to a field rep, then you'll need to resort to a multi-stage sales process. For instance, you will likely have considerable success using Google AdWords to generate qualified leads, which sales reps can then call on. The key here is to recognize when you can sell directly to a customer versus when a more personalized approach is required.

Finally, you may run into difficulties with PPC campaigns when bid prices are so high that you are priced out of the market (this is a common problem when selling low-cost consumer goods). Many advertisers simply give up on PPC at this point. However, we've discovered that even in these hyper-competitive markets, there is still plenty of inexpensive search traffic available to advertisers who are willing to work hard on improving the quality of their campaigns. You'll learn exactly how to do this using the techniques described in the following chapters.

When Google AdWords Is the Least Effective Way to Reach Your Target Customer

Perry Marshall
Co-author, The Ultimate Guide to Google AdWords
www.adwordsbook.com

Because I'm the author of some of the most popular books on Google AdWords, my clients are surprised to hear me say that sometimes Google might be last on your list of best ways to sell your product. Let me give you some examples that lend insight into Google's place in the world.

Once I had a client who manufactured AC adapters—you know, those big black plugs that provide power for your CD player or charge your cell phone. We tried mightily to make Google AdWords work, and couldn't. Why? Because this company sells custom lots of 500 units or more to manufacturers, but all the traffic for "AC adapters" and related keywords was made up of everyday consumers looking to buy one unit at a time. Our Google campaign was a total failure, despite valiant efforts to disqualify non-customers. The ads would say, "minimum lots of 500," but Joe Consumer would click on the ad anyway, then leave. A manufacturing directory is a much better way to reach other manufacturers in that situation.

Here's another example: let's say you sell some kind of high-end equipment, software, or consulting to high-level executives and lower-level people are a waste of time for you. (A very common scenario!) Is bidding on keywords a good way to target those executives? No, not really. Maybe only 1% of the people searching are executives, and the rest just waste your clicks. Direct mail would be much, much better for that. A FedEx envelope on the executive's desk is a rifle shot.

Keyword-based advertising only works *when people know they have a problem, can describe it to themselves, and believe that somebody on the internet has a solution.* But many people have severe problems they don't even realize they have. If that's the case, search engine marketing isn't a very good way to reach them. You need to interrupt them instead. So again, direct mail, ads in magazines they read, TV, radio—all of those media might be better. Search engine marketing only gets you people who are proactively looking to solve their problems right now.

Sometimes search traffic gets you, ironically, the lowest-quality, least interested, and least qualified prospects. People who regularly visit specific websites are much more interested and much more qualified. For example, let's say you are doing fundraising for environmental activism. You could bid on the keyword "environment," but what you'd probably get is high school kids doing homework assignments and writing papers about the environment.

Now, it may be nice to reach those kids with your message, but you ain't gonna get any money out of them. And if you think about it, people who are already active and interested in environmental issues probably are not typing "environment" into a search engine. They already have sites they like to go to. You'll get much better traffic, and more donations, advertising on those sites. (That's why, in some categories, AdSense gets you better traffic than Google searches.)

Every kind of advertising media slices the world in a different way. Bidding on keywords slices the world according to who's got an itch to scratch right now. Direct mail slices the world according to what magazines people subscribe to, what mail-order products they've purchased, and what charities they've donated money to. Compiled mailing lists slice the world according to where people live, what income level they're in, what positions they hold in their jobs, and what kind of homes they live in.

"Rock, Paper, Scissors"

Print advertising slices the world according to topics people are interested in. If you advertise in *Bass Fisherman Magazine*, you get guys who are rabidly interested in bass fishing. If you advertise on the radio at 7:30 in the morning, you get people who are on their way to work. Every form of advertising has pros and cons, just like in that game "Rock, Paper, Scissors," where each choice has its unique advantages and disadvantages.

I told an exec from an online industrial directory that he just needs to come out and say that yes, sometimes Google is hands down the easiest, cheapest way to get new customers. (His prospect will be rather surprised to hear him say that! Coming clean will boost his credibility.) But he can also point out that sometimes, as with those AC adapters, Google may be one of the worst ways to get a new customer.

For most people, the truth is somewhere in the middle. For most people, Google is a great way to get a certain number of high-quality leads, but there are only so many available. It's like an oil well that pumps out just so much every day and no more. Plus, you never want to have all your eggs in one basket: that makes you very vulnerable. So you need to explore other avenues.

Many of my customers who advertise on Google have also used any or all of the following ways to acquire new customers:

- Buying space ads in e-zines
- Endorsed email blasts from affiliates
- Pop-under and pop-up ads on other sites
- Postcard mailings
- Direct mail
- Magalogs (catalogs that look like magazines)
- Spots in other people's catalogs
- FedEx envelopes to highly targeted prospects from carefully selected mailing lists
- Banner ads
- Radio
- TV
- Telemarketing
- Social media sites like Facebook and Twitter
- Issuing a press release
- Writing a book
- Being an "expert" on a talk show
- Exhibiting at trade shows
- Flyers distributed house-to-house or business-to-business
- Doing a custom teleseminar for another person's email list
- Ads in magazines
- Remnant space in local newspapers, purchased at a deep discount rate
- Speaking at seminars
- Card decks (packets of postcards that come in the mail)
- Writing magazine articles and e-zine articles
- "Buyer advocate" sites like Thomas Register and Globalspec

- Insert media (flyer inserts in newspapers, magazines, or mail-order shipments)
- "Lumpy mail" (sending people interesting objects, like one guy I know who mailed out a six-foot canoe paddle)

When all you have is a hammer, everything looks like a nail. So save this list for the next time you have one of those days when it seems impossible to find a new customer!

Remember that every other advertiser out there has access to some customers, and many of them know they can make a little more money (and not lose any business) by giving you controlled access to their customers. And many times, even though those other media may have a higher customer acquisition cost, the customers may be higher-quality.

What If You Already Have a Great SEO Campaign?

A COMMON QUESTION MANY ONLINE COMPANIES HAVE IS WHY BOTHER WITH A POTEN-tially expensive PPC campaign if they have an effective search engine opti-mization (SEO) campaign already in place? PPC offers a number of compelling advantages over SEO that advertisers should be aware of.

Demographics

The visitors who arrive to your site from search ads and natural search results are very dif-ferent. Prospects who arrive at your site as a result of clicking on a "sponsored" ad gener-ally have a higher predisposition toward buying something. On the other hand, visitors who click on organic results tend to just be looking for information and are less likely to spend money. While this is certainly not true for every business (I have run across a number of exceptions to the rule myself), most advertisers report that PPC campaigns convert at a higher rate than organic ones.

Another tendency I've noticed is that visitors who arrive via sponsored ads tend to skew more toward women and technically unsophisticated visitors. If you are selling products that cater to these demographics, you will likely see a big improvement in results with PPC.

Speed

Getting new content indexed by the search engines is a painful process that tends to take a long time. With PPC, it's quick and (mostly) painless to get visitors to your desired landing pages. And with the ad quality score that Google provides you, you have a feedback mechanism by which you can improve your campaign, potentially resulting in more traffic at a lower cost-per-click. There is no equivalent in SEO.

Control

No matter how good your SEO campaign, you have very little input into where your links will show up. Your organic rankings vary by geographic region, language, even browser and personal preferences! If you want to be on the top of the search results pages with SEO, you have an uphill battle ahead of you. You can work for months (sometimes years) and still never capture the coveted top position.

On the other hand, PPC lets you decide when and where ads are displayed. You can choose to display your ads in the search results only or also on partner networks (such as Ask.com or AOL). You can pick and choose particular geographic regions in which to show your ads. You can also use targeting options to filter out unwanted impressions, such as visitors looking for "free" products and services only. And if you really want those top positions (and are willing to pay for it), you can directly influence your quality score and bid prices in order to get them.

Safety

The PPC algorithms change, but not nearly as often as SEO. It's rather unusual for a good ad campaign to stop working suddenly and without warning. The same can't be said for SEO. Not a few companies have gone out of business when their SEO rankings vanished overnight.

If most of your customers are finding you through organic listings, your business is on very shaky ground. PPC provides you with a good way to diversify your traffic sources.

SUMMARY

If you're already running a successful SEO campaign, you've proven that the search engines can be a valuable source of traffic for your business. Adding a PPC campaign to your marketing bag of tricks will result in more visitors and provide a valuable safety net in the event that your organic rankings ever drop.

3% of Advertisers Dominate Pay-per-Click

A S A SMALL ADVERTISER STARTING OUT IN 2003, I WAS DRAWN TO GOOGLE ADWORDS because it allowed me to level the playing field with far larger competitors. With nothing more than a credit card and a little elbow grease, I could tap into a huge reservoir of highly motivated buyers that most other advertisers had overlooked.

This great democratization of advertising played no small part in catapulting Google to becoming a multi-billion-dollar company. However, this is no longer the case.

AdGooroo conducted a study in December 2007 to determine just how evenly distributed advertising impressions were among search advertisers. We looked at a wide variety of industries and measured each advertiser's *coverage*[1]—the percentage of the time that each company's ads appeared when people searched on related keyword phrases.

On one hand, there's nothing inherently unfair about search engine advertising: everyone in the market has access to the same knowledge, the same training materials, the same experts, and so on. It would be reasonable to assume that advertising exposure is fairly well distributed among all participants in the marketplace.

We were shocked to learn that it just isn't so.

A FEW ADVERTISERS DOMINATE ALL THE REST

In industry after industry, we found that a few advertisers stood out over all their competitors. In nearly every vertical, 98% of all advertisers were receiving less than 20% of the available search impressions. This held true virtually everywhere we looked (with one notable exception—car rental—which is clearly a cutthroat business). Figure 12-1 shows some examples.

Industry	Dominant Advertisers	Total Advertisers	Percent
Car Rental	14	175	8.0%
Car Insurance	7	573	1.2%
Consumer Loans	2	775	0.3%
Online Education	6	277	2.1%
Online Movie Rental	2	438	0.5%
Tax Preparation	2	453	0.4%
Web Hosting	3	758	0.3%
Weight Management	9	666	1.4%

FIGURE 12-1.

Even when we lowered our threshold to include advertisers whose ads appeared for only 1 out of 10 searches (10% coverage), we could find no category in which search engine ads were equitably distributed among the various advertisers. In nearly every industry, fewer than 3% of the advertisers virtually shut out their competitors from most of the available search traffic (Figure 12-2).

Industry	Dominant Advertisers	Total Advertisers	Percent
Car Rental	24	175	13.7%
Car Insurance	15	573	2.6%
Consumer Loans	8	775	1.0%
Online Education	12	277	4.3%
Online Movie Rental	8	438	1.8%
Tax Preparation	13	453	2.9%
Web Hosting	18	758	2.4%
Weight Management	16	666	2.4%

FIGURE 12-2.

EVERYONE WANTS TO BE ON TOP ... BUT FEW ARE

Perhaps it's not so surprising that in nearly every industry, an elite group of advertisers exists that dominates the search engine results pages. After all, in any given market there are on average about 700 advertisers competing for fewer than a dozen ad slots on the search results pages.

What is surprising is that this state of affairs can continue to be true nearly two years after our first study. In that time, numerous books on pay-per-click advertising have been published. There have been dozens of widely attended trade shows devoted to search marketing. The algorithms that hand out ad impressions are automated and impartial. But still, if you judge search campaigns by the percentage of the impressions they're receiving, 97% of them are mediocre at best.

If all the advertisers want their ads to show up as often as possible on the search engines, why aren't they?

It's because advertisers fail to understand that the pay-per-click algorithm that doles out the ad impressions isn't a single program; it's a complicated combination of many different algorithms. One determines the quality of your ads, another the quality of your landing pages. Yet another is called millions of times a day to figure out what ads should be shown, and it has a co-worker to assign an order to these ads.

Each of these different algorithms is like a little policeman, and each has the ability to choke off your ads if it isn't satisfied. That means you can't skip steps or take shortcuts.

You have to fire on all cylinders in order to succeed in pay-per-click, and few advertisers do. After you finish this book, you won't need to be one of them.

Note

1. The concept of coverage is important, so we'll devote an entire chapter to it later.

CHAPTER 13

The Water Is Always Rising in Search

THE WATER IS ALWAYS RISING IN SEARCH. IF YOU DON'T RISE WITH IT, YOUR CAMPAIGN WILL drown.

Here's why. As you'll read about in Chapter 18, the search engines prize relevant, high-quality ads. Good ads keep the visitors coming back. And the more visitors there are, the more money they make from the ads.

Whether or not your campaign is deemed to be better than others depends on a variety of factors:

- The clickthrough rate of your ads
- How well your ad copy mirrors the visitor's search phrase
- The relevance and user experience of your landing pages

And a wide variety of other minor factors that are constantly changing, including:

- Historical CTR of your campaign
- The subject matter of your website as a whole
- Etc. …

Just as in your grade school class, Google grades on a curve. If your ads are deemed to be of higher quality than your competitors' ads, they will appear higher and more often.

YOUR COMPETITORS ARE OUT TO GET YOU (AND THEY MAY EVENTUALLY SUCCEED)

Chances are that you are going to spend a good amount of time working on your campaign while reading this book. You may improve your ad copy, your keyword selection, or your landing pages. These will all likely have a positive impact on your campaign.

Now let's say you get things running smoothly. Your campaign is garnering lots of impressions, plenty of clicks, and a reasonable clickthrough rate. You step away to focus on other important things such as running your business or vacationing in Mexico. Before you know it, a year has passed. You log in to AdWords and find that your campaign now looks something like Figure 13-1:

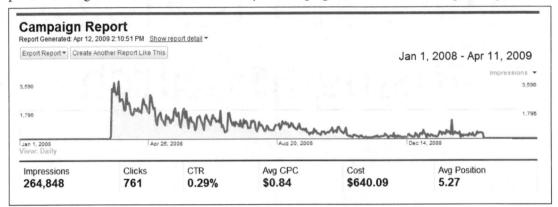

FIGURE 13-1. Actual results of an unmanaged Google AdWords campaign.

Wow! What happened?

The campaign initially received a high number of impressions, but these gradually dwindled until January, when the ads stopped showing on Google's search result pages.

It would be wonderful if we could simply put our campaigns on autopilot and walk away. However, we can't, because our competitors are constantly taking steps to optimize their own quality scores. Working together as a group, they are raising the bar on quality. As they do, the relative quality of your campaign is going down.

In other words, your campaign is under constant assault from all sides, so you can't get complacent. You simply must remain vigilant if you want to beat the competition.

CHAPTER 14

The $100 Bidding Myth

Many advertisers mistakenly believe that the cure for a bad campaign is a higher bid. And why not? If I'm willing to pay the search engine $100 for an ad, it makes money and my ad runs. We're both happy, so why doesn't it work this way?

To see why, consider for a moment the following ad:

> **Free Puppies and Diamonds**
> Lottery millionaire wants to give
> away his fortune. First 100 only!
> www.MillionaireGiveaway.com

Most of us won't be bothered to click on an ad like this these days, no matter how much we like free puppies and diamonds. At one time, however, these ads were fairly common, and they appeared for a variety of search terms, typically with a landing page that looked something like the one in Figure 14-1.

FIGURE 14-1. A spam landing page.

Most people don't like these ads or the landing pages behind them. These ads (and landing pages) are deceptive, and people get burned out on them pretty quickly.

The search engines realized long ago that it's not enough to serve just the needs of the advertisers. They had to serve the needs of the users, or they would eventually stop coming back (Figure 14-2).

If the search engines hadn't cracked down on this a few years ago, search marketing would probably not have ballooned into the 20-billion-dollar industry that it is today.

Spam campaigns are generally low-quality and not all that believable. They only work when the spammer can acquire massive amounts of traffic at a very cheap rate. The solution for eliminating these ads, then, is simple: devise an automated solution for gauging the quality of a search campaign and then require advertisers to pay a certain minimum amount for their ads to appear.

This could easily be done by looking at both the ad copy (Does it have multiple exclamation points? Does it use the word "free"? Does it match the targeted keyword phrase?) and the landing page (Is it a brand-new domain? Who's linking to the site? Does it take a long time to load?).

At the end of the day, however, any automated criteria can be gamed in exactly the same ways that spammers have been gaming the search engines for years. Through the use of clever tricks such as keyword stuffing, crash and burn domains, doorway pages, and so forth, spammers

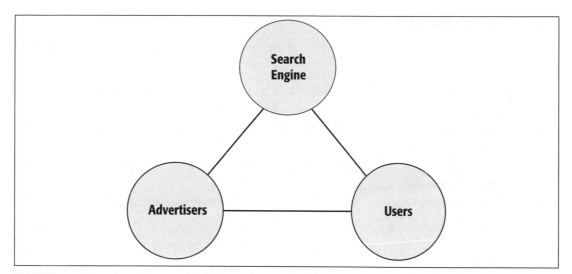

FIGURE 14-2. Search engines need to balance the needs of advertisers, users, and themselves.

could get around these minimum bids. By itself, this approach would eventually evolve into a cat-and-mouse game between the spammers and the search engines (with legitimate advertisers being unfairly penalized when they couldn't keep up).

The only way to truly gauge the credibility of an advertiser is by manual review. Yahoo! went down this road, but it's slow and fraught with errors in judgment that frustrate legitimate advertisers. Imagine how it feels to wait two or three days for your ads to start running and then have someone tell you that your landing pages aren't "high quality" enough.

Google took it in a different direction. It discovered that clickthrough rates were the best way to gauge the quality of ads. Ads with low clickthrough rates would be dropped, while relevant ads with high clickthrough rates would be retained (and promoted higher on the search results pages).

By itself, this is still subject to gaming. Nothing would stop a spammer from creating a brand-new campaign every few days and squeezing as much traffic from the system as possible with misleading ads until they were shut down.

So Google did a clever thing. They subjected new campaigns to the automated review, and if they passed, allowed them to run … slowly. Instead of giving brand-new campaigns equal access to the system, Google subjects them to a benchmarking period during which the ads are tested in every ad slot, but only receive a small percentage of the available impressions.

Ads that don't perform have their minimum bids raised. Legitimate advertisers can still buy clicks (albeit at grossly inflated levels) while spammers will drop out because the costs are too high.

This approach is superior in that it doesn't rely on an "unbeatable" algorithm, nor does it give new (untrusted) advertisers the same access to search traffic as older, more established advertisers. If a spammer does get through, it will get only a few clicks before its bids are raised.

THE "$100 BIDDING MYTH"

In general, this system works well. However, there are some implications that you should be aware of:

- It will typically take 10-15 days for a brand-new campaign to reach its traffic potential. Until that time, the campaign will receive a paltry number of clicks.
- The clickthrough rate and perceived "quality" of your ads and landing pages matter more than your bid price.
- If your campaign isn't deemed to be of high quality, you will have to pay more than other advertisers to have your ads shown in the same spot.
- And even then, you'll receive only a small portion of the available traffic (typically 1-5%).

In other words, even if you are willing to pay $100 for a click, you'll be charged a high opportunity cost (in the form of missed impressions) that you can't buy your way out of.

The really insidious thing about this is that this problem doesn't just affect low-quality advertisers. It affects every advertiser.

That's right. It doesn't matter who you are, how large your budget is, or how great your campaign is: you are almost certainly missing out on a huge chunk of the available search traffic. We know this because we can measure it.

CHAPTER 15

The Little-Known Metric That Can Increase Your Search Traffic by 400%

WHAT IF I TOLD YOU THERE WAS A METRIC THAT YOU COULD USE TO DIAGNOSE POOR ad copy, quality score problems, and budget and billing issues and increase your search traffic by 400% or more?

Well, there is. I discovered this metric in 2004 and used it to quietly blow the doors off every search campaign I worked on. A freelance copywriter friend of mine had to stop advertising on Google within 48 hours of using this data because his phone was ringing off the hook. I personally used it to become the #1 affiliate marketer in the computer security industry in the space of a few short months.

This metric is called coverage.[1]

Coverage is the percentage of the time that people see your ads when they search on your targeted terms. Stated in other terms, it is the percentage of the total possible impressions your ads received.

Most advertisers don't measure coverage. And most don't have any idea of how much traffic they are missing out on. As we saw in our opening chapter, 97% of advertisers have less than 20% coverage. If you're one of these advertisers, you could increase your traffic fivefold—or more—by maximizing your coverage.

In 2004, I started a company to disseminate this metric to the marketplace. You might think that after all this time, advertisers would have caught on and diminished its importance as a key campaign statistic. Yet they haven't. Even today, in 2010, not one advertiser in 500 is making use of this data to build its competitive advantage (but those few who are, are making a killing).

Coverage is rarely discussed in any online forum, but it is one of the key differences that separate great campaigns from mediocre ones. In this chapter, we'll discuss this concept and teach you what may be the most important rule in search marketing: *Always maximize your coverage.*

LOW COVERAGE = LOST OPPORTUNITIES

Take a look at Figure 15-1. On this graph, we've plotted coverage along the left axis and the average position on the bottom axis. At the upper right are a few advertisers who appear 100% of the time when people search for the term *free spyware*. On the lower right is an advertiser who is bidding high enough to end up at the top of the search results, yet it only appears about 1% of the time. This unlucky advertiser probably thinks that this is a low-traffic keyword, because she sees few impressions on the campaign reports. Little does this advertiser know that it could increase its traffic by a whopping 10,000% if it fixed its coverage problem.

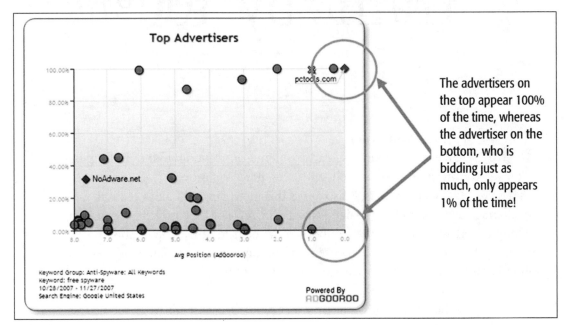

The advertisers on the top appear 100% of the time, whereas the advertiser on the bottom, who is bidding just as much, only appears 1% of the time!

FIGURE 15-1.

Many people think that increasing their bids will give them more traffic. There is some truth to this, because higher bids tend to increase your position on the search results pages. Higher positions in turn translate to higher clickthrough rates. You could typically increase your traffic by 20%, 50%, or even 100% by increasing your bids as a result of the improved clickthrough rate alone. That pales in comparison with the 400% gains I regularly see advertisers get from improving their coverage.

As we mentioned in the previous chapter, bidding more for a term doesn't work as well because it doesn't guarantee you higher coverage. In fact, bidding more can actually reduce your coverage if several well-entrenched advertisers are already bidding for the top positions on the page! This is likely what happened to the unfortunate advertiser above. It may have gone from getting 5-10% at the bottom of the page to getting only 1% of the coverage at the top. No increase in clickthrough rate is going to make up for the loss in ad impressions that comes from trying to compete with advertisers who basically have superior campaigns.

At the end of this chapter, we'll talk about strategies for increasing your coverage. But for now, you just need to realize that impressions don't cost you anything, and they can actually build your brand awareness. So, ideally, you want to have 100% coverage.

Now let's look at the uglier side of the low coverage problem:

LOW COVERAGE MEANS YOU ARE OVERPAYING FOR TRAFFIC

Figure 15-2 is another example chart, this time for the phrase *keyword tool*. From this chart, you can see that we (adgooroo.com) have 100% coverage. Referencing our campaign statistics, we learn that we're getting an average 1.0% clickthrough rate for this keyword. We pay $1.40 for each visitor (CPC) and get about 12 clicks per day, for an average daily total of $16.80.

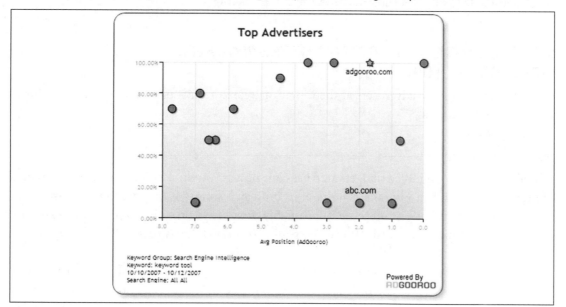

FIGURE 15-2.

The advertiser below us at position 2.0, which we'll call ABC.com, is bidding roughly the same amount but is getting only 10% coverage. We could assume that if its ad performance is roughly the same as ours, it is getting 1.2 clicks per day for an average daily cost of $1.68.

The reason it is only showing up at 10% coverage is that it is facing a number of well-entrenched advertisers (including us) who can't be easily dislodged. One strategy it could try is to reduce its bid for this keyword. Although this will drop its average position on the search results page, this often has the effect of increasing coverage.

Let's assume that this strategy works. ABC.com drops its bid to $0.75. Its average position drops to 5.0, its coverage increases to 100%, and its clickthrough rate drops by 40%. Here's what their keyword performance looks like now:

Average position: 5.0
Average CPC: $0.75
Coverage: 100%
Impressions: 1200
Clickthrough rate: 0.6% (40% lower at position 5.0)
Clicks: 7.2 (= 1200 × 0.6%)
Daily cost: $5.40 (= 7.2 × $0.75)

So what happened here? ABC.com is now paying 45% less for each visitor, and it's increased its traffic by 600%.

If you had a dollar to spend, would you rather spend it all to get one visitor to your site? Or would you rather pay a quarter for each of four visitors? Or perhaps a dime each for 10 visitors?

This leads us to an important maxim in search marketing:

WIN THE BATTLE AT THE BOTTOM OF THE PAGE BEFORE YOU FIGHT FOR THE TOP

Generally speaking, the advertisers at the top of the search results page have one of two things over their competitors:

1. Bigger budgets
2. Superior campaigns

Believe it or not, unlimited budgets aren't as common as you think. While there are thousands of brand advertisers,[2] most of them are as short on search smarts as they are long on cash. They tend to use up their budgets on those unprofitable broad keywords and have terrible exposure in the profitable niche keywords (this is the reason you don't see as many eBay ads on Google these days).

So most of the time, high placement on the search results pages is going to be determined by how relevant your ads are. The best ads end up on top. Why? Because good ads bring in more clicks from visitors. This brings in more advertising dollars, and that's good for the search engines.

If you think that you have any chance of beating that game, think again. You won't be able to merely outbid everyone else and get a decent percentage of the search traffic. The search engines will let you pay top dollar for placement, but they won't give you much of it. That's the approach that won Yahoo! the battle back in 2005, but lost them the war in 2008 (nobody likes seeing FTD ads on every search).

Instead, to win in search you need to take out the weak competitors at the bottom of the page. You know you've done that when your coverage is at (or close to) 100%. Then—and only then—should you think about bidding higher. But chances are, you won't have to. When you beat those competitors, Google and the other search engines are likely to give you a placement bonus, which means your ads automatically appear higher without you having to pay a single cent more.

The moral of the story is, before you think about increasing your bids to compete for more traffic, make sure that you've already maximized your coverage; otherwise, you're just wasting money.

COVERAGE PROBLEMS ALERT YOU TO CAMPAIGN PROBLEMS

If you find more than a few keywords in your account that are receiving a low percentage of the available impressions, it indicates that you have some serious structural issues with your campaign. You'll need to address these problems if you hope to outperform the competition, as they'll continue to drag down your campaign indefinitely.

What makes coverage truly interesting is that it is often the only way you can diagnose these issues. The vast majority of advertisers are not dominating pay-per-click because they fail to monitor this important metric.

TROUBLESHOOTING COVERAGE PROBLEMS

Once you identify a coverage problem, there are six possible causes:

Your Budget Is Capped

Make sure your budget cap is higher than the search engine's recommended daily amount. More on this in Chapter 26.

You're Trying to Muscle Your Way to the Top

Per the advice given on the previous page about winning the battle, you want to look at your average rank for the problem keyword. Is your ad appearing only a small percentage of the time, but high up on the page?

If so, you need to start by dropping your bid until it hits the bottom half (position 6 is a good rule of thumb). It's so much easier to compete at the bottom that your coverage problem may go away by itself. And even if it doesn't, it makes the next troubleshooting step much easier.

Ineffective Ad Copy

Google grades ads on a curve. If your ad only has a 0.2% CTR (horrible by most standards) but your competitors are all getting 0.05% CTR, you're actually doing okay. Your ads will likely appear a pretty good percentage of the time, while theirs will appear less often.

On the contrary, if you have a 2% CTR, but your top competitors have a 3-5% CTR, then your ad coverage will suffer. The only solution here is to craft an ad that's as good as or better than theirs.

Watching your coverage figures is a great way to estimate how well your CTR compares with that of your competitors. If you are showing up under 90% for a keyword, the first thing you want to look at is tweaking your ad copy. Read more on this in Chapter 28.

Advertising on Off-Target Keywords

Improving your ad copy only works if the keyword is a good fit for your business. For instance, the keyword *identity theft* is a very tempting, high-traffic opportunity for SurfSecret. However, searchers who enter this keyword are interested more in the prevention of identity theft than in computer privacy software.

To compete with identity theft companies on this keyword, I would essentially have to copy their ads and completely misrepresent the business in order to get a comparable CTR.

If I'm not willing to go that far, then I should also be open to the fact that maybe this isn't the right keyword to be advertising on.

Poor Landing Page or Domain Alignment

Even if a company was willing to go so far as to use misleading ad copy in an effort to artificially boost its CTR, it still wouldn't work. The reason why is that starting in 2007, Google began factoring landing page and general website content into its quality scores. This system (more or less) succeeds at limiting attempts to game AdWords clickthrough rates with bogus ads.

The reason I say "more or less" is because the quality scoring algorithm isn't perfect. You may be advertising on a highly relevant keyword with relevant ad copy, but still end up with a quality score penalty (it's common; in fact, it's happened to me many times). Once a low coverage estimate alerts you to the issue, it often only takes a minor tweak to the website or landing page to fix the problem.

Keyword Matching Problems

Another possible way to fix low coverage problems is to consider your match types. Many advertisers make the mistake of only entering broad match terms into their search accounts. This puts you at a disadvantage against advertisers who are using phrase or exact matches on the same keywords.

If you've followed the instructions for setting up your ad groups, you won't have this problem. However, you may have neglected to add the specific keyword to your account and have just been catching it with an umbrella term.

For instance, when I initially set up the SurfSecret account, I had low coverage for the search phrase *how to remove cookies*. When I looked at the search account, I realized that I had only been targeting the keyword phrase *remove cookies*. After I added *how to remove cookies* (including the phrase and exact match variations), my coverage shot up to 100%.

Another way this can factor into your account is through Google's AutoMatch algorithm, which automatically targets synonyms and plurals of your targeted phrases. If you target *remove cookies* in your search campaign, your ads will also show up for *remove cookie*. However, you won't have as close of a match as if you had entered the singular version explicitly into your account.

As you can tell, there are some pretty subtle things you have to be watching out for. If you could predict all of these problems ahead of time, you would be a much better search marketer than I am (you'd probably be the best search marketer on the planet, in fact). But you would also have an enormous, unwieldy, and difficult-to-manage campaign with a lot of sunk hours.

If you follow the steps in the previous chapters, you'll end up with a campaign that will get you partial coverage (at least) in all of the important keywords and their variations. Then you can use coverage to diagnose and fix those few remaining problem areas. It's a huge time saver.

HOW TO MONITOR COVERAGE

Although spotting problem keywords is easy to do using the coverage metric (just look for keywords with coverage below 90% or so), you'll need a third-party tool to collect this statistic for you.

AdGooroo SEM Insight was designed specifically for this purpose. Both of these tools analyze search campaigns for common campaign problems, including low coverage situations. In addition to providing charts similar to those shown earlier in this chapter, these tools specifically look for harmful trends in your coverage (Figure 15-3).

PPC Overview	PPC Alerts (21/104/90)	Natural Overview	Trademark	Keyword Research		
Alerts below reflect current day only.						
Displaying 1 - 13 of 13 items		First | Prev | Next | Last		Display 50 ▾	items per page	
	Keyword	Alert		Engine	Region	
		coverage				
▼ Priority: ●						
● ● ●	adwords keywords	Coverage trending down		Google	US	
● ● ●	most popular keywords	Coverage lower than normal range		Google	US	
＞ Priority: ●						
Displaying 1 - 13 of 13 items		First | Prev | Next | Last		Display 50 ▾	items per page	

FIGURE 15-3. Automated solutions are very useful for spotting coverage problems.

When you see alerts such as these, you'll want to start working through the troubleshooting steps as soon as possible. They are often a sign of quality issues, and once Google decides that your website is a poor performer for a particular keyword, it can be incredibly difficult to get your ads activated again.

SEM Insight also includes an Advertiser Detail report that allows you to plot the coverage and rank of all keywords for your campaign (each circle represents a keyword). Using this chart, just look for keywords with coverage less than 50%. These are problem areas that should be diagnosed and corrected quickly before they turn into permanent penalties (Figure 15-4).

IMPRESSION SHARE

A better-known statistic that is closely related to coverage is impression share. Impression share can be thought of as the percentage of the available search impressions in which your ads appear.

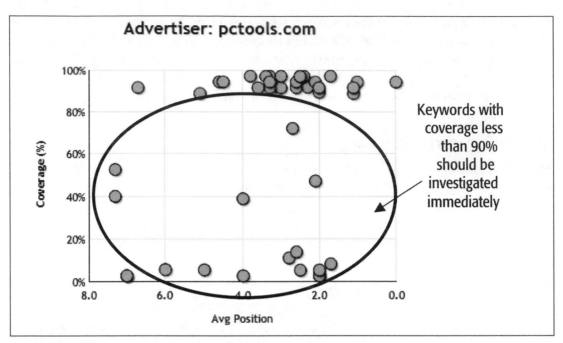

FIGURE 15-4. Use coverage charts to quickly identify problem keywords.

It differs from coverage in that it takes total search volume into account and is calculated across all of your keywords.

For instance, let's say that you are advertising on only two keywords, one of them a broad, high-traffic term, and the other a very specific, niche term (see Figure 15-5).

$$\text{Impression Share} = \frac{\text{Captured Impressions}}{\text{Total Search Volume}}$$

$$\text{Impression Share} = \frac{500,490}{1,000,500} = 50.02\%$$

Keyword	Monthly Search Volume	Coverage	Captured Impressions
Rear Projection TV	1,000,000	50%	500,000
Kabuchi Model A751 DLP Rear Projection TV	500	98%	490
Total	1,000,500		500,490

FIGURE 15-5. Simple impression share calculation using both a broad and a niche keyword phrase.

The coverage numbers are shown for each of these keywords in the third column. By multiplying the coverage for each keyword by the monthly search volume, we can generate an estimate of how many impressions our pay-per-click campaign is capturing.

To find the impression share, you divide the number of captured impressions by the total search volume.

The reason coverage is of more importance to search marketers is because it is more actionable. In this example, the coverage clearly showed that this advertiser needs to work on improving its exposure for the keyword *rear projection TV*. In contrast, the impression share figure told us that something was wrong, but it didn't give us any clues on how to fix it.

Furthermore, if there are a few high-traffic keywords in your campaign, they will dominate the impression share, making it difficult to measure the effect of the more profitable, but lower-traffic, niche keyword campaigns. The coverage statistic doesn't suffer from this problem, because it doesn't take search volume into consideration.

Nevertheless, both statistics are useful. Impression share serves as a high-level indicator of the overall health of your campaign. Coverage serves as a way to pinpoint problems down to the individual keyword.

How to Find Impression Share

You can find your current impression share within your Google AdWords account, but it's not easy! Here's how to do it:

1. Log in to your AdWords account.

2. Open the "Reporting" menu and select "Reports."

3. Create a new report.

4. Select "Campaign Performance" as the report type.

5. Expand the "Add or Remove Columns" link under section 3, "Advanced Settings," and click the "Impression share" check box. Note: this check box is only displayed for the Campaign Performance report (see Figure 15-6 on the next page).

6. Run your report. After a few minutes, you will be able to open it and find your current impression share.

SUMMARY

Coverage can be used to reveal quality problems in your campaign that result in high minimum bids and low share of impressions. Furthermore, when you have a keyword with low coverage, you are missing potential traffic and overpaying for the traffic that you are receiving. This makes it one of the most important statistics at your disposal for outperforming your competitors.

To increase coverage for problem keywords, try the following (in order):

- Increase your maximum daily budget (Chapter 26).
- Reduce your bids until your ads show up around the sixth position (Chapter 27).

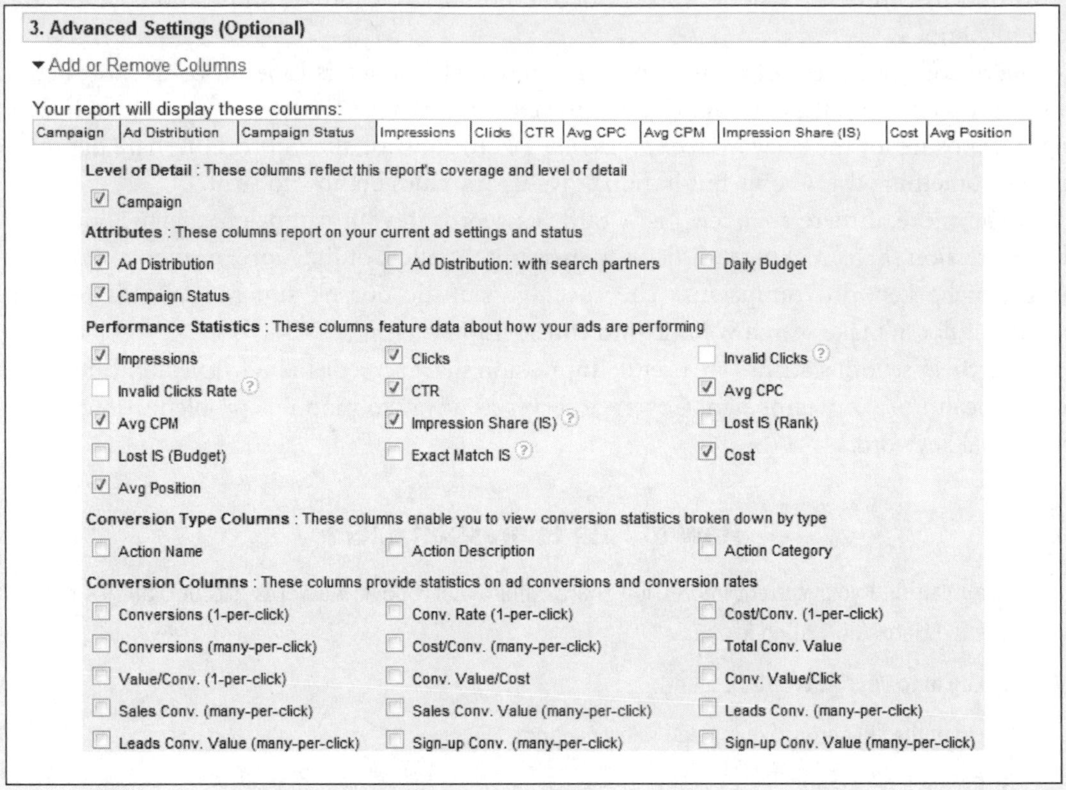

FIGURE 15-6. To find impression share, you have to activate it in the "Advanced Settings" section in the AdWords reporting interface. It is only available at the campaign level.

- Optimize your ad copy (Chapter 28).
- Optimize your landing pages (Chapter 8).
- Delete keywords that are not relevant to your business (Chapter 21).
- Check your match types (Chapter 23).

Notes

1. Not to be confused with clickthrough rate, which is the percentage of visitors who click your ads after actually seeing them.
2. Around 45,000, as far as we can tell by mining the AdGooroo database.

Clickthrough Rates Explained

C LICKTHROUGH RATE LIES AT THE VERY HEART OF THE ALGORITHMS THE SEARCH ENGINES use to determine which ads get shown and which don't. While most search marketers typically have a vague understanding that clickthrough rate increases as an ad moves higher up on the search results page, the whole concept is shrouded in mystery.

In this chapter, we'll talk about the factors we know improve clickthrough rates (and even a little about those factors we aren't so sure about).

WHY IS CLICKTHROUGH RATE SO IMPORTANT?

Outside of coverage (impression share), clickthrough rate is likely the most important metric you need to track in your campaigns. The formula to calculate it is simple:

$$\text{Clickthrough Rate} = \frac{\text{Clicks}}{\text{Impressions}}$$

For example, if one of your ads received 1,500 impressions and generated 35 clicks, then your clickthrough rate is 2.33% (pretty respectable!).

As you can see, clickthrough rate measures the amount of traffic any particular ad (or your campaign as a whole) is driving to your website. It merits your attention for this reason alone.

Moreover, the clickthrough rate of your ads is an important component of your quality score. Your quality score, in turn, determines the share of impressions that your ads receive. A high quality score can also result in your ads appearing higher on the search results page (at no additional cost), which in turn can further increase your clickthrough rates!

THE DIFFICULTY OF ESTIMATING CLICKTHROUGH RATE

Clickthrough rates are notoriously volatile and difficult to predict. Computer modeling may be the only way to tackle this problem. The reason is simply because clickthrough rates vary widely based on keyword, position, day of the week, and even time of day. Figure 16-1 shows just how much noise there can be.

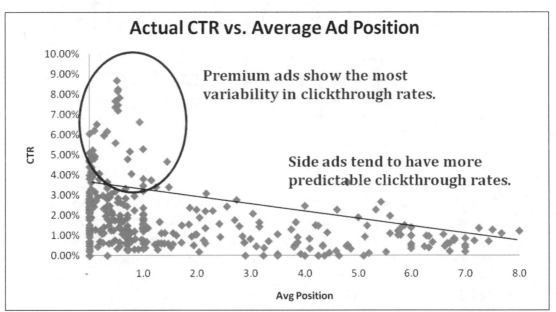

FIGURE 16-1. Predicting clickthrough rates is difficult because of the extreme variability in real-world results.

Here we see confirmation that clickthrough rates do indeed increase with average position of one's ads. However, this same chart shows that there still remains much noise to be explained. At position three (third side ad on Google), the clickthrough rate has a wide range of 0% to 2.5%. The premium ads are even more unpredictable, with clickthrough rates ranging up to 9.0%.

The apparent volatility motivated us to study the underlying factors which drive clickthrough rate. After testing 120 different models, we uncovered some useful data for search marketers and wound up with a predictive model that explains more of the mysteries behind clickthrough rate than has ever been possible before.

Figure 16-2 shows how well our final model predicts actual clickthrough rates. As you can see, it does a good job predicting the clickthrough rate of side ads, and while it fails to capture the extreme volatility that we typically see in premium ads, it does take a step forward in the right direction.

Overall, more than 60% of the variability we see in clickthrough rates can be explained by the factors we'll discuss in this chapter. That is more than enough to give us some useful guidance on how we can improve our search campaigns. Instead of spending months or years in trial and error, we can feed the model our ads and get clues about what we might be doing right or wrong.

Below, you'll find the most useful insights that we've gleaned with the use of this powerful tool.

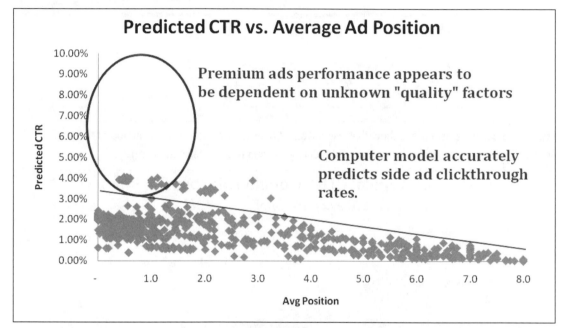

FIGURE 16-2. Results of computer modeling of clickthrough rates. The lack of data in the circled area indicates that the computer model cannot accurately predict the clickthrough rates of all premium ads.

CLICKTHROUGH RATE IS AFFECTED BY THE POSITION OF YOUR ADS

Remember how we talked about the importance of keeping your action area above the page fold in the chapters on conversion optimization? The very same thing is at work on the search engine results page, and it explains why the position of your ads determines your clickthrough rate.

As most marketers know, the higher an ad appears on the search results pages, the more attention it draws to itself. This naturally increases your clickthrough rate. Check out these heat map comparisons of Google and Bing ads (Figure 16-3).

Our model is in agreement with this fundamental observation. The predicted clickthrough rate for a broad (single-word) phrase on Google AdWords is shown in Figure 16-4. The model assumes that the ads haven't been optimized. As you can see, ads at the bottom of the page drive

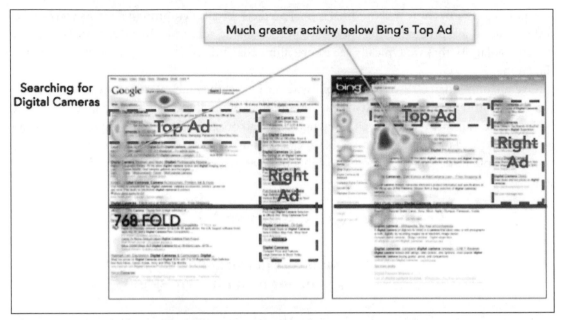

FIGURE 16-3. These heat maps show that visitors' attention is focused on ads near the top of the page. Source: "Search Engine Preference," June 2009, Catalyst Group (www.catalystnyc.com)

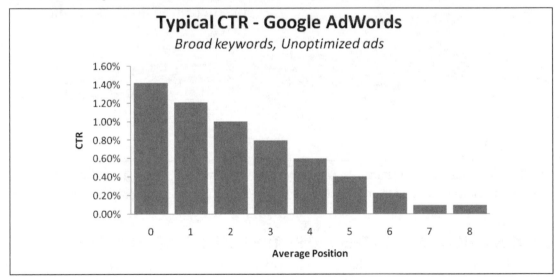

FIGURE 16-4. Typical clickthrough rates for broad keywords on AdWords (position 0 = premium ad placement, position 8 = bottom of page).

small amounts of traffic (typical clickthrough rate of 0.1%), while ads in the premium positions have typical clickthrough rates of up to 1.4%.

Obviously, as ad position increases, so does the clickthrough rate. Because of this relationship, more of the traffic driven from a broad keyword ends up going to advertisers in the top few positions. This in turn means that most of the advertising revenue the search engine makes from these keywords will come from the top advertisers, giving them a powerful incentive to display less bottom-of-page inventory.

If you've managed your own campaigns before, you'll probably have realized that the relationship between average position and clickthrough rate is never this consistent: it varies considerably from day to day. Figure 16-5 shows a typical example of how actual clickthrough rate can vary for each day in a given month.

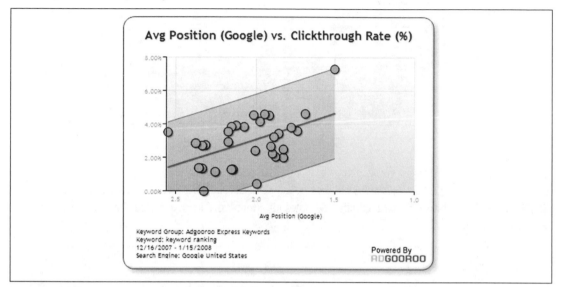

FIGURE 16-5. Chart showing how actual CTR can vary by day and position.

While it's not possible to predict the clickthrough rate on any particular day, there is clearly a relationship with the average position of the ad that holds over longer date ranges. In our studies, we have found this to be universally true across hundreds of thousands of keywords.

SIMILARITY BETWEEN AD COPY AND KEYWORD PHRASE

While many search marketers know that the closer the similarity of your ad copy to the searcher's keyword phrase, the higher the clickthrough rate, few realize that ad copy plays an even more important role than the position or price of your ads!

The lift on clickthrough rate is profound. In the premium positions, the clickthrough rate increased from 1.4% to nearly 4.0%. This increase held for ads at the bottom of the search results pages as well. The typical clickthrough rate for those ads increased from 0.1% to 0.33%—more than three times higher (Figure 16-6).

Here's another illustration of just how powerful the effect of optimization can be (Figure 16-7). We've overlaid the predicted clickthrough rates for each ad on top of an example search results page. The optimized ad in the fifth position on the right of the page is expected to outperform the four ads appearing above it. This is due entirely to the effect of optimized ad copy.

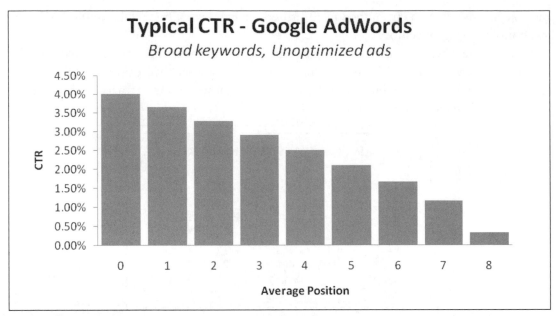

FIGURE 16-6. Chart showing typical clickthrough rates for a four-word keyword phrase with corresponding optimized ad copy.

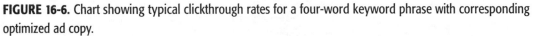

FIGURE 16-7. The optimized ad shown in position five is predicted to receive a higher clickthrough rate than the four ads above it.

OVERALL COMPETITIVENESS OF THE KEYWORD PHRASE

An underappreciated factor that affects clickthrough rate is the degree of competitive bidding for the search phrase. This can be measured in a number of ways, including:

- Actual number of advertisers bidding on the term
- The estimated CPC for the top ad position
- The competition level as reported by the search engines
- The number of words in the phrase

Here's how this plays out in practice (Figure 16-8).

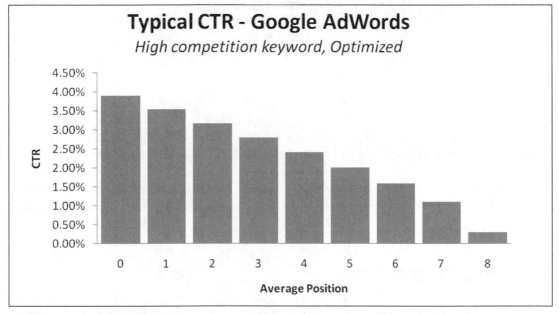

FIGURE 16-8. Typical clickthrough rates for an optimized ad targeted to a high-competition phrase

In this case, the clickthrough rate ranges from 0.30% to 3.90%. Compare this with a low-competition keyword phrase (Figure 16-9).

The clickthrough rate for low-competition phrases ranges from 0.43% to 4.34%. This represents clickthrough rate improvements over high-competition terms of 11% and 43%, respectively.

Two important conclusions can be drawn from this data.

First, it is much better to target hundreds or thousands of niche terms in your campaigns than it is to target a handful of broad terms. The level of competition will be much lower, and as a result, you'll get a much bigger bite of the apple.

Second, the benefits of niche keyword targeting are typically higher for advertisers appearing in low positions than for those advertisers who appear in high positions. So if you can't afford to bid as much as your competitors, it's important that you find less competitive keywords to target.

This is why I advise you to spend so much time in the planning phase of your campaign finding longer, more specific keyword phrases. Most marketers fail to do this and instead add

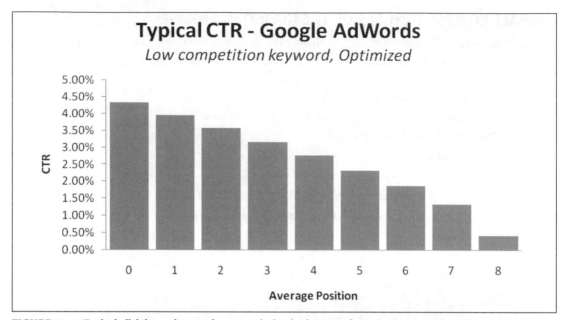

FIGURE 16-9. Typical clickthrough rates for an optimized ad targeted to a low-competition phrase

phrases in a piecemeal fashion over time. If you follow my advice, your campaign will drive a higher overall clickthrough rate right out of the gate, resulting in placement bonuses and lower average CPC prices.

OTHER QUALITY SCORE ISSUES

As we'll discuss in our chapter on quality score, Google takes into account a number of other factors that aren't exactly easy to measure. These include how closely your landing page and keyword are aligned, the historical clickthrough rate of your ads, and even the loading time of your website.

Overall, the factors discussed above are the most important, but you can't ignore quality score considerations. In our studies, these unknown ingredients account for about 38% of the variation in clickthrough rates.

This presents a difficult challenge for search marketers. While we are expected to chase quality score (after all, it determines more of our clickthrough rate than any other factor), Google isn't exactly forthcoming about how it's calculated. As of this writing, it's still a secret formula (but we know a few things—check out Chapter 18).

SUMMARY

Behind coverage, the clickthrough rate of your campaign and ads is the second most important metric that determines the ultimate success of your campaign. This chapter presented some of the theory and latest research behind this all-important statistic.

The Ever-Changing CPC Formula

W HEN YOU BUY ADVERTISING PLACEMENT ON THE SEARCH ENGINES, YOU SPECIFY THE maximum price that you are willing to pay when someone clicks your ads. This is known as your maximum bid. This maximum bid is the price that you are willing to pay for a visitor to your site. It is not usually the actual price you pay per visitor, the cost-per-click (or CPC).

The actual formulas used to calculate CPC are well-guarded secrets and change often. This makes it impossible to predict with a high degree of accuracy. Nevertheless, by studying the history of the PPC algorithms in conjunction with a bit of computer simulation, we can develop a reasonable idea of how it works and even find some insights to help us gain an advantage over our competitors.

THE EVOLUTION OF PAY-PER-CLICK

In the late 1990s, the pay-per-click advertising model ran a distant second to the pay-per-impression (CPM) model, which dominated at the time. Although a number of ad networks had been experimenting with pay-per-click since at least 1996, it was not widely accepted due to rampant click fraud.

The attractive thing about PPC was that advertisers paid only when people clicked on their ads. This greatly reduced waste and improved the ROI of internet advertising. For those who knew how to use the medium, the return on search engine advertising was far in excess of the traditional gold standard, email marketing (back then, you could buy traffic for a penny).

In the early Overture/Yahoo! days, the CPC you paid was pretty straightforward. You specified a price that you were willing to pay (with no minimums!) for a specific position and that was that. Advertisers' ads would appear in the order of bids, much like an eBay auction (see Figure 17-1).

Advertiser	Maximum Bid	Position
A	$25.00	1
B	$1.77	2
C	$1.35	3
D	$0.75	4
E	$0.01	5

FIGURE 17-1.

This simple model left a lot of risk on advertisers' plates. As you can see from the example above, the top advertiser was paying $25.00 per click, while the advertiser below was paying only $1.77. Obviously, the advertiser paying a higher price would exhaust its budget more quickly and receive a lower return on what it spends (if it made a profit at those prices at all).

In response to this, both Google and Yahoo! tweaked their bidding algorithms so that advertisers would only pay a penny more than the nearest competitor below them. Even if advertisers specified a maximum bid that was far too high, the system would automatically drop their bids to just one cent more than the next advertiser (Figure 17-2).

Advertiser	Maximum Bid	Actual CPC	Position
A	$25.00	$1.78	1
B	$1.77	$1.36	2
C	$1.35	$0.76	3
D	$0.75	$0.10	4
E	$0.01	$0.01	5

FIGURE 17-2.

Another important consequence of this auction-based model is that it led to the development of defensive and offensive tactics for interfering with competitors' campaigns. One of these tactics, bid jamming, consisted of bidding one penny below the top bidder. This forced the top bidder to pay the maximum bid. So if advertiser B was bid jamming, it could bid $24.99 and drain advertiser A's budget (Figure 17-3).

Advertiser	Maximum Bid	Actual CPC	Position
A	$25.00	$25.00	1
B	$1.77	$1.36	2
C	$1.35	$0.76	3
D	$0.75	$0.02	4
E	$0.01	$0.01	5

FIGURE 17-3.

This "pay for position" model was modestly successful and straightforward, but it led to a proliferation of low-quality ads. Search engine users tended to despise these ads due to their poor relevance, and clickthrough rates suffered. Had this trend toward untargeted ads gone unchecked, most people would have trained themselves to ignore the ads, and search engine marketing would probably never have matured into the billion-dollar industry it is today.

Yahoo! recognized this problem and attempted to clean up its listings through a manual review process. Advertisers would submit ads and then be forced to wait up to five days for a customer service representative to approve them. This improved the quality of the ads being shown and led to higher clickthrough rates, far in excess of those available from banner advertising.

However, the delays introduced by this cumbersome process prevented advertisers from reaching the maximum profit potential of their campaigns. It was difficult to split-test ads, so advertisers took few steps to improve their clickthrough rates. And of course, this slow process made it difficult to add the thousands of highly specific niche keywords necessary to create a world-class pay-per-click campaign. (Yahoo!'s cumbersome user interface at the time didn't help things any either.)

It was primarily because of these obstacles that search engine advertising remained the realm of a few thousand savvy webmasters for so long. It wasn't until 2003, when Google launched its "do-it-yourself" advertising platform, that pay-per-click advertising finally caught on with advertisers.

A fascinating consequence of this simple bidding model is that it failed to maximize the total revenue Yahoo! could have made selling search ads. At best, this approach allowed it to earn only half of what it could have made from a model such as the one Google later introduced.

For more on the complex math behind ad auctions, see "AdWords and Generalized On-line Matching" by Mehta, Saberi, Vazirini, and Vazirini (www.eecs.berkeley.edu/~vazirani/pubs/adwords.pdf).

ADVERTISERS GO GAGA FOR GOOGLE

Google entered the online ad scene in 2000[1] with its AdWords Select program. At the time, the program was only open to big-budget advertisers, and ad buys were sold face-to-face by sales reps, in much the same manner as traditional ad buys. In 2003, it opened up the platform so that any advertiser could participate with nothing more than a website and a credit card.[2]

Google added an important new twist to the Yahoo! model: ads would be awarded placement not only by the maximum bid price advertisers were willing to pay, but also by their click-through rate. This not only led to better-quality ads (and higher clickthrough rates); it also allowed Google to get rid of the manual ad approval process. As a result, advertisers could manage their campaigns far more easily than before, and Google quickly picked up small and medium customers that Yahoo! had missed.

However, this change removed much of the transparency of how ads were priced, because popularity was now being factored into the pricing equation. Specifically, if one ad were twice as effective as another, the first ad would be ranked as if its maximum bid were double what the advertiser actually set. The advertiser would, however, pay only its original price.

Sound complicated? It was simple in comparison with what was yet to come. The algorithms were tweaked and sometimes overhauled over the next few years to address a variety of issues, ranging from quality control to deliberate attempts by spammers to bypass the checks and balances of the system.

TODAY'S ADWORDS PRICING ALGORITHM

Fast-forward to 2010, where the CPC pricing model is far more complicated. Google now calculates a quality score for every ad on its system.[3] We'll talk about how the quality score is calculated in Chapter 18, but to understand this discussion, you simply need to know that the quality score ranges from 0 to 10, where a higher number indicates a better ad (at least in Google's opinion).

In any given keyword, the quality score is multiplied by the advertiser's maximum bid price to determine the ad rank (Figure 17-4).

Advertiser	Maximum Bid	Quality Score	Ad Rank
A	$4.00	1	4
B	$3.00	3	9
C	$2.00	6	12
D	$1.00	8	8

FIGURE 17-4. Maximum bid is multiplied by quality score to come up with ad rank.

The ads are then sorted in order by their ad rank to determine the order in which they appear (Figure 17-5).

Advertiser	Maximum Bid	Quality Score	Ad Rank
A	$2.00	6	12
B	$3.00	3	9
C	$1.00	8	8
D	$4.00	1	4

FIGURE 17-5. Next, the ads are sorted by ad rank.

To find out how much each advertiser actually has to pay for a click, Google calculates the minimum amount necessary to retain the advertiser's position. It does this by comparing the prices and quality scores for each adjacent ad.

For example, to find the price for Advertiser C above, we compare it to Advertiser B using the following equation:

$$\text{Price}_c \times \text{Quality Score}_c = \text{Price}_b \times \text{Quality Score}_b$$

$$\text{Price}_c \times 6 = \$3.00 \times 3$$

$$\text{Price}_c = \frac{\$3.00 \times 3}{6}$$

$$\text{Price}_c = \$1.50$$

You then repeat this process for each of the remaining advertisers. The lowest-ranked advertiser pays the minimum bid, which can be as little as just a few cents (Figure 17-6).

Advertiser	Maximum Bid	Quality Score	Actual Price
A	$2.00	6	$1.50
B	$3.00	3	$2.67
C	$1.00	8	$0.50
D	$4.00	1	Minimum Bid

FIGURE 17-6. The actual prices are determined by comparing the maximum bid prices and quality scores of each adjacent advertiser.

As you can see from this example, paying more does not guarantee you the top ad spot. Rather, the price you pay is determined by the quality of your ads in relation to those of the advertiser just below you. Mathematically, this is expressed as:

$$\text{Your Price} = \frac{\text{Competitor's Bid} \times \text{Competitor's Quality Score}}{\text{Your Quality Score}}$$

This formula explains much of why the methods you are reading about in this book are so effective. We spent so much time on conversion optimization because improving your conversion rate affords you the opportunity to raise your maximum bid. This directly impacts your ad rank, resulting in higher placement for your ads.

What About Your Daily Budget?

Budget plays an important part in determining how many impressions your ads receive, but it doesn't appear to play a significant role in determining the average CPC of your ads. We'll talk more about this important topic in Chapter 26.

We also manage our quality score on several fronts, including optimizing ad copy, reducing landing page load time, and (perhaps most importantly) monitoring competitors' paid search efforts. Getting even a single point or two of quality score advantage over them allows us to pay less per click than they are willing to and (as we'll see in a moment) provides a powerful defense against bid jamming.

SIMULATING CPC USING COMPUTER MODELS

The discussion above should give you a pretty fair idea of how Google's pricing mechanism works. But it does very little for understanding how prices work in a real-world environment. For this, we need to again turn to computer modeling.

The quality score throws a serious monkey wrench into any attempt to calculate CPC. In order to estimate quality score, you have to look at the targeted keyword phrase, ad copy, and landing page for every advertiser appearing for a given term. This is not easy to do even with fast computers.

However, we can assume that as time passes, advertisers will become smarter about optimizing their ads. (Many of them will buy books such as this one!) Thus, the quality scores for the most prominent ads will skew toward the high end (the 7-10 range), and they will play less of a role than they do for terms targeted by less motivated advertisers.

At the same time, the average CPC becomes more important. And fortunately, Google provides us that information through its API in the form of a CPC curve.

However, even this valuable source of data isn't without its problems. Google buckets its terms according to average price into high-, medium-, and low-priced buckets. The price it gives for low-priced terms tends to be quite accurate. The price for high- and medium-priced terms is decidedly less so.

Computer simulations can course-correct for these problems, though, and in the end, it turns out that you can develop a fairly good understanding of how CPC works in the real world.

OVERALL DEMAND

Perhaps as should be expected from an auction-based system, the overall price you will pay for your ads is determined by the level of competitive bidding for your targeted terms. Some terms are highly prized and advertisers will pay an absurd amount of money for the top positions. Here are the top bid prices for a few terms on Google AdWords in June 2009:

- Mesothelioma: $63.42
- Student consolidation: $48.70
- Car donation: $22.35

As a pay-per-click advertiser, you should be aware of how expensive the terms you've chosen for your campaign are. If the prices are out of your league, then diversify out into more specific (and less competitive) keyword phrases and make extensive use of negative matching to eliminate impressions on these high-dollar-value terms.

GLADIATOR BIDDING

Gladiator bidding refers to the practice some marketers have of trying to buy the top spots at any cost and without regard to ad quality. This is often the mentality at large corporations that are long on dollars and short on search expertise.

What ends up happening in these cases is that the advertiser succeeds at capturing the top side ad placement and pushes other, higher-quality advertisers further down the page. However, their low quality score fails to secure them the coveted premium ad spot (above the organic results), and it ensures that they will pay a price close to their maximum bid.

Here's an overly simplified example. Our gladiator bidder is BigCo, which buys the top spot with a massive $25.00 bid, but a low quality score of three. Below is a better-optimized competitor that has a quality score of seven and is willing to pay $10.00.

We can plug in the formulas above to see what price BigCo is paying for the top spot.

$$\text{Price}_{BigCo} \times \text{Quality Score}_{BigCo} = \text{Price}_{LittleCo} \times \text{Quality Score}_{LittleCo}$$

$$\text{Price}_{BigCo} \times 3 = \$10.00 \times 7$$

$$\text{Price}_{BigCo} = \frac{\$10.00 \times 7}{3}$$

$$\text{Price}_{BigCo} = \$23.33$$

Figure 17-7 shows the same information in tabular format.

Advertiser	Maximum Bid	Quality Score	Actual Price
BigCo	$25.00	3	$23.33
LittleCo	$10.00	7	Minimum Bid

FIGURE 17-7.

As you can see, this is somewhat reminiscent of the old bid jamming days, except instead of making competitors pay for the top spots with high bids, it's done with moderate bids and high quality scores. This is an incredibly important concept for all search marketers. If you work on optimizing your expensive terms, you can quickly exhaust better-funded competitors' budgets (if they fail to keep up with your optimizations). You can even monitor their search campaigns to track your progress.

At the same time, you have to keep a very close eye on the efforts of other advertisers to ensure that they aren't doing the same to you. You do this by monitoring closely for changes in their ad copy and landing pages, as these are strong evidence of optimization. More on this in Chapter 19.

Our computer models show that outside of overall demand, this is the single most important factor which determines bid prices. Advertisers who bid blindly for the top positions pay an astonishing 49% premium! (See Figure 17-8.)

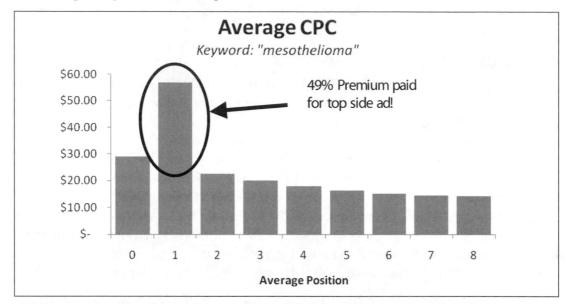

FIGURE 17-8. Advertisers who buy the top positions without regard for the quality of their ads pay a 49% premium on average.

POSITION

Surprisingly, the average position of your ads plays much less of a role in determining your average CPC than it used to, largely because of quality score. Our model shows that on average, the difference in the average CPC paid at the bottom of the page versus the top is less than 25%.

The takeaway from this is that once your bids are high enough to place your ads on the first page of search results, your maximum bid isn't as important as you might think. At this point, quality score kicks in and tends to carry your ads farther up the page.

SUMMARY

In this chapter, we took a look back at the history of pay-per-click to learn how the CPC formula evolved and why it's not very transparent today. We saw how the concept of quality score was developed as a means of dealing with poor-quality advertisers.

At the same time, we used the power of computer simulation to demonstrate once again why it pays to focus on highly specific niche terms ignored by other advertisers. We also learned that quality score can be used offensively as a weapon to exhaust competitors' budgets, and that we should be keeping a careful eye on competitors' efforts in order to prevent them from doing the same to us.

Notes

1. "Secret of Googlenomics: Data Fueled Recipe Brews Profitability," Wired Magazine, May 22, 2009, http://www.wired.com/culture/culturereviews/magazine/17-06/nep_googlenomics.
2. "Google Launches AdWords Select," Search Engine Watch, February 20, 2002, http://searchenginewatch.com/2159301.
3. "Introduction to the Google Ad Auction," Google, March 11, 2009, www.youtube.com/watch?v=K7l0a2PVhPQ.

Quality Score Explained

I N APRIL 2007, A MAJOR CHANGE TO ADWORDS EFFECTIVELY SHUT DOWN MANY ADVERTISERS' campaigns overnight. This change, also known to some as the Google Slap, was intended to get rid of low-value affiliate and one-page sales letter sites from the paid listings, but there was plenty of collateral damage. Many high-quality sites (including some affiliates) were shut out of the paid search listings, while many not-so-high-quality sites (including some affiliates) posing as high-quality retail or review sites were awarded rankings and coverage bonuses.

Like many others, I had sites that were affected by this change. The minimum required bid for keywords where I had been advertising profitably for years increased to $10.00 because of Google's insistence that my sites were no longer relevant.

I don't believe it was Google's intention to shut down legitimate sites that provide value for search engine visitors. Rather, it instituted this new algorithm as a means to encourage advertisers to raise the quality of their own ads. Where it went wrong was in providing relatively little guidance to advertisers about what constituted "quality." Furthermore, the algorithm has continued to evolve over time, making it somewhat of a moving target that advertisers constantly have to chase.

In hopes of clearing away some of the fog, I asked the AdGooroo research team to conduct a series of experiments to provide more insight into what we can do to create higher-quality ads in the eyes of Google. Our findings will prove useful to most companies looking to improve their PPC results.

WHAT ARE QUALITY SCORES?

For every keyword in your AdWords campaign, Google will assign you a quality score between 0 and 10. A low score indicates a low-quality ad, while a high score indicates a high-quality ad.

WHY IS QUALITY SCORE IMPORTANT?

As we discussed in the previous chapter, the quality score is one of the ingredients of your ad rank. Higher quality scores push your ads higher up on the page and also increase the difference between your maximum bid and the average CPC. In other words, high-quality ads cost less and gain exposure to more search traffic (impression share).

Another benefit of having a high quality score is that it will lower the estimated bid to reach the first page of the search results. This metric, also called the first-page bid estimate, approximates the CPC needed to reach the first page of the Google search results when your ad is triggered by an exact match. A high-quality ad may cost as little as $0.03 to be shown on the first page, while a low-quality ad can cost as much as $50.00; it's easy to see why you must be cognizant of your quality scores.

One major change occurred recently to this aspect of the quality score algorithm that you should be aware of. Previously, the minimum bid was the absolute minimum required amount you were forced to bid in order to have your ads shown. This price affected ads shown anywhere on the search network or partner sites. The "all or none" philosophy behind this approach angered advertisers and also resulted in a large drop in ad coverage.[1] This may have negatively impacted Google's revenues (management even said so during the second quarter 2008 shareholders meeting), and the algorithm was changed from a static all-or-nothing approach to a dynamic one in September 2008.

The new approach calculates quality scores on the fly. This means that your ads may be awarded higher quality scores for different keywords, in certain regions, and on different partner sites. While this new added flexibility allowed some of the more middling advertisers to take a (small) bite of the apple, I actually feel that this change was a disservice to search marketers because it made the algorithm even more complicated than before.

Previously, you could stay somewhat aware of holes in your campaign by simply looking at your AdWords reports. Back then, when Google said you had a low quality score, Google meant it. Your ad wasn't being shown.

Today, when you see a low quality score, you may still have ads appearing for the keyword in certain regions or on partner sites. If Google tells you that your ad isn't showing, another one of your ads, possibly an unrelated one, could very well be showing up in its place. Conversely, having a high quality score does not guarantee that your ad is being displayed. It may only be showing up on partner sites (such as AOL or Ask.com), in certain geographical regions, or on specific keyword phrases. There's no easy way to tell.

The only definitive way to be sure where your ads are appearing is to use a third-party service so that you can see exactly what your customers do. Advertisers who rely on the quality scores reported within the Google interface don't stand a chance. The good news, however, is that relatively few people are aware of these issues, and this makes it far easier for us to compete.

Hopefully, Google's philosophy of fixing things by making them more complicated will change in the future.

The Official Explanation of Quality Score

A good place to start in our understanding of the quality score calculation is to read what Google has to say about it.[2]

Quality Score for Google and the Search Network

While we continue to refine our Quality Score formulas for Google and the search network, the core components remain more or less the same:

- The historical clickthrough rate (CTR) of the keyword and the matched ad on Google; note that CTR on the Google Network only ever impacts Quality Score on the Google Network—not on Google

- Your account history, which is measured by the CTR of all the ads and keywords in your account

- The historical CTR of the display URLs in the ad group

- The quality of your landing page

- The relevance of the keyword to the ads in its ad group

- The relevance of the keyword and the matched ad to the search query

- Your account's performance in the geographical region where the ad will be shown

- Other relevance factors

Note that there are slight variations to the Quality Score formula when it affects ad position and first page bid:

- **For calculating a keyword-targeted ad's position,** landing page quality is not a factor. Also, when calculating ad position on a search network placement, Quality Score considers the CTR on that particular placement in addition to CTR on Google.

- **For calculating first page bid,** Quality Score doesn't consider the matched ad or search query, since this estimate appears as a metric in your account and doesn't vary per search query.

The most important component of your quality score is the historical CTR of your keyword and ad. This is Google's bread and butter and hasn't changed throughout the years.

Next up in importance is the historical CTR of your entire account. This is a grossly over-looked point. Advertisers who target thousands or hundreds of thousands of keywords with no regard for their relevance get penalized hard by Google. The same goes for those who fail to remove or improve keywords with mediocre clickthrough rates (if I can't achieve a CTR of at least 0.5% with a keyword after several attempts to optimize it, I delete it from my account).

Google also considers the overall CTR of the display URLs in your ads. Incorporating this as a factor prevents spammers from continually creating new AdWords accounts to show their ads once they've been banned. In other words, don't experiment with any URL that's important unless you are prepared to live with the consequences.

The quality of your landing page is also factored in, but not in regards to position. This used to be incorporated into the ad position algorithm, but frankly, Google doesn't do a very good job of assessing the quality of landing pages. Many advertisers (including myself) were outspoken about mistakes that the automated landing page analyzer made, so this factor now plays less of a role than it used to.

The similarity and appropriateness of your ad copy to both the keywords you are targeting and what the visitor actually types in are important determinants of your quality score. We talk about this at great length in the chapters on keyword selection and ad copy.

ON-PAGE QUALITY SCORE FACTORS

Throughout this book, I touch on many ways to improve the relevance of your keywords and ad copy. There's also an entire section devoted to the methods behind optimizing conversions on your landing pages. However, to receive high quality scores, you will also have to tweak your landing pages to satisfy Google.

Very little has been written about this subject, so per our standard approach, we devised a series of controlled experiments to learn more about how landing page quality is assessed.

Site Genre

Relevance is the key to understanding how the quality score algorithm works. Google strongly prefers sites that are tightly focused on specific topics. This helps it to more accurately categorize the site and serve it for relevant queries.

Thus, one of the first things Google does when it learns of a new site is to analyze it and assign it to one or more categories (site genre), each containing dozens of closely related keyword phrases.

You may access this information by entering your domain name into the Google AdWords keyword tool (https://adwords.google.com/select/KeywordTool). The categories that SurfSecret was assigned include "security software," "anonymous proxy," "internet security," and "internet privacy" (Figure 18-1).

Google's attempt to categorize your site genre prevents insurance sites from showing up for travel-based queries. However, the effect is much more subtle than that. If your site is devoted

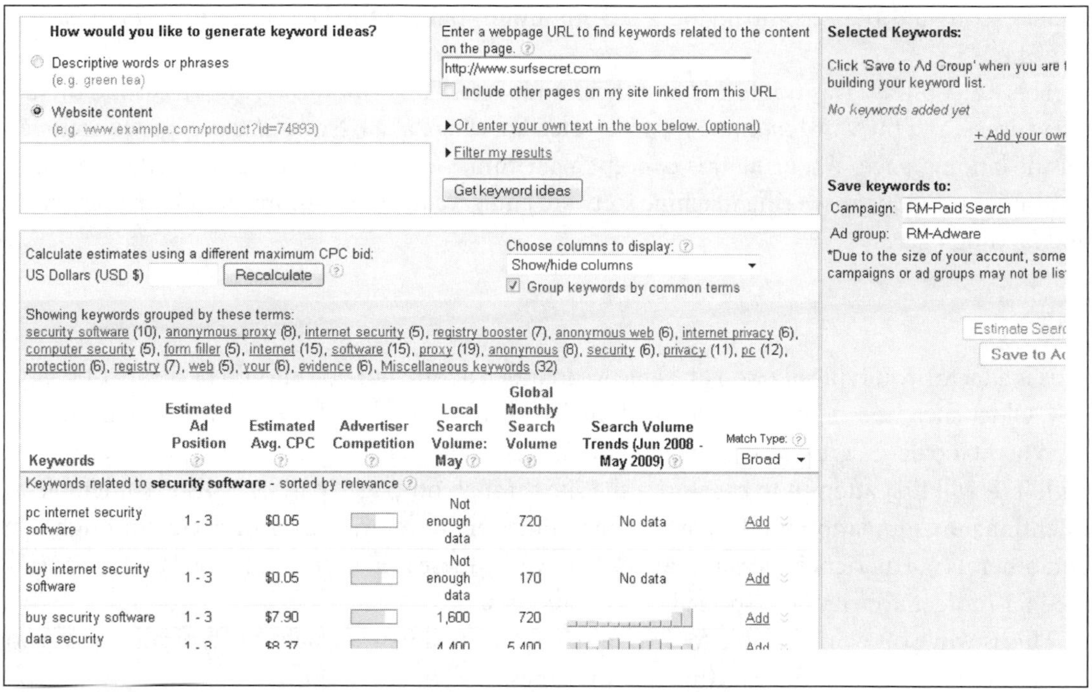

FIGURE 18-1. The Google Keyword Tool will show you the topics it thinks your site is about.

to vacationing in Mexico, it will probably receive poor quality scores for general travel terms, like *Mexico airfares* or *cheap travel.*

Virtually every concept you can think of has been cataloged by Google. It's almost like a card catalog that encompasses every possible idea. This universal tagging system occurs completely behind the scenes. (In our opinion, it's perhaps one of the greatest achievements ever made by the company, on par with Celera's mapping of the human genome. One day, this same technology will probably provide the basis of an artificial intelligence system with at least a rudimentary understanding of the internet.)

Google uses this categorization to predict whether certain keywords are truly relevant to your site. It works even if the phrases aren't found on the landing page.

For instance, much to our surprise, one day we discovered that a specific landing page on the site www.callbutler.com was receiving a high

You can (and should) use the Google Keyword Tool to find high-quality terms for your site. But take the results with a grain of salt, as it can return categories and keywords that are either too broad or not on target for your site.

For instance, when I enter the landing page for AdGooroo SEM Insight into the tool, it returns the category "make money" along with keywords such as *make money now* and *make money at home*. These keywords are neither cheap nor effective for a product such as ours.

Scrutinize the results you get from this or any other tool before entering them into your PPC accounts.

quality score and the accompanying $0.03 minimum bid for the keyword *answering machine software.*

This exact phrase was not found anywhere on its site. The word *answering* was found on just a few pages, and the word *machine* wasn't located anywhere at all. None of these words occurred on the landing page. Yet, using this concept algorithm, Google was able to correctly guess that CallButler provides answering machine software and gave it a low minimum bid for this phrase and landing page.

Site Age

This is a factor you typically won't be able to do much about, but you should be aware of it anyway. Older sites seem to be rewarded with higher quality scores and lower minimum bids.

When Google first learns of a new domain, it goes through a "getting to know you" period with it. It will first attempt to categorize the site through on-page analysis. This is vulnerable to intentional manipulation on the part of the webmaster, however, so over time clickthrough rate and other user experience measures are used to verify these initial findings. The latter is considered far more authoritative, especially as the site ages.

This is why you won't be able to drive much traffic to a new domain for typically up to two weeks, even if you have high starting quality scores.

We tested this by hosting identical landing pages on different URLs, while keeping ad copy, bids, and keywords the same. URLs that were already found in Google's index consistently received higher quality scores than brand-new URLs. After a few weeks, the quality scores for the new URLs tended to improve.

Linking Neighborhood

Another important factor is your linking neighborhood. Linking is a critical component in SEO, and it appears it's now being used to inform Google of the subject matter of your site.

Just as in SEO, incoming links will transfer authority and trust to your domain. If you manage your incoming links at all, you should focus on quality, not quantity. Focus on links coming from reputable, authoritative sites (especially on .edu domains). The anchor text may be factored into this as well.

The problem with relying on inbound links is that it can take months to make significant changes in your inbound links—hardly the stuff that will allow you to make quick fixes.

However, you can also use outbound links to adjust your quality scores. In our tests, we found that adding outgoing links to closely related resources substantially improved our scores in many cases, especially for newer sites.

Using both inbound and outbound links in conjunction with each other is even more powerful. For instance, we were able to drop our first-page bids from $0.30 to $0.05 in under a month by adding outbound links to our page and getting just a few inbound ones from quality sites.

Presence of Pop-Ups and Pop-Unders

Make no mistake, Google hates pop-up and pop-under ads. If your page triggers obnoxious advertising, you can pretty much rule out advertising it with AdWords.

Load Time and Page Size

Load time has become a significant factor in the quality score algorithm. However, if you follow the same advice that was set out in the conversion optimization section, your pages will score well in this regard.

Trust Signals

There is some evidence that Google looks for the presence of particular elements that lend credibility and trustworthiness to a business. The two most important of these elements are a privacy policy and a business address.

I have anecdotal evidence that both of these factors seem to improve quality scores, and it doesn't hurt to include them (they also help to boost conversion rates).

Scope of Your Site

We discovered that Google will take into consideration not only the links and on-page elements of individual landing pages, but also your site as a whole. As your site gets larger, Google will weight your specific landing page less and favor your overall site theme more.

Tips for Commercial Sites

- Place all of your contact information on one page and give it an obvious name, such as "Contact Us."
- Don't bury your contact page.
- Include a phone number if you can.
- Don't use a PO box.
- Don't use a fake address. It's unethical and Google can figure this out.

This has important implications for sites with more pages on them. Small sites focused on specific topics tend to receive higher quality scores for lower-volume, highly specific terms. As the number of pages grows, the quality scores will shift to favor higher-volume, less specific terms.

For instance, a minisite devoted to cafes in Paris may receive favorable quality scores for niche terms (Figure 18-2a).

As the site grows and more pages are added on topics such as "hotels in Paris" or "things to do while in Paris," the quality scores will drop for the above terms and improve for terms like those in Figure 18-2b.

If you aren't ready to fight for these high-traffic/high-cost terms, then pay close attention to keeping the scope of your site tight and specific.

Key Word Phrase	Monthly Search Volume	Estimated Average CPC
Hotel Paris	1,000	$0.57
Last minute hotels	110	$0.05
Paris café menu	880	$0.05

FIGURE 18-2A. Highly relevant terms for a minisite devoted to Paris cafes.

Key Word Phrase	Monthly Search Volume	Estimated Average CPC
Hotel Paris	4,090,000	$2.93
Last minute hotels	7,840,000	$2.89
Paris hotel deals	49,500	$2.69

FIGURE 18-2B. As the same site grows, it will become more relevant for higher-traffic (and more expensive) terms such as these.

One strategy for dealing with this wrinkle is through the use of subdomains. For instance, that large site could duplicate its global website content onto tens of thousands of minisites with domains like paris.xyztravel.com.

We do this exact thing on our free.adgooroo.com website. This site contains keyword samples and ranking reports for over a million domains, so Google will probably have a hard time guessing its core topic area. In fact, if you enter that domain into the AdWords keyword tool, you'll see that Google has tagged it with wildly off-base categories, including "car rental" and "new balance."

If you take this approach, be careful not to trigger a duplicate content penalty for the main site, as this could cause your natural rankings to drop. You could get around this by using a robots.txt file to ensure that the Googlebots only find one of the two versions.

Keyword Density

We saved the best technique for last. Keyword density is simply the ratio of text on your page relating to the desired keywords versus everything else. Increasing the keyword density proved to improve our quality scores more than any other factor we tested.

For instance, I wanted to raise our quality score for the keyword *Ghent hotels*. This keyword phrase was recommended to us by the Google Keyword Tool when we seeded it with a specific landing page on that topic.

The minimum bid required to reach the first page was $0.30—too high for us. We then modified the ad by pointing it to a different landing page on the same site. Our minimum bid dropped to $0.20, which was an affordable price.

The second page was on the same website. Our keyword didn't change, nor did our ad copy. The site navigation and supporting page script were all consistent between both versions. The only difference was the page content, specifically that the keywords, *Ghent* and *hotel*, were mentioned many more times throughout the new page. We experienced this repeatedly with a variety of sites and landing pages.

There are two ways to improve your keyword density. The most obvious way you can do this is by incorporating your desired keywords into your page structure multiple times, including one or two insertions into different types of HTML tags (such as <H1>, <strong>, etc.).

You have to be careful about overdoing this, however. Not only can it turn off visitors, but Google also has a diminishing returns formula in place. You will get less effect for each additional repetition of the phrase. And beyond a certain point, your page may even be flagged as low-quality. (We haven't seen this happen, but there are so many similarities between Google Quality Score and organic rankings algorithms that we don't think it's worth taking a chance.)

You should also break the phrase up when possible. Don't repeat *Paris hotels* throughout your page. Instead, use phrases such as *hotels in Paris, the newcomer's guide to Paris, things to get used to in your hotel*, and so forth. This is more natural-sounding and avoids triggering filters that are intended to stop spammers.

You can also increase your keyword density by incorporating the keyword phrase into your meta description tag and as part of your image alt tags. We found that these changes made a slight but definite improvement in our quality scores.[3]

Another way to improve your keyword density is by eliminating as much nonessential HTML from your pages as possible. This is most effective if your pages are larger than 50k in size.

AJAX and JavaScript are two prime areas to consider for removal. Also, if your pages are coded using ASP.NET Platform, you should be aware that .NET inserts large chunks of binary code into your rendered page. These chunks of computer-generated code bloat your page size and reduce your keyword density. If your pages are greater than 50k in size, ask your website developers to reduce or eliminate viewstate binary from the page source.[4]

Match Type Not Important

You may have noticed that match type is not mentioned (it used to be). One recent change is that match type now appears to be ignored for the purposes of calculating quality score. When you check your AdWords reports, you may indeed notice that a keyword always has the same quality score, even if you target it using different match types.

Should You Block the Google AdsBot from Crawling Your Site?

When you submit your ads, Google crawls your site to determine the quality of the landing page. Given that we may come to a fundamental disagreement with Google about the relevance of our pages, does it make sense to prevent Google from crawling our sites?

AdsBot is the name of Google's Quality Score crawler.[5] It is different from the Googlebot, which is responsible for indexing your site for inclusion in the natural search results.

You can prevent it from being able to see your landing page by adding the following to your robots.txt file:

User-agent: AdsBot-Google
Disallow: /

We tested this change by comparing one campaign that had been crawled by the AdsBot with an exact duplicate using a landing page that the AdsBot couldn't see. We divided the minimum bid into 10-cent buckets and counted the number of keywords that fell into each.

Figure 18-2c shows our results.

Minimum Bid	# Keywords in Original Campaign	# Keywords in Blocked Campaign
< $0.10	13	3
$0.11 - $0.20	45	28
$0.21 - $0.30	182	56
$0.31 - $0.40	319	110
$0.41 - $0.50	1,520	913
> $0.51	502	1,455

FIGURE 18-2B.

As you can see, our minimum bids were much higher when we blocked the AdsBot with our robots.txt file. For this reason, you should never try to block it.

How to Check Your Quality Scores

In the Google AdWords interface, drill into your keywords. Clicking the small balloon icon in the status column will reveal your quality score.

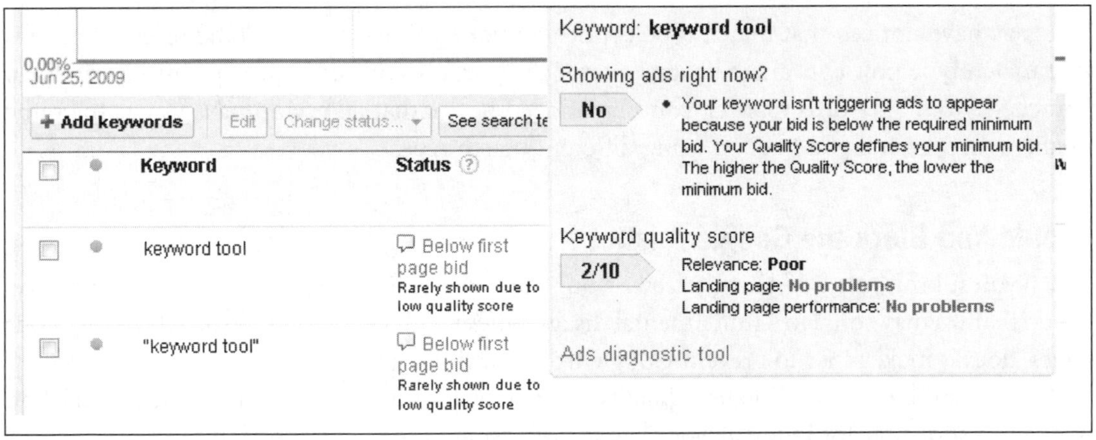

FIGURE 18-3. You can check your quality score directly within the AdWords interface.

The Instant Quality Score Calculation

When you make changes to your existing ad groups, there can sometimes be a delay before you see a change in your quality scores. This is not conducive for quick testing.

I discovered a technique for getting an instant refresh of your quality scores. This will be useful as you go through the following steps to improve your quality scores.

You need to install the Google AdWords Editor (a desktop application). Instead of altering your existing groups, you simply make copies of them, modify them, and then upload your changes. The new ad group will immediately reflect your updated quality scores.

This technique can be used to test the effect of alternative landing pages, ad copy, or even URLs on your quality score. In a single day, you can test dozens of different variations.

SUMMARY

The Google AdWords quality score introduces a significant new management challenge into your AdWords campaigns. You will easily spend most of your time adjusting your keywords, ads, and landing pages to Google's satisfaction.

There are a variety of actions you can take to improve your scores. Begin by using the AdWords Keyword Tool to understand your site and landing page genres. If the keyword categories and suggestions seem to be off-target, consider using both inbound and outbound links to inform Google about your site's subject matter.

You can also expand or tighten the scope of your website by changing the number of pages on your site. Increase the number of pages on your site to get better quality scores for broad, high-traffic keywords. Decrease the number of pages on your site to improve your quality scores for certain niche keywords (one way of doing this is by creating a minisite).

Next, look to increase the keyword density of your desired landing pages. Do this primarily by increasing the number of times the keyword is mentioned on your page. You should also seek to minimize page-bloating code such as AJAX, JavaScript, or binary objects that may not be visible to the user.

Notes

1. "AdGooroo Search Engine Advertiser Update—Q308," www.adgooroo.com/ adgooroo_q308_search_marketing.php
2. http://adwords.google.com/support/bin/answer.py?answer=10215
3. Interestingly, these same tactics are said to hold no weight in Google's natural ranking algorithm. This suggests a certain openness on Google's part to work with advertisers' commercial placements, an attitude it definitely doe not have with its organic results.

4. This page has valuable information on reducing binary viewstate size: http://www.webref-erence.com/programming/asp/viewstate/.

5. https://adwords.google.com/support/bin/answer.py?answer=38197&hl=en

CHAPTER 19

Put the Competition to Work for You

ONE ARE THE DAYS WHEN YOU COULD RUN YOUR PAY-PER-CLICK CAMPAIGNS IN A SILO. The search engines' increasing focus on relevance as well as high demand for ad placement means that advertisers are judged against one another to determine which ads will be shown and which will not.

If you want to take a bigger bite of the apple than your competitors, you have to keep close tabs on them. This practice is known as *search engine intelligence* (or SEI for short). In this chapter, I'll show you how to use search engine intelligence to outwit your competitors and take advantage of their mistakes.

TACTICAL ADVANTAGES OF SEI

At a tactical level, you need to know when competitors are making improvements to their quality scores and bids. As they succeed in doing so, your relative advantage over them will be diminished. Having even one competitor close the gap can put the hurt on your campaign. Having a few do it can be catastrophic. This is the main reason why campaigns that are left to their own devices invariably decline after a few months.

The interrelationships between advertisers can be clearly shown by marking up our quality score formula (Figure 19-1).

FIGURE 19-1.

As you can see, the price you pay for your ads is determined in no small part by your competitors' aggressiveness and the ratio of your optimization efforts to theirs. And as we discussed in the last chapter, quality score determines the placement of your ads and the amount of traffic you'll receive from paid search. It also plays a huge role in determining how much of the available search traffic your ads will be exposed to (coverage).

Another important tactical benefit of watching your competitors is that it allows you to defend against tactics like bid jamming, which can result in dramatic drops in impressions and clickthrough rates, or even result in your being banned from valuable keywords altogether (see Chapter 27).

Paying attention to competitors' paid search efforts can pay off strategically as well. Because PPC is so measurable, many companies test new products, features, and services on the search engines prior to widespread launch. You can get advance notice of these changes if you're watchful.

You can also use paid search to peek inside of your competitors' business models. If a competitor launches a new pricing model or brand while aggressively increasing CPCs, keep a close eye on the competitor for awhile. If it later drops CPCs and/or pulls the model, you've found something that didn't work. Our competitors have saved us at AdGooroo countless times from launching features that the market truly didn't want.

PLANNING A NEW CAMPAIGN

One of the best uses of search engine intelligence is in the planning stages of a new campaign. SEI helps you to answer questions such as:

- How much traffic can I expect?
- How much should I budget?
- How much revenue can I expect to generate?

It's important to realize that only the roughest of estimates can be made without either an active search campaign or sophisticated computer modeling techniques at your disposal. If you don't absolutely need to plan your campaign ahead of time, I advise you to simply start your campaign and see what the numbers tell you after a week or two. On the other hand, if you need to get approval for your budget in advance, you'll likely need some sort of defensible estimate.

Before I start arming you with techniques to answer these questions, I need to set your expectations accordingly.

A GOOD ESTIMATE IS HARD TO FIND

Whenever you rely on the preliminary data that the search engines provide with their keyword or traffic estimator tools, be sure to take it with a grain of salt. As we say in search marketing, this data is as good as bad data gets.

It's not that their data is "wrong"—it's simply based on system-wide averages, and your campaign will (hopefully) be anything but average. The statistics you get from the search engines ignore the effects of ad coverage, optimized copy, landing page quality scores, and historical clickthrough rates, so your actual campaign results may vary wildly from your initial estimates.

So use the data as a directional indicator only. If you estimate that there are 580,000 searches in the U.S. in your industry in a given month, don't be surprised if you actually see 150,000 or 2,000,000. In practice, if you can get within 300%, you've done a pretty good job.

There are many reasons why the data you pull from the search engines might be wrong. Here are some of the most common:

Traffic Sources

The traffic estimates reported by the search engines may or may not include traffic from partner sites. For instance, the Google AdWords API includes traffic from Ask.com and AOL. Not only is this traffic highly volatile and difficult to predict, but your quality scores play a large part in determining how much of it you'll get access to.

Quality Score Issues

Your actual search results will vary tremendously based on your quality scores. For instance, if your ads and landing pages are considerably better than those of most advertisers out there, you can expect your average position (and thus clickthrough rate) to be higher than anticipated, while your average cost-per-click may end up far lower.

Conversely, if your landing pages or ad copy aren't very good, you may receive little or no traffic at all. See Chapter 30, "Don't Blindly Trust the Search Engines," for a real-world example of how quality score issues can complicate your campaign.

Seasonality

Search data also varies widely depending on when it was collected.

For example, Google currently reports an average of 2,900 searches per month for the term *Chicago flower delivery*. But the February 2009 estimate was 5,400 (February is the biggest month of the year in the online flower industry). If you inadvertently create a yearly forecast using the February estimate, your final figure will be overstated by 86% (Figure 19-2).

Keywords	Estimated Ad Position ⑦	Estimated Avg. CPC ⑦	Advertiser Competition ⑦	Approx Search Volume: February ⑦	Approx Avg Search Volume ⑦	Search Volume Trends (Mar 2008 - Feb 2009) ⑦
Keywords related to term(s) entered - sorted by relevance ⑦						
chicago flower delivery	1 - 3	$7.54	▭	5,400	2,900	▦
chicago flowers delivery	1 - 3	$6.66	▭	1,600	880	▦
chicago flower deliveries	1 - 3	$0.05	▭	Not enough data	Not enough data	No data
day flower delivery chicago	1 - 3	$0.05	▭	Not enough data	73	No data
flower delivery chicago il	1 - 3	$0.05	▭	Not enough data	91	No data
flower delivery in chicago	1 - 3	$7.99	▭	880	480	▦
flower delivery in chicago il	1 - 3	$0.05	▭	Not enough data	36	No data

FIGURE 19-2. Sample output from the AdWords Keyword Tool for March 2009.

One-Time Events

Another source of error is that one-time occurrences such as news articles, press releases, and offline advertising campaigns can temporarily push traffic well above normal levels.

Markets in Decline

All markets experience periods of growth and decline. If you're entering a market in decline, you may find that your search traffic comes nowhere near the levels you initially estimated. This happened in 2005 to the antispam software category, when the industry dried up virtually overnight.

Keyword Matching

If you follow my recommendations for using both phrase and exact matching in your keyword lists, your number of paid search clicks will likely end up far higher than the "average" estimates provided by the search engines. This is because the vast majority of advertisers don't make use of these keyword matching techniques.

Keyword matching is very difficult to factor into traffic estimates. Not only will your click-through rates be higher; your traffic and cost-per-click will tend to be lower when matching is used extensively.

The Engines Ignore the Vast Majority of Niche Terms

If you've done a good job at keyword expansion, you'll be making use of hundreds or thousands of niche terms. The engines often lack data for these phrases. For instance, Google returns no traffic estimates for *Chicago flower delivery* (Figure 19-2), despite the fact that this is a very profitable term for advertisers.

You Probably Won't Capture All of the Broad Traffic (Nor Will You Want To)

If you go against my advice and include broad keywords in your campaign, it will be rather unlikely that you'll capture a significant percentage of the available search impressions. If you include these phrases in your forecasts, you'll usually end up with wildly optimistic traffic estimates.

The AdWords Keyword Tool indicates that there are about 24,900,000 searches a month on the term *flowers*. There are hundreds of advertisers bidding on this term, so the chances are low that your ads will show for a meaningful percentage of the search volume. Given that this term will likely have an abysmal conversion rate, it's altogether best to not count on much traffic for this term.

Geo-Targeting

Another subtlety that can throw off your estimates is failing to use the geo-targeting filter when retrieving traffic data. If your campaign is targeting the U.S., then be sure to exclude traffic from the rest of the world from your estimates.

Day-Parting

If you plan on day-parting (see Chapter 31), be aware that you will capture only a percentage of the available traffic. You'll need to guess how much of the available traffic you'll miss out on and adjust accordingly.

With this discussion out of the way, let's move on to some of the more useful data points you can gather about your category and competitors.

ESTIMATING SEARCH VOLUME

Earlier we began constructing a spreadsheet to contain our keyword research data. You can also add a column to capture the monthly search volume for your keywords. This data will help you plan your PPC campaign, but you can also benefit greatly from it by incorporating it into your SEO campaigns (Figure 19-3).

You can use the AdWords Keyword Tool to populate your search volume column:

- Navigate to the tool at https://adwords. google.com/select/KeywordTool (you will need to log in to your AdWords account first).
- Click the "Edit" link to tailor your results to your desired geographic region if necessary.
- Make sure "Descriptive words or phrases" is selected.
- Enter your keywords in the provided text area.
- Check "Use synonyms" (optional: I usually find that this provides more accurate search volume figures).
- Click the "Filter my results" link.
- Check the box that reads, "Don't show ideas for new keywords."
- Click "Get keyword ideas" to generate the latest traffic estimates.

Search Engine Optimization

Search engine optimization (SEO) is an important part of search marketing, but is out of the scope of this book. Nevertheless, you can use many of these search engine intelligence techniques to enhance your organic rankings and stay on top of your competitors' organic efforts as well.

ESTIMATING IMPRESSIONS

There is a common perception that the search volume estimates provided by Google tend to be inaccurate. We've found that these search volume estimates are actually fairly reliable, provided you account for the various sources of error discussed above.

For the most part, this perception is based on the fact that marketers don't typically see as many impressions in their AdWords accounts as they do in the traffic estimator tool.

Some of the reasons for this include:

Your ads may not display on the first page of search results (where most of the search volume is generated) due to low bids or quality score issues.

Your ads may appear on the first page of search results, but may only capture a small percentage of the available impressions. This is usually due to the presence of other advertisers with higher-quality campaigns and ads than yours.

The traffic estimator tool does not filter out fraudulent impressions generated by bots or scraping tools, while AdWords does.

For these reasons, you need to discount the search volume to come up with an impression estimate. One rule of thumb you can follow is that 98% of advertisers receive less than 20% of the available impressions. If you are serious about search marketing, however, you stand a good

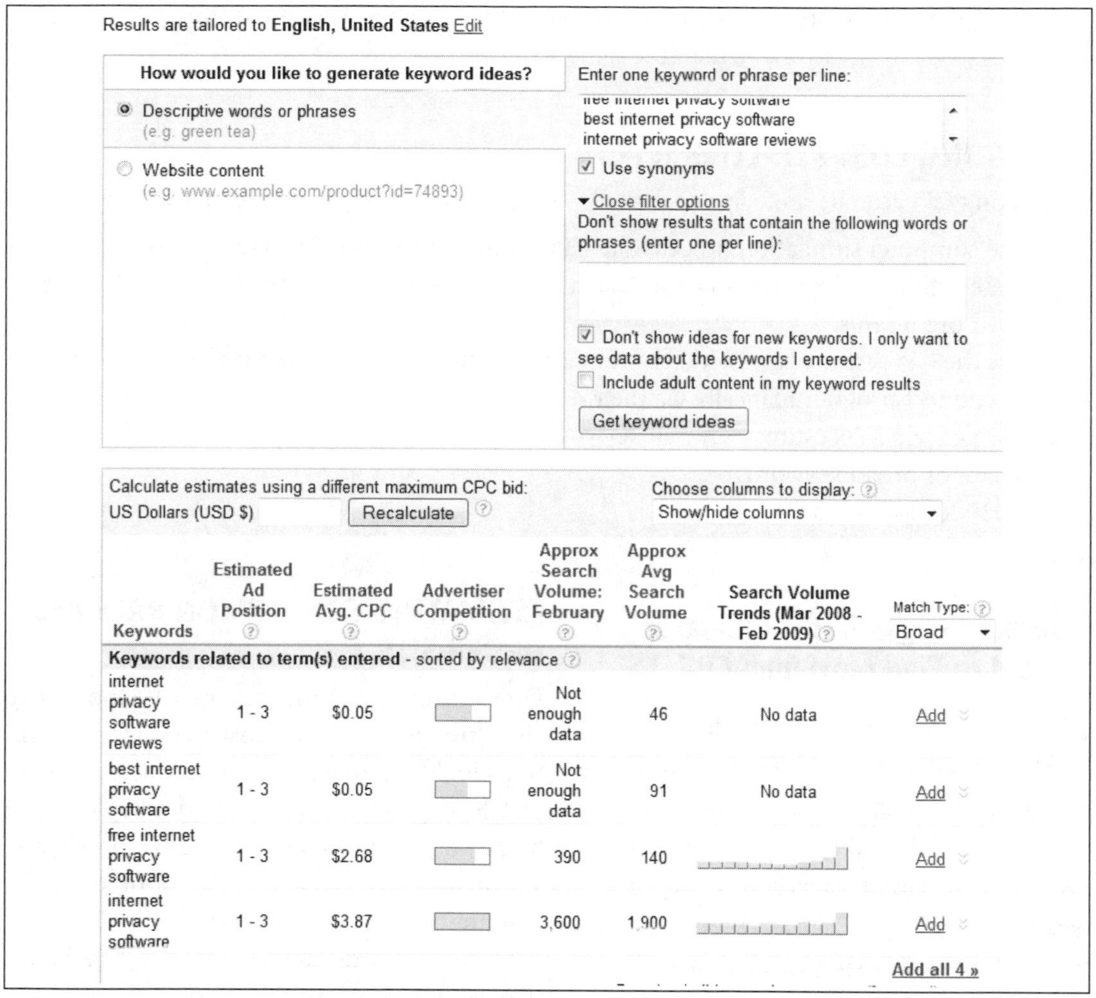

FIGURE 19-3. You can use the AdWords Keyword Tool to generate traffic estimates.

chance of capturing a higher amount. Fifteen percent is easily attainable in most markets, while 30-50% is about the highest an advertiser can hope for unless it has serious chops.

ESTIMATING CLICKTHROUGH RATE (CTR)

Creating reliable clickthrough rate estimates without sophisticated computer models is pretty much impossible (we talked about this at length in Chapter 16).

However, if you absolutely, positively need to generate an estimate for some reason, you can do so with these best-guess estimates based on the customer life cycle category:

- Browse keywords: 0.5%
- Shop keywords: 1.0%
- Buy keywords: 1.5%

Just keep in mind that if you use these estimates, they won't be very good (forget being in the ballpark—you'll be lucky if you're in the same state).

ESTIMATING COST-PER-CLICK (CPC)

Forecasting CPC can be done in a variety of ways. In order from most to least accurate:

- Use computer simulations to generate CPC estimates for individual keywords, then adjust these estimates for various factors (such as average position of your ads). See Chapter 17 for more on this.
- Use the CPC estimates provided by the search engines (e.g., use their traffic estimator tools or connect programmatically via their APIs).
- Use generic CPC estimates for all keywords:
  $3.50 for broad keywords
  $1.50 for lower-traffic keywords

Use the Google Traffic Estimator Tool to Find Maximum CPC

On Google, the most reliable way to gather CPC data is to enter a high maximum bid into the traffic estimator tool (I use $100). This will return an estimated CPC for the topmost position on the page. Then multiply this figure by 60%. As long as your ad doesn't appear on the top of the right sidebar, your estimate will be "good enough for government work."

ESTIMATING CONVERSION RATE AND ORDER SIZE

Forecasting these metrics makes the above clickthrough rate and cost-per-click calculations look like an exact science. They are completely dependent on the credibility of your brand, how fine-tuned your sales funnels are, seasonality, overall demand in your category, and hundreds of other factors.

In other words, any estimate is little better than a guess.

If you have an existing website, you may be able to use your site-wide conversion rate as a starting point. If not, plug in these numbers based on your website conversion strategy:

- E-mail capture: 20%
- B2B lead generation: 3-5%
- Sale of common low-priced consumer goods (under $40): 1-2%
- Sale of common high-priced consumer goods: 0.5%

The above figures assume that you are making use of targeted keywords, superior landing pages, and sales funnels. If for some reason this isn't a safe assumption, you should cut them by 80%.

Order size can be trivial to estimate, or it can be impossible. If you are selling $49 ebooks, it's pretty straightforward. If you are capturing email addresses, then you'll need to devise a proxy value per lead. If you have a catalog site with hundreds of categories, you'll probably need to hook into your financial systems directly.

ESTIMATING COMPETITORS' TRAFFIC

There are a number of tools that will help to give you an idea of how much traffic competing websites are receiving each month (from all sources, not just paid search). This can be very helpful for planning a new website as well as forecasting traffic and sales of an existing one.

Alexa (Alexa.com)

Alexa is one of the first places you should visit to get an idea of how your competitors stack up in terms of raw traffic. Simply type in the domain name to generate traffic statistics. The most interesting statistic is reach, which indicates the percentage of global internet users who visit that site in a given month.

Alexa collects its data using toolbars that are installed on millions of computers all over the world. Because it relies on statistical sampling, the figures are generally only accurate for the top 100,000 sites in the U.S. (Figure 19-4).

FIGURE 19-4. Alexa is a free resource you can use to estimate competitors' traffic.

Quantcast (Quantcast.com)

Quantcast generates traffic estimates using a combination of panel data and direct measurements (larger sites). It offers a greater variety of statistics than Alexa, but the traffic estimates aren't particularly reliable for anything but the largest sites (which makes it valuable for profes-

If your site primarily targets English-speaking visitors, you can convert Alexa's reach figure into a monthly traffic estimate by multiplying it by 670,000,000.

sional media buyers, but less so for smaller advertisers). The data also appears to be very delayed: as of this writing, Bing is receiving over 20,000,000 visitors per month, but Quantcast shows it receiving only 56,000 visitors per month. That's quite a difference. Nevertheless, the demographic information can be useful when it comes time to write your ad copy (Figure 19-5).

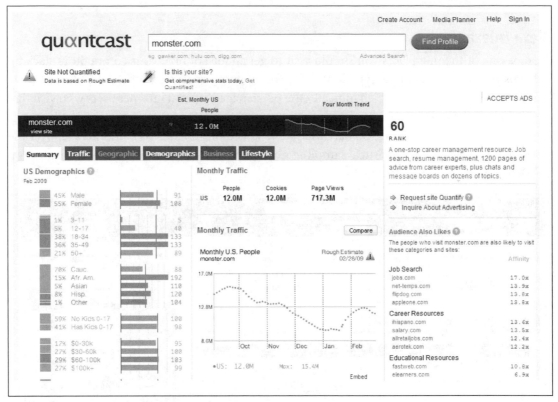

FIGURE 19-5. Quantcast offers free traffic data on virtually every site.

Hitwise (Hitwise.com)

Hitwise is another option for gathering traffic and demographic data on competitors' websites. The price point on this service puts it out of reach for most smaller advertisers, however (Figure 19-6).

USING ADGOOROO TO COLLECT COMPETITIVE INTELLIGENCE

Many of the readers of this book are AdGooroo subscribers, so this chapter on search engine intelligence would not be complete without sharing some of the useful ways that people have found to use the service.

As useful as the above tools are to internet marketers, there are two important areas in which they are lacking.

The first is that all of them rely on panels of known internet users to generate their estimates of traffic, clickthrough rates, reach, and demographics. People sometimes knowingly volunteer

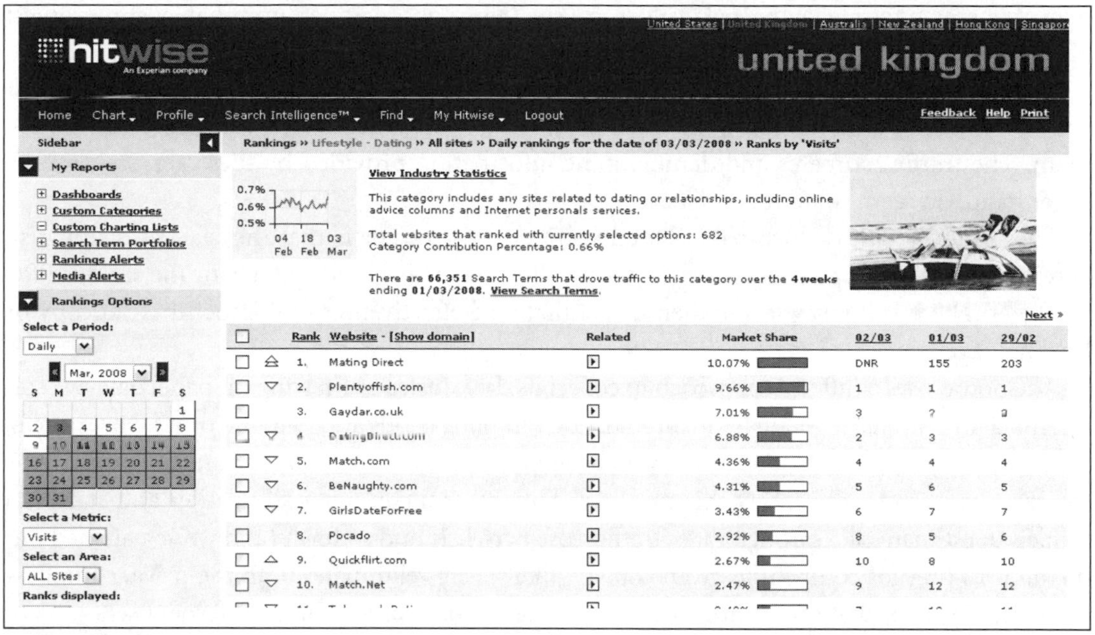

FIGURE 19-6. Hitwise is a commercial intelligence service that provides useful traffic and demographic data on competitors.

W hile all of these services are valuable in some way, take the time to understand how they acquire their data as well as the strengths and weaknesses of each. This will help you avoid drawing bad conclusions.

I recently received an email from a so-called internet marketing "guru" showing people how to find "winning landing page ideas" by watching for dips in Alexa traffic and then looking for changes in website landing pages using Internet Archive (http://archive.org). Anyone with a cursory under-standing of Alexa's methodology could see that this technique is worthless because Alexa doesn't drill down into landing pages.

for these panels, but often this data is collected without the users' knowledge or consent through ISP monitoring, browser plugins, or toolbars.

Ignoring the privacy implications, panel data is invaluable, provided the sample size is large enough. However, it begins to fall apart as you drill down into individual pages or short date ranges. There has even been a recent trend by some of these companies to provide guidance on conversion rate data or average order sizes for competing sites—but don't believe the hype. You simply cannot generate reliable clickthrough rates, let alone conversion data, based on a panel approach. As mentioned in our chapter on split-testing, it can take hundreds of clicks or sales to generate a valid estimate of conversion rate. It is ridiculous to believe that you can trust any estimates generated by a few hundred visitors to a site (which is the upper limit that even the largest panels can deliver to most sites).

This does not diminish the value of these services in any way. Just realize that clickthrough or conversion rate estimates based on small samples are not reliable and you shouldn't believe them. The traffic estimates and demographic information provided by these services, on the other hand, do seem to be very reliable.

The second area in which panel-based services are deficient is that they fail to distinguish between paid search and organic search traffic. This is a major disadvantage for the serious PPC marketer. There is no way to use them to estimate the effectiveness of competitors' ad copy or landing pages.

AdGooroo uses a different approach to collect its data. Instead of relying on panel data, we collect much of our data through frequent statistical sampling of ads and join it to other data sources, most notably the APIs provided by the search engines (we have worked out arrangements with the search engines to legally collect this data). We then rely on computer simulation and statistical models to estimate clickthrough rates, traffic, cost-per-click, and so forth (and we've patented our methods to prevent competitors from copying them). This eliminates both the privacy implications and the error that results from sampling small populations of known internet users.

With that explanation behind us, here are some of the ways you can use this service to boost your pay-per-click campaigns.

ESTIMATING THE NUMBER OF COMPETITORS IN YOUR MARKET

This data is available within AdGooroo in the Keyword Group report (Figure 19-7).

FINDING YOUR TOP COMPETITORS

It's important to distinguish between your company's overall competitors and your competitors on the search engine. From a search marketing standpoint, it only matters who is showing up, how often, and what they are saying. Virtually all the businesspeople I talk to have a good idea of who their top competitors are, but very few of them can say who their biggest threats are on Google.

For the dedicated search marketer, knowing your top five competitors in each search engine or country goes a long way toward allowing you to focus on what's important and reducing the amount of work you need to do.

Once you've identified your top competitors, you'll want to dig into their ad copy to find out what they're telling the market.

FIND THE TOP AD COPY

It's easy to find all of the ad copy in any category. On the Keyword Group report, click the "Show Ads" tab. This will produce a report with all of your competitors' ad copy sorted by how often it

Advertiser	Ranking	Coverage (%)	Avg Position	Captured Impressions	Missed Impressions	Est Clicks	Est CTR	Est CPC	Est Spend	Search Share (%)
WinClear.com	1	39.6	1.5	7,440	39,865	198.2	2.66%	$1.00	$198.96	15.7
pc-confidential.com	2	37.6	3.4	14,057	33,248	445.4	3.17%	$0.53	$237.40	29.7
evidence-blaster.com	3	31.3	1.6	3,665	43,640	89.3	2.44%	$0.59	$62.07	7.7
consumersreporter.org	4	30.3	1.8	1,423	45,882	29.4	2.07%	$0.86	$25.32	3.0
pctools.com	5	28.5	3.0	15,818	31,487	237.6	1.50%	$0.84	$200.58	33.4
deloitte.com	6	10.9	1.4	50	47,255	4.1	8.25%	$2.55	$10.53	0.1
google.com	7	9.9	1.0	5,950	41,355	173.1	2.91%	$0.90	$156.02	12.6
hyperdynesoftware.com	8	8.8	2.5	12,767	34,538	284.0	2.22%	$0.71	$200.26	27.0
privacytweaks.com	9	12.8	5.5	8,119	39,186	151.1	1.86%	$0.56	$85.06	17.2
internethistorycleaner.ws	10	10.1	4.7	867	46,438	11.2	1.29%	$0.73	$8.22	1.8
econsumers-guides.org	11	6.9	2.9	167	47,138	4.0	2.39%	$0.95	$3.78	0.4
contentpurity.com	12	6.1	3.1	17	47,288	1.3	7.55%	$1.77	$2.28	0.0
toptenreviews.com	13	5.8	2.9	4,641	42,664	96.7	2.08%	$0.75	$72.18	9.8
spectorsoft.com	14	4.7	2.0	3,764	43,541	31.8	0.85%	$1.11	$35.26	8.0
webwatchernow.com	15	4.4	2.0	2,873	44,432	49.1	1.71%	$1.56	$76.56	6.1
pcpitstop.com	16	7.7	4.7	3,255	44,050	45.3	1.39%	$0.39	$17.83	6.9

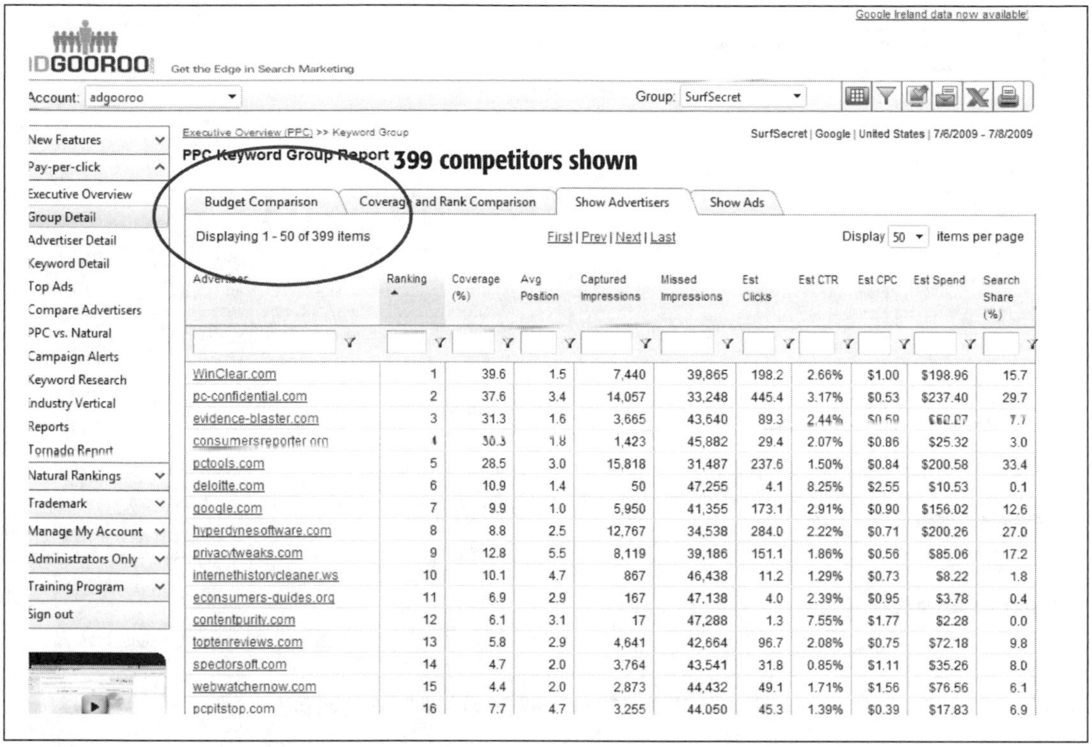

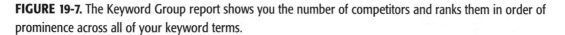

FIGURE 19-7. The Keyword Group report shows you the number of competitors and ranks them in order of prominence across all of your keyword terms.

is served. It also includes landing page URLs and the keywords the ads were found in (Figure 19-8).

Once your account has been collecting data for at least 30 days, you can even mine past impression data to narrow down those ads that potentially have the highest clickthrough rates in your category. This can be done using the "Top Ads" report (see Figure 19-9).

Using these two reports, I am typically able to start a brand-new campaign with clickthrough rates in the high 1-2% range. I then use split-testing to push my clickthrough rates even higher. This results in high quality scores for most terms (7-10 range) without having to wait months for results.

FIND EFFECTIVE LANDING PAGES

Landing page optimization is one of the most important management practices you have to master in pay-per-click advertising. Unfortunately, it's also the most time-consuming one. You can greatly reduce the learning curve by assessing the most prominent landing pages in your category and seeding your tests with variants of the pages your competitors are using. This will often bring you to parity with them in a short time (Figure 19-10).

Then use the time you saved to perform follow-up tests, allowing you to both exceed their conversion rates and outbid them.

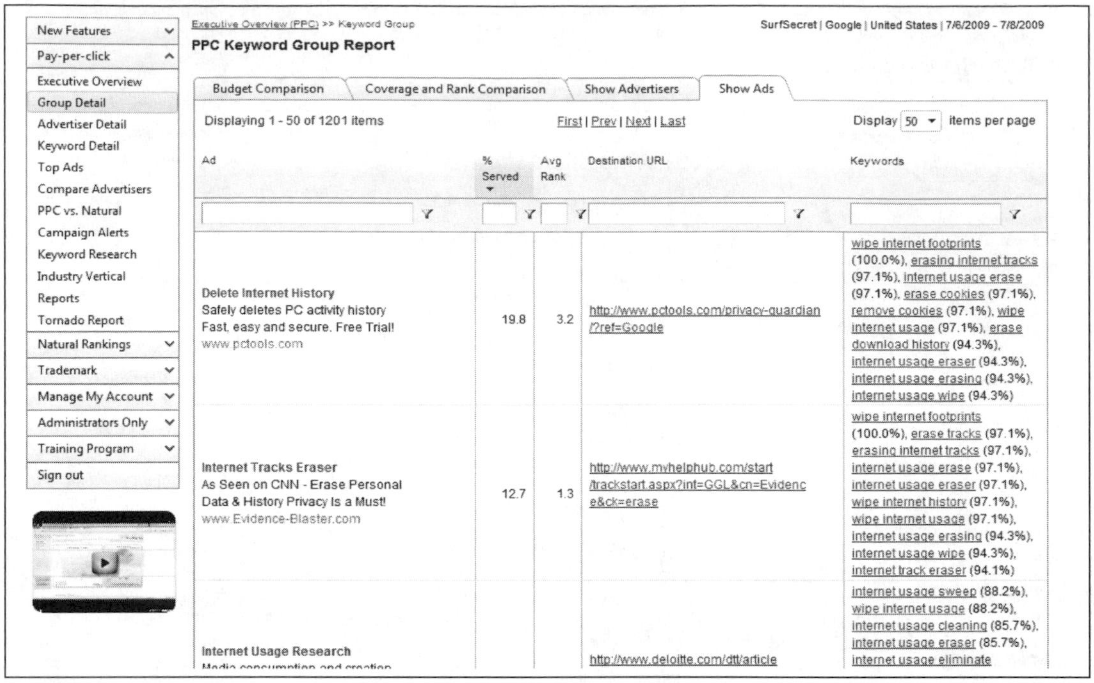

FIGURE 19-8. The Ad Copy report finds all ad copy in any given business category.

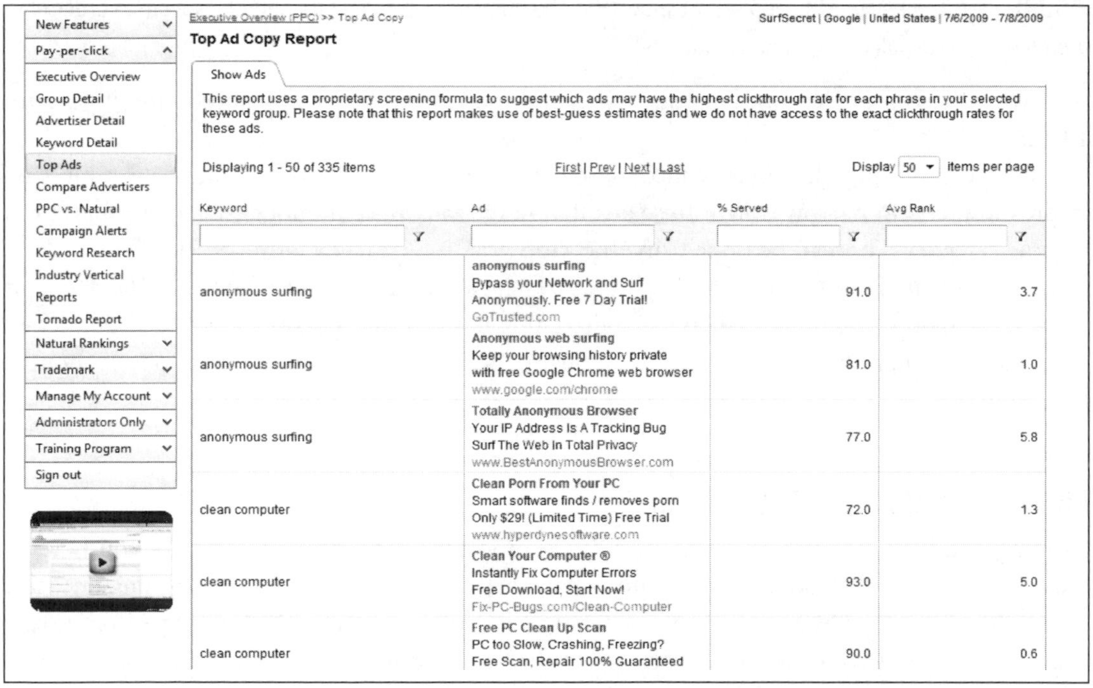

FIGURE 19-9. The Top Ads report takes it a step further and mines past impression data of thousands of ads to find those with the highest chance of being top performers. This report requires 30 days of data.

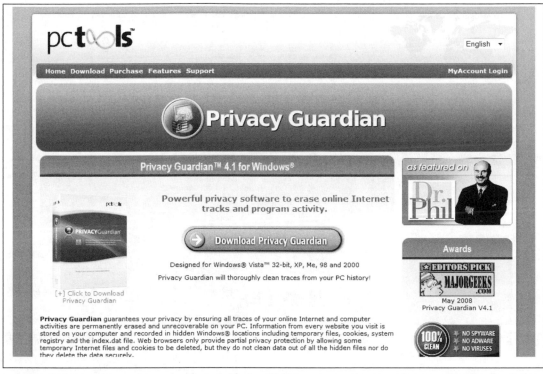

FIGURE 19-10. The Ad Copy report also includes landing page URLs, sorted by frequency of appearance. This is valuable information, as it guides you to your competitors' most successful landing pages.

ESTIMATE COMPETITORS' TRAFFIC AND BUDGETS

Knowing what competitors are able to spend in pay-per-click is a valuable advantage. It can save you the trouble of entering markets that don't have a lot of demand, or it can prevent you from giving up on your campaign before it has had a chance to reach its potential.

Remember those computer simulation models for figuring out competitors' clickthrough rates and average cost-per-click prices? They're built into all AdGooroo reports, and they allow you to get a very good estimate of what kind of results your competitors are getting.

Here's an Advertiser Detail report on an up-and-coming company in the privacy software market (Figure 19-11). Notice how it started out in early June with a tiny PPC spend, but increased it dramatically into July. There's a very good chance that its early campaign turned a profit.

Seeing a chart like this makes me want to look at the landing pages and see what they're doing. If it looks promising, I would test something similar for my own site (Figure 19-12).

Scrolling further down the page also shows me if there have been any recent changes in its bid prices or clickthrough rates. It looks like it's been slowly increasing its bids throughout June (Figure 19-13).

I can even drill into its individual keywords to see what its current estimated bids are. It turns out that most of its spend is on a single keyword (*clean computer*). A smart advertiser would

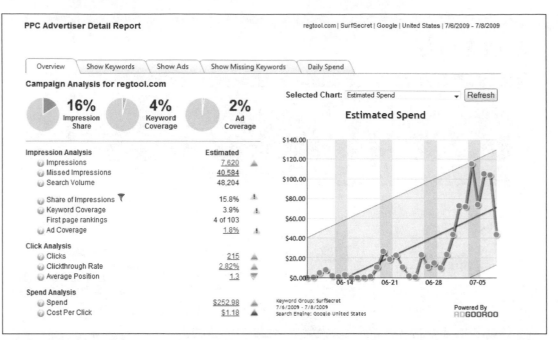

FIGURE 19-11. This advertiser has dramatically increased its PPC spend—a sign that it's doing something right.

FIGURE 19-12. Here's its top landing page. It's a prime candidate for testing.

probably diversify out into many different keywords, so I make a mental note that this advertiser probably isn't all that sophisticated when it comes to PPC. It will probably be a waste of time to split-test its ads (Figure 19-14).

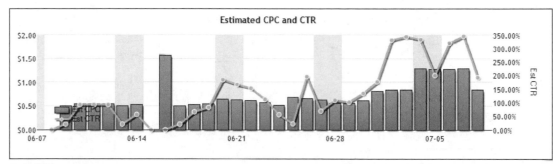

FIGURE 19-13.

Keyword	Coverage (%)	Avg Rank	Estimated							
			Total Search Volume	Captured Impressions	Missed Impressions	Clicks	CTR	CPC ▼		Spend
erase image cache	67.6	1.0	N/A			0.2		$3.14		$0.68
how do i clean my computer of porn	5.7	5.5	N/A					$1.52		$0.04
clean computer	88.9	0.2	8,137	7,233	904	212.1	2.93%	$1.18		$250.44
pc cleaner	17.1	7.3	2,441	387	2,054	2.9	0.74%	$0.64		$1.82
anonymous surfing	0.0		4,463		4,463					
clean my computeronline privacy	0.0		N/A							

Displaying 1 - 50 of 103 items · First | Prev | Next | Last · Display 50 ▼ items per page

Tabs: Overview | Show Keywords | Show Ads | Show Missing Keywords | Daily Spend

FIGURE 19-14.

I should point out that the CPCs listed in this report aren't exact. They are simply the best estimates that we're able to generate with computer modeling. Nevertheless, this data has given me incredibly valuable clues about this particular advertiser's internet marketing program and a new landing page I can add to my list of things to test.

FIND COMPETITORS' MISTAKES

Another common occurrence you'll come across while peeking into your competitors' spending habits is starting a PPC campaign but quickly turning down the dials. This is often a sign of poor landing pages.

Here's an example of an advertiser who started out with a tiny PPC spend (Figure 19-15). They increased their bids and quickly dropped them again—a sign that their campaign was losing money.

This is unlikely to happen with a strong landing page. Here's what theirs looks like (Figure 19-16). In comparison with the competing landing page above, this page uses longer copy and is much less flashy. This tells me I may be dealing with an audience that is less technically inclined and probably more easily influenced by slick marketing.

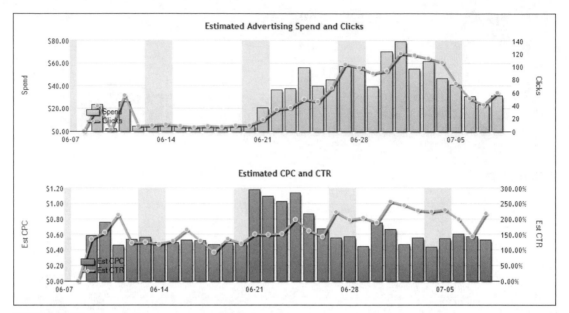

FIGURE 19-15.

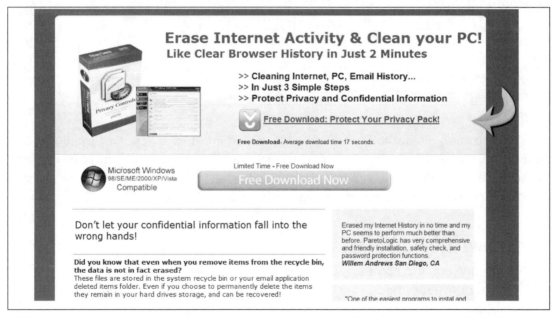

FIGURE 19-16. A landing page that doesn't seem to be performing well enough to support high bids. Compare this with the slick, short-copy landing page above.

Again, I stuff this information into my mental file. It will almost certainly come in handy later.

SPOT OPPORTUNITIES TO GRAB MARKET SHARE

If you're in a commodity market such as paper or office supplies, you may run across sites that mysteriously pause their campaigns around the 25th of the month. The reason for this is simple: companies in these categories often have fixed budgets and blow through them too quickly. You'll know this is the case if their campaign is reactivated on the first of the month.

You can often take advantage of these competitors' absence to grab market share. It's a good opportunity to raise your bids and get in front of more customers while they're away.

USE BID JAMMING (AND DEFEND AGAINST IT)

One of the (perhaps unintended) consequences of the AdWords quality score algorithm is that bid jamming is once again possible on the search engines. Having access to SEI allows you to find opportunities to knock competitors out of prime keywords (sometimes even permanently).

I'll share a detailed example of how to use bid jamming in Chapter 27.

PLUG HOLES IN YOUR ORGANIC CAMPAIGNS

Some of the smartest internet marketers in the world are religious in their use of this next technique for their websites with an active SEO campaign in place. They use the AdGooroo PPC vs. Natural report to find organic listings in which they are not on the first page of search results, then focus on quality score optimization and raise their bid prices to gain prominent placement in the sponsored listings. They compensate for the increased CPCs by lowering their bids (or even pausing altogether) for keywords in which they have high first-page rankings (Figure 19-17).

Keyword comparison															
Displaying 1 - 50 of 103 items					First | Prev | Next | Last								Display 50 ▼ items per page		
		Pay-per-click								Natural					
Keyword	Monthly Search Volume	Coverage	Rank	Captured Impressions	Missed Impressions	Est Clicks	Est CTR	Est CPC	Est Spend	Natural Rank ▼	Impressions	Clicks	CTR		
pc cleaner	24,750	94.3	2.2	2,316	125	28.0	1.21%	$0.91	$25.48	99				PPC Report	Natural Report
erase download history	240	94.3	3.3	20	4	0.2	1.14%	$1.75	$0.39	98				PPC Report	Natural Report
how do i delete history	4,050				399					94				PPC Report	Natural Report
wipe internet files	240	88.2	3.0	21	3	0.3	1.51%	$1.75	$0.55	90				PPC Report	Natural Report
remove history	11,100	88.6	1.6	970	124	20.5	2.11%	$0.75	$15.43	85				PPC Report	Natural Report
erase all internet tracks	130	47.1	3.4	6	7		0.38%	$1.35	$0.03	8	13		2.98%	PPC Report	Natural Report
erasing internet tracks	130	97.1	3.5	12		0.1	0.79%	$1.71	$0.17	8	13		2.98%	PPC Report	Natural Report

FIGURE 19-17. The PPC vs. Natural report allows you to spend more where you are weak in organic listings, and less for those keywords in which you have high rankings.

SUMMARY

Search engine intelligence (SEI) has become a critical component of modern pay-per-click strategy. Advertisers who rely on it are faster and more nimble, and can defend against their competitors' efforts to chip away at their campaign performance. If you're facing off against larger, well-funded competitors, it may be the only advantage you have against them.

CHAPTER 20

The Foundation of Search Marketing: The Visitor Intention Model

B EFORE YOU CREATE YOUR FIRST CAMPAIGN, CHOOSE YOUR KEYWORDS, OR WRITE A SINGLE ad, you should understand the basic mechanisms behind how people search. The psychology of search is a deep subject, but fortunately for us, a few smart marketers[1] have come up with an easy-to-understand and surprisingly practical framework that anyone can use to create powerful campaigns from scratch. This model forms the foundation for keyword selection, ad copy, and even bidding strategies. It takes only a few minutes to learn, and the payoff is well worth it.

THE VISITOR INTENTION MODEL

This model of search behavior postulates that there is a correlation between the phrases that people type into search engines and their intent to purchase. In other words, you can guess how likely it is that individuals will purchase from you based on their search phrase.

Under this model, search engine users tend to fall within one of three primary categories or two secondary categories (Figure 20-1).

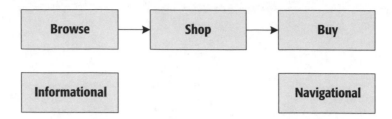

FIGURE 20-1.

Browsers are in information-gathering mode. The search phrases they enter tend to be short and not very specific (e.g., *Las Vegas, coupons, spyware,* etc.). This group is least likely to make an immediate purchase, so aggressively promoting products to them is not the best approach.

Because browsers are generally looking for information rather than commercial offerings, they tend to click on natural results more often than ads. When they do click on ads, they will often click more than one as they gather as much information as possible. They usually start at the top of the page and work their way down (becoming more selective as they go along).

The browser group is closely related to the *informational* group. The difference is that the former are potentially buyers, whereas people in the informational group are highly unlikely to buy at all. People interested in celebrity gossip are an example. It would be difficult to monetize this group of visitors in any other way than through contextual or banner advertising.

Most people using search engines fall within one of these two groups, but you're far more likely to make a sale to a *shopper.* These people have an identified need and are considering their options. They are often using a search engine to compare different products or services.

You can almost think of shoppers as tire kickers. They might be seriously interested in buying now or later, but the immediate need is to assess their options. By appealing to that information-gathering need, you can often convert them to buyers (or at least capture their information for when they are ready to buy).

Buyers, on the other hand, are ready to buy now. They might be looking for a specific product, or just the first product that seems to meet their needs. Their information gathering is largely done, and they spend less time on the search engine and more time on vendors' websites.

Aggressive emotional or impulsive appeals often work with these visitors, because the logical part of their brains has already been satisfied through prior research. Often, they need just the slightest push to buy from you. You want to tempt with promotional offers, and you should cater to instant gratification: fast shipping, high quality, low price, and so forth.

Finally, the *navigational* group is a subset of the buyer category. The purpose of their queries is to reach a particular website that they have in mind, typically because they've visited it in the past or because they assume that such a site exists. For instance, someone who searches for *greyhound bus* is almost certainly looking to reach http://www.greyhound.com.

These visitors are quite hard to convert. Unlike other types of searchers, they usually have only one "right" result. They know the site they want to visit, and only that site will do. Although making a sale to these visitors isn't impossible, it's certainly an uphill battle—one that will tie up an inordinate amount of your time and money.

IDENTIFYING YOUR VISITORS' PURCHASE INTENTION

The information above is critical for any marketer to know. In the offline world, companies pay dearly for this type of market research. Fortunately, you don't have to.

You can guess which group a visitor falls within simply by the length and specificity of their keyword phrase.

- Short, one-word keyword phrases that generate a lot of traffic are commonly used by browsers.
- Two- and three-word phrases that contain comparison words such as *best, cheap*, or *review* are shoppers' terms.
- Phrases with four or more words that refer to specific products, SKUs, or model numbers are used by buyers to find what they want quickly.
- Specific URLs, companies, or brand names identify navigational searchers.

Here are some examples to get your wheels turning. In the coming chapters, we'll show you how to use this insight to transform your search advertising radically.

Browse	Shop	Buy	Navigate
Television	HDTV HDTV Reviews	Panasonic 43" plasma TV HVD3002 best price	Panasonic
Las Vegas	Las Vegas Airfare	Cheap Las Vegas	Expedia
Spyware	Best Antispyware Program	Spyware Doctor 4.0	pctools.com

Power Tip

It is often difficult to distinguish between "shop" and "buy" keywords. Eventually you get a knack for it. One rule of thumb that I follow is when dealing with products, verbs are often "shop" terms and nouns are often "buy" terms. For instance, *internet files clean* is likely a "shop" phrase, while *internet files cleaner* is most likely a "buy" term. I would write different ads for each and even be willing to pay a little more for the latter phrase.

SUMMARY

The phrases your potential customers are searching on reveal their purchase intentions. Most of your revenues will be generated through niche (shop or buy) keywords. Most of your traffic (and costs) will be generated from broad (browse) keywords. For this reason, most advertisers should focus on niche keywords and leave the broad keywords to brand-name competitors who are less concerned with immediate payback.

Note

1. The original model of search behavior was created by Andrei Broder, who wrote about it in his paper "A Taxonomy of Web Search" while working for AltaVista Corporation. It has evolved over the years and today is in widespread use among many top-tier search agencies.

Building Your
Keyword List

I N BOTH ORGANIC AND PAID SEARCH MARKETING, KEYWORDS ARE THE BAIT THAT LURES prospective customers to your website.

People will find your site based on the keywords where your ads appear. For this reason alone, it's important to expand your campaign with as many relevant terms as possible. Yet the average B2B (business-to-business) advertiser only bids on 50 terms.[1] This is not a recipe for success!

Keyword selection may not be the most important success factor for paid search, but it's certainly in the top five. The time you spend perfecting your keyword list will dramatically improve the potential results of your pay-per-click advertising campaign.

THE FOUR MOST COMMON KEYWORD RESEARCH MISTAKES

Let's start out by discussing the four most common mistakes search advertisers make when establishing their campaigns.

Mistake 1: Not Using Enough Keywords

As we stated earlier, the average B2B business has only 50 keywords in its paid search campaign. This is a huge mistake. No matter what your business is, you should be able to come up with thousands of niche terms that are relevant to potential customers. Aim to have no less than 5,000 keywords, but preferably 25,000 or more.

Mistake 2: Relying Solely on Brainstorming

As crazy as it sounds, many small businesses casually type in a few dozen keywords off the top of their heads into the Google AdWords interface and expect to start seeing results. This fails for several reasons:

- Brainstorming usually results in a limited set of keywords.
- The keywords resulting from this method are obvious "browse" keywords. These keywords generate lots of traffic (and costs) but few sales.
- These keywords usually don't reflect searchers' purchase intentions.

Mistake 3: Relying Solely on Popular or Free Tools

The two most popular keyword research tools are (hands down) Wordtracker and the Google Keyword Tool.

Both of these tools return good results. The major problem with them is that they are widely used, which means the keywords they return are quite competitive. The other problem is that the algorithms behind them are based on total search traffic, which means these keywords will tend to drive more traffic but convert at a much lower rate than low-volume niche keywords.

Mistake 4: Never Updating Your Keyword Lists

After you complete this chapter, you're going to have a great set of keywords. But don't forget to revisit your list from time to time. New buzzwords and niche areas will pop up from time to time, and if you never update your list, you'll miss out on new potential traffic sources.

QUANTITY IS IMPORTANT ... TO A POINT

Given what we just said about these four common mistakes, it seems reasonable that we could play it safe, dump every possible keyword into our campaigns, and let the search engines worry about it.

Unfortunately, this doesn't work very well.

There are two competing factors at work here. On one hand, using many generic keywords will allow you to reach more visitors. On the other, niche keywords that reflect your business will attract more qualified (but fewer) prospects who convert at a much higher rate.

So which is it? Quantity or quality?

The answer is both. You want to start with a core set of keywords that reflect your business. But you should also build that list into hundreds (or preferably thousands) of niche, hyper-specific keyword phrases that reflect both what visitors are searching for and what your business sells.

This has many advantages.

Although generic keywords such as *plasma TV* are searched on by lots of people, these searchers are less likely to make a purchase, so you end up wasting your campaign budget on ineffective advertising. Targeted keywords like *cheapest 43" plasma TV* are generally much less expensive to bid on and have far better conversion rates.

Google (and now Yahoo!) has mechanisms to prevent you from bidding on keywords that aren't relevant to your business. Although you can get around this, it's difficult, expensive, and time-consuming to do so.

However, if Google thinks a particular keyword accurately reflects your business, it rewards you with placement and coverage bonuses, essentially giving you a discount on your advertising and an advantage over less search-savvy competitors.

So if you take nothing else from this book, remember this: *target hundreds or thousands of specific, relevant keywords in your search marketing efforts*. Following this strategy alone could be the difference between a winning campaign and a losing one.

TO COME UP WITH KEYWORDS, THINK LIKE YOUR CUSTOMERS

We learned in Marketing 101 to focus on the customers and meet their needs. But before the internet and other highly measurable media forced us marketers to be accountable, many of us got away with focusing on the features of our products rather than emphasizing benefits.

Nowadays, if you're out there flexing your muscles, talking about how great you are, and trying to impress prospects, you're probably not going to get very far. Companies that succeed in today's cluttered marketplace start by doing the market research on what problems their prospects have.

They are desperate to understand the pains, fears, and hopes of their prospects. They know how to empathize with their prospects. Once they have their market research, savvy marketers then know how to position themselves. They know how to say, "I feel your pain," and how to present a solution to ease that pain.

When people enter keywords into a search box, they have a pain. They have a need. They have a question that they want answered. They want to be served the solution in the form of information as to how they can resolve their problem.

Your job as a marketer is to put yourself in their shoes. You must ask yourself: What keywords are my ideal prospects going to type into Google or Yahoo!?

That is the question all marketers should have been asking themselves all along, but if you don't know the right keywords that your prospects are asking, your PPC campaigns aren't going to send you much qualified traffic.

This is where the customer life cycle model begins to come into play. To create effective PPC campaigns, you should always be asking yourself:

- What behavioral category does this keyword fall in (browse, shop, or buy)?
- Can I refine a browse keyword into one or more shop keywords?
- Can I refine a shop keyword into one or more buy keywords?

As you come up with each keyword, you will want to categorize it into one of the three categories. This step will come in handy while you are structuring your campaigns, writing your ads, and setting your initial bids.

KEYWORD GENERATION: STEP BY STEP

Keeping in mind the three common mistakes we started this chapter with, we're now going to show you how to build a keyword list rich with high-converting terms.

When you start building your keyword list, you're going to be doing little more than guessing. By using the right analytical tools and performing the right analysis, you will expand your keywords and hone the list down by improving or eliminating underperforming keywords.

Start by brainstorming about the kinds of keywords that are relevant to your customers and jot them down on a pad of paper or in an electronic document.

As in any brainstorming, it is best to have blue sky thinking at first. In other words, don't edit yourself. Later, you will see that the actual results of your campaign will edit you by telling you which keywords work and which don't.

Err on the side of having more keywords rather than less.

Try not to just think in terms of one-word or even two-word keywords. You want to own niches: you want to think in terms of key phrases, so that you can dominate when a searcher looks for something specific that is relevant to what you have to sell.

You might find that the keyword *red leashes for German shepherds* doesn't get any clicks, but don't make that determination yourself. Don't assume anything. That's what's great about the search engines. They'll tell you in a very cold and calculated manner whether you get any clicks or conversions.

So, for the purposes of starting a new campaign, assume nothing and test everything. The more keywords, the merrier. The exception to this is that you should make sure all your keywords are relevant to your business.

If you are selling vacations to Mexico, the keyword *Mexico* probably isn't a good choice—it's too untargeted, broad, and competitive. These general keywords will probably be high-priced as well.

You are looking for relatively low-cost keywords that convert well, and by testing you will be able to home in on that subset of keywords where you should be spending the lion's share of your search budget.

So it's okay to test general terms, but spend more time looking for niche key phrases. As we discussed in Chapter 20, browsers and information gatherers are more likely to search with general terms, whereas people closer to the buying stage tend to be more specific and type in longer search phrases.

By choosing specific keywords, you are more likely to attract higher-quality prospects at a relatively lower cost. You won't get much traffic on these more specific key phrases, but because there are so many of them, the overall traffic can be comparable to that available from broad terms. Moreover, these terms will cost less and convert better.

Step 1: Brainstorm

Let's start with a little brainstorming session for our real-world case study, SurfSecret. SurfSecret is a company that specializes in privacy and identity protection software. Here are a few of the starting keywords that I came up with off the top of my head:

- online privacy
- anonymous surfing
- erase tracks
- tracks eraser
- identity theft protection

Step 2: Mine Through Marketing Collateral

If you have an established business, you'll want to sort through pamphlets, brochures, websites, and any other marketing copy you have available. I'll start expanding our list using the SurfSecret website (Figure 21-1).

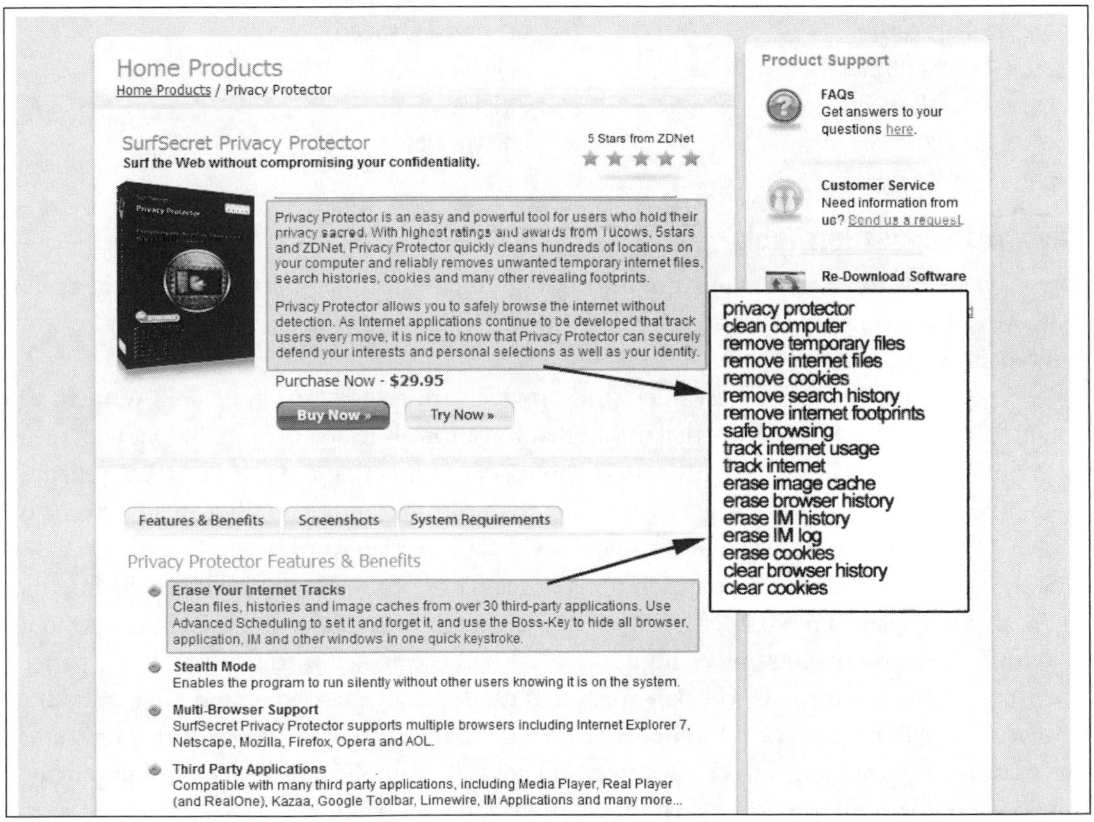

FIGURE 21-1. Website product pages are a good source of keyword ideas.

SurfSecret also provided me with retail boxes that were full of good copy. I took all the ideas I could from these sources and ended up with a list of 39 keywords. I also came up with a variety of useful synonyms for "erase," such as "clean," "clear," "hide," "remove," and "wipe."

Here's my current keyword list:

online privacy	clear browser history
anonymous surfing	clear cookies
erase tracks	steal identity
tracks eraser	protect internet passwords
identity theft protection	protect login
privacy protector	protect username passwords
clean computer	protect credit card info
remove temporary files	key loggers
remove internet files	keyloggers
remove cookies	phishing
remove search history	hide downloads
remove internet footprints	erase download history
safe browsing	remove download history
track internet usage	clear download history
track internet	optimize PC performance
erase image cache	optimize PC speed
erase browser history	hide files
erase IM history	lock files
erase IM log	encrypt files
erase cookies	

Keyword Suggestion Tools

Your next step is to augment your brainstorming results with third-party keyword suggestion tools. Most search engines provide these tools, which will generate related terms for any keyword you type in.

It's in each search engine's best interest to provide such a tool. Search engines want you to expand your keyword lists because that means that you are likely to spend more money with them.

In our experience, most PPC advertisers have keyword lists that are too short. One client in the online coupon business was generating hundreds of thousands of dollars in advertising on a mere 18 keywords! Imagine what it could do with a proper keyword list.

So be sure to use keyword expansion tools to get ahead of the curve. You'll usually find that you're able to expand a modest list of a hundred keywords to several thousand with a few tools.

Why do we recommend using multiple tools? It's because no keyword research tool is perfect. The worst of them return obvious keywords that can be easily guessed at and are highly competitive. The better ones return hundreds or even thousands of niche keywords that only a few savvy competitors are targeting. Play it safe, and consult multiple sources. Don't skimp here—this is one of the most important steps in planning your campaign.

Step 3: Expand Horizontally Using the Google AdWords Keyword Tool

Next, we're going to expand our list horizontally: that is, we want to cast as broad a net as possible to come up with different topics and search phrases that people may be searching on.

A good place to start is with the free tools that anyone can use. But keep in mind that although the price might be right, there's a serious disadvantage that comes with using them—many of your competitors will be using them too. This makes the terms they suggest a bit on the competitive side.

And because the algorithms behind these tools are based on search volume, the terms they suggest will tend to be from the "broad" group. The overall quality of keywords generated this way tends to be on the low side, and we're going to end up with keywords that generate lots of traffic but relatively few sales.

So you can't really count on these exact terms ever becoming big money makers for your campaign (although it would be nice). Instead, we're hoping simply to find new areas that we haven't found yet. Later on, we'll work on turning these into "shop" or "buy" keywords.

The first tool we'll use is the Google AdWords Keyword Tool, found at https://adwords.google.com/select/KeywordTool.

Enter small groups of the keywords you've discovered so far into the tool. Add new phrases to your list until you can't seem to find any new ones.

You'll notice the tool returns primarily bad suggestions (such as *online drugs*, *employee privacy*, and *privacy fences*). Just ignore them and keep going.

Also, don't bother adding any of these keywords to your AdWords account yet—we have a lot of work ahead of us before we get to that point (Figure 21-2).

After supplementing my list with the Google AdWords Keyword Tool, I ended up with 106 total keywords, many of them just slight variations of each other.

Note: the same page also gives you the option of generating suggestions by entering a URL from your website. This is worth trying, but I find that it rarely returns any additional keywords beyond the first technique.

Step 4: Continue Expanding Keywords with the Microsoft adCenter Add-In

We're now going to repeat the same process using the Microsoft Live Search Keyword Research tool. This little-known keyword suggestion tool is provided free to Microsoft Live Search advertisers and is used from within Excel to generate an alternative set of keywords we can use to supplement our list.

To install this tool:

1. Sign up for a Microsoft Live Search advertising account at http://adcenter.microsoft.com.
2. Navigate to http://advertising.microsoft.com/search-advertising/adcenter_addin. Download and install the adCenter add-in for Excel (Figure 21-3).
3. Open up Excel. You should now see a new menu titled "Ad Intelligence."
4. Type in your keywords, starting at the top left cell and working downwards.

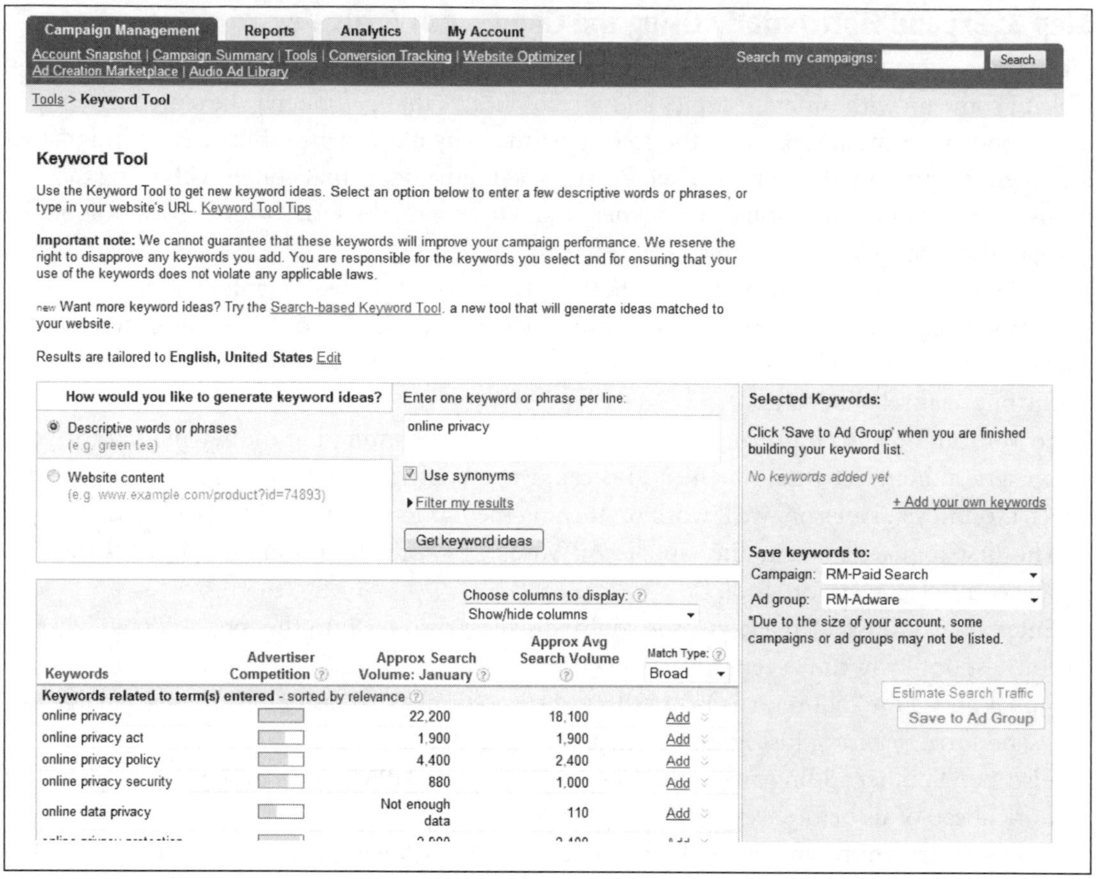

FIGURE 21-2. The first free tool we'll use is the Google AdWords Keyword Tool, found at https://adwords.google.com/select/KeywordTool.

5. From the "Ad Intelligence" menu, click the "Keyword Suggestion" toolbar button. After a few moments, your spreadsheet will be populated with new keyword suggestions (Figure 21-4, page 224).

Carefully sort through the keyword suggestions and eliminate any bad matches. This tool is useful, but just like the Google AdWords tool, it can come up with completely off-base suggestions (*college mainland*, *corn cutter*, and *cirque de soleil* were returned in my list).

After completing this step, I ended up with 249 keywords.

PROFESSIONAL TOOLS

Next, you're going to want to use two professional keyword expansion tools to beef up your keyword list even more.

The major advantage of these tools is that, because they cost money, fewer companies are using them. This means the keywords they generate will on average be less competitive than the broad terms suggested by the search engines, which can translate into a substantial reduction in

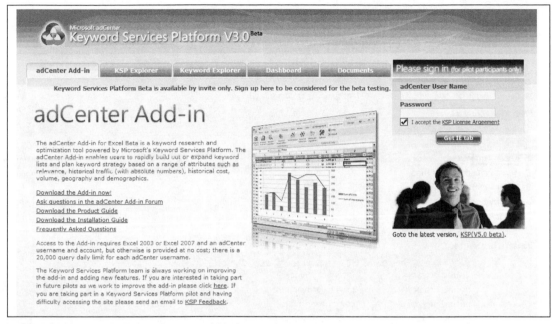

FIGURE 21-3. Download the adCenter add-in for Excel.

your visitor acquisition costs. A small investment in the right tools can result in tens of thousands of dollars in additional revenue over the course of a year.

Another big advantage of using these tools is that the algorithms they use to generate keywords are completely different from the two previous sources. Wordtracker uses a large database of keywords compiled over the years, while AdGooroo searches for your competitors' ads, essentially doing a "reverse lookup" of keywords.

Step 5: Find Additional Niche Terms with Wordtracker

Wordtracker (www.wordtracker.com) has been a staple of PPC marketers for many years, and until the burst of keyword expansion tools hit the market in 2006, it was the only game in town.

Wordtracker pulls data feeds from a few dozen second-tier search engines (Dogpile, Lycos, AltaVista, etc.) and offers subscribers various tools to generate keyword lists.

One of the more interesting aspects of Wordtracker is the KEI analysis feature. KEI is reportedly an indicator of high-profit, low-competition keywords and is used for search engine optimization (SEO), not PPC. We have had mixed success with KEI. Although high-KEI keywords are easier to target, we have not found them to demonstrate above-average conversion rates. Your results may vary.

Wordtracker generates quite a few broad terms and digs deeper into the niche terms than the free tools. The search traffic estimates are unreliable, however—they don't correlate at all with Google or Yahoo! traffic. Nevertheless, it's inexpensive ($59/month at the time of this writing) and you may potentially find some lucrative keywords, so I strongly recommend adding this tool to your arsenal.

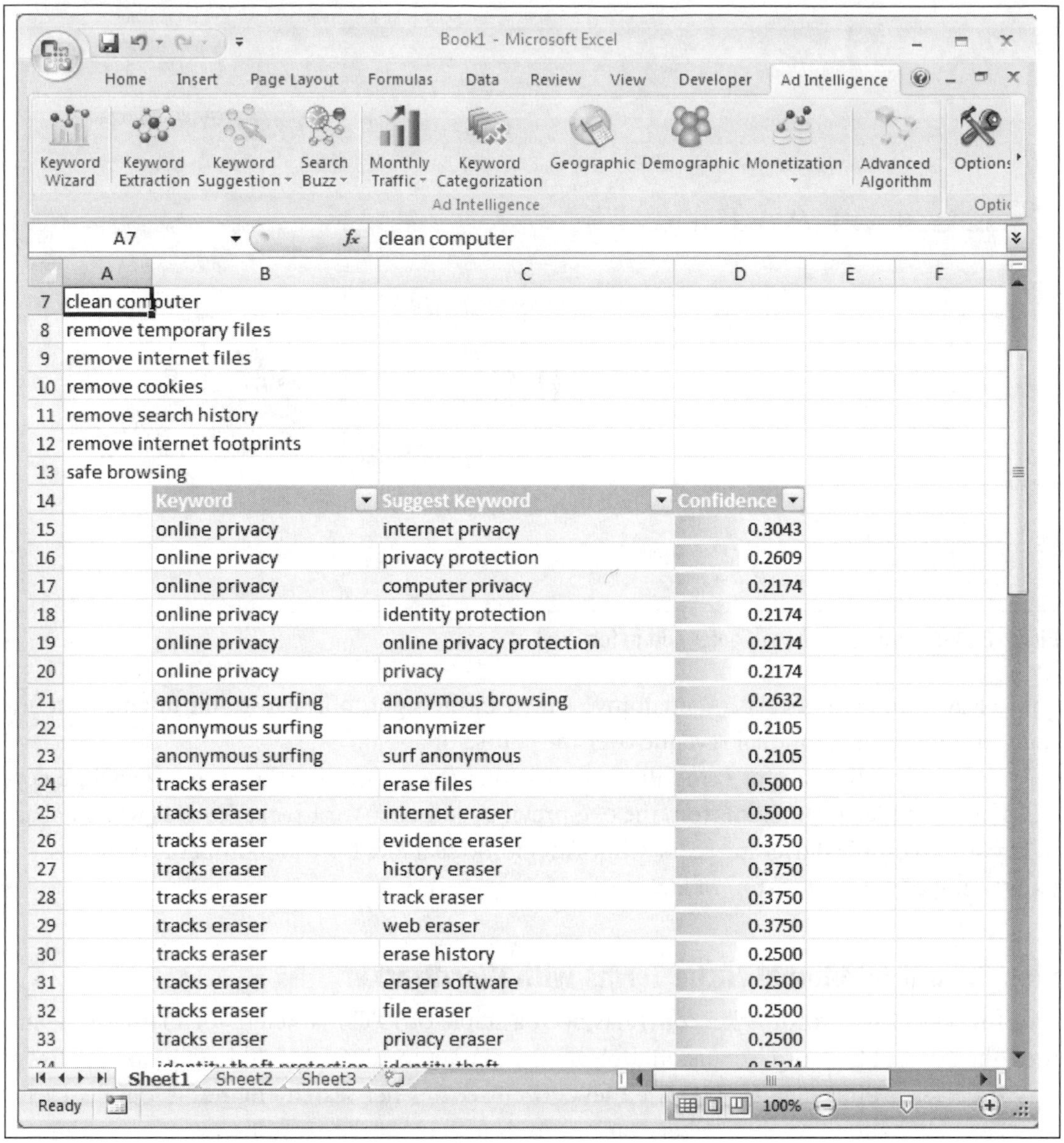

FIGURE 21-4.

Step 6: Reverse-Engineer Competitors' Keyword Lists with AdGooroo

Next, I'll show you how to use AdGooroo SEM Insight (www.adgooroo.com) to build out your keyword list using an entirely different approach. (Full disclosure: I am the founder of AdGooroo and the original creator of SEM Insight.) This is a commercial-grade tool that will allow you to dig very deeply into your competitors' keyword lists by determining where their search ads appear.

This approach is very different from that of the above tools, which attempt to look for correlations between keywords and then rank them by traffic. Instead, this tool looks for the terms that people actually type in—even if these terms only generate a handful of queries a month. If a competitor's ad appears for a term, it is highly likely that the term is relevant.

The disadvantage with this tool is that you may run across quite a few "noise" words, especially if your competitors aren't doing a good job of targeting their keywords. However, you can turn this into an advantage by noting these junk phrases and adding them to your negative list (see Chapter 23).

Let's walk through an example.

I logged into my AdGooroo account and created a new keyword group called SurfSecret. I added 79 of the common terms from the keyword list I've compiled so far, set targeting to Google US, and came back the next day.

Although one day is usually not enough time to come up with a good map of the competition (three full days is ideal), AdGooroo returned a list of my top competitors (Figure 21-5).

Show Advertisers	Show Ads			
Displaying 1 - 50 of 96 items		First | Prev | Next | Last		Display 50 ▾ items per page
Advertiser		Ranking ▲	Coverage (%)	Avg Rank
	⅂	⅂	⅂	⅂
lifelock.com		1	37.3	0.5
WinClear.com		2	33.3	1.4
consumersoftwarereviews.com		3	33.3	1.9
pc-confidential.com		4	27.5	4.0
identityguard.com		5	21.6	0.7
trustedid.com		6	21.6	1.8
consumercompare.org		7	19.6	0.2
google.com		8	19.6	0.8
consumer-reporter.net		9	19.6	1.8
idwatchdog.com		10	17.6	3.1
idarmor.com		11	19.6	4.5
premiumsafeidentity.com		12	17.6	3.9
evidence-blaster.com		13	15.7	2.9
identitytruth.com		14	13.7	2.0
protectmyid.com		15	13.7	2.0
identitytheftlabs.com		16	17.6	5.6
theidentitytheftreview.com		17	19.6	6.3
pctools.com		18	7.8	2.7
hyperdynesoftware.com		19	9.8	4.2
beawarecorporate.com		20	7.8	3.3
pcperformancetools.com		21	7.8	3.7
spectorsoft.com		22	5.9	2.4
visistat.com		23	3.9	0.2
myfasterpc.com		24	3.9	0.5

FIGURE 21-5.

Note that I didn't go to any great pains to narrow down my keyword list. It contained terms that are slightly off-target for my purposes, such as *identity theft*. As a result, there are companies on this list that aren't direct competitors (lifelock.com, google.com, etc.). This is valuable information. I clicked on each of these competitors' names in the list to see which keywords matched.

For example, I clicked on "lifelock.com" to get the following chart. The chart clearly indicates that three of the keywords in my list are probably bad matches for my campaign. The keywords *identity theft protection*, *protect credit card info*, and *steal identity*, are definitely not part of SurfSecret's value proposition, so I delete them from my list (Figure 21-6).

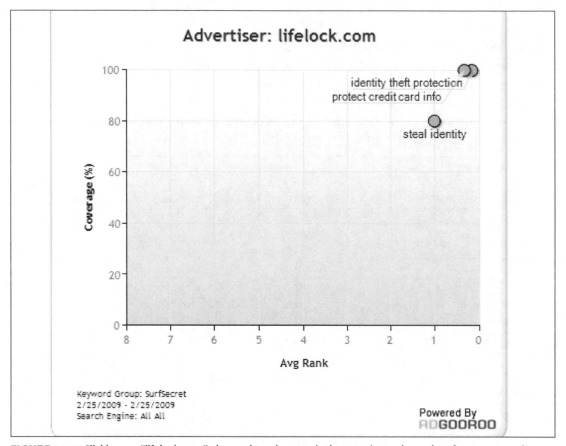

FIGURE 21-6. Clicking on "lifelock.com" shows three keywords that aren't good matches for my campaign.

It's very important to weed out off-target keywords as early as possible. Not only will these keywords increase your campaign costs while doing little to improve revenue; they will also drop your campaign clickthrough rate, potentially penalizing your ad placement.

I repeated this process to remove eight more keywords.

Next, I want to make use of the AdGooroo "Keyword Research" report to augment my list with some high-quality keyword matches.

Navigate to the "Keyword Research" report via the left navigation menu. When you get there, don't worry about the basic report. We're going to make use of the advanced version, which is found by clicking the "Search for keywords by exact URL" link (Figure 21-7).

Next, I selected a few companies that I know are direct competitors to SurfSecret (Figure 21-8).

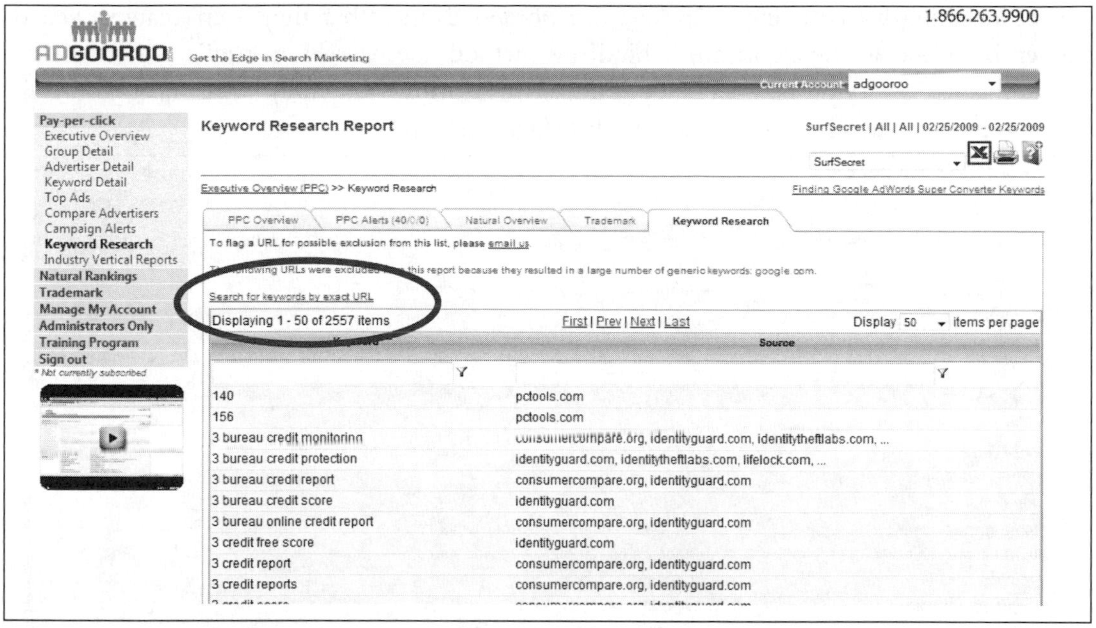

FIGURE 21-7. For now, we'll ignore the basic keyword research report. Click the highlighted link to search for specific competitors' keywords.

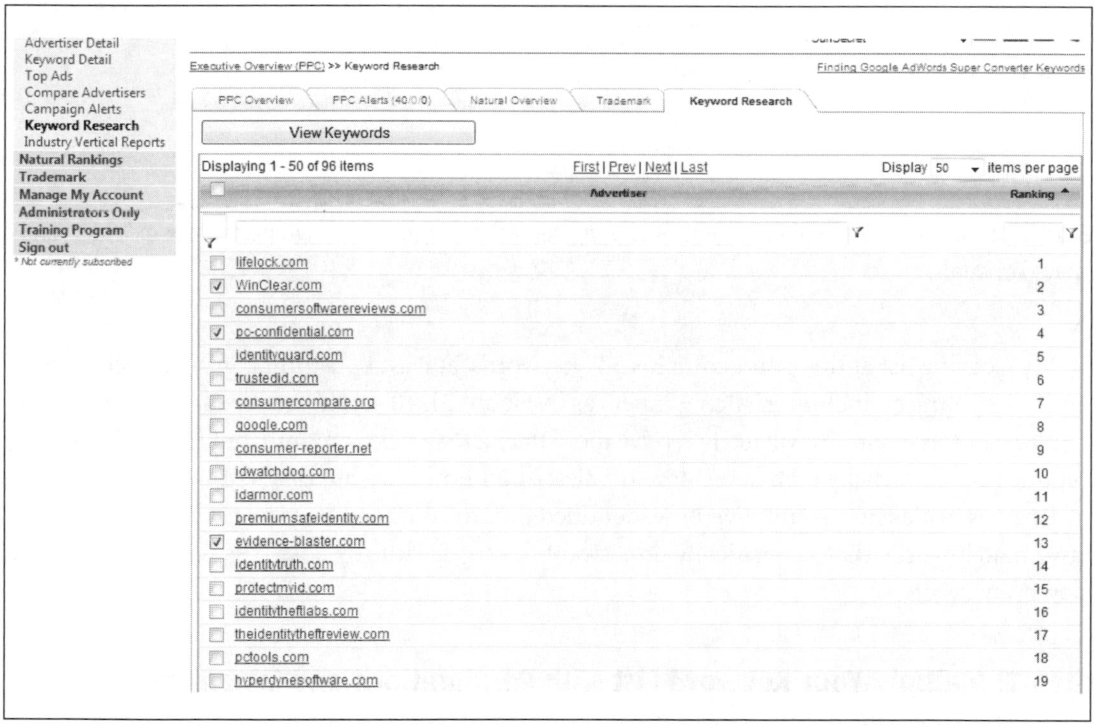

FIGURE 21-8. Select a few direct competitors. Focusing on these domains will yield the best keyword list.

The resulting list contained 326 keyword phrases. Notice that they aren't categorized or ranked by traffic, as the algorithm behind this method doesn't rely on traffic estimates. As a result, this list is very dense with "shop" and "buy" keywords. Carefully work through this list and add relevant keyword phrases to your list (Figure 21-9).

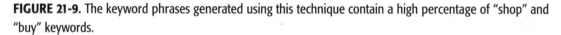

Keyword Research Report   All | All | 02/25/2009 - 02/25/2009

Executive Overview (PPC) >> Keyword Research   Finding Google AdWords Super Converter Keywords

PPC Overview   PPC Alerts (40/0/0)   Natural Overview   Trademark   **Keyword Research**

Search Again

Displaying 1 - 50 of 326 items   First | Prev | Next | Last   Display 50   items per page

Keyword	Source
1940's cleaners	evidence-blaster.com, pc-confidential.com, WinClear.com
activity connection	WinClear.com
address bar	WinClear.com
allume internet cleanup	evidence-blaster.com, pc-confidential.com
allume internet cleanup 4.0	evidence-blaster.com, pc-confidential.com
autocomplete	pc-confidential.com
best privacy software	pc-confidential.com
browser cleaner	evidence-blaster.com, pc-confidential.com
browser eraser	evidence-blaster.com, WinClear.com
cache memory	pc-confidential.com
clean browser	evidence-blaster.com, pc-confidential.com
clean computer	WinClear.com
clean cookie	WinClear.com
clean file	evidence-blaster.com
clean free hard drive	WinClear.com
clean hard drive	WinClear.com
clean hard drive data manually	WinClear.com
clean history	evidence-blaster.com, WinClear.com
clean internet	evidence-blaster.com, pc-confidential.com

FIGURE 21-9. The keyword phrases generated using this technique contain a high percentage of "shop" and "buy" keywords.

My working list at this point contains 509 keywords, at least two-thirds of them niche "shop" and "buy" phrases, including such winners as in Figure 21-10 on the next page.

None of these phrases will likely receive more than a few clicks a month, but they will probably produce an abnormally high percentage of sales. And I now have hundreds of them on my list.

Perhaps just as important, I've now identified dozens of interchangeable synonyms and negative match words that I specifically don't want to target with my ads. This will make my next step even easier.

Step 7: Multiply Your Keyword List with Permutations and Synonyms

Next we want to take those synonym lists and merge them together to create new permutations to add to our list.

Keyword Phrase	Category
Best privacy software ever	Shop (comparison)
delete sites that have visited on internet explorer	Buy (very specific phrase)
download window washer free	Buy (competitor's product)
hidden files web pages delete pc program	Buy (very specific phrase)
how do I clean my computer of past history	Buy (very specific phrase)
my history will not delete	Buy (very specific problem)
privacy software review evidence blaster	Shop (review)

FIGURE 21-10.

For instance, if we have two synonym lists as shown in Figure 21-11, we'd like to combine

List 1	List 2
Clean	My computer
Clear	Tracks
Erase	Download history
Wipe	Internet footprints
Get rid of	Internet usage
Eliminate	Browser cache
Sweep	Image cache
Hide	Cookies
Erasing	Browser history
Remove	Keyloggers
Eraser	Evidence
Cleaner	File
Cleaning	Internet history
Erasing	Address toolbar
	Browser toolbar
	History
	Internet files
	IM history

FIGURE 21-11.

them to end up with a master list of terms as shown in Figure 21-12.

Clean [X]	Erase [X]
Clean my computer	Erase my computer
Clean tracks	Erase tracks
Clean download history	Erase download history
Clean internet footprints	Erase internet footprints
Clean internet usage	Erase internet usage
Clean browser cache	Erase browser cache
Clean image cache	Erase image cache
Clean cookies	Erase cookies
Clean browser history	Erase browser history

FIGURE 21-12.

You can do this by hand, but a much easier way is to use Excel. Open up a spreadsheet and paste your lists in the first two columns (Figure 21-13).

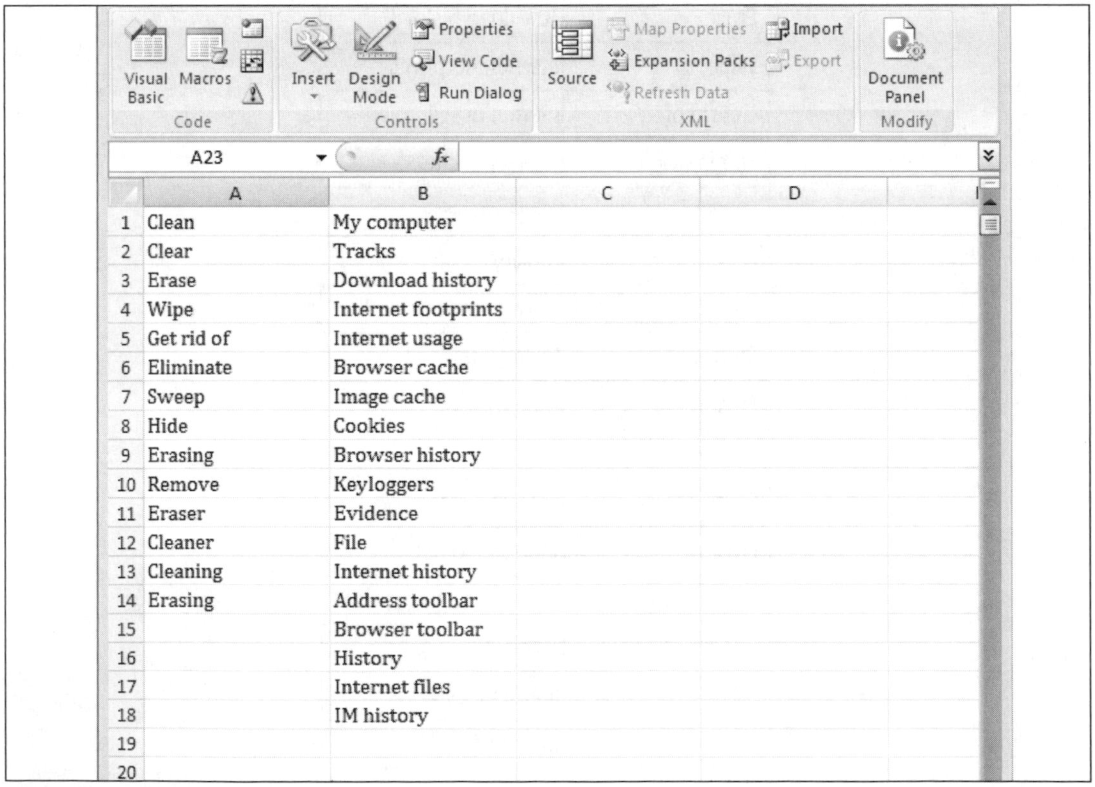

FIGURE 21-13. Paste your synonym lists into an Excel spreadsheet.

Next, you'll create a macro to do the work for you. Select the "Developer" menu item and click "Visual Basic." A blank screen will appear. Copy the following code into this window (Figure 21-4):

```vba
Sub CreateKeywordPermutations()

    Dim rngL1 As Range
    Dim rngL2 As Range
    Dim rngA As Range
    Dim rngB As Range
    Dim rngOutA As Range
    Dim rngOutB As Range

    Set rngL1 = Range("A1", Range("A1").End(xlDown))
    Set rngL2 = Range("B1", Range("B1").End(xlDown))

    Set rngOutA = Range("D1")
    Set rngOutB = Range("D" & (rngL1.Rows.Count * rngL2.Rows.Count * 2))

    For Each rngA In rngL1.Cells
        For Each rngB In rngL2.Cells
            rngOutA = rngA.Value & " " & rngB.Value
            rngOutB = rngB.Value & " " & rngA.Value
            Set rngOutA = rngOutA.Offset(1, 0)
            Set rngOutB = rngOutB.Offset(-1, 0)
        Next
    Next

End Sub
```

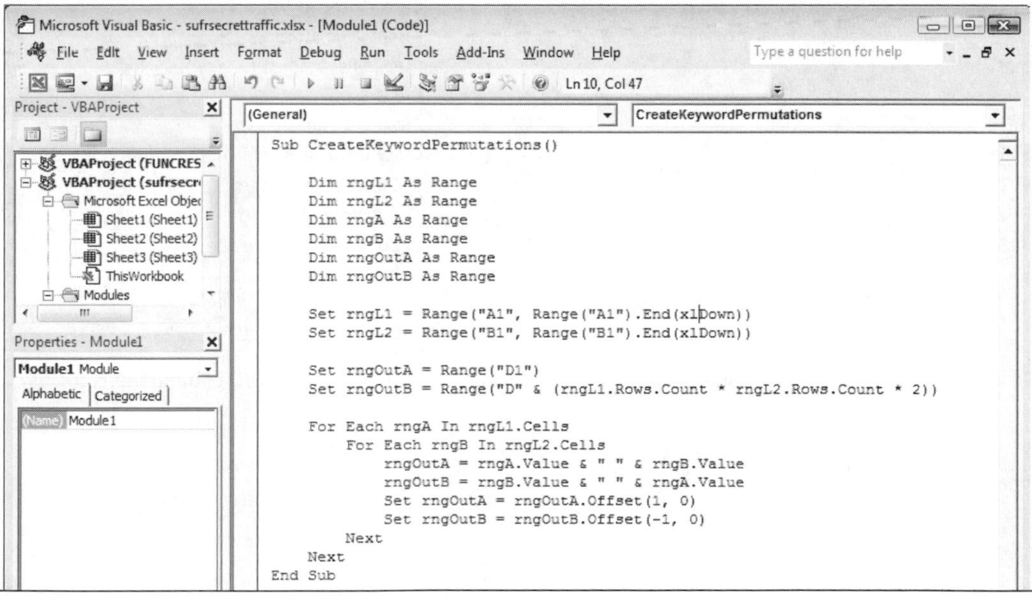

FIGURE 21-14. Type the above code into the Excel macro window.

When you're done, save the spreadsheet so you don't have to type the code in again.

Finally, run the macro by selecting "Macros" (on the Developer toolbar), then clicking "Run." Your new keyword list will appear in the fourth column of the spreadsheet (Figure 21-15).

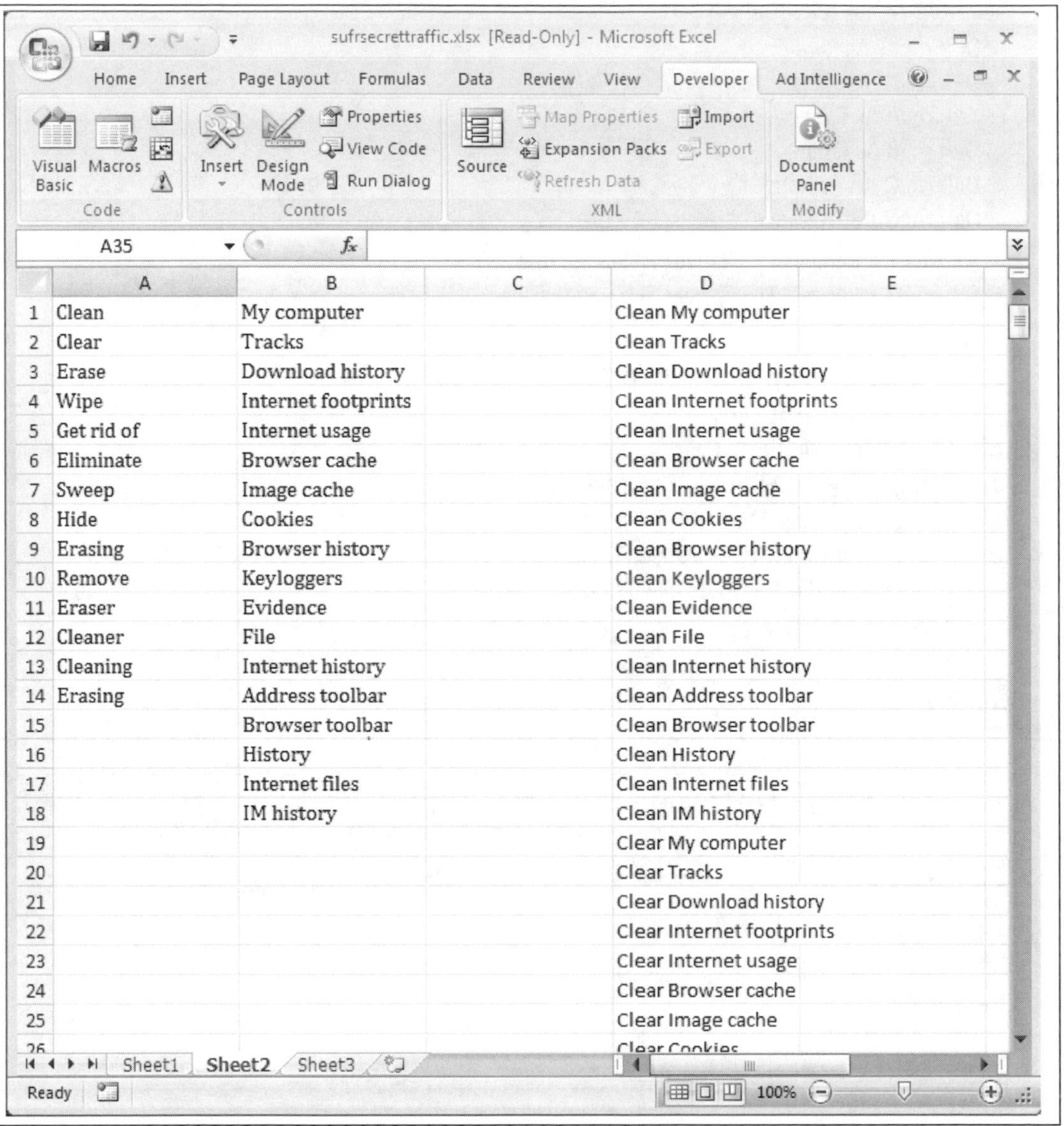

FIGURE 21-15. Our Excel spreadsheet will automatically calculate all of the keyword combinations for us.

After I completed this step, the SurfSecret list contained 1,004 keywords.

Step 8: Remove Duplicates

While you have Excel open, you can perform the final step of removing duplicate keywords from your list. Paste your entire list into the first column of a fresh spreadsheet, select the "Data" menu item, and click the "Remove Duplicates" option in the "Data Tools" section.

Excel removed 169 duplicate keywords, leaving a lengthy list of 835 behind (mostly "shop" and "buy" keywords). This is a pretty good starting point for our campaign.

SUMMARY

Choosing the keywords you're going to target is probably the most important part of running your search marketing. You should strive to develop a long list of highly specific "shop" and "buy" keywords. The best way to do this is by using a combination of elbow grease and third-party tools.

Note

1. Chart 5.20, Search Marketing Benchmark Guide 2007, MarketingSherpa.

CHAPTER 22

Planning and Structuring Your Campaign

MAKE NO MISTAKE: THE WAY YOU STRUCTURE YOUR CAMPAIGNS WILL IN NO SMALL PART influence the amount of traffic you'll be able to drive to your website from paid search.

Last year I revamped a PPC campaign for a client using the technique described in this chapter. Traffic increased by over 1,000%. Eight months later, the client reported that traffic had dropped 60%, but offered no explanation why. I quickly found that they had replaced my carefully constructed campaign with one that had a simpler structure and was "easier to manage."

The client didn't realize that the campaign was created in a particular way to ensure that every important keyword was assigned its own optimized ad. The new campaign architecture didn't make as much allowance for targeting, and the clickthrough rate suffered as a result.

Unfortunately, there's a tradeoff between convenience and performance, so you'll need to decide which is more important to you; I assume the majority of readers will opt for performance. However, if you set up your campaign using an organizational scheme such as the one we discuss next, you'll find that you can minimize the amount of additional work while maximizing your campaign's traffic-generating potential.

HOW NOT TO SET UP YOUR CAMPAIGN

There are two primary mistakes people make when setting up new campaigns.

The first of these is using too few ad groups. Ads perform best when they are targeted at a specific keyword phrase or perhaps a small group of closely related keyword phrases. Lumping all of your keywords into too few ad groups means that you'll have too few ads. This makes it virtually impossible to optimize the ad copy beyond a nominal clickthrough rate.

Ad copy optimization is one of the primary efforts you can undertake to beat your competitors, so your campaign should be set up in a way that allows you to tweak ads all the way down to the individual keyword level, if necessary.

The second mistake is failing to group closely related keywords together. This is on the opposite end of the spectrum from the first mistake we just mentioned. Sometimes first-time marketers get overzealous and assign every keyword to its own ad group. A typical campaign should have over 1,000 keywords, so they end up with over 1,000 ad groups. Although this affords a high degree of precision in tuning ads, managing the campaign becomes too cumbersome.

The solution lies somewhere in the middle: group related keywords together into a reasonable number of ad groups. Later on, keywords that drive the most traffic or sales can be broken out into their own separate groups for fine-tuning. For most campaigns, I find 20–30 ad groups to be sufficient.

START BY CATEGORIZING YOUR KEYWORDS

Begin planning your campaign not in AdWords, but in Excel. Create columns for "Category," "Keyword," "Browse," "Shop," "Buy," and "Ad Group."

Then, use the tools mentioned in the previous chapter to build an extensive list of keywords. Don't worry about categorizing them or assigning them to behavioral buckets yet. Just capture them in the keyword column.

After collecting an exhaustive list (with a minimum of 1,000 keywords), group the related keyword phrases together. There's no exact science to this (despite repeated attempts by software companies to automate the process). Just group the keywords together into whatever reasonable categories you can think of. Twenty is a nice round number to start with. If you go higher than 50, you'll probably end up spending a lot of time managing groups that may not bring in much traffic.

Next, assign each keyword to one of the three primary behavioral buckets ("browse," "shop," or "buy"). You may optionally also add a "navigational" bucket for keywords such as competitors' company names or URLs, but we generally don't recommend advertising on these terms (use your discretion).

Assigning each keyword to one of these categories is a very important step. We are going to use these buckets to split our categories into more targeted ad groups. This will substantially reduce the time needed to make our campaign profitable.

Pay close attention to any keyword in the "browse" bucket. Consider the keyword carefully: do you really need/want to advertise on this term? The traffic (and costs) will be high, but the conversions and clickthrough rates will be low. If you're not sure, then I suggest setting them aside in your initial campaign. You can always add them later.

Finally, if any landing page ideas jump out at you, jot them down in the last column.

Here's how my spreadsheet looks for SurfSecret (Figure 22-1).

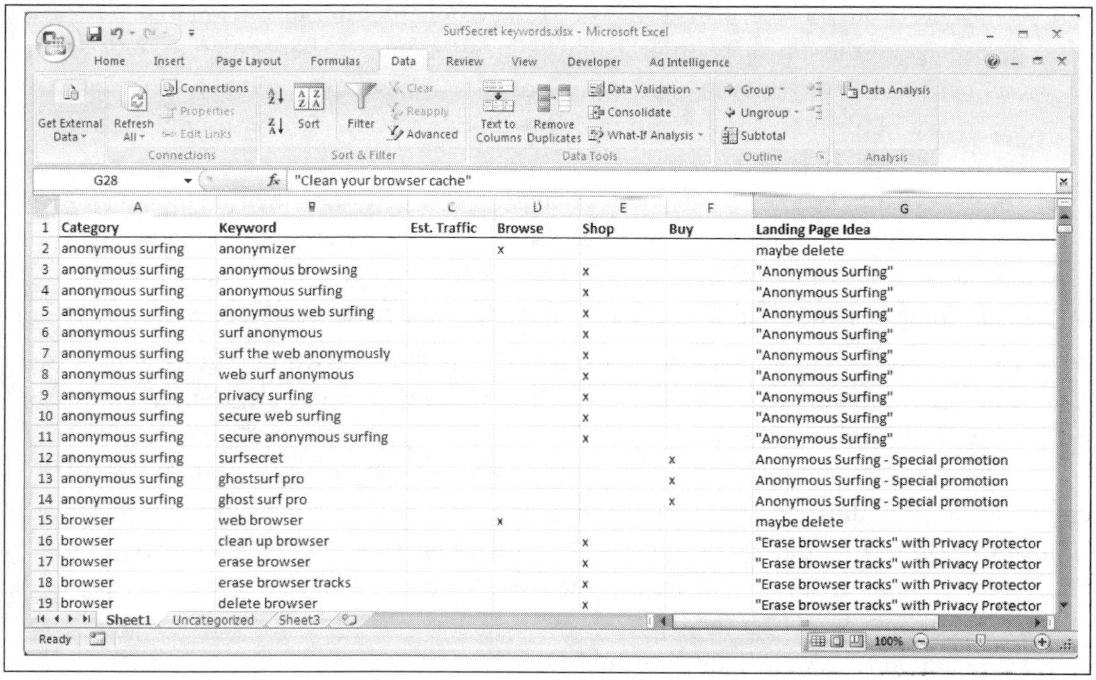

	Category	Keyword	Est. Traffic	Browse	Shop	Buy	Landing Page Idea
2	anonymous surfing	anonymizer		x			maybe delete
3	anonymous surfing	anonymous browsing			x		"Anonymous Surfing"
4	anonymous surfing	anonymous surfing			x		"Anonymous Surfing"
5	anonymous surfing	anonymous web surfing			x		"Anonymous Surfing"
6	anonymous surfing	surf anonymous			x		"Anonymous Surfing"
7	anonymous surfing	surf the web anonymously			x		"Anonymous Surfing"
8	anonymous surfing	web surf anonymous			x		"Anonymous Surfing"
9	anonymous surfing	privacy surfing			x		"Anonymous Surfing"
10	anonymous surfing	secure web surfing			x		"Anonymous Surfing"
11	anonymous surfing	secure anonymous surfing			x		"Anonymous Surfing"
12	anonymous surfing	surfsecret				x	Anonymous Surfing - Special promotion
13	anonymous surfing	ghostsurf pro				x	Anonymous Surfing - Special promotion
14	anonymous surfing	ghost surf pro				x	Anonymous Surfing - Special promotion
15	browser	web browser		x			maybe delete
16	browser	clean up browser			x		"Erase browser tracks" with Privacy Protector
17	browser	erase browser			x		"Erase browser tracks" with Privacy Protector
18	browser	erase browser tracks			x		"Erase browser tracks" with Privacy Protector
19	browser	delete browser			x		"Erase browser tracks" with Privacy Protector

FIGURE 22-1.

With this spreadsheet, I have a pretty good idea of the number of landing pages I'll need. I've also eliminated a number of questionable terms (including *computer hard drives* and *computer tips*). And most importantly, I've created a master plan for my starting list of ad groups.

THIS IS THE BLUEPRINT FOR YOUR ENTIRE CAMPAIGN

I ended up with 18 categories, each consisting of a mix of "browse," "shop," and "buy" keywords. So this means I will start my campaign with up to 54 ad groups.

Why so many?

If you were to manage each of these terms individually, it would be far too much work. It would be a full-time job (and then some).

On the other hand, if you put all of your terms in one group, your ads and landing pages wouldn't be very targeted. You'd also likely end up with a "one size fits all" bid price.

So we need a happy medium. In our case, we made an attempt to break out our phrases into the three categories:

- **"Browse" keywords.** These are terms we're not so sure about. They will likely generate high traffic and costs, but the lack of specificity means that we're going to have lower click-through and conversion rates. *Web browser* is a phrase that falls in this category. If we do decide to keep these terms, we don't want to bid very high for them.
- **"Shop" keywords.** These terms will generate a decent amount of traffic as well, but a good percentage of these people are probably looking for "how to" information, reviews, and comparisons. Nevertheless, a good portion of them can be convinced to buy. We'd be willing to pay a little more for these terms and write special ads. We may even want to experiment with special landing pages.
- **"Buy" keywords.** These are the phrases that people type in when they are looking for what we have to offer (*surfsecret, image cache cleaner, privacy software*). Each of these keyword phrases indicates a likely buyer. We should be willing to pay a lot for these visitors. We're also willing to write highly specific ads and even create custom landing pages.

As you can see, we want to spend the most time on the "buy" keywords, but we don't want to ignore the "shop" keywords completely. It's a lot easier to work on your campaign when you start off with these terms in separate ad groups.

Could we get by with just three ad groups, one for each category? In a pinch, we probably could. But some of these terms have different implications. Your landing pages and ad copy will probably be completely different for the "buy" phrases *browser cache eraser* and *internet history eraser*, even though these terms mean roughly the same thing. As we'll see when we get to the chapter on ad copy, the ads for these phrases will be best served with different headlines. This is much easier to do if they are in different ad groups.

SUMMARY

The long-term potential of your campaign is determined by the keywords you choose and how you assign them to ad groups. The vast majority of advertisers dump their keywords into arbitrary ad groups. Don't be one of them. Instead, organize your keywords within Excel according to category and behavioral bucket. This blueprint will serve as the foundation for your campaign and will allow you to outperform the vast majority of competitors from the very start.

CHAPTER 23

Cut Campaign Waste with Keyword Matching

M OST ADVERTISING CAMPAIGNS HAVE AN ENORMOUS AMOUNT OF WASTE. WITH OTHER channels, you have to live with unwanted slippage, but not so in search because of a technique called *keyword matching*.

Keyword matching is an important method of cost control that allows you to refine your ad targeting and improve your returns. It works by eliminating unprofitable traffic that comes from your ads showing up for searches not closely related to your offering.

Mastering this technique offers you some of the best returns on time spent. You can audit a typical campaign in under an hour, and you shouldn't need to do it more than once every few months (if that). I've recently audited one of my larger campaigns and was able to cut 70% of my spend after the first round and over 60% in the second. That's an 88% reduction in spend with no loss in sales. Excited yet?

GOOGLE AND BING MATCH TYPES
Broad Match

This is the default match setting. When you enter a keyword phrase in AdWords or Live

Search without any additional punctuation, your ads will be served for all searches that contain the keywords in your phrase (in any order), as well as any likely synonyms or plurals.

For instance, if you use broad match on the keyword phrase *plasma television* (without quotes), your ad will appear when people search for *plasma TV*, *plasma display*, *televisionplasma*, *plasma televisions*, or even *buy 42-inch plasma televisions*.

We use broad match for most keywords in our campaign. However, it can sometimes generate unwanted clicks, driving up your total cost.

Phrase Match

A useful technique for refining your targeting is to incorporate phrase match. Do this by surrounding your keyword phrase in quotes.

Your ads will then appear only for searches that contain your target keyword phrase. Additional keywords may appear before or after, but your exact phrase must appear in the search query.

For instance, if you use phrase match on *plasma television,* your ads will appear for *buy plasma television* but not for *plasma 42" television*.

Phrase matching results in less traffic than broad matching, but the clickthrough (and sometimes conversion) rate is usually higher.

Exact Match

Another major match type is exact match. To enable exact matching for a keyword, enclose it in square brackets, e.g., *[plasma television]*.

Your ads will then appear only when people type your exact phrase. Plurals, synonyms, or additional words will not trigger your ads.

The volume with this match type will be the lowest, but the clickthrough rates can be absolutely astounding (15% is not unusual). If you utilize exact matching with a "superconverter" keyword (see Chapter 27) and some highly tuned ad copy, the result can often drive the majority of your search revenues.

Negative Match

This match type is used when you have a specific word you know you want to filter out. For instance, we broad match on *keyword* in our advertising. This ensures that we show up when people search on phrases such as *keywords for dentists*.

However, it turns out that this phrase drives the majority of its traffic from programmers looking for lists of reserved keywords—definitely not our target market. We found that we could filter out most of this traffic by negative matching the term *java* (a programming language).

To do this, you simply need to precede the unwanted term with a negative sign and add it to your campaign or ad group. In our case, it looks like this: *-java*.

Virtually every campaign can see a dramatic improvement in results by using this technique.

▼

Advanced Negative Matching: Boxing In, Boxing Out

Matt Van Wagner
Find Me Faster
www.findmefaster.com

In the NBA, great centers know that boxing out and boxing in under the boards are key to winning games. One of my favorite tactics in PPC tactics is to use negative keywords both to box out ad impressions and unwanted clicks and to box in clicks so that the right ads get shown.

Boxing Out

Much has already been written about using negatives to keep your ads from showing for keywords that are not related to your searches. By reducing ad impressions, you keep your CTRs up, which improves your quality score and keeps your ad spend under control by reducing unproductive clicks.

Boxing In

A second, less used application for negative keywords is boxing in clicks to make sure that only the right keyword matches to a specific search query.

It is very common that an AdWords account has closely related keywords across multiple ad groups, all of which could qualify for the ad auction for a single search query. When that happens, these keywords compete against each other for placement in Ad Rank auction, and unless you use negative keywords to prevent a match, the search engines can pick the keyword they like best—which could simply be the one with the highest bid and not necessarily the one you'd prefer to present on that search query.

In this case, you can use negative keywords to box in the choice of keywords to the one you want.

Let's say you have three ad groups, each with one broad match keyword, like this:

Ad Group	Key Word
Stone	Stone Siding
Rock	Rock Siding
Faux Stone	Faux Stone Siding

On the user query *fake stone siding*, any of these three keywords may trigger ads. By adding in negatives, you can force the logic so that only one match can be made:

Ad Group	Key Word
Stone	Stone siding -faux -fake
Rock	Rock siding -stone
Faux Stone	Faux Stone Siding

Instead of three possible matches, Google now only has one, which is the one we forced. Boxing in like this lets you control which ad displays and thereby tailor your bids, ad copy, and landing pages to your best advantage; it augments your broad, phrase, and exact match tactics.

Negative Exact Match

Years ago, I discovered a technique that even my Google AdWords rep didn't know about—the negative exact match.

We discovered that over 99% of the conversions from the term *keyword* came only when there was another word in the search phrase. We wanted to see what would happen if we stopped advertising on the term *keyword* but continued advertising on longer search phrases containing that word.

We found that we were able to do this by adding the term *-[keyword]* to our campaign. The minus sign indicates a negative match while the square brackets indicate exact matching. Combining the two prevents our ads from showing up when people search on *keyword* by itself.

The day after we made this change, our ad spend dropped by 50% while sales stayed strong. This is a powerful technique that I advise everyone to explore.

YAHOO! MATCH TYPES
Advanced Match (Yahoo! Only)

Yahoo! offers only two match types for advertisers. The Advanced Match is a bit of a misnomer because it's the default setting. It's essentially equivalent to the Google AdWords broad match, in that it will also match common misspellings and plurals.

However, there is one key difference: It may trigger a match on any of the keywords in your ad (!) or website (!!). This can definitely introduce some unwanted traffic to your campaign.

Standard Match (Yahoo! Only)

Yahoo! Standard Match narrows a match to the searcher's exact query order, making it similar to a Google phrase match. It will also match common misspellings and plurals as well as words in your ad.

WHICH MATCH TYPES SHOULD YOU USE?

As you progress through the match types from least restrictive to most restrictive (e.g., Broad ➜ Phrase ➜ Exact), an interesting thing happens. Although you'll receive less traffic, your click-through rate will increase dramatically (your conversion rates may also increase if you are using a well-targeted landing page).

This can lead to confusion, and newcomers to search marketing sometimes try to guess which of the match types they should be using. Fortunately, there's no need to choose. Not only can you use all three, you should.

So instead of just entering *Las Vegas vacations* into your PPC campaign, you'll enter the same keyword three times:

- *Las Vegas vacations* (broad)
- "*Las Vegas vacations*" (phrase)
- *[Las Vegas vacations]* (exact)

When you specify all three match types, the search engines will automatically choose the best one. This will allow you to maximize both your search volume and your clickthrough rates.

A SIMPLE REFINEMENT TO YOUR SPREADSHEET THAT WILL SAVE YOU HOURS OF WORK

In the previous chapter, we created a spreadsheet with seven columns. We'll now add two more columns to automatically add the brackets and quotes around your base keywords. This will save you the time of manually retyping each keyword three times.

Here's what you need to do:

Insert two new columns to the right of the "Keyword" column

Name the first of these columns "Phrase Match." Enter the following formula into cell C2 (note that the four quotation marks in a row are intentional):

=CONCATENATE("""",B2,"""")

Name the second of these columns "Exact Match." Enter the following formula into cell D2:

=CONCATENATE("[",B2,"]")

Select the cells C2 and D2 and copy them down to the end of your spreadsheet. The easiest way to do this is to double-click the tiny black square at the lower right of your selection. Another way to do it is to press CTRL-C to copy the selection, select the remaining cells in the columns, and then press CTRL-V to paste them.

My SurfSecret spreadsheet now looks like this:

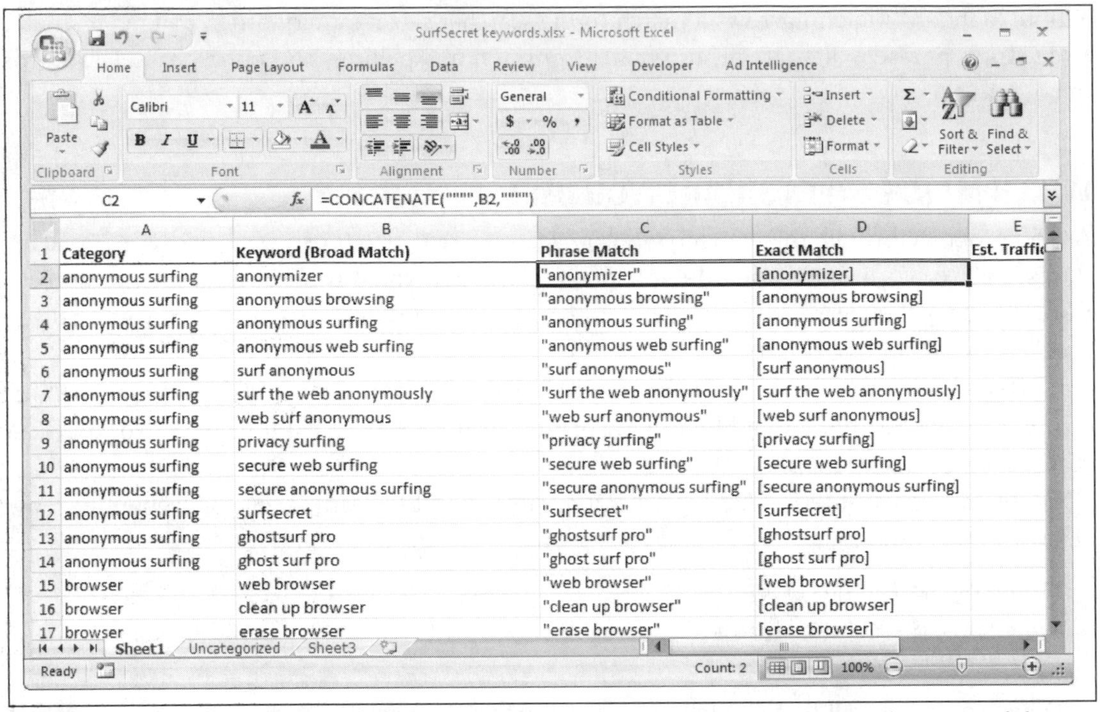

Category	Keyword (Broad Match)	Phrase Match	Exact Match	Est. Traffic
anonymous surfing	anonymizer	"anonymizer"	[anonymizer]	
anonymous surfing	anonymous browsing	"anonymous browsing"	[anonymous browsing]	
anonymous surfing	anonymous surfing	"anonymous surfing"	[anonymous surfing]	
anonymous surfing	anonymous web surfing	"anonymous web surfing"	[anonymous web surfing]	
anonymous surfing	surf anonymous	"surf anonymous"	[surf anonymous]	
anonymous surfing	surf the web anonymously	"surf the web anonymously"	[surf the web anonymously]	
anonymous surfing	web surf anonymous	"web surf anonymous"	[web surf anonymous]	
anonymous surfing	privacy surfing	"privacy surfing"	[privacy surfing]	
anonymous surfing	secure web surfing	"secure web surfing"	[secure web surfing]	
anonymous surfing	secure anonymous surfing	"secure anonymous surfing"	[secure anonymous surfing]	
anonymous surfing	surfsecret	"surfsecret"	[surfsecret]	
anonymous surfing	ghostsurf pro	"ghostsurf pro"	[ghostsurf pro]	
anonymous surfing	ghost surf pro	"ghost surf pro"	[ghost surf pro]	
browser	web browser	"web browser"	[web browser]	
browser	clean up browser	"clean up browser"	[clean up browser]	
browser	erase browser	"erase browser"	[erase browser]	

FIGURE 23-1. Our spreadsheet now contains two additional columns with the phrase and exact match keywords.

SUMMARY

Keyword matching is a powerful technique you can use to eliminate unwanted impressions and clicks and thus reduce your costs. Utilize all of the matching options at your disposal to eliminate bad traffic and maximize those clicks that have the highest chance of converting to a sale.

Create Your
Ad Groups

Y OU'RE FINALLY READY TO SET UP YOUR CAMPAIGN! CREATE YOUR AD GROUPS WITHIN THE
Google AdWords interface (or better yet, use the Google AdWords Desktop
Editor—see the power tip). Create one group for each unique combination of
category and "browse"/"shop"/"buy" bucket. If you decide to skip the "browse"
keywords for now, that's a third less work you'll need to do. (See Figure 24-1.)

For instance, here are some of the ad groups I created for the SurfSecret campaign:

- Anonymous Surfing—Shop
- Anonymous Surfing—Buy
- Cookies—Shop
- Cookies—Buy
- Footprints—Shop
- Footprints—Buy

What About Ad Copy?

If you're using the AdWords reporting interface to enter your ad groups, it will ask you to

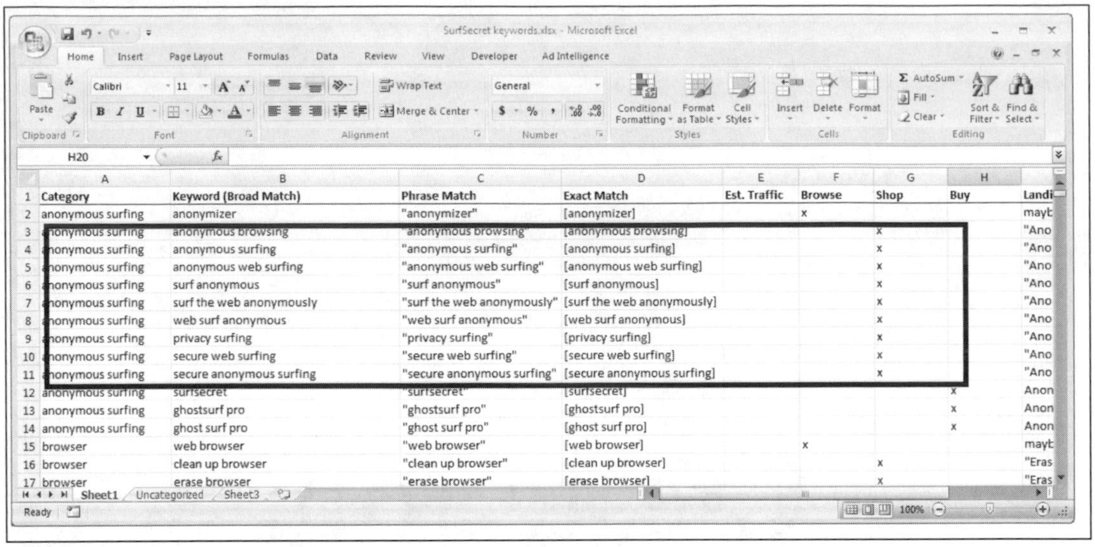

FIGURE 24-1. Your completed spreadsheet becomes the basis for your ad groups. For example, the keywords outlined above were included in the "Anonymous Surfing–Shop" group.

enter ad copy. For now, just enter some placeholder ad copy so you can complete the process and get your campaign set up.

If you are in a hurry to get your campaign started, you can begin with this generic ad copy. However, I strongly recommend first reading over the later chapters on writing targeted ad copy and at least starting off with reasonably targeted (albeit unoptimized) ad copy. The first two weeks of your campaign are very important, particularly with Google AdWords, because it's during this time that your campaign will be benchmarked against the competition. Scoring decent clickthrough rates early on will result in higher quality scores later. This, in turn, will translate to more traffic at a cheaper average cost-per-click.

Power Tip

Setting up new campaigns in the Google AdWords interface is a slow, tedious process. I prefer to use the Google AdWords Editor (a free download). This tool is faster, and you don't have to specify ad copy when creating your groups with it.

YOUR CAMPAIGN WILL CONTINUE TO EVOLVE OVER TIME

Realize from the beginning that your work doesn't stop here. By starting with a blueprint, you've cut months of work from your learning curve (and have likely saved yourself the extra work of having to later start your campaign over from scratch as it continues to grow).

However, over the next several months, you'll likely discover new keywords, better ad copy, and breakthrough landing pages. You'll need to make extensive changes to your campaign structure to accommodate these new discoveries.

The most common situation you'll face is that your initial guesses on how to properly group related keywords together into ad groups were way off. You'll handle this with a technique called "Peel & Stick."

The Peel & Stick Technique Explained

Bryan Todd
Co-author, *The Ultimate Guide to Google AdWords*
www.adwordsbook.com

Peel & Stick is the magic fundamental key to everything Google and, to be frank, all things Internet. It's as basic to AdWords as dribbling and shooting are to basketball, as "buy low, sell high" is to trading, as middle C is to playing the piano. It's a trusted friend, a familiar way of life to anyone, anywhere, who makes any living at all with pay-per-click.

Peel & Stick is, very simply, peeling an important keyword out of an ad group and sticking it into another (or a new) ad group with a pair of ads better matched for it.

It's what you do when you want a higher clickthrough rate and lower costs.

It's how you keep your message laser-targeted to every person who sees your ad and every person who comes through your sales funnel.

Peel & Stick is first about ads and keywords—but it can also be about ads and domains, or about keywords and landing pages. More on that below.

Some weeks ago, I went online looking for cycling jerseys. On summer evenings I practically live on my bicycle, and I prefer riding during the hour or two around dusk, so I needed a jersey that was brightly colored to make me visible to evening traffic. And the style had to fit my taste.

So I went searching on Google, hoping to find a series of sites that would give me a nice array I could choose from. My keyword? "Cycling jerseys." Clear and simple.

I was shocked at what I found … or rather, didn't find. One ad announced "sporting gear." Another, "cycling shoes." Still another, "athletic jerseys." And another, "cycling gear." (Promising though it seemed at first, that one took me to a page about helmets, gloves, shorts, and shoe straps. No jerseys.)

One solitary ad at the very top offered "cycling jerseys." So it got my click … and I stayed.

It's worth noting that Google put that ad up top, front and center. Its performance over time in earning clicks had clearly told Google that it was relevant—the perfect match for the perfect keyword. Some smart advertiser had used Peel & Stick the right way. So Google rewarded the person by sticking their ad at the top. (And they most likely gave them lower click prices as well—another benefit of a high quality score.)

Peel & Stick is a process, not an event. You first turn on your traffic and then do Peel & Stick over time as you watch and see which keywords work for you and which ones yet don't.

The 95/5 Rule will instantly take over once your traffic is running: Ninety-five percent of your impressions and clicks will come from just 5% of your keywords. So at first Peel & Stick is just for that top 5%—the words that matter most.

In any ad group, there are keywords that belong and keywords that don't. Some are merely mismatches for the ads you've got, and will do far better in another ad group with ads of their own. Others are a waste of time and money and bring impressions with no clicks or clicks with no sales, and it's best to just get rid of them.

Here's an ad we ran back when we opened our very first Google account:

> ### PROSPECTING STINKS
> Telemarketing Annoys People
> Guerilla Marketing Is King
> www.PerryMarshall.com

And here are some of the keywords we tried with it:

		Keyword	Status	Max. CPC	Clicks	Impr. ↓	CTR ⑦
☐	●	**Total - all keywords**			597	99,854	0.60%
☐	●	prospecting	🗩 Eligible	$0.40	214	20,575	1.04%
☐	✖	telemarketing	🗩 Deleted	$0.00	85	14,715	0.58%
☐	✖	sales training	🗩 Deleted	$0.00	26	7,447	0.35%
☐	✖	telemarketers	🗩 Deleted	$0.00	37	6,492	0.57%
☐	✖	marketing	🗩 Deleted	$0.00	23	5,023	0.46%
☐	✖	marketing consultant	🗩 Deleted	$0.00	21	4,085	0.51%

You can see how many we deleted from the ad group. And you can see why: they're not used in the ad, and they're getting CTRs of far below 1.0%. They got peeled and stuck, so now they're in other ad groups with better ads, getting far more clicks.

What's left are keywords that *are* used in the ad in some form, and which get CTRs well above 1.0%:

		Keyword	Status	Max. CPC	Clicks	Impr. ↓	CTR (?)
☐	●	**Total - all keywords**			**597**	**99,854**	**0.60%**
☐	●	prospecting	💬 Eligible	$0.40	214	20,575	1.04%
☐	●	sales prospecting	💬 Eligible First page bid estimate: $1.25	$0.45	7	199	3.52%
☐	●	prospect list	💬 Eligible First page bid estimate: $3.00	$0.45	6	112	5.36%
☐	●	prospecting letter	💬 Eligible	$0.45	1	89	1.12%
☐	●	business prospect	💬 Eligible	$0.45	0	56	0.00%
☐	●	sale prospecting	💬 Eligible	$0.45	0	18	0.00%
☐	●	prospecting system	💬 Eligible First page bid estimate: $0.55	$0.45	0	18	0.00%
☐	●	find prospect	💬 Eligible	$0.45	0	13	0.00%
☐	●	prospecting list	💬 Eligible First page bid	$0.45	0	11	0.00%

(Notice the keywords lower down the resulting list. Some of them don't belong, but they don't have enough impressions to matter, so we didn't bother removing them.)

If you do this right, your CTR will go up, your quality score will go up, your per-click cost will go down, and Google will serve your ads more often.

Once you've done this, you may find that even in your new ad groups, there are *still* keywords that could use Peel & Stick even further. I work with clients all the time for whom this is the case, especially when they're just getting started out. They're often surprised at my suggestion.

"You mean, do this even further?"

Yes, my friend, do this even further still. Your job is never completely done. In our example above, there are a couple of terms that I bet we could write even better ads for and get better CTRs on, such as "prospect list" or "prospecting letter." So those are next up for testing.

When Do I Do Peel & Stick?

Peel & Stick is for keywords that meet three criteria:

They get a high enough volume of impressions for it to matter.

They're getting a much lower CTR than they ought to be (especially if the CTR is significantly below 1.0%).

You're convinced that the right ad match will make all the difference.

How Can I Make Peel & Stick Work Best for Me?

The easiest, quickest application of Peel & Stick is to write an ad that uses your keyword in the headline. Of course, that can only happen if your keywords are grouped together as tightly as possible. Doing this will almost instantly increase your quality score.

But Peel & Stick is not just about echoing keywords in headlines. It's about saying to your prospect what he's really thinking—which changes from keyword to keyword. Over time, you can get to know some of your keywords so well that you'll know exactly what lines two and three need to say for *this* keyword rather than for that *other* keyword over there, above and beyond what you merely say in the headline of the ad.

Let's say you were bidding on "lose 10 pounds" and "lose 10 pounds fast." Both keywords were in the same ad group, but you did your homework and discovered that the latter searchers were largely people planning on an upcoming class reunion. You would do Peel & Stick on the second keyword and write an ad like this:

```
┌─────────────────────────────┐
│    LOSE 10 POUNDS FAST       │
│  Fit into those new clothes and │
│    look great for that reunion  │
│    www.XYZWeightLoss.com        │
└─────────────────────────────┘
```

Doing It Everywhere

The magic of Peel & Stick is that it applies everywhere. You can Peel & Stick keywords with new ads. You can do Peel & Stick with landing pages, and start creating ad groups that send to pages that are laser-targeted just for specific high-traffic keywords in your list.

Eventually, as you get into doing placement targeting as well, you'll discover that peeling and sticking placements (i.e., domain names and URLs) is virtually no different than with keywords.

And creating separate content versus search campaigns is yet another form of Peel & Stick. Doing so gives you separate data. And as you test new ads and ideas, you discover over time that "what works" slowly evolves in a different direction on the content network than on Google search.

With Peel & Stick, what your customers are searching for they find, and find instantly. That makes the cash register ring. It makes Google happy. Most importantly, it makes your customer happy.

I should know. I got my cycling jersey. If it weren't for Peel & Stick, I might still be looking.

SUMMARY

By completing the steps up to this point, you've done more to ensure the success of your campaign than the vast majority of search advertisers. You've organized your campaign in a manner that can grow over time and won't end up a confusing mass of disorganized ad groups. Furthermore, you'll be able to quickly spot potential traffic and revenue opportunities, break them out into their own dedicated ad groups using the Peel & Stick technique, and take advantage of specialized ad copy and landing pages that can far outperform anything the competition can throw at you.

CHAPTER 25

Monitoring Your Campaign Performance

Y OU WOULDN'T RUN YOUR BUSINESS WITHOUT OCCASIONALLY LOOKING AT YOUR INCOME statement and balance sheet, would you? Yet you would be surprised at how many small business advertisers rarely take more than a casual look at their online advertising campaigns.

The next few chapters will focus on the numbers side of pay-per-click advertising. If math isn't your thing, don't worry! We'll boil it down to only the essential statistics that you'll need to keep an eye on to properly manage your campaign.

WHY IT'S IMPORTANT TO STAY ON TOP OF YOUR CAMPAIGN DATA

Knowing your overall campaign data will help you answer questions like these:

- What's a reasonable clickthrough rate to expect for my ads?
- How much should I (or could I) be spending each month on paid search?
- What's the maximum revenue I could expect each month from my paid search campaign?
- Is my advertising in this particular keyword hurting or helping me?

There's no way to answer these questions without a working knowledge of how your campaign has performed in the past. And, believe me, these things are important to know.

The first thing a high-priced agency or consultant will do is analyze your past data to get an understanding of what you've done and how much better they can do in the future (and how much they can charge you).

Along with the behavioral model, this data serves as the foundation for everything that comes later. Without it, you'll never be able to make an informed decision about your campaign. With it, your eyes will open to problems and opportunities that were invisible before.

KEY STATISTICS TO WATCH

- Your average daily and monthly campaign spend
- Your average impression share and coverage—the percentage of search engine users who are seeing your ads (also known as reach)
- The number of visitors (clicks) you typically receive, on both a daily and monthly basis
- Your average clickthrough rate—or CTR—the percentage of people who see your ads and actually click them
- Your average conversion rate—the percentage of visitors to your site who buy from you
- Your spend relative to that of your competitors (optional, but highly recommended)

Typical Daily and Monthly Spend

The two most important statistics you need to track are your daily and monthly campaign spend.

This will help you answer questions such as:

- Are you spending $10 a day or $100?
- How has your campaign spend changed over the past month?
- What does a normal month look like?

Start by looking at your absolute dollar spend every day (or try to). If you don't do this, you may be in for some rude surprises.

A few years ago, I was mining my server logs to find new keyword phrases to target. One of the keyword phrases was *Flooder.AKE*, a computer virus that was rapidly spreading over the internet. After noticing that no other advertisers were targeting this phrase, I added it to my campaign with a modest $0.15 bid.

Three days later I discovered that my tactic had worked too well and my site was flooded with new visitors. My campaign spend increased from $200 per day to over $2,500! Had I been more diligent, I would have saved myself a massive AdWords bill.

It's also a good idea to maintain a trending chart. This will help you distinguish between normal daily fluctuations and abnormal ones. A typical trending chart is shown in Figure 25-1. With it, you can see that the costs are usually highest in the first half of the week and trend down into the weekends (indicated by the shaded vertical bars). The chart also tells us that while our typical spend is $40, it's perfectly normal for daily costs to fluctuate between $20 and $60. Anything outside that range should set the alarm bells off (Figure 25-1).

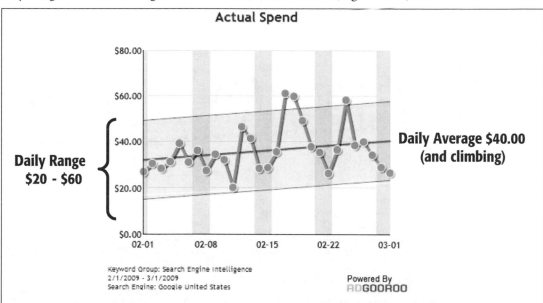

FIGURE 25-1. Use monthly spend charts to find your average daily spend, the normal range, and trends.

Impression Share and Coverage

Impression share is the percentage of the available search impressions in which your ads appear across all of your keywords. Coverage is similar, except that it doesn't take traffic into account and can be used on individual keywords. These metrics tell you how much traffic you're leaving on the table and are so important that we devoted an entire chapter to them earlier.

While impression share is nice to know, I find coverage to be more useful because it tells you exactly where any problems lie.

Daily/Monthly Clicks

You'll also want to track both the daily and monthly clicks that you're receiving from your PPC campaigns. Just as we discussed with campaign costs, you need to be able to distinguish between normal daily fluctuations and trends either up or down.

How to Use Impression Share

I use impression share for one purpose: to monitor the overall health of my campaign. If it drops below 70%, I start digging for answers.

Figure 25-2 is an example of a monthly chart showing clicks. They are highest in the beginning part of the week and trend down into the weekend. Clicks often mirror costs, but not always. If they diverge significantly, you should drill into your historical CTR to see if there are any interesting patterns there.

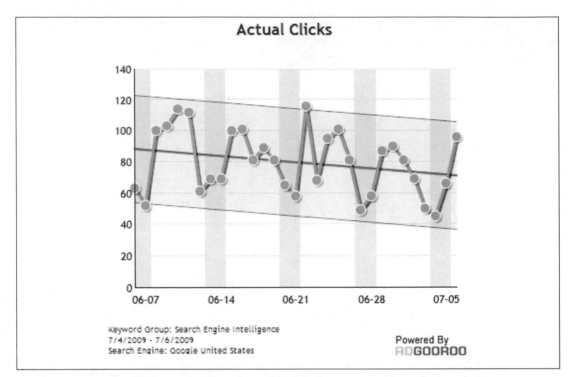

FIGURE 25-2. You should also track daily and monthly clicks from your paid search campaigns.

Average Clickthrough Rate

Having charts of your costs and clicks is helpful, but it doesn't give you the whole picture. It's very easy to miss important changes in your campaign if you try to eyeball the charts against one another. For this reason, we also want to track the average daily clickthrough rate.

In the next sample chart, you can see that the daily clickthrough rate is decreasing (the blue band indicates a statistically significant trend). This isn't at all obvious from the previous two charts. This indicates that something may possibly be wrong with this campaign and we need to dig deeper to find the root cause (Figure 25-3).

Average Conversion Rate

The final "must-have" statistic is average website conversion rate (attributed to PPC traffic). This figure adds color to your overall website sales.

If your website pulled in twice the revenue this month than last, you might just pat yourself on the back and move on. Before you do, though, be sure to check out the average conversion rate. If it lags behind your sales, you may be missing out on something big.

In 2007, I worked on a site that was generating over $15 million a year in sales. One weekend, the average conversion rate in the United Kingdom dropped dramatically while the overall website sales remained in the normal range. Upon further investigation, it turned out that a minor development change on the website had resulted in endless loops in the shopping cart, but only

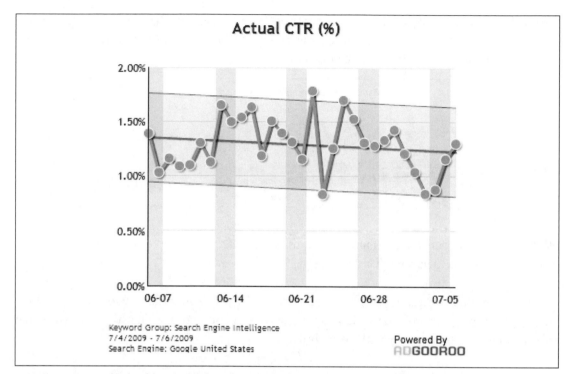

FIGURE 25-3. Monitoring historical CTR is another way to spot potential problems in your campaign.

for that country. I never would have noticed this problem had I not been paying attention to the average conversion rate.

Competitors' Spend

This last metric has recently bubbled into the top tier of statistics I keep a close eye on. As mentioned in Chapter 19, watching what levers your competitors are pulling can give you valuable insights into their businesses.

If you see a long-time competitor increase their bids, it's often a sign that something is working (the same does not hold true for brand-new competitors, who may simply be trying to figure out the optimal position for their campaigns). Check their landing pages for new products, feature improvements, or even new layouts and copy.

If their bids and/or budget back down after a sustained push, it's often a sign that something isn't working. For instance, we used to have a fierce competitor who backed off all of their AdWords spending about a year ago (they began with day-parting and later added a budget cap, which was evident because their keyword coverage was uniformly capped at around 50%). Today, we hardly hear anything from them. This data was incredibly valuable to us because they had a business model that seemed promising at the time. Their apparent poor performance in the marketplace saved us the time and expense of testing that model for ourselves.

Figure 25-4 shows an example of a competitor who activated their AdWords account for only

15 days before shutting it down. We could probably learn a lot about what doesn't work by investigating their website. (As it turns out, they were a new affiliate in an overly crowded category. The odds were against them from the beginning.)

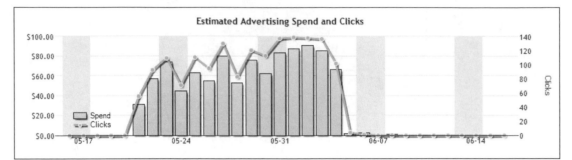

FIGURE 25-4. By monitoring your competitors' spends, you can learn what works and what doesn't much more quickly than you could through firsthand testing.

Aside from the strategic advantage this data gives you, it's also very handy for benchmarking your own campaign spend and traffic versus those of your competitors. This helps to ensure that you can at least achieve parity with your rivals.

TRACKING THIS INFORMATION

If the analogy to financial statements we made at the beginning of this chapter made your eyes glaze over, don't worry. There are a few tools available to you that can track and analyze this information.

The first tool is AdWords itself. Nearly all of the information you need (with the exception of coverage) is available within your AdWords account on the Campaign Summary page. Yours should look something like this:

Current Status	Current Budget ⑦	Clicks	Impr.	CTR	Avg. CPC	Avg. CPM	Cost	Conv. Rate	Cost/Conv.	Conversions
Active	$100.00 / day	194	294,736	0.06%	$3.61	$2.37	$699.49	7.22%	$49.96	14

When you look at this data, be sure to check the date range. If you're looking for general averages, then 30 days is a good period to use. On the other hand, if you've recently made changes to your campaign and want to measure their effect, it's best to shorten the period.

The last three columns (conversion rate, cost/conversion, and conversions) will only be visible if you've enabled conversion tracking for your campaign. Conversion tracking allows you to correlate your ad spend and your website sales. There are full instructions for enabling it in the AdWords interface (to get to it, click "Conversion Tracking" in the green menu bar at the top of the "Campaign Management" tab).

Although this is handy for checking your average values, notice that it lacks any context. Without some kind of historical perspective, this data tells you nothing.

THE TREND IS YOUR FRIEND

Charting is a tool most commonly used by those who analyze stocks and options, but professionals in all occupations use charts to visualize trends over time. It's a valuable technique in online advertising as well.

Trending charts give you a huge advantage as an advertiser, because they allow you to spot problems that can seriously impair your campaign performance. Most advertisers never use them, and this is a major reason why 97% of advertisers aren't doing so hot on AdWords.

In the land of the blind, charts make you the man with one eye.

There are three ways to get this data:

Method 1: Generate Reports Within AdWords

One way you can get at this data is by creating campaign performance reports within the AdWords interface. To do this, navigate to the "Reports" tab and click "Create Report." The most useful report at your disposal is called the Keyword Performance Report (it may be called the Keyword/Site Performance Report if you're also using contextual advertising).

When you run this report, you'll see something similar to this:

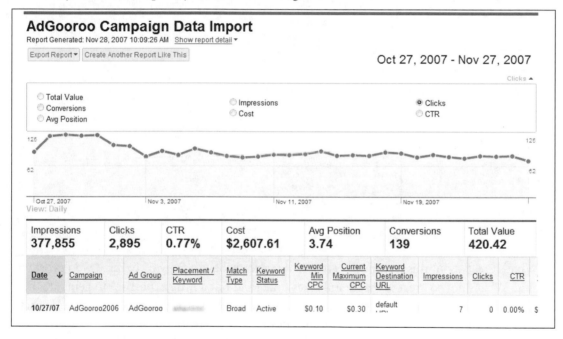

Not only does this report contain the summary-level information we mentioned previously, but it also gives you the ability to create simple charts quickly.

As helpful as this feature can be, I rarely use it because it takes a while to log in to your account, create a report, wait for it to download, and then play with charting options until you get what you're looking for. If you have a few thousand keywords to manage, this tool is just too cumbersome.

It's also not very flexible. You're limited to charting trends over time. There's no way to plot complex relationships, such as how your clickthrough rate varies with your bid.

Finally, you have to run a new report for every keyword you wish to analyze. This is not an effective use of anyone's time.

Method 2: Import AdWords Data into Excel

If you're a spreadsheet jockey, you're in luck. AdWords allows you to export all of your data to Microsoft Excel. From there, you can create sophisticated charts that perfectly meet your needs.

For instance, in less than two minutes you can create a chart showing how clickthrough rate varies with average position (see below). This is a key piece of data that will help you set your bids more intelligently.

It's exactly these types of charts that we used while studying clickthrough rates on Google.

What's great about this technique is that if you already have a copy of Excel, it won't cost you a thing. What's not so great is that it still takes time (and not a little expertise) to generate these charts. It's more powerful than creating charts within the AdWords interface, but it's not practical if your campaign has hundreds or thousands of active keywords.

Method 3: Third-Party Charting Tools

As much as I love Excel, the truth is that unless you want to spend the majority of your waking hours managing your search campaign, you won't have enough time to schedule reports, export them to Excel, and then generate all the graphs you need by hand.

One way to automate the process is to use a third-party reporting tool. Tools like AdGooroo

SEM Insight will automatically import your AdWords data every morning and then slice and dice your data any which way you need:

On the left, you'll see the important statistics for your campaign. Clicking any of the hyperlinks will display the daily trend on the chart to the right. For instance, if you click the Total Cost figure, you'll see a daily breakdown of your campaign costs (Figure 25-5).

You can plot both simple daily trends and sophisticated scatterplots, which can be used to find hidden relationships in your campaign. To re-create the chart that we just made in Excel, you just select "CTR by Position." A chart is then generated, along with any statistically significant trends. The whole process takes seconds (Figure 25-6).

I can't overstate the value of having access to a simple and fast charting solution. Not only will it save you bundles of time, but it actually makes the process of data mining your campaign *fun*. And, unlike most types of fun, this kind will actually make you money.

WHAT ABOUT COVERAGE?

Earlier I stated that nearly all of the data you need is available within your AdWords reports.

Coverage is the exception. Coverage—the percentage of the time that your ads appear to search engine users—is not a widely available statistic, and yet, it's absolutely indispensable. In the land of the blind, this is your other eye.

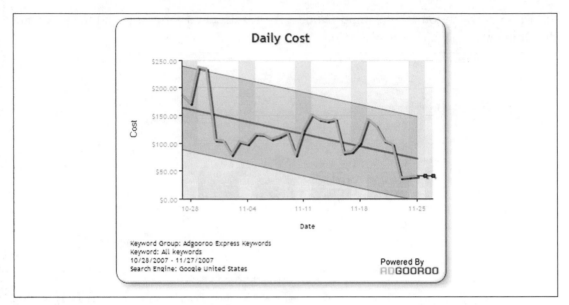

FIGURE 25-5.

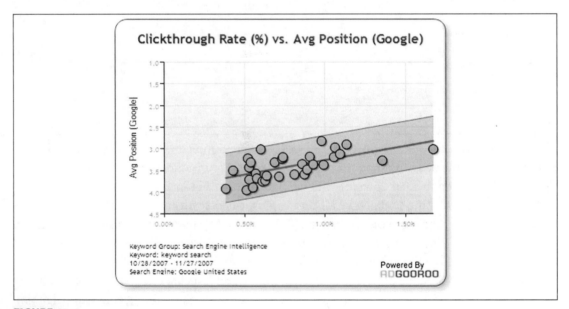

FIGURE 25-6.

There are only two ways to get it. One is to type your keywords into Google and continually refresh the page, recording how frequently your ads appear (you'll also need to close your browser or clear your cookies between requests).

The other way to get it is within AdGooroo. In fact, I invented it for this purpose. This data provided valuable feedback about the advertising marketplace that none of our competitors had, and to this day it allows us to outperform them.

THINK YOU DON'T HAVE TIME FOR THIS? THINK AGAIN!

If you're as pressed for time as the rest of us, you may be tempted to skip out on monitoring your campaign stats. I want to convince you that this is a bad idea. Spending even a small amount of time on this monitoring can have a huge payoff.

So now I'd like you to do this: using your campaign statistics, figure out how many keywords were responsible for 70% of your campaign spend for the past month. Now compare that with how much revenue these keywords produced. You'll probably find that the 80/20 rule is in effect here.

The first time I did this exercise back in 2004, I was shocked. I found that over 80% of my budget was spent on a single keyword (to the tune of $800 per day), and this keyword generated less than 5% of my total revenues. I immediately dropped my bids and started improving my ad copy. As a result, I achieved a drastic drop in campaign spend and immediate improvements in my campaign return.

I repeated this exercise in 2007 while writing the first version of this book. I discovered that two keywords were generating nearly 70% of our traffic, but the conversion rate was running at about 10% of the site average. In that case, we used a negative exact match to drop our campaign costs by half without losing a single sale.

When I repeated the exercise again in 2009 (with a heavily optimized AdWords campaign), I still found that 10 keywords generated over 50% of the revenue on our site while accounting for only 16% of the total campaign cost (Figure 25-7).

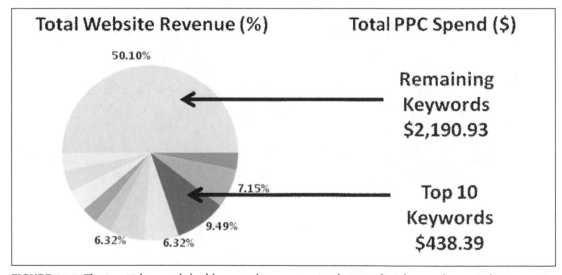

FIGURE 25-7. The top 10 keywords in this campaign represent only 16% of total campaign costs but generate 50% of the revenues.

Hopefully, this example demonstrates to you the value of devoting even a little time to digesting your campaign metrics. The payoff can be huge.

SUMMARY

Actively monitoring your campaign statistics and having the ability to plot trends are important requirements for diagnosing and fixing problems that are common in every search campaign. Ultimately, this data comes from AdWords, but there are time-saving tools that you can use to turn these chores into a pleasant (and profitable) exercise.

CHAPTER 26

Don't Starve Your Campaign

MOST OF US DON'T HAVE UNLIMITED BUDGETS. THE SEARCH ENGINES KNOW THIS, SO they give us a way to make sure we don't exceed our budgets by allowing us to specify a reasonable maximum daily spend. In this chapter, you're going to see why you should never use this feature. We'll also touch on bid management, and I'll show you a do-it-yourself system that could save you thousands in bid management fees.

HOW TO SET YOUR MAXIMUM DAILY BUDGET

Log in to your AdWords account and click on your campaign in the "Campaigns" tab. On the following page, you'll find a section that looks like the one shown in Figure 26-1. This is where you can specify your maximum daily budget.

HOW THE MAXIMUM DAILY BUDGET FEATURE WORKS

When you set up your paid search campaign, you're asked to specify a maximum daily budget. The search engines will allocate this amount across your various keywords, and

FIGURE 26-1. Set your maximum daily budget by clicking on your campaign on the main AdWords screen.

they typically do a good job ensuring that you spend no more than the specified amount each day. In other words, if you specify a $75 daily campaign limit, then, over the course of a month, you will have spent on average $75 each day. There may be days when you go over or under, but it averages out over time.

This sounds like a good thing, but really it's not.

WOULD YOU LET A STRANGER RUN YOUR MARKETING?

That's exactly what you do when you set a low daily budget limit on your campaign.

The problem arises when the potential amount you could be spending on search marketing goes over your daily budget limit. In other words, if you could potentially spend $2,000 a day on your search campaign but you specify a $75 daily limit, then you're going to run into problems.

Setting low limits is bad because it's in the search engines' best interest to conserve the shelf space of ads. In other words, they have a limited inventory of advertising they can sell each day. This means that to generate the most revenue, they need to sell as much premium shelf space to the advertisers with the largest (or unlimited) budgets to capture that revenue.

So what about your $75? Don't the search engines want it? Yes, and they'll usually get it by selling you less predictable (and usually less profitable) ad space. This ad space appears next to the rare and unusual search terms that people type in every day.[1]

Advertisers who specify a high maximum budget have a better chance of getting placement in higher-traffic keywords, because this traffic is more predictable and thus allows the search engines to maximize their revenue reliably.

The real kicker is that by setting a limit, you cede control over a critical part of your campaign (where to show your ads) to a complete stranger—a strange computer program, actually. This computer program generally makes poor decisions on your behalf, because it doesn't know or care about your profit margins or your ROI. It's optimized to spend your campaign budget as quickly as possible within the parameters you've given it.

In contrast, if you don't specify a budget, you've taken this control away from the search engine. You've in essence told them, "Please maximize my impressions wherever possible, without exception." This removes a major uncertainty from your marketing efforts and allows you to pursue your goal of reaching 100% coverage more easily.

Let's look at some examples of how limiting your budget can hurt you.

MISSING OUT ON HIGH-TRAFFIC PERIODS

Figure 26-2 is a graph indicating the daily cost for a campaign that did not have a maximum budget. As you can see, the daily spend was lumpy. On a few days, the spend was over $200, but it averaged $118/day overall. This advertiser received the benefit of getting more exposure on those high-traffic days. An advertiser with a budget restriction would probably miss this opportunity.

You can learn more about how budget plays into the AdWords algorithm by reading the academic paper "AdWords and Generalized On-line Matching" (Mehta, Saberi, Vazirani, and Vazirani, www.stanford.edu/~saberi/adwords. pdf).

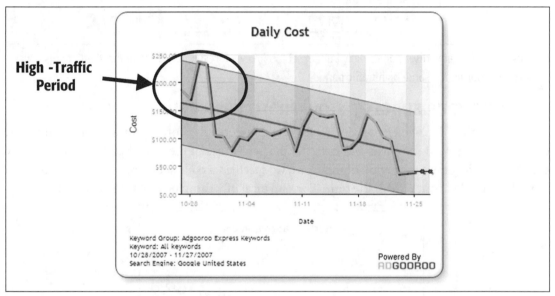

FIGURE 26-2. This advertiser had a high daily budget set and was able to take advantage of a high-traffic period.

In contrast, look at one of their competitors who had a maximum budget cap (Figure 26-3). As search volume increased in its category, its costs stayed flat because it hit its maximum budget. As a result, its coverage declined over time.

As you can see, campaigns with low daily budgets do not automatically adapt to changing market conditions—just one more thing that can go wrong during the course of a typical AdWords campaign.

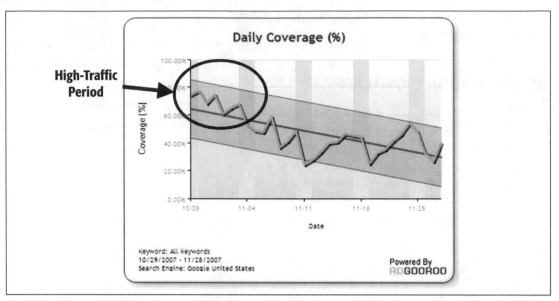

High-Traffic Period

FIGURE 26-3. This advertiser had its daily budget set too low. As a result, its ads were throttled and its coverage dropped during the same high-traffic period.

DIVERTING YOUR BUDGET TO LOW-PROFIT KEYWORDS

In the scatterplot shown in Figure 26-4, each icon represents a keyword in our AdWords campaign. Coverage is shown on the y-axis and indicates the percentage of the time that the ad was seen by searchers. During the time period of this chart, we specified a daily spending limit, and so our ads were shown only about 75% of the time. This is typical of a campaign that is budget-starved.

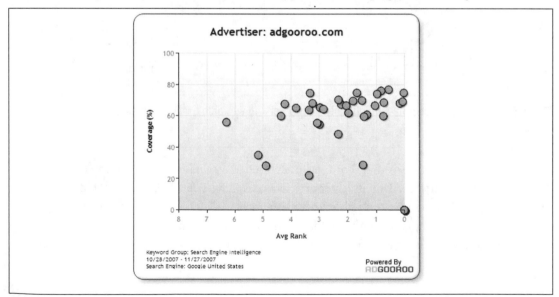

FIGURE 26-4. Example of a throttled campaign. Notice how the coverage is not equally distributed across all keywords.

If all keywords were throttled equally, this might not be such a bad problem. However, you can see from the chart that the impressions weren't prorated evenly across all of the keywords. Rather, a number of keywords were given impressions less than 50% of the time, including some very profitable keywords with very high bids!

The actual coverage you get for each keyword when operating under a fixed budget is determined by a computer program. It incorporates many variables, and nobody outside of the search engines can say with authority what those variables are. But we do know that these algorithms don't take into account your profit margin for each keyword, so the chances are very high that some of your budget will be shifted away from high-profit keywords into low-profit ones, which is not good.

Advertisers with unlimited budgets don't experience this problem nearly as often. Here's an example of how our campaign looks today. There are actually 107 keywords represented in this chart, and all but a few have coverage values near 100%.

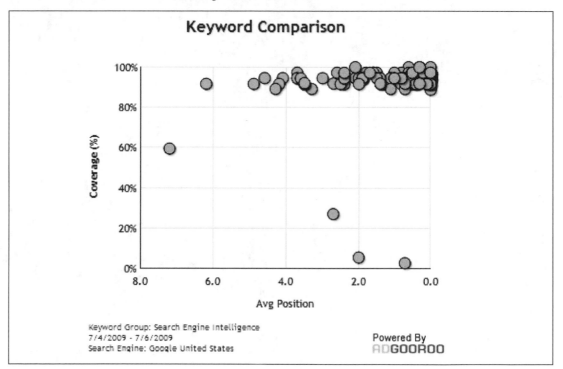

FIGURE 26-5. A pay-per-click campaign that is not budget-starved. Most keywords appear with high coverage.

SUMMARY

Putting control over your campaign spend in anyone else's hands is a bad idea and unnecessary once you know the techniques we'll teach you in the next chapter. Clear the maximum daily budget setting on your account, and you'll eliminate several problems that drag down the efficiency of many paid search campaigns.

Note

1. According to Udi Manber, Google's VP of engineering, 20–25% of the search terms typed into Google each day have never been entered before (readwriteweb.com/archives/udi_manber_search_is_a_hard_problem.php).

Setting Your Keyword Bids

NOW YOU'RE READY TO SET BIDS FOR EACH KEYWORD. YOUR BID, ALSO KNOWN AS MAX CPC or maximum cost-per-click, is the amount that you're willing to pay for each visitor who comes to your site.

After ad copy optimization, this is where you'll spend most of your time maintaining your campaign. It's vital that you maintain a regular schedule to review your bids, because now that you've eliminated the cap on your campaign budget, your daily spend can fluctuate quite a bit.

Over the course of any given month, you can expect your campaign costs to be relatively stable. However, periods of seasonality or growing demand can cause your spend to increase beyond your budget.

By committing to a set time, perhaps once a week (or even daily if you're using a third-party campaign tracking tool), to review your campaign statistics, you'll ensure that there are no unpleasant invoices waiting for you at the end of the month.

So what happens if you find your spend is going up? This is actually great news! You can either leave your bids the same and enjoy the extra traffic or lower your bids to drop your average cost per visitor. If traffic drops too far, inch your bids back up to a comfortable level.

In theory, this sounds quite simple. But the question remains: how much should you bid for any given keyword?

DON'T GUESS WITH YOUR BIDS

One of the most difficult things to do when setting up a new campaign is determining what your initial bid price should be. Often, marketers set a campaign-wide default bid to $0.50 (or some other arbitrary value) and hope for the best, but the result of this strategy is often an unacceptably high net loss.

It would be far more useful to devise a set of simple rules to inform our bidding strategy. Then, instead of blindly setting bids, we could use these rules to make intelligent decisions—minimizing our spend on unprofitable keywords and maximizing our traffic on profitable ones.

Earlier, we explored the factors that impact clickthrough rate and average cost per click. We even went so far as to devise complicated computer simulations that can make reasonably accurate predictions about how an ad will perform based on these factors. We are now going to use these tools to come up with a surprisingly simple system for properly setting your bids.

RULE 1: SET INITIAL BID PRICE FOR BROAD KEYWORDS

Choosing the optimal bid price for broad keywords is important, as these keywords will compose most of your campaign costs. Set your bid price too high and you'll blow through your monthly budget in a few days. Set it too low and you could miss out on the lion's share of the available traffic.

Getting in the right ballpark quickly would both greatly shorten the ramp-up time on our campaigns and reduce the risk of overspending on terms that may not pay off.

We set out to answer the question of what price to pay by combining our computer models of clickthrough rate and cost-per-click into a financial forecasting model that could predict both costs and revenues under a variety of situations.

As a sample, I modeled the keyword phrase *Las Vegas hotel*. I pulled traffic and maximum CPC estimates from the Google AdWords keyword tool. The other measures are just reasonable ballpark assumptions:

- 2,740,000 searches per month
- 98% coverage
- $5.01 maximum CPC
- 1.20% conversion rate
- $49.00 average order size

Combining these assumptions into a simple profit and loss forecasting model produces some interesting insights. I've dumped this information into the chart shown in Figure 27-1.

In this typical scenario, revenues fail to scale with our campaign costs, and as a result, the ads fail to turn a profit no matter where they appear on the page. We lose just a little money ($308)

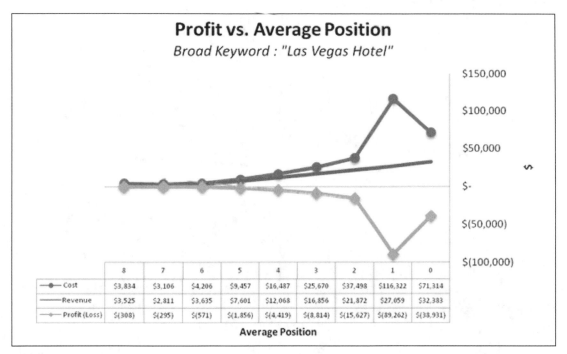

Profit vs. Average Position
Broad Keyword : "Las Vegas Hotel"

	8	7	6	5	4	3	2	1	0
Cost	$3,834	$3,106	$4,206	$9,457	$16,487	$25,670	$37,498	$116,322	$71,314
Revenue	$3,525	$2,811	$3,635	$7,601	$12,068	$16,856	$21,872	$27,059	$32,383
Profit (Loss)	$(308)	$(295)	$(571)	$(1,856)	$(4,419)	$(8,814)	$(15,627)	$(89,262)	$(38,931)

Average Position

FIGURE 27-1.

at the bottom of the page. At the top, we're out a whopping $39,000.

But what if we change the assumptions? What levers can we pull to make broad keywords pay off?

Let's try tweaking the ad quality. The following chart shows what the model predicts for a heavily optimized ad (Figure 27-2).

Here, we've actually managed to lose even more money as a result of optimizing our ads!

This rather counterintuitive result is explained by the fact that optimization succeeded in increasing our clickthrough rate, but did not reduce our average CPC far enough to come in below cost.

Why Do Costs Spike at Position One?

Costs for ads that appear at position one (the top side ad) are almost always higher than you'd expect them to be. This is because these ads are often placed there as a result of a high bid and low quality score (see the section on gladiator bidding in Chapter 17).

If these ads had higher quality scores, they would likely appear in the premium spots (above the natural search results) at a lower average CPC.

Next, let's see what happens if we manage to double our conversion rate as a result of website optimization, as shown in Figure 27-3. We'll use our original, unoptimized ad .

We've finally managed to turn a (modest) profit! Notice that the bottom of the page is profitable, but only up to position two. Moving just one position higher than that turns our net profit into a net loser to the tune of $62,000. Just one small mistake like this can ruin a pay-per-click campaign. So much for gladiator bidding.

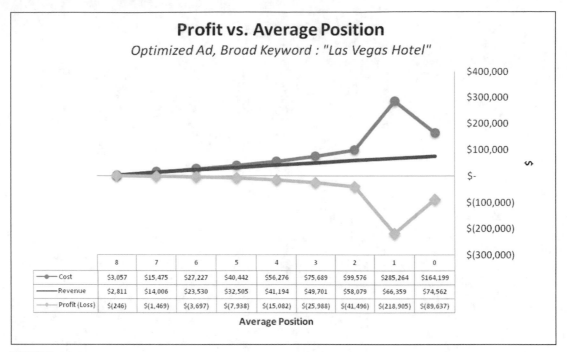

Profit vs. Average Position
Optimized Ad, Broad Keyword : "Las Vegas Hotel"

	8	7	6	5	4	3	2	1	0
Cost	$3,057	$15,475	$27,227	$40,442	$56,276	$75,689	$99,576	$285,264	$164,199
Revenue	$2,811	$14,006	$23,530	$32,505	$41,194	$49,701	$58,079	$66,359	$74,562
Profit (Loss)	$(246)	$(1,469)	$(3,697)	$(7,938)	$(15,082)	$(25,988)	$(41,496)	$(218,905)	$(89,637)

Average Position

FIGURE 27-2.

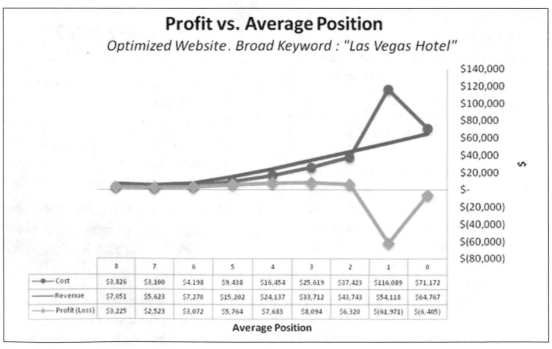

Profit vs. Average Position
Optimized Website. Broad Keyword : "Las Vegas Hotel"

	8	7	6	5	4	3	2	1	0
Cost	$3,826	$3,100	$4,198	$9,438	$16,454	$25,619	$37,423	$116,089	$71,172
Revenue	$7,051	$5,623	$7,270	$15,202	$24,137	$33,712	$43,743	$54,118	$64,767
Profit (Loss)	$3,225	$2,523	$3,072	$5,764	$7,683	$8,094	$6,320	$(61,971)	$(6,405)

Average Position

FIGURE 27-3.

Now let's try optimizing our ad copy again, as shown in Figure 27-4.

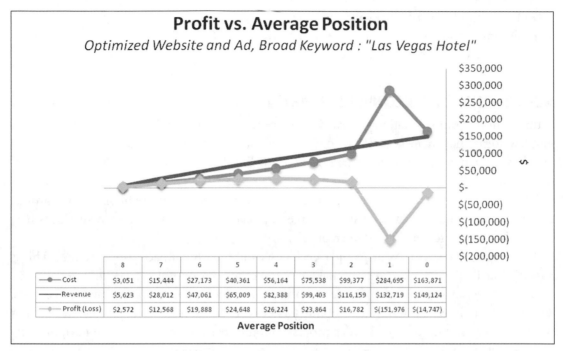

FIGURE 27-4.

Now we're talking. By taking a profitable keyword and optimizing it, we were able to triple our peak profits (from $8,100 to $26,200).

In general, the higher your conversion rate and average order size, the more you can afford to bid. But this can be simplified into a general rule: *If you aren't making money at position seven, you aren't going to make money anywhere on the first search results page.* Optimizing your ad copy won't help, either.

So for broad keywords, you want to start out by setting your bids to position seven and carefully monitoring your revenue and profits for each keyword to ensure that your traffic is profitable. (This can done easily with Google Analytics.)

If it is, you'll want to find out if you can make more money at higher positions. We tested our model and found that under most situations, you'll want to bid no higher than position five. Bidding any higher than this means that you'll run the risk of turning a small profit into a large loss (with one exception, which we'll talk about next).

It turns out that these general principles hold true under a wide variety of conditions. So the first strategy of our simple bid management system will be:

Strategy 1. For broad keywords, set your initial bids just high enough to reach the bottom of the first page of search results.

If your ads are unprofitable at this position, then take one of the following actions:

■ Lower your bids (your ads will appear on the second page, which will dramatically reduce your traffic).

- Delete this keyword from your account.
- Optimize your website to increase your conversion rate.
- Increase your average order size.

RULE 2: FIND "SUPERCONVERTER" KEYWORDS

It turns out that our simulations revealed another interesting facet of keyword bidding. For certain keywords, there may be a critical point in your conversion rate or average order size beyond which you can make money no matter how high you bid. This is the one time that gladiator bidding really works!

These superconverter keywords can often generate 80% or even more of all of your profits. However, they're not all that common. A large campaign with a thousand or so keywords may have only a few which qualify as superconverters.

With regular keywords, your pay-per-click costs will rapidly outpace your revenues. This is why it's usually the case that you can make money at the bottom of the page, but not the top.

Superconverter keywords are different in that your revenues far outpace your average costs. This is almost always the result of combining a keyword that is closely related to your business with a strong landing page and order process (another reason why I recommend optimizing your website prior to launching a full-scale pay-per-click campaign).

Through experimentation, we discovered a simple formula for finding superconverters. The turning point occurs when you make more from an average visitor than the maximum CPC for the top positions on the page. Your average visitor value can be found by multiplying your conversion rate by your average order size.

Expressed mathematically, it looks like this:

$$\text{Conversion Rate} \times \text{Average Order Size} > \text{Average CPC}_{\text{Position 1}}$$

Let's illustrate this by continuing our example from above. The maximum CPC given to us by Google for the term *Las Vegas hotel* was $5.01. Our average order size was $349 and our conversion rate was 0.30%. Plugging these numbers into our formula yields:

$$\text{Conversion Rate} \times \text{Average Order Size} > \text{Average CPC}_{\text{Position 1}}$$

$$0.30\% \times \$349 > \$5.01$$

$$\$1.05 < \$5.01$$

The equation did not hold true, so the chances are slim that we'll be able to bid for the highest position on the page.

As I illustrated above, doubling the conversion rate did a lot to improve profitability. But it wasn't enough to reach escape velocity. This should be clear when you plug the numbers into our equation:

$$0.60\% \times \$349 > \$5.01$$

But what happens if we change our term to *Las Vegas family hotels*? The maximum CPC (given to us on the Google AdWords keyword tool) is only $2.23. That's pretty close to our $2.10 average visitor value.

Let's see how our model looks for this term (Figure 27-5):

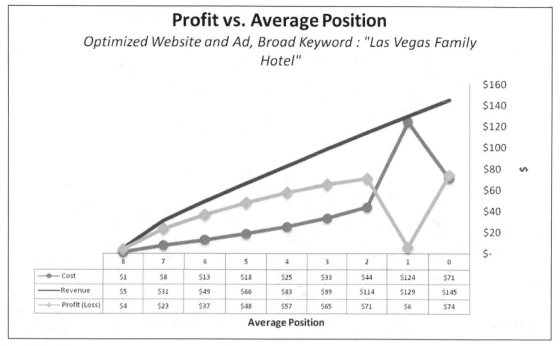

FIGURE 27-5.

As you can see, we are able to turn a profit for this keyword regardless of our bid price (and the more we bid, the more we make). The one spot we have to watch out for is that top side ad. At that spot, we end up giving most of our profits back.

Fortunately, your ad will only appear there if it has a high maximum bid and a low quality score. Optimizing your ad copy should get it over the hump and into the premium positions.

As you can see, the rule isn't an exact one. As long as your average visitor value is close to the maximum CPC and your quality scores are high, you'll turn a good profit regardless of your bid price.

This brings us to our second strategy:

Strategy 2: For those ads which are profitable, slowly raise your bids to position five unless your average visitor value exceeds the estimated maximum CPC for that keyword (superconverter keywords). Follow up with ad copy optimization.

RULE 3: SET INITIAL BID PRICE FOR NICHE KEYWORDS

We ran the same models for more specific, niche keywords. Not surprisingly, it's much easier to make money when targeting these phrases. And because they are usually cheaper by virtue of being less competitive, you can usually afford to be more aggressive with your bids. Shoot for position two, and then try to optimize your ad copy until you land in the premium spots (Figure 27-6).

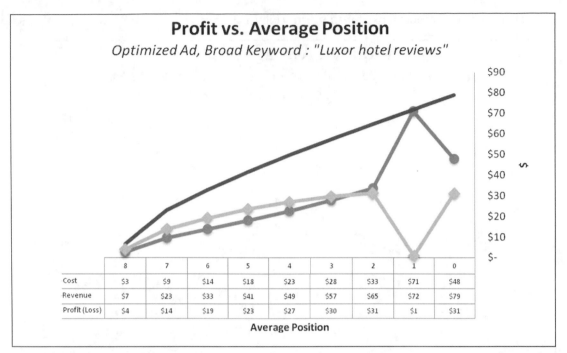

Profit vs. Average Position
Optimized Ad, Broad Keyword : "Luxor hotel reviews"

	8	7	6	5	4	3	2	1	0
Cost	$3	$9	$14	$18	$23	$28	$33	$71	$48
Revenue	$7	$23	$33	$41	$49	$57	$65	$72	$79
Profit (Loss)	$4	$14	$19	$23	$27	$30	$31	$1	$31

Average Position

FIGURE 27-6. The standard approach for niche terms is simple. Aim for position two in order to maximize profits.

Then the general bidding strategy for niche keyword phrases is:

Strategy 3: For niche terms, increase your bids until your ads appear in position two. Then use ad copy optimization to capture premium placement.

RULE 4: BID JAMMING

Bid jamming is a way to make competitors pay dearly (or lose impression share) for terms for which you have high quality scores. This is one of my favorite tactics for diminishing the competition's campaign performance, especially on high-traffic terms where it will potentially have a long-term effect.

Once you have your initial bids set and you've nudged them to the point of optimal profitability, use this tactic to interfere with competitors' campaigns and take market share.

Here's an actual example of this at work. On June 30, we were ranked behind four other competitors for the term *keyword research*.

Figure 27-7 shows how we compared prior to conducting any bid jamming (names have been removed from the charts and graphs for obvious reasons).

Figure 27-8 shows the same information in graphic form.

Does Your Average Position Affect Conversion Rate?

There is an interesting phenomenon in paid advertising that we call *searcher fatigue*. This term refers to the fact that people tend to click on more ads during the first stages of their search, but as they refine their terms (moving from browsers to buyers), they become more selective and spend more time on the websites they visit.

In other words, the ads at the top of the page sometimes do a better job of educating visitors than selling to them.

About 80% of the time, it won't make a difference. But we've found a measurable trend in about 20% of the keywords that we've studied (most of these being broad keywords), so you must be aware that your conversion rate might vary depending on where your ad is found on the page.

For high-traffic "browse" terms, the conversion rate tends to be higher at the bottom of the page. For low-traffic "shop" and "buy" terms, the conversion rate tends to be higher at the top of the page.

The following chart shows an example of a keyword in which there was a trend. Notice how the conversion rate decreases from position 3.5 to 2.5.

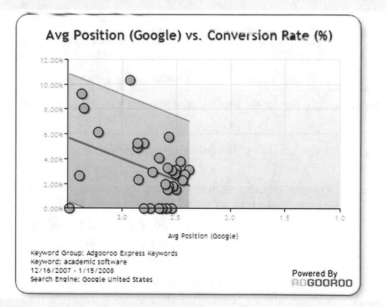

If you have extra time to spend on your campaign, this is fertile ground for exploration.

Advertiser	Rank	Coverage	Avg. Position
Competitor B	1	97.1%	0.0
Competitor A	2	97.1%	0.4
Competitor C	3	97.1%	1.0
Competitor D	4	97.1%	1.4
AdGooroo.com	5	94.3%	1.4

FIGURE 27-7. Before we started bid jamming, we were the fifth ranked competitor.

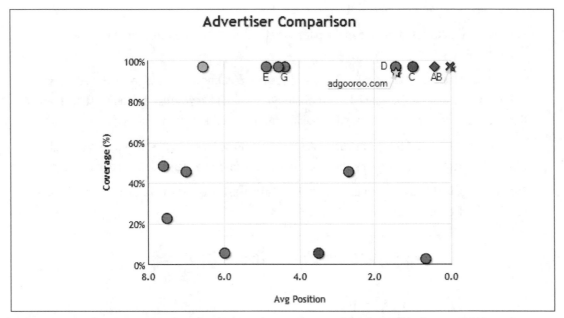

FIGURE 27-8. Advertiser comparison for the term *keyword research*, as it stood before our bid jamming efforts.

Looking at my AdWords data, I saw that our quality score for this term was seven, indicating both that we are a very relevant advertiser for this term and that a small increase in bid would potentially be enough to dislodge one or more of our competitors. I was bidding $1.60 at this time, but paying an actual CPC of $1.35.

Over the next week, I slowly raised our bid to $2.00. We moved up substantially in the rankings, taking the number two position. Competitors B, C, and D retained their positions relative to one another. Competitor A, however, lost nearly 85% of its search traffic for this term. This is most likely due to the fact that it was bidding higher than us, but had a lower quality score.

What's more, our clickthrough rate went from around 0.4% to 1.48% and our average CPC increased only to $1.55 (Figure 27-9)!

As of this writing, Competitor A is still on the way down. It's very likely that the Google AdWords algorithm will decide it is no longer a relevant advertiser and ban it from this term at

Advertiser	Rank	Coverage	Avg. Position
Competitor B	1	97.1%	0.0
AdGooroo.com	2	97.1%	0.5
Competitor C	3	97.1%	1.0
Competitor D	4	97.1%	1.8
Competitor E	5	97.1%	3.4
Competitor A	11	16.7%	0.3

FIGURE 27-9. As a result of bid jamming, Competitor A lost nearly 85% of their traffic for this highly profitable term.

some point in the not-so-distant future. When that happens, I'll be doing the same to Competitor B (Figure 27-10).

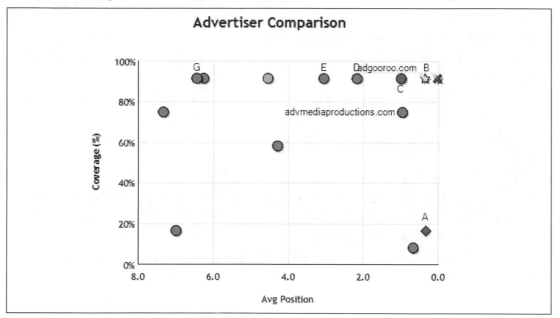

FIGURE 27-10. Intelligent use of bid jamming allowed us to triple our clickthrough rate and dislodge a well-established competitor at minimal cost. Notice that Competitor A has lost 85% of its traffic.

MANAGING YOUR BIDS OVER TIME

These rules are great for getting new campaigns up to speed quickly. From here, you'll need to put your analytics reports to work in order to fine-tune your bid prices. Watch your average revenue and costs for each keyword and nudge your bids up or down as necessary. A good rule of thumb is to keep costs at one-half of revenue for each of your keywords.

However, this is rarely a practical option for most of your keywords. "Shop" and "buy" keywords, profitable as they may be, generally don't generate enough traffic to be statistically meaningful. If you get a few dozen clicks a month for a given keyword and you have a conversion rate of only 2–5%, it will take you a very long time to gather enough data to calculate a statistically sound bid price—and by that time, the competitive environment will have changed radically, rendering most of your data useless.

So when you are lacking sufficient traffic (at least 200 clicks per month), fall back on these simple formulas. They work, they will save you time, and they will help to make you one of the top 3% of AdWords advertisers.

SUMMARY

Giving control over your bid prices to anyone else (even a computer) is a bad idea and for most advertisers, completely unnecessary. With a little work, you can eliminate much of the advantage that larger advertisers with dedicated staff have over you. Use these simple strategies to manage your bids:

Strategy 1. For broad keywords, set your initial bids just high enough to reach the bottom of the first page of search results. If your ads are unprofitable at this position, then take one of the following actions:

- Lower your bids (your ads will appear on the second page, which will dramatically reduce your traffic)
- Delete this keyword from your account
- Optimize your web site to increase your conversion rate
- Increase your average order size

Strategy 2: For those ads which are profitable, slowly raise your bids to position five unless your average visitor value exceeds the estimated maximum CPC for that keyword (superconverter keywords). Follow up with ad copy optimization.

Strategy 3: For niche terms, increase your bids until your ads appear in position two. Then use ad copy optimization to capture premium placement.

CHAPTER 28

Drag Visitors to Your Site with Killer Ad Copy

I N A PREVIOUS CHAPTER, WE LEARNED THAT FOR COST REASONS, WE OFTEN HAVE TO SETTLE FOR placing our ads in the lower positions on the search results pages. Although these positions are usually quite cost-effective, they don't generate nearly as much traffic as the higher ones. This makes it essential that we maximize our clickthrough rate with powerful, targeted ad copy.

Well-written ads attract more visitors and generate more revenue. On the other hand, bad ads receive few clicks and can even be deactivated if they underperform over an extended period.

What's more, making improvements to your ad copy will usually result in your ads earning a position placement bonus. Your ads will be shown higher on the search results page, but you'll pay the same price you were paying before (or even less). This bonus can easily push your ads up a few positions, resulting in as much as a 50% increase in traffic.

Ad copy optimization is also an offensive tactic, in that it forces advertisers appearing above you to pay more, as well as a defensive tactic, in that it helps to minimize the chances that advertisers appearing below you can raise your actual CPC close to your maximum bid.

For all of these reasons, ad copy optimization is the best opportunity you have to outperform the competition. It is the cornerstone of achieving long-term competitive advantage on Google AdWords.

WRITE YOUR ADS TO MIRROR YOUR VISITORS' INTENTION

Ads work best when they are aligned with the visitor's search query. Too many advertisers simply ignore this advice and use generic ads for all or most of their keywords.

By taking the time up front to identify the customer life cycle category for each of your keywords, you'll put yourself far ahead of the pack when it comes to writing your ad copy. Here are some general considerations to keep in mind when crafting your copy.

Browsers

Browsers are looking for information. Your ads should offer them educational articles, technical advice, white papers, and so on. Don't focus on price, delivery, or guarantees, because many of them won't care and may actually be turned off by aggressive pitches. A good strategy here is to educate potential consumers about your product or service category while capturing their contact information. If you succeed, you'll be more likely to stay in touch and they'll be more likely to return to your site again in the future.

Shoppers

Shoppers are closer to a purchase decision, but are generally looking for more information about different products. Descriptive terms work well (e.g., *best, cheapest,* or *review*) as do comparisons, third-party testimonials, and so on. Your goal should be to convert shoppers to buyers, and one effective way of doing this is to tempt them with limited-time promotions.

Buyers

These visitors have committed themselves to making a purchase. You can safely make an aggressive pitch toward winning the sale right away. You'll want to tempt them with promotional offers, and you should cater to their purchasing needs: fast shipping, high quality, low price, and so on.

Not Sure of the Keyword Category?

Try split-testing multiple ads. The best performers will often tell you the category to which the keyword belongs. If your split tests don't determine a clear winner, then try experimenting with negative matching to eliminate ad impressions for clearly off-target search queries.

22 BEST PRACTICES TAKEN FROM A DATABASE OF THE WORLD'S BEST ADS

Search ads are short. You have only the following to work with:

- Twenty-five characters for the headline
- Thirty-five characters each for two lines of copy (70 characters total)
- A display URL (which doesn't have to match the clickthrough URL)

This requires you to be direct and concise, of course. But there are plenty of other rules you can follow to write more effective ads.

In early 2008, we compiled a database of the most effective ad copy on Google AdWords. We performed a statistical analysis on this data to determine the best practices you should follow when writing your ads. Some of our findings are detailed below.

If you are willing to make ad copy optimization a core part of your marketing practices, then you should download the complete set of rules and ads at http://www.adgooroo.com/adcopy.

Please be aware that a specific rule may or may not work in every situation. You should always split-test your ads to measure results.

Include Keyword Phrases in Ad Titles

Many of the top ads include the keyword phrase within the title of the ad. In our database, nearly 33% of the top-performing ads had an exact match between the search phrase and ad title.

Higher clickthrough rates result not only from the ad more accurately reflecting the searcher's intention, but also because matching keywords are bolded in the ad, thus drawing more attention to it.

Respect Your Customers' Language

The more you customize the ad copy to your audience, the more successful it will be. Make sure you target the right language and the right country for each ad. Many Google advertisers ignore this advice at their own peril. For instance, in the computer security software category on Google Japan, I see a number of U.S. advertisers displaying English ads. None of these advertisers are showing up very often for the same terms on Google U.S. The low clickthrough rates they're undoubtedly receiving will penalize their campaigns in other markets.

Localize Your Ads

In some cases, a mediocre local ad can outperform well-written national ads. For instance, here's an ad that displayed for the keyword *buy digital printer*:

Minuteman Press
Quality, cost-effective printing
"We're as close as your phone"
www.chicago.minutemanpress.com

Although this ad is well written, it's off-target for this keyword. Nevertheless, it outranked many other ads that incorporated the words *digital* and *printer* in the headline, but only in the Chicagoland area.

Localizing your ads is a good practice for local businesses. But it is usually impractical for national advertisers to write separate ads for every region in the country in an effort to boost regional CTRs.

Have Endorsements and Testimonials

Statements from past customers or professional review organizations are a powerful form of persuasion. If your product has been written up in a name-brand magazine such as *InfoWorld*, try including that information in your ad: "Ranked #1 in Security by InfoWorld." This is a very powerful technique for increasing ad clickthrough rates.

Sell the Benefits

The phrase *128-bit security* describes a feature. *Prevents eavesdropping* is a benefit. See the difference? Features describe the product. Benefits describe what the product will do for the customer.

Always lead off with benefits, not features. Feature descriptions don't draw well (except in niche markets made up of primarily well-educated buyers), although they do have their place in pushing customers to make a purchase.

Have a Unique Selling Proposition

In a nutshell, a unique selling proposition answers the question "What is compelling and different about your product or service?" For example, "eBay—The World's Online Marketplace," or "Netflix—Rent all the DVDs you want for $20 a month."

A single sentence tells you what is special about this business. This simple, concise statement is known as a unique selling proposition. USPs are a big reason why ads can stale out over time. A few years ago, Netflix's USP was unique, but now there are a number of knock-off companies trying to cash in. So the Netflix marketing manager needs to stress what is different today (and not in 2004) about their offering.

USPs are closely related to positioning. For more on this subject, read the classic marketing book *Positioning* by Al Ries and Jack Trout.[1]

Attention Grabbers

New, free, how to, and *improved* are words that have been used for a long time with success in the print world. They still work well with search ads.

There are some drawbacks, though. First, if your competitors are using these words in their ads, they'll tend to lose effectiveness. Also, these attention grabbers probably won't be as effective in a B2B setting because business buyers tend to be more skeptical.

Important note on *free*: be careful with this word. We recently conducted a study of the most effective AdWords ads. Although a full 24% of the ads in our study incorporated the word *free*, it's notorious for attracting people who aren't willing to pay for anything. For most businesses, this is a waste of ad dollars.

An alternative technique for reaching into this large barrel of customers and possibly turning a few of them into buyers is to use the attention-grabbing phrase *how to*. This phrase reaches out to prospects in the "browse" category and can expand your audience profitably.

Use Action Words

Less obvious from a marketing standpoint is to ensure that you use simple and enthusiastic action verbs in your ad copy: *discover, enhance, get, learn, receive,* and so on.

Have a Call to Action

More specific than using action words is including a call to action in your ads. This phrase signals to the prospect what you would like them to do. We found call-to-action phrases in a full 29.1% of our top-performing ads.

These are common calls to action:

- Get official quote now!
- Join now for free!
- Shop now and save
- Learn more today
- Search flights now
- Get tips at AOL!
- Order today for quick delivery!
- Request free info!
- Read this

Most ads benefit from having a call to action. Not sure what yours is? Ask yourself what the ideal customers would do when they see your ad. The answer is obvious—click through! So tell them that directly, or find an analogous way to do so.

Be aware that both Google and Yahoo! frown on certain overused call-to-action phrases, such as *Click here!*

Disclosing Price

You don't want just any traffic at your site. You want people who are willing to pay for your product or service. Including the price deters "tire kickers" and saves on your ad spend. Sometimes there are valid strategic marketing reasons why you shouldn't disclose price (e.g., value-based pricing models), but if not, try incorporating price in your "buy" bucket ads.

Of the top ads in our database, 15% contained the price. Of these, the price was mentioned most frequently in line one (52%), followed by line two (39%), and then the title (15%).

A word of advice: be careful to split-test your ads both with and without the price. Generally, this technique works well only for low-priced items (under $20).

Try Exclamation Points in Line One or Two

Did you know Google allows exclamation points in ads? It does, but not in the title (which is why many people mistakenly believe Google doesn't allow them). This tactic seems to work. 34% of the top ads in our database contained exclamation points in line one or line two.

Squeeze More Text in Using Ampersands

Space is at a premium when writing ads, so every character counts. Replacing the word *and* with an ampersand (&) is an effective way to get two more characters when you really need them. Ampersands were found in 27% of ads, which indicates that this technique does not seem to hurt clickthrough rates.

Incorporate Special Symbols

Trademark symbols (™, ©, ®) may only be required for legal reasons, but they can improve clickthrough rates as well. These unusual characters occurred in only 2.1% of ads. They frequently appear next to company or product names that match one or more words of the search phrase.

Use Specific Numbers

A full 41% of ads contained at least one number. Numbers were most commonly found in "shop" ads such as:

> **50th birthday gift ideas**
> A free service to help you find
> creative 50th Birthday Gifts.
> Or Buy ads, like:

> **Save 45% On Abrasives**
> Grind & Cut Wheels, Discs, Belts
> Quality Same Day Ship On Stock Item

Capitalization

Although we were not able to pull up specific percentages to compare ads with proper capitalization (first letter and proper names only) with those that capitalized every word, it was very clear that capitalizing every word is a common ad copy tactic. You should test this technique in your ads.

We also found ads that made creative use of capitalization in the title ("WOW Big Sale!"). These ads draw the eye, yet don't appear spammy.

Include a Brand Name

We specifically excluded most brand names from our study, as they are not typical keywords. That said, there is much anecdotal evidence that including well-known brand names in the ad copy can substantially boost clickthrough rates. In the most competitive categories (such as travel), this may be the only way to compete successfully on Google.

Experiment with Extremely Short Ads

In competitive keywords where up to 11 ads can be shown at a time (eight on the side and up to three premium ads), anything that makes your ads stand out can help. Some advertisers rely on extremely short ads to make their point:

> **8gb iPod**
> Find 8gb iPod
> at Great Prices.

> **Expense Reports**
> Top 5 Websites
> For Expense Reports

There's no rule that says you have to use all of your characters, so this is definitely a concept worth testing.

Capture the Lead to Boost Your Conversion Rate

In competitive fields, trying to make the sale directly from the ad may be a tough proposition. Often, it's better to offer information for free, capture the lead, and attempt to sell via other means such as email marketing. This is a common tactic in such competitive fields as the following:

- Travel—free destination guides
- Online education—degree information
- Pharmaceuticals—prescription info
- Hair restoration—free transplant info

Optimize Niche Keywords

As profitable as longer, niche keywords can be, the ad copy that appears for them is rarely of the same quality as it is for high-traffic broad terms. This makes sense—marketers spend the most time improving their ads for high-cost terms. Given the profit potential of these terms, we recommend that you allocate some time to improving these terms.

For instance, while the keyword phrase *teen car insurance* returned a number of ads containing *teen car insurance* in the title and/or copy, only two advertisers had optimized their ads for *cheap teen car insurance* (most ads were targeted to *cheap car insurance* and said nothing about *teen*).

Similarly, a search on the term *credit identity online report theft* returned five ads with high clickthrough rates, but only one of them had anything to do with identity theft. A savvy competitor could easily improve their performance in these niche phrases with even the most cursory ad copy optimization.

Guess the Intention on Broad Keywords

One vexing problem with search advertising is that broad (typically one-word) search phrases generate the most traffic, but offer little clue as to what the visitor is searching for. Relying on the search phrase alone often results in low clickthrough rates.

One tactic that appears to work is to run "shop" ads for these broad keywords. The intent is to turn a browser into a shopper, potentially beating other competitors to the punch.

An example for the keyword *spyware* will help to illustrate this. Rather than running ads with the title *spyware*, advertisers are enticing searchers with offers for more information:

Top 5 Spyware Removers
Compare and Download the 5 Top
Spyware Virus Removers for Free.

Which Spyware Remover?
Don't download any Spyware removers
until you read this article.

Are You an "Official Site"?

Although Google has quietly eliminated most affiliates from its advertiser list, some advertisers are still using "official site" in their ad copy. Only 3.7% of the ads in our database made this appeal, but it may be worth testing, especially for "buy" keywords.

Examples:

Shop For iPod Nano
Official Site. Free Shipping on orders
$24 & up or pick up in store

Tiffany & Co. (Official)
Shop the Official Tiffany & Co.
site for exclusive Tiffany designs.

Include "www" in Your Domain Name

Surprisingly, we've found that including "www" in the display URL tends to boost clickthrough rates. 80.6% of the ads in our database included it, leading us to believe that this is a general rule. If you are among the nearly 20% of advertisers who are not including "www" in your URL, you should consider testing it.

NINE WAYS TO WRITE TERRIBLE ADS
Blindly Using Keyword Insertion

Keyword insertion is an advanced AdWords feature that allows you to insert the keyword that triggered your ad directly into the ad copy. To use it, you place a short piece of code into your ad text. Each time the ad shows, the code will be replaced with the targeted keyword.

For example:

{keyword: Erase Internet Tracks}
Erase your internet history
Fast, easy, and secure. Free trial!
www.SurfSecret.com

This works out pretty well if your keywords have been chosen appropriately. For instance, if you are targeting the term *erase internet history*, the ad will look like this:

Erase Internet History
Erase your internet history
Fast, easy, and secure. Free trial!
www.SurfSecret.com

However, it seems that most advertisers get it wrong, resulting in comical ads such as the following, found for the term *spyware*:

Spyware
Protect your system with Dell
and save on Spyware today!

Only use keyword insertion for ad groups with carefully chosen keywords.

Relying Too Much on Broad Keywords

Broad keywords appeal to a wide audience, but they suffer from the disadvantage that it's difficult to adjust ad copy based on searcher behavior.

Is the person who typed in *plasma TV* looking to buy a specific plasma television, to learn about the different types of flat-panel displays, or to compare prices? There's no way to tell for sure, and that's why conversion rates are so low for this keyword. Conversely, traffic is very high, so you end up spending a disproportionate amount of your ad budget to generate relatively few sales.

Broad keywords also suffer from low clickthrough rates. We recently tested AdWords ads for the term *shareware*. Our ad produced a single click in about 1,700 impressions and was quickly disabled. Is this a big deal? You bet. The two factors of high volume and low CTR deliver a double whammy to your historical stats, dragging your entire campaign down. This can result in your ads for all of your other keywords being penalized!

You'll avoid this problem if you follow our advice on keyword selection. Your campaign should ideally consist of a minimum of tens of thousands of keyword phrases. And if you must use broad keywords, you should be making liberal use of negative matching to eliminate impressions in unwanted keyword phrases.

Forgetting to Spell-Check Your Ads

No matter how long you've been in business or how great your reputation may be, misspellings make your company look unprofessional. Furthermore, ads with obvious misspellings in them often convert at a lower rate. Double-check all your ad copy before hitting the save button.

Using Abbreviations to Save Space

Many people, especially nonnative English speakers, will not understand the following abbreviations:

- lb
- ea
- qty
- ASAP
- Inc
- ext
- w/o

Sometimes you can't avoid using abbreviations because of space considerations, but you should generally try to write without them.

Using Technical Jargon

Jargon can be useful, but generally only in niche B2B categories. If you aren't selling to specialists (for example, scientists or mining engineers), avoid industry jargon. If, on the other hand, you are running a frequency campaign designed to differentiate your product in the minds of expert users and the space is very competitive, technical jargon is worth trying. I suspect that most of the time you will be disappointed, however, because the truth is that people buy what makes them feel good, and technical terminology doesn't speak well to that part of our brains responsible for emotion.

At the end of the day, people buy benefits, not features—and benefits can usually be stated in clear, nontechnical terms.

Using the Word *Free*

Including the word *free* in your ad is a sure way to boost clickthrough rates. However, it can easily backfire and deplete your search budget on people with no intention of purchasing from you.

I generally advise advertisers to never use this term, and to even include it as a negative match. Nevertheless, if you believe your business can generate revenue with a "free" appeal, it will almost certainly work: a full 24% of the ads in our database contained this term.

Including Your Company Name in the Headline

The idea behind this is that you are repeating your company name in the headline as well as the URL. These ads have nearly zero clickthrough unless you are a well-known brand name (such as Target, Orbitz, Expedia, and so on).

Use of Superlatives

Superlatives such as *best, greatest, #1,* and so on generate a sense of mistrust in most people. Avoid using these terms at all costs. We ran a series of ads that touted our "amazing" new software and had dismal clickthrough rates. The software really was amazing, but searchers didn't respond to this particular claim.

That said, you should always test superlatives in your ad copy. We have found that some do work, but it is highly dependent on your business category. A detailed analysis of superlatives is contained in our ad copy study.

Promising What You Can't Deliver

Not only do people resent being sold a bill of goods, but Google's editors will remove your ad if they learn that you are making unjustifiable claims. Even if you do have the lowest prices, making this claim is a bad idea for a variety of reasons unless you are credibly positioned as a value company (Southwest Airlines, Wal-Mart). You will probably get more effective results by clearly stating the price in your ad and letting people judge for themselves.

On a related note, does it need to be said that if you can't deliver the goods, then you shouldn't advertise them? This is not only a great way to waste your ad budget; it's also unethical and potentially illegal.

Paint a Bull's-Eye on Your Ads
Howie Jacobson
Author, *AdWords for Dummies*

The animal inhabitants of the Costa Rican rain forest spend most of their time and energy looking for food and trying not to become food. They've evolved an amazing array of predatory and defensive strategies in the neverending battle for survival. For example, bird species that feast on insects have a huge array of choices—thousands of different potential meals. It's more overwhelming than the dinner menu at the Cheesecake Factory.

But not all of the insects are edible. Some are poisonous to birds. Some are yucky-tasting (a scientific word meaning "unpalatable"). And a whole bunch of yummy bugs have evolved to look like the poisonous ones.

So what's a hungry bird to do? Before you answer, think about these two constraints:

Constraint #1: Too Much Information

When my family and I hiked in a Costa Rican rain forest for four hours, we saw exactly one animal: a hairy tarantula standing in the middle of the path, with a "you want a piece of me?" expression. The animals were there—we could hear them and see their pictures on the laminated card we got at the gift shop—but the place looked like a greenhouse ghost town. They were all hiding or camouflaged in the varied and verdant environment.

Finding the animals was like playing "Where's Waldo?" But instead of hundreds of people in red and white stripes vying for our attention, the multiplicity of leaves, mosses, ferns, and barks obscured the hundreds of animals that had evolved to hide in plain sight. I tip my hat to those insectivorous birds who choose to make the rain forest their home and restaurant. Anyone looking for animal protein in that place has got to have amazing eyesight.

Constraint #2: Limited Processing Power

Birds have small heads, which means limited cranial capacity, which means they are, well, bird-brained. Their brains are small. Not a lot of processing going on in there. Think about the computer you bought in 1994 trying to run Second Life and YouTube.

The Strategy: Search Imaging

To recap: the birds can see tons of stuff—about seven times more detail than humans—but can't deal with all the information, because there are more stimuli than they have the capacity to process. (Sound like us on the internet?)

Even though there are lots of palatable species of insect available to them, the birds focus on one or two at most, because they lack the brain processing power to take in and evaluate the entire visual landscape. So they create a "search image" in their heads before they start looking for food, and only pay attention to what matches that search image.

They miss a lot of potential dinners (having no capacity for opportunism), but rarely go hungry. That's how your prospects are looking at Google's search results.

They are overwhelmed by the sheer size of the web and the amount of information available on every single topic: websites, articles, videos, audios, PDFs, emails, banners, pop-ups, blog posts, blog comments, tweets, SMS, voicemails …

So when they search, they are not looking for more information. They are looking for *less*. They need to eliminate everything that isn't breathtakingly relevant, interesting, and important. And they search with an image in their minds—a search image that allows the brain to ignore almost everything that doesn't match the image.

How do you know what their search image is? They tell you—by typing it.

Keyword = Search Image

If someone is searching for the phrase *industrial clean room*, they see the following Google ads (Figure 28-1):

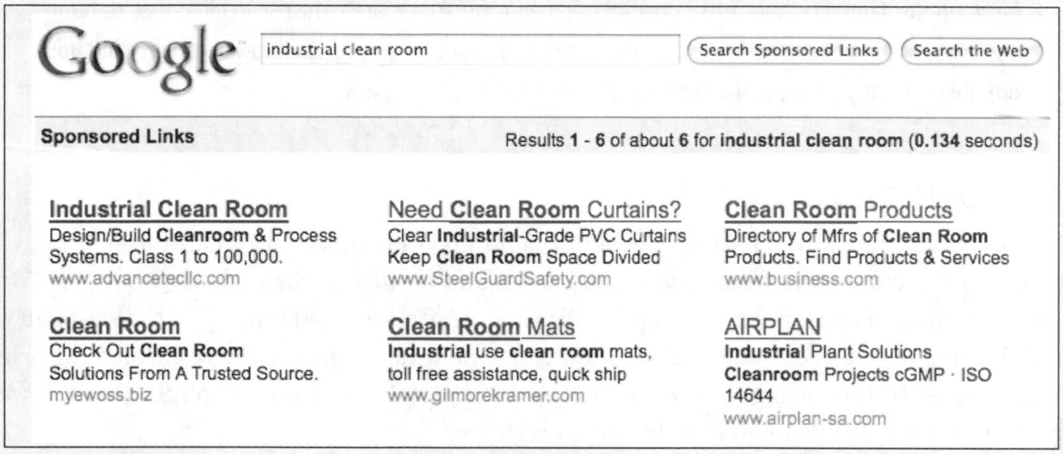

FIGURE 28-1.

Which headline matches the search image? Only one—*Industrial Clean Room*. It captures the eye immediately, because that click requires less thought, less expenditure of processing energy, than any of the others.

Now, are the other ads also relevant to the search? You might argue that the word *industrial* is superfluous: all clean rooms are industrial. So why bother showing it in your ad? Because your prospect has told you exactly what their filter is. They want industrial, you give them industrial. Otherwise they will tune you out.

Opportunism—clicking on a "Gee, this might be interesting" ad—is not a preferred strategy in an environment of information and opportunity overload.

In a perfect world, you might suppose, your ad would mirror the search image for every keyword in your AdWords account. But that's not realistic, nor even desirable. (Your long-tail keywords belong in groups, if only to garner enough traffic to determine split test winners.)

The best practice here is to isolate and reflect the search image for your "money" keywords—the high-traffic, high-converting words that keep you in business. Each of them deserves its own ad group and its own ads, perfectly keyed to the pre-filtered desire of your prospect.

Don't Be Mechanical

I don't want to give the impression that you should always paste the search term into the headline. A lot of the time you should, but not always.

> The main exception is when everyone else is doing just that. If the prime directive of search market-
> ing is relevance, then the sub-prime directive is uniqueness. If you want to be seen, you've got to
> stand out.
>
> More on this later. For now, just remember that your prospects aren't just searching: they're hunt-
> ing—with eyes that can see more than their brains can process. If you want to get caught (and you
> do), then match your ad to the search image they're already carrying.

"BORROW" THE BEST ADS

One of the quickest ways to achieve breakthrough improvements in your clickthrough rates is
to identify top companies from different industries and repurpose their ads.

For instance, I ran a single ad for a particular high-traffic keyword throughout the last half of
2007. During this period, I was unable to come up with a variation that outperformed the original. However, by borrowing an ad concept from a successful stock photography company, I was
able to triple my clickthrough rate (literally) overnight!

Borrowing an ad is one thing. Finding the right ad to borrow is a whole different ball game.
Grabbing ads at random from your browser doesn't cut it for a number of reasons:

There are usually too many candidate ads to test. For instance, SurfSecret is currently squaring
off against 1,060 distinct competing ads. There's not enough time to test that many variations.

There's no way to guess which ads are likely winners. Your competitors are probably not going
to give you access to their AdWords accounts to find out.

You miss a lot of ads because of personalization and geo-targeting. It also tells you nothing
about the frequency or average rank of competing ads—important clues to how effective they are.

So while you might be able to stumble across some gains by testing ads you've grabbed at ran-
dom from your browser, you'll need some kind of automated solution to collect ads for you.
Then you can make some serious progress (this was a big part of my motivation for developing
AdGooroo).

Having a database like this at your disposal allows you to generate endless candidates for
split-testing. It also eliminates the possibility of missing out on powerful ads. And as I have
learned over the past five years of using this technique, you can also use it to very quickly narrow in on the very best ads in any industry.

A few years ago, I began to notice certain patterns in the top-performing ads. For instance, I
noticed that these ads often appeared higher in the search results. I also noticed that they tended
to stick around for a while.

I used these observations as the basis for a series of experiments and ultimately ended up with
a set of filters that allowed me to eliminate the majority of the ads in any market that were less
likely to be top performers. I patented this algorithm in 2008 and released it publicly within
AdGooroo as the Top Ad Copy *r*eport (Figure 28-2).

Keyword	Ad	% Served	Avg Rank
anonymous surfing	**Anonymous Proxy Surfing** Anonymous proxy surfing. We replace your IP with ours, Untraceable. www.securenetics.com	75.0	5.8
anonymous surfing	**Anonymous Surfing ©** Access any blocked site and hide from your ISP, boss, anyone. www.Anonymizer.com	97.0	2.1
anonymous surfing	**Anonymous Web Surfing** Keep your browsing history private with free Google Chrome web browser www.google.com/chrome	98.0	1.0
anonymous surfing	How to hide my IP address About 99% of hacking attacks uses the IP address. Hide your IP now. www.HideYourIPAddress.net	52.0	3.4
anonymous surfing	**Surf Anonymously** Bypass your Network and Surf Anonymously. Free 7 Day Trial! GoTrusted.com	92.0	5.0
clean computer	**Clean PC - HERE** Don't Clean Your PC Until You Read This Article. www.RegistryReview.ws/CleanPC	62.0	2.2

FIGURE 28-2. The AdGooroo Top Ad Copy report applies three filters to all ads in a given industry to find the likeliest top performers.

It's not at all obvious that you can reverse-engineer high-quality ads from impression data. However, there's a very good reason why it works. Effective ads are awarded quality score bonuses that cause them to appear higher and more often, so it makes sense that the ads you find with this technique should perform far better than those gathered at random.

In practice, the results are very good. The majority of the ads returned from this report have high clickthrough rates. I use this report as my starting point, and then design follow-up tests using my best practice rules outlined in the preceding chapters.

The end result is that I can typically create a campaign using high-performing ad copy in a matter of a few hours. While most advertisers struggle with building their campaign over many months, my initial efforts almost always capture a high percentage of the available impressions (Figures 28-3, 28-4, and 28-5).

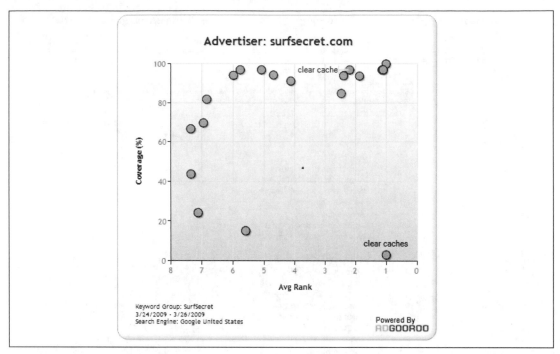

FIGURE 28-3. This chart depicts SurfSecret's coverage in various keywords just two weeks after launch. It's rare for a new account to capture such a high impression share.

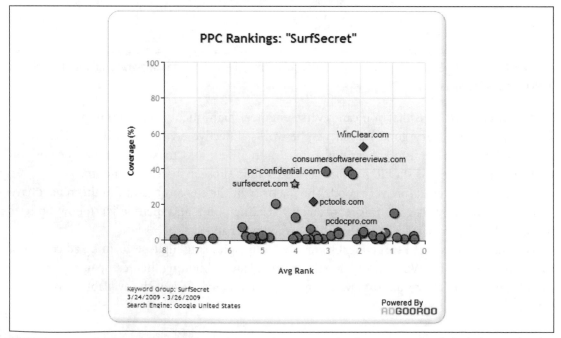

FIGURE 28-4. In just two weeks, SurfSecret became the #5 most dominant competitor in its industry. The circles at the bottom represent dozens of other companies competing for placement in this category.

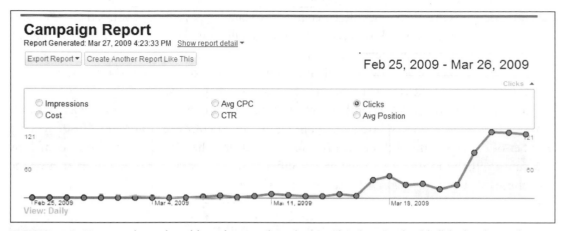

FIGURE 28-5. Here are the real-world results: an AdWords chart showing actual paid clicks for the 11 days following launch.

TESTING ADS

Search marketing has a great advantage over most other forms of advertising in that it delivers feedback on ads very quickly. Creating a successful print or television ad generally requires extensive marketing research, copy tests, focus groups, and so on. But with search, you can simply let two ads run side by side for a certain period and choose the one with the higher clickthrough or conversion rate.

This feedback is so valuable that you should always be testing at least two ads simultaneously using an A/B split test. This will tell you conclusively that one ad is more effective than the other over the same period.

Unlike many forms of promotion, online ads have a straightforward measure of quality: clickthrough rate (CTR). Google will dock your quality score if your CTR falls below a certain threshold, so you have to be sure to split-test your ads until your CTR is at a reasonable level. (1.0% is pretty good for broad keywords, while 2.0% should be your goal for niche keywords.)

How Long Should You Test an Ad?

We touched on testing times in the section on website optimization. A little review never hurts, however.

When you are testing ads, it's important to get enough traffic to be confident of the results.

How many clicks do you need? There are complex statistical formulas[2] you can use to tell you exactly how much data is needed, but in

If you're using conversion tracking on your site, you can also measure the conversion rate for each ad and choose the variant that maximizes your profits (new sales less advertising costs). This measure is known as incremental profit.

When testing, be sure keep an eye on both of these metrics. It's easy to write ads that generate high clickthrough rates but low sales (just include the word *free*). If you're in a high-traffic vertical and can generate enough conversions to measure incremental profit, then by all means use it. It's a far better metric.

general it depends greatly on the difference in clickthrough rates between your ad variations. If one ad is pulling in 2.00% CTR versus another that is pulling in 0.65%, you'll be quite confident that there is a long-term difference in as few as 10 or 20 clicks.

On the other hand, if your two test ads are pulling 0.75% and 0.65% respectively, then it may take several hundred clicks to gain a good degree of confidence in your results.

Ad copy split-testing is far easier than website optimization, so I use Perry Marshall and Brian Teasley's free website, www.splittester.com, to figure out when my tests are done. Just enter the number of clicks and the clickthrough rate for each ad, and the site will tell you how confident you can be in the results (shoot for 95% confidence). This tool saves me hours of number crunching every month. Figure 28-6 shows an example.

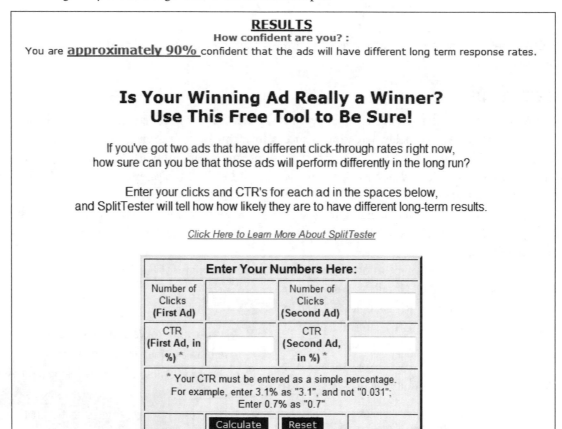

FIGURE 28-6. A screenshot of www.splittester.com. This handy website saves a lot of time when calculating split test results.

Measuring Results

After your testing period is over, compare the clickthrough rate (or incremental profit) for each ad to determine which was most effective. Disable the losing ads and either start a new test or let your winning ad continue to run by itself. The best-performing ad is sometimes known as a control.

Our control ad today is producing a 3.2% CTR in an extremely competitive keyword. The average cost-per-click is only $0.12. How did we do it? Careful side-by-side testing of multiple ads performed over a sufficient length of time.

SUMMARY

Your ad copy is an important factor that determines your clickthrough rate, so you should continually strive to improve it. Aligning your ad copy with visitor intention using the customer life cycle model (discussed in Chapter 4) is an effective shortcut to success. Browsers want information, shoppers want to learn about and compare products, and buyers are looking to make a purchase. Writing your ad with these needs in mind will increase your clickthrough rates.

We also covered 22 best practices and nine worst practices that you should keep in mind when writing new ad copy.

The effectiveness of your ad copy will vary over time, so be sure to refine your ads using A/B split-testing continually. In addition to testing, you can also shortcut your campaign results dramatically by identifying and testing the best ads in your industry.

Notes

1. Al Ries and Jack Trout, *Positioning: The Battle for Your Mind.* McGraw-Hill, 2001.
2. Specifically, you calculate a z-value for the two clickthrough rates and compare it to the percentiles of a standard normal distribution. If p is the clickthrough rate and n is the number of clicks, the formula is

$$z_1 = \frac{\hat{p}_1 - \hat{p}_2}{\sqrt{\dfrac{\hat{p}_1(1 - \hat{p}_1)}{n_1} + \dfrac{\hat{p}_2(1 - \hat{p}_2)}{n_2}}}$$

The World's Best Affiliate Ads

T HE BEST WAY TO LEARN COPYWRITING IS BY STUDYING OTHER PEOPLE'S ADS. THIS HOLDS true even in the tightly constrained world of pay-per-click advertising. This chapter will be devoted to analyzing some of the world's most successful affiliate ads.

To find these ads, the AdGooroo research team mined our database using the Top Ad Copy algorithm mentioned in the previous chapter. This resulted in over 17,000,000 ads for the month of June 2009 alone. We then filtered them down to only those ads appearing from known affiliate networks. The final data file contained a mere 8,000 ads. Most of these ads shared common elements, so I boiled them down to two dozen for illustrative purposes.

What makes these ads even more remarkable is that most of them were placed by affiliate marketers who receive a commission on completed sales of less than 10%. This low payout rate means that they can't support a high maximum bid. Despite this constraint, many of them quickly reached the premium ad positions in our tests.

These ads may seem generic, unoriginal, and perhaps even a little trite. However, they work very well. (Some of them generated clickthrough rates over 12% in our split tests!) Looking at them, you'll see just how universal the rules laid out in the previous chapter really are. Some of these rules, such as capitalizing every word in the ad, are used in virtually every top-performing ad. Others, such as the use of ampersands, exclamation points, and special symbols, aren't quite as obvious, but did become apparent through the use of statistical analysis.

Using even one of these techniques in your ads can significantly boost clickthrough rates. But the world's best affiliates use as many of them as possible to push their clicks into the stratosphere.

Keyword	Ad Copy	Comments
15-inch monitor	**Save on 15" LCD Monitors** Best Bargains On 15" LCD Monitors Same Day Shipping, Buy Now! www.TigerDirect.com	Includes keyword phrase in ad title Exclamation point Specific numbers Each word capitalized
2009 outlook	**Outlook 2009** 2009 CA Anti-Spam Plus Is Here! Guard Against Spam, Phishing & More Shop.ca.com	Includes keyword phrase in ad title Exclamation point Specific numbers Each word capitalized Brand name
30gb microsoft zune digital media	**Famous 30GB MP3 Player** $129 - 2.5" LCD, USB 2.0, Black $1.99 Same Day Shipping, Save Now. www.TigerDirect.com	PriceCall to action ("Save Now.") Specific numbers Each word capitalized
32 lcd	**Amazing Deals on Monitors** Shop & Save on Brand Name Monitors Order Online Now & Save! www.TigerDirect.com	Ampersand Call to action ("Order Online Now & Save!") Exclamation point
37 flat panel tv	**Flat Panel TV** Buy Computer Accessories From Over 400 Brands At Dell" Official Store! www.Dell.com/Business	Specific numbers Each word capitalized Trademark symbol Official site Exclamation point
a printer cartridge	**Printer cartridge** Up To 75% Off Printer Ink & Toner. Free Shipping On Orders Over $55! www.123Inkjets.com	Includes keyword phrase in ad title "Free" Price included Specific numbers Exclamation point Each word capitalized
baby gift basket	**Sweet Baby Gift Baskets** Baby Gift Baskets At Affordable Prices. Save 5% On Registration. www.BabyBasket.com	Includes keyword phrase in ad title Specific numbers Call to action ("Save 5% on Registration") Each word capitalized

Keyword	Ad Copy	Comments
build a computer	**Build A Computer** Customize a Stylish & Powerful Dell Computer with Intel Technology www.Dell.com	Includes keyword phrase in ad title Brand names Ampersand
car top carrier	**Car Top Carrier–$29 & up** Low Prices & Large Selection In Stock. Same Day Shipping DiscountRamps.com/Roof-Racks	Includes keyword phrase in ad title Price included Specific numbers Ampersand Each word capitalized
dick's sporting goods	**Dick's Sporting Goods®** Every Season Starts At Dick's Sporting Goods. Official Site. DicksSportingGoods.com	Includes keyword phrase in ad title Brand name Official site Each word capitalized Special symbol ®
fashion sneakers	**Fashion Sneakers & Shoes** Upgrade To Free Overnight Shipping By Ordering One Item Of Clothing! www.Zappos.com/Fashion-Sneakers	Includes keyword phrase in ad title Call to action ("Upgrade To …") Exclamation point Each word capitalized "Free"
ftd fruit basket	**Fruit Gift Baskets, FRESH** Always Fresh! Register & Save 5% On Every Order. Nationwide Delivery. CapalbosOnline.com/Since-1906	Each word capitalized One word in all caps ("FRESH") Specific numbers Exclamation point
garmin nuvi 350	**Garmin Nuvi 350** Shop Now & Save $91 On The Garmin 350. Now $109.00 + Get Free Shipping www.RadioShack.com	Includes keyword phrase in ad title Call to action ("Shop Now," "Save $91," "Get Free Shipping") Brand name Specific numbers Price included Each word capitalized
harley super glide	**Harley Davidson OEM Parts** Harley Davidson Parts Done Right. Fast Shipping. Solid Service. www.BikeBandit.com	Includes keyword phrase in ad title Brand name Each word capitalized
installing laminate floors	**Installing Laminate Floors** Your Expert Flooring Resource For Do-It-Yourself Floor Installation! www.LumberLiquidators.com	Includes keyword phrase in ad title Each word capitalized Exclamation point
kidkraft dollhouse	**Kidkraft** Find Infant & Toddler Dolls At ToysRUs. Shop Now! www.toysrus.com	Brand name Ampersand Call to action ("Shop Now!") Each word capitalized

Keyword	Ad Copy	Comments
leap frog	**Leap frog** Find Leapfrog Educational Toys At eToys.com. Save Time – Shop Online! www.eToys.com	Includes keyword phrase in ad title Brand name Exclamation point Call to action ("Save Time," "Shop Online!") Each word capitalized
men's gold chains	**Man Jewelry Chains** Check Out Our Great Selection Of Modern Men's Necklaces. Free S/H! www.JustMetal.com	Each word capitalized "Free"
neutrogena sunscreen with spf	**Neutrogena Spf Sunscreen** Shop Neutrogena SPF Sunscreen Free Shipping On Orders over $25! www.ulta.com	Includes keyword phrase in ad title Each word capitalized "Free" Exclamation point Specific numbers Call to action ("Shop Neutrogena")
ryan newman	**Ryan Newman** Shop Now! Great Deals This Fall At The Official NASCAR Store. Store.NASCAR.com	Includes keyword phrase in ad title Each word capitalized Call to action ("Shop Now!") Brand name
school chairs	**Buy Stacking Chairs** Guaranteed In Stock – Free Delivery Factory Direct Pricing – Order Now. www.StackChairs4Less.com	"Free" Each word capitalized Call to action ("Order Now.")
thermal underwear	**Save on Long Underwear** Save Up to 70% Off Retail Prices! Clearance Prices On Long Underwear. www.SierraTradingPost.com	Specific numbers Call to action ("Save up to&") Each word capitalized Exclamation point
used golf equipment	**Golf Equipment** Discount Name-Brand Golf Equipment Save 40% or More – Lowest Prices! RockBottomGolf.com	Includes keyword phrase in ad title Special symbols (dashes) Exclamation point Specific numbers Call to action ("Save 40% or More")

CHAPTER 30

Don't Blindly Trust the Search Engines

S OMETIMES YOU JUST CAN'T TRUST WHAT THE SEARCH ENGINES TELL YOU.

You may think your ad is appearing when it's not. You may think it's not when it is. Sometimes your campaign reports are, well… just downright wrong.

It's not their fault, really. If you think about all of the possible ways an ad can get triggered (various match types, synonyms, plurals, maybe even affiliates bidding on your same terms with identical ads, etc.), it's easy to see how your search reports might say one thing, while your customers are seeing another.

Figure 30-1 an example taken from one of my campaigns today. In the screenshot below, you can see that Google is reporting that my ads aren't appearing for the phrase *keywords search*. I've received exactly zero impressions in the past seven days (according to the report).

The supposed reason is a "low quality score." Clicking the magnifying glass takes me to the AdWords Keyword Analysis page. Here it says that I have a problem with my landing page (Figure 30-2).

However, my ads are appearing. In fact, according to AdGooroo, in the past three days my ads have appeared exactly 93.9% of the time in the United States at an average position of 1.3. This is shown in Figure 30-3.

		Active											
☐	Q► keywords search	Ads rarely show due to low quality score	Poor	$1.15	▼ Settings Default Max CPC [Edit]	0	0	-	-	-	- 0.00%	$0.00	0

FIGURE 30-1.

FIGURE 30-2.

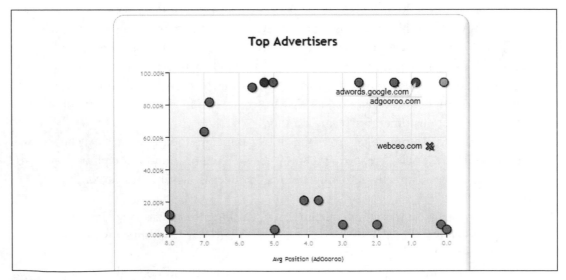

FIGURE 30-3.

A casual Google search also confirms this. I found my ad on the first search results page.

Why does AdWords clearly say that my ad isn't appearing while at the same time serving it to end users?

The key is to look at the ad text. In the AdGooroo screenshot, we see an ad that starts with "Find Keywords for AdWords." Yet the AdWords reporting interface shows that the ad below (Figure 30-4) is the one we're attempting to serve:

| | Search 5,000,000 keywords Increase Traffic, Reduce Costs Search the Largest Keyword Database www.AdGooroo.com | Edit | Active | 0.0% | 0 | - | 0.00% | $0.00 | 0.0% | $0.00 |

FIGURE 30-4.

After searching through my campaign, I finally discover that the ad being served is being targeted to the broad term *keyword*. This triggers the ad for *keywords search*.

Amazingly, both ads have the same exact landing page. So while the AdWords quality bot for some reason decided that the combination of a niche keyword, a highly targeted ad, and a well-crafted landing page wasn't up to snuff, it simultaneously decided that a broad keyword, a generic ad, and the same landing page were a pretty good fit—good enough to show my ad in the top spots of the search results page.

Does it make sense? No.

Do you have to put up with it? No, not if you triangulate your data using multiple tools.

Had I believed the AdWords reporting interface, I would have (incorrectly) thought that my ad wasn't showing. But it was. Showing in a top position, in fact.

This is why it's important to look at your keywords exactly as your customers do. They are probably seeing things a lot differently than you may think.

CHAPTER 31

Open All Night
(Day-Parting)

IGH UP ON THE LIST OF OVERHYPED PAY-PER-CLICK PRACTICES IS DAY-PARTING, THE
practice of increasing bids during the hours of the day when conversions
are at their highest. At other hours of the day (usually during the wee early-
morning hours), bids are lowered or keywords may be paused altogether.

This idea is a holdover from the world of broadcast ("push") advertising. In the traditional media world, day-parting is the practice of dividing the day into several parts, each
of which caters to a different audience. Television and radio stations could then charge different prices based on the audience that was expected to see an ad at any given time.

This not only gives media buyers the ability to stretch their ad dollars, but lets them better reach the people who are most interested in their products. This is why commercials for
family products run during the day (better demographic targeting) and infomercials run at
night (the ad spots are cheap).

Unfortunately, neither of these concepts translates well into pay-per-click marketing.

THE DEMOGRAPHIC MARKETERS

Day-parters tend to fall into two camps. Let's consider the first: demographic targeters. These marketers use day-parting in an attempt to maximize the number of impressions they are serving to their target audience. They believe that because there are more sales when traffic is highest, this is a sign that their target demographic is more active. Thus, they raise their bids or activate their campaigns during the busiest hours of the day.

However, pay-per-click allows us to directly measure the correlation between a searcher's interest in a product and its decision to buy. We no longer have to make guesses about our audience using the indirect relationship that exists in broadcast advertising. We can measure this relationship directly.

And measurement almost always shows that there is no direct correlation between the time when things are busy and when people are ready to buy. These days, people may be ready to buy at noon during their lunch break, or they may be ready to buy at 2 A.M. when they can't sleep because they are so worried about their problems—which your product will solve, right?

The internet is an instant-gratification medium. Advertisers who try to use day-parting to segment their audience just don't get this fundamental fact.

This doesn't mean that you shouldn't try to better target your ads. It just means that you should be using proven methods which work (such as keyword matching).

THE COST CUTTERS

The other camp of day-parters consists of those who use it as a means of cutting costs (and conversely, increasing ROI).

They argue that if conversion rates are lower at night, the money they save by pausing their campaigns at that time outweighs the opportunity cost of the sales they miss. This results in an effective net profit.

This argument holds a lot more water than the first, to be sure. But just because a boat has smaller holes doesn't mean it will float.

Here are a few of the reasons why day-parting doesn't make for an effective cost-cutting measure.

Day-Parting Ignores "Assists"

Not every one of your keywords will appear to be a winner. There may be dozens of keywords to which you can never attribute a sale, but as soon as you remove them from your campaign, your conversions will drop like a rock.

When visitors fail to buy the first time they click on one of your ads, but do so later after clicking another ad, the first click is known as an assist. These keywords assist other keywords in doing their job. They are the Scottie Pippen to your Michael Jordan.

Unless you install special tracking, however, you will fail to see the assists at work. And herein lies the reason why so many people mistakenly try to cut costs during low-conversion hours.

They fail to see that many of those late-night visitors come back the next day with their wallets out, ready to buy from that site they found the night before.

Day-Parting Doesn't Cut Costs As Much As You Think

You've already seen how CPC prices are determined in no small part by the overall demand for a keyword. Because demand for ad placement goes down at night, CPC prices tend to drop during this time. In addition, traffic volumes are much lower at night.

The combination of low search volume and reduced average CPC means that the total cost savings realized by pausing campaigns during non-peak hours is often small in comparison with the spend during peak hours. It almost doesn't seem worth it.

Yahoo! provides an alternative web analytics software package (http://web.analytics.yahoo.com/) that can be used to track assists. If you're looking for a project, it can be used in conjunction with Google Analytics.

Day-Parting Helps Your Competitors

Conversely, when you pause your campaigns, you reduce the competitive bidding pressure for the remaining advertisers. You are actually making it cheaper for them to advertise in your absence. In essence, you're increasing the efficiency of their campaigns, probably far more than your own.

Day-Parting Adds Management Overhead

All three of the big search engines offer day-parting in their feature sets these days, so the cost overhead of buying a third-party solution to manage day-parting has largely gone away. However, there are still some lingering complications that require your attention.

Chief among these are the differing ways in which the search engines handle day-parting. With Google, day-parting is based on the time zone where your campaign was set up. If you're a California advertiser who's day-parting your campaign from 8 A.M. to 5 P.M., your ads will actually appear from 11 A.M. to 8 P.M. in New York. This is why day-parting becomes far less useful as the geographic footprint of your customer base grows. (Note that Bing works the way it should—day-parting is based on your visitors' time zone.)

As the pay-per-click algorithms evolve over time, you'll need to assess the impact of any changes on your day-parting strategy. For example, Google used to use your absolute click-through rate (regardless of the position of your ads) when calculating the relevance of your campaign. If you used day-parting to lower your bids, your campaign-level quality score would be negatively impacted. This is (allegedly) no longer the case, but there will always be subtle complications that you need to stay on top of.

SOMETIMES DAY-PARTING WORKS

Although I recommend against the use of day-parting for most advertisers, there are a few situations where it makes sense.

> These same arguments apply to "weekend-parting" as well. If your local business is only open Monday through Friday, you may want to consider pausing your campaign on Saturday and Sunday.

First, certain types of audiences do tend to exhibit a demographic skew at various times throughout the day. For instance, there tends to be a pronounced bias toward corporate buyers in most B2B categories during regular business hours (7 A.M. to 6 P.M.). Conversely, entrepreneurs and small business owners tend to predominate during the evening and early morning hours.

Second, day-parting becomes more valid if your budget is limited and you've determined that assists aren't playing a prominent role in your campaign (such as with impulse buys).

And finally, day-parting is practically required for local advertisers with regular business hours (such as dentists, plumbers, local retailers, etc.) due to the nature of local search. Many local searchers will simply go down a list of ads and choose the first business that picks up the phone. If nobody is there to answer, then you should probably consider pausing your ads so you don't incur the cost for wasted clicks.

SUMMARY

Day-parting is a strategy that most advertisers should avoid, but it does serve a valuable role in a few niche categories as well as for local advertisers. If you decide to incorporate it into your campaign, be sure to stay on top of changes to the paid search algorithms, as even seemingly minor tweaks can have a big impact on your traffic and conversions.

CHAPTER 32

Tying It All Together

I HOPE THAT AS YOU'VE READ THIS BOOK (AND POSSIBLY REWORKED AN EXISTING PAY-PER-CLICK campaign), you have come to understand that this method is a far cry from the seat-of-the-pants way most pay-per-click campaigns are run.

I've shown you dozens of easy and often not at all obvious techniques that you can use as part of your daily management routine. The benefits of this disciplined approach are immense. Individually, they eliminate the many small slippages that reduce the effectiveness of most advertisers' campaigns. Together, they have a compounding effect that will ensure that few (if any) competitors will come close to getting results anywhere near as good as yours.

I'd love to hear your success stories. Write me at info@adgooroo.com. While I can't personally reply to everyone who writes, I promise to read every email sent to me.

Here's to standing out from the crowd,

—*Rich*

Index

Gain Access To AdGooroo's Competitive Intelligence Tools … For Free!

PPC
SEO
Banner Ads

The best way to succeed in internet marketing is to learn what's working for your competitors. Since 2004, AdGooroo has been helping online businesses improve their results by giving them insight into the most successful tactics in Pay-Per-Click, Search Engine Optimization, and Display Advertising.

Now you can access much of this data using AdGooroo's free site. It's as simple as entering in a keyword phrase or competitor's domain name. You'll get access to

- Related keywords
- Current ad copy
- Landing pages
- Organic rankings
- Keyword traffic
- And more!

To try out the AdGooroo free site, go to **free.adgooroo.com.**

To learn more about AdGooroo's other products, visit:
www.adgooroo.com/GetStarted